THE DECONSTRUCTION OF EQUITY

The Deconstruction of Equity

Activist Shareholders, Decoupled Risk, and Corporate Governance

WOLF-GEORG RINGE

OXFORD
UNIVERSITY PRESS

OXFORD
UNIVERSITY PRESS

Great Clarendon Street, Oxford, OX2 6DP,
United Kingdom

Oxford University Press is a department of the University of Oxford.
It furthers the University's objective of excellence in research, scholarship,
and education by publishing worldwide. Oxford is a registered trade mark of
Oxford University Press in the UK and in certain other countries

First Edition published in 2016

Impression: 1

Published in the United States of America by Oxford University Press
198 Madison Avenue, New York, NY 10016, United States of America

British Library Cataloguing in Publication Data
Data available

Library of Congress Control Number: 2016936069

ISBN 978–0–19–872303–5

Printed and bound by
CPI Group (UK) Ltd, Croydon, CR0 4YY

Preface

This book is the fruit of several years of research. It brings together several aspects of legal and economic scholarship, as it is the attempt to develop solutions to equity risk-decoupling, a problem that is present in capital markets around the world. Corresponding to these challenges, my approach is both comparative and interdisciplinary, and seeks to put economic problems at the centre of the discussion. Legislative responses from different jurisdictions are provided and discussed as examples. The book differs from other studies on the subject in that it develops a concrete regulatory proposal to address the problem in an EU context. However, the concepts developed in the study may hopefully also serve as inspiration for regulators in other jurisdictions.

I presented aspects of this work in research seminars in various universities and research centres around the world, and I am very grateful for the many fruitful discussions, and the feedback and suggestions that I received. I benefited from discussions with staff at the European Securities and Markets Authority, who gave me valuable insights into the political implications and hands-on practicalities of EU lawmaking.

I am particularly grateful to John Armour, Jordan Barry, Paul Davies, Luca Enriques, Holger Fleischer, Jeffrey Gordon, Alexander Hellgardt, Klaus Hopt, Henry Hu, Maiju Kettunen, James Lawrie, Pasquale Munafo, Dorothea Ringe, Edward Rock, Hans-Bernd Schäfer, Steve Schwarcz, Ulrich Seibert, Karl Sternberg, Fred Tung, and Dirk Zetzsche, as well as for feedback received at workshop and conference presentations at HEC Paris; Tilburg Law & Economics Centre; George Washington University, Washington DC; IDC Herzliyah, Israel; Max Planck Institute for Comparative and International Private Law, Hamburg; the Oxford Law & Finance workshop; the Italian and the German Law & Economics Societies; University Rey Juan Carlos, Madrid; Université d'Aix-en-Provence; Seattle University School of Law; and UCL London.

The book builds on, and draws on, some of my previous research. Parts of the text extend and further develop articles that I have published over the past few years,[1] and the topic should be seen in the context of my broader interest in shareholder engagement and activism and my forthcoming work in this field.[2]

[1] For example, Maiju Kettunen and Wolf-Georg Ringe, 'Disclosure Regulation of Cash-Settled Equity Derivatives—An Intentions-Based Approach' [2012] Lloyd's Maritime and Commercial Law Quarterly 227; Wolf-Georg Ringe, 'Hedge Funds and Risk-Decoupling—The Empty Voting Problem in the European Union' (2013) 36 Seattle University Law Review 1027; Wolf-Georg Ringe, 'Empty Voting Revisited: The *Telus* Saga' (2013) 28 Butterworths Journal of International Banking and Financial Law 154.

[2] Wolf-Georg Ringe, 'Shareholder Activism: A Renaissance' in Jeffrey N Gordon and Wolf-Georg Ringe (eds), *The Oxford Handbook of Corporate Law and Governance* (forthcoming, Oxford University Press 2016).

Tara Mrejen and Ingvild Oeystese provided excellent research assistance and support at various stages of the project.

My final thanks go to the professional and supportive team at Oxford University Press. I am grateful for their patience with this project.

Georg Ringe

Copenhagen
October 2015

Table of Contents

Table of Cases

AUSTRALIA

CANADA

EUROPEAN UNION

GERMANY

NEW ZEALAND

UNITED KINGDOM

UNITED STATES

Table of Legislation

UNITED STATES

INTERNATIONAL

I

Introduction

What is the risk of artificially distorted incentives in shareholder voting? That is, in a nutshell, the central question of this book. This question matters because many players in today's equity markets can manipulate their incentives by modifying their risk exposure in investment targets. Sophisticated players, such as hedge funds, have found ways to invest without carrying the corresponding economic risk, with the help of financial derivatives and other instruments.

To make this more concrete, the subject matter of this book is best explained by providing an example.[1]

Consider a hypothetical shareholder A who holds 100 shares in company C. Under regular circumstances, A's voting power in the company's general meeting corresponds to the number of his shares—100. At the same time, A's economic risk exposure in the business corresponds to the same economic value: he is interested in 100 shares, which stand to gain in value if the company does well, and which will depreciate if the company is run poorly. The assumption, therefore, is that A will use the voting influence he has by virtue of his 100 shares to make decisions that contribute to the company's optimal performance, since he stands to win or lose depending on the choices he makes. This is the traditional understanding of how shareholders are motivated and how their role as the corporation's residual risk-bearers allow them to exercise control rights.[2]

Now consider two alternative scenarios. The first is a scenario where the risk is eliminated or reduced. Let us assume that A as before holds 100 shares, but that he concludes a financial derivative contract with a bank, referencing the same number of shares, which makes him immune against any share price development in these shares. In other words, the derivatives put him in a position where he does not care whether the share price goes up or down. A is still the official owner of the shares, and he remains entitled to vote as before. But he will not feel the economic consequences of his actions as in the first example. This creates the possibility that A will use his voting influence for motives other than wealth maximization, which the existing shareholders will not be happy about.

[1] The problem will be discussed in more technical detail in Chapter III.

[2] Frank H Easterbrook and Daniel R Fischel, 'Voting in Corporate Law' (1983) 26 Journal of Law and Economics 395, 401.

In the second scenario, the relationship between risk and influence is reversed. Assume that A does not hold any shares, but that he intends to invest in company C. In order to avoid appearing publicly as a shareholder in C, he acquires indirect economic interest in the 100 shares, again using derivatives, options, or other instruments through entering into corresponding transactions with a bank. This allows A to be risk-exposed in the business like any other shareholder, but avoids triggering public disclosure laws by not appearing as a regular shareholder. The public, and in particular fellow shareholders, are unaware of A's exposure in C, and complain that his actions are a circumvention of block disclosure laws.

This book is concerned with such strategies to uncouple risk from influence in equity ownership. The traditional assumption in law and economic scholarship is that power should match accountability, and it is one of the unwritten assumptions of corporate law that the voting power should correspond to the economic risk exposure. More than thirty years ago, Easterbrook and Fischel put it like this:

> Voting flows with the residual interest in the firm, and unless each element of the residual interest carries an equal voting right, there will be a needless agency cost of management. Those with disproportionate voting power will not receive shares of the residual gains or losses from new endeavours and arrangements commensurate with their control; as a result they will not make optimal decisions.[3]

As we shall see, however, nowadays a number of techniques make it possible to decouple risk and equity ownership. Using a range of different strategies, sophisticated players for example attempt to eliminate or reduce the economic risk that is normally inherently attached to the shares they buy.[4] The brief examples given above are based on the use of derivatives, but there are also alternative techniques, like share lending, where shares are simply borrowed over a certain time frame, or record date capture, where the registration date for a general meeting is exploited. They are all used to overcome the assumption that shareholders are risk-exposed participants in the firms, and they all deconstruct and dismember equity ownership and shift the risk to others.

One newspaper article describes the phenomenon as follows:

> [I]nnovations in the financial markets over the last 30 years have created the possibility, and, in fact, the reality, that the link can be severed between share ownership and one's economic interest, which leads to an incentive to maximize the value of a corporation and its shares. Indeed, capital markets today make it easy to divorce share ownership, and the associated voting rights, from any proportionate economic interest in the value of the corporation's shares. This separation can be caused by a multitude of transactions, in the form of equity swaps, forwards, futures, puts or calls, all of which call into question the fundamental assumption of 'one share, one vote'.[5]

[3] ibid. 409.

[4] See Katayun I Jaffari and Whitney W Deeney, 'One Share, One Vote? Not Necessarily: Manipulation of the SEC Proxy System to Effect Empty Voting' *Legal Intelligencer* (25 February 2011) 7.

[5] ibid.

These strategies touch the core of corporate governance and the traditional assumptions of share ownership and voting rights. Under the corporate laws of all major jurisdictions, risk and voting rights are necessarily tied together in a bundle of different rights and obligations, which together make up the essential elements of an equity share. This 'deconstruction' of the legal elements of a share into different parts is accompanied by several economic problems. For instance, if it is possible to separate the risk from the share—or, put differently, if the share and its voting right remain an empty shell without 'skin in the game'—the shareholder pursuing such a strategy will no longer necessarily exercise the voting right in the way exercised by an optimal shareholder with perfect risk alignment. Quite the contrary, they might ultimately be able to pursue goals that are quite opposed or even detrimental to the company's interests. The shareholder might misuse his control rights to further his own private benefits to the detriment of other shareholders and potential investors. This may be a contributing factor in what others have dubbed the 'waning power of equity ownership'.[6]

Against this background, the present study examines this phenomenon from two sides. First, we explore implications that the decoupling of risk exposure may have on share ownership in general, and on the nature of equity. Second, the investigation discusses the risks that other shareholders and investors encounter when investing in companies in which the risk is decoupled.

Risk-decoupling raises a number of broader issues, which affect the most fundamental elements of corporate organization.

1. In particular, the occurrence of risk-decoupling strategies touches on the proper role of shareholders in corporate governance and capital markets. As we shall see, the traditional hypothesis of shareholders as the righteous owners of corporations—who have an optimal risk exposure as the residual owners—will be seriously tested.
2. Risk-decoupling techniques further jeopardize the effectiveness of capital markets. The information circulated on these markets is typically based on the distribution of voting rights, as a proxy for equity allocation. If, however, the voting right is an empty shell, and the risk behind it has disappeared, the voting rights disclosure is not worth much. Conversely, voting right disclosure may not be helpful where economic influence can be acquired without formally appearing as a shareholder.

A. Context

The phenomenon of risk-decoupling and equity-unbundling first caught the interest of scholars several years ago. Among the pioneers to describe the

[6] John Plender, 'The Waning Power of Equity Ownership' *Financial Times* (London, 23 April 2012) FTFm 24.

phenomenon and to develop early regulatory concerns were Shaun Martin and Frank Partnoy, as well as Henry Hu and Bernard Black.[7] In a series of subsequent articles, the latter duo further developed the analysis of risk-decoupling in its various facets.[8] Several other legal scholars have built on this seminal work over the past few years.[9]

It took some time from the problem's first description until the topic also caught the interest of the economics literature. But over the past few years, economists have studied the extent and the pervasiveness of risk-decoupling in its various shades.[10] In particular, these scholars have measured the frequency of such risk-decoupling strategies in real life. These empirical realities are further discussed later.[11]

Finally, the issue has also interested legal practice, as several court decisions have had to deal with risk-decoupling situations, and law-makers and regulators have started to develop responses in some parts of the field. As we know from political economy, regulation is frequently scandal-driven. It is therefore not surprising that policy-makers have responded mostly in those jurisdictions that were affected by a high-profile case of risk-decoupling, and mostly addressing those substantive parts of the risk-decoupling problem that was at stake in their territory. Thus, for example, the occurrence of a large decoupling transaction in Telus, the Canadian

[7] The early literature is Shaun Martin and Frank Partnoy, 'Encumbered Shares' [2005] University of Illinois Law Review 775, and Henry T C Hu and Bernard Black, 'The New Vote Buying: Empty Voting and Hidden (Morphable) Ownership' (2006) 79 Southern California Law Review 811.

[8] Henry T C Hu and Bernard S Black, 'Empty Voting and Hidden (Morphable) Ownership: Taxonomy, Implications, and Reforms' (2006) 61 Business Lawyer 1011; Henry T C Hu and Bernard S Black, 'Hedge Funds, Insiders, and the Decoupling of Economic and Voting Ownership: Empty Voting and Hidden (Morphable) Ownership' (2007) 13 Journal of Corporate Finance 343; Henry T C Hu and Bernard S Black, 'Equity and Debt Decoupling and Empty Voting II: Importance and Extensions' (2008) 156 University of Pennsylvania Law Review 625. More recently, Henry T C Hu, 'Financial Innovation and Governance Mechanisms: The Evolution of Decoupling and Transparency' (2015) 70 The Business Lawyer 347.

[9] See, for example, Dirk Zetzsche, 'Hidden Ownership in Europe: BAFin's Decision in Schaeffler v. Continental' (2009) 10 European Business Organization Law Review 115; Roberta S Karmel, 'Voting Power without Responsibility or Risk: How Should Proxy Reform Address the Decoupling of Economic and Voting Rights' (2010) 55 Villanova Law Review 93; Maiju Kettunen and Wolf-Georg Ringe, 'Disclosure Regulation of Cash-Settled Equity Derivatives—An Intentions-Based Approach' [2012] Lloyd's Maritime and Commercial Law Quarterly 227; Michael C Schouten, *The Decoupling of Voting and Economic Ownership* (Kluwer 2012); Jordan M Barry, John William Hatfield, and Scott Duke Kominers, 'On Derivatives Markets and Social Welfare: A Theory of Empty Voting and Hidden Ownership' (2013) 99 Virginia Law Review 1103; Wolf-Georg Ringe, 'Hedge Funds and Risk-Decoupling—The Empty Voting Problem in the European Union' (2013) 36 Seattle University Law Review 1027; Paul Ali, Ian Ramsay, and Benjamin Saunders, 'Securities Lending, Empty Voting and Corporate Governance' [2014] Law and Financial Markets Review 326; David Marais, 'Decoupling Voting Rights from Economic Interest: The Case of Empty and Negative Voting' (2015) 18 Trinity College Law Review 180.

[10] See, among others, Susan E K Christoffersen and others, 'Vote Trading and Information Aggregation' (2007) 62 The Journal of Finance 2897; Avner Kalay, Oğuzhan Karakaş, and Shagun Pant, 'The Market Value of Corporate Votes: Theory and Evidence from Option Prices' (2014) 69 The Journal of Finance 1235; Reena Aggarwal, Pedro A C Saffi, and Jason Sturgess, 'The Role of Institutional Investors in Voting: Evidence from the Securities Lending Market' (2015) 70 Journal of Finance 2309.

[11] See Chapter III.D.

telecommunications giant, shook up the debate in Canada and prompted regulatory action where the problem had not really been noted before.[12]

The time is ripe for taking stock in the debate, and for analysing and weighing the different findings that have been made over time. This book seeks to add to the debate by providing three major contributions. First, I provide a comprehensive assessment of the risk-decoupling problem in a geographical and substantive perspective. That is, the present study looks at the problem with a global perspective, overcoming any national parochialism, as the economic problem of risk shifting arises in many jurisdictions in a similar way. Further, as we shall see, there are different types and forms of risk-decoupling, and they will all be considered together here as they pose similar or related problems.

The second contribution is that the present study seeks to develop a fundamental problem analysis that is informed by economic theory and empirical findings. These insights will become relevant at several points in this study, mostly informing the three 'problem perspectives' which form the backbone of the problem analysis in Chapter V.

Third, the main goal of the present study is to develop a regulatory response to risk-decoupling. Thus, we will develop a concrete regulatory text that will address the concerns building on the findings from the problem analysis.

Risk-decoupling is a global phenomenon. It is intuitive that the possibility to modify their risk profile appeals to shareholders in all developed economies. As an academic phenomenon, the issue of risk-decoupling and empty voting has already gained much attention by scholars in the United States.[13] This book, however, attempts to analyse the problem in the particular governance context of the European Union. The objective is to develop concrete regulatory responses to constitute a solution in the EU context. The substance, however, will be the same as in any jurisdiction in the world, and the arguments made and considered will be equally relevant everywhere.

B. Structure

This book is organized as follows. Chapter II provides the foundations by discussing the role of shareholders in the corporation and develops the key understanding of shareholder voting and power in corporate governance. This allows us

[12] See on the *Telus* case Chapters III.B.1.c and VI.A.5. The Canadian regulator is currently debating regulatory action. See Canadian Securities Administrators, *Update on Proposed Amendments to Multilateral Instrument 62-104 Take-Over Bids and Issuer Bids, National Instrument 62-103 Early Warning System and Related Take-Over Bid and Insider Reporting Issues and National Policy 62-203 Take-Over Bids and Issuer Bids*, CSA Notice 62-307 (10 October 2014); Paul D Barbeau and Eric Chernin, 'The CSA Proceeds with Amendments to the Early Warning Reporting Regime but Abandons Two Key Proposed Changes' (14 October 2014), available at <http://www.bennettjones.com/Publications/Updates/The_CSA_Proceeds_with_Amendments_to_the_Early_Warning_Reporting_Regime_but_Abandons_Two_Key_Proposed_Changes/> accessed 19 August 2015.

[13] See in particular the references provided in notes 7, 8, and 9.

to understand the phenomenon of 'decoupled' shareholder risk, which is explained in Chapter III. We will see that this part distinguishes between negative and positive risk-decoupling (see section III.A). Each of these two different strategies is highlighted by ample examples and empirical evidence.

Chapter IV then proceeds to describe the failure of traditional concepts of corporate and securities law to address the issue under established principles. This leads us to deeper exploration of the regulatory problems at the heart of the phenomenon. Chapter V undertakes this analysis by offering four different problem perspectives, each of which sheds light on the topic from a different angle: principal-agent theory, information and transaction costs, corporate finance, and the market for corporate control. The first three of these are mostly relevant for negative risk-decoupling, the fourth for positive risk-decoupling.

Building on the lessons learned from the problem analysis, Chapter VI then builds elements of a regulatory solution. While rejecting a few proposals that have been made by others or that are already in force in some jurisdictions, it is the objective here to develop a comprehensive solution that encompasses an answer to all different aspects of risk-decoupling. The result for negative decoupling is a three-pillar framework, using disclosure as the first, vote suspension as the second, and *ex post* court litigation as the third pillar. To address positive decoupling, this study proposes an intentions-based disclosure system.

The final chapter, Chapter VII, then takes the problem to the appropriate level of regulation. In the European context, it is the EU who should act; individual Member States' activities are therefore helpful but should ultimately be overcome.

Chapter VIII offers a number of final conclusions and an outlook.

II

Shareholders in Corporate Governance

The role of shareholders is one of the most debated topics in modern corporate governance, and is central to our understanding of risk-decoupling.

Nothing creates stronger feelings than discussions on the rights shareholders should have in the governance of a corporation. Some see shareholders as the rightful owners of the firm, who have been largely stripped of their influence by powerful managers and other interest groups. Others, however, point out that unrestricted shareholder influence may have negative consequences for the corporation and for society at large. Some critics regard putting shareholders centre stage as a dangerous outflow of capitalism. For them, the notion of 'shareholder value' itself incorporates all the excesses of a society oriented towards monetary profit. They contrast this with a more 'stakeholder'-oriented model of the corporation according to which shareholders are only one of many constituencies of the corporation.

More recent scholarship has relied on more specific criticism, and targets the tendency of (some) shareholders to have a short-term orientation rather than long-term values. The popular anger at this development, according to this view, is evidenced by the financial crisis and the contributory role that greedy shareholders played in pushing short-term profits at the expense of long-term value.

Depending on their school of thought, scholars derive different prescriptions for the design of legal rules. Shareholder advocates support maximum empowerment of equity-holders in their jurisdictions. Sceptics posit that shareholders should be legally constrained in various ways, for example by prescribing the goal of the corporation as serving the society as a whole (rather than internal profit maximization), or by devising various tools to bolster the role of other constituencies such as employees or creditors at the expense of full shareholder reign. More indirect regulatory attempts include the bolstering of long-term-oriented shareholders instead of those focusing on the short term.

The linchpin of this is the voting entitlement of equity-holders. To assess and evaluate the impact of modern manipulation and risk-decoupling strategies, we need to first understand the background and the policy debate around the importance and problems of shareholder voting rights. In this first section, we thus lay the foundation and briefly discuss the role of shareholder voting rights in corporate governance, the legal policy objective of the allocation of voting rights to shareholders, and the basic assumptions that are connected in our economic system with the exercise of voting rights.

A. Costs of Voting and Apathy

Shareholders exercise their influence in the corporation mostly through voting. In theory, the right to vote is one of the most important rights of the shareholder as the beneficial owner of the company.[1] While conducting the daily business is in the hands of the administration, the right to vote allows the shareholder to participate in strategy-setting by way of shareholder resolutions. Shareholders are thus offered a reasonable control mechanism on certain fundamental aspects of the company's activity and strategy. Once almost neglected, the importance of shareholders' voting rights has more recently enjoyed a renaissance.[2]

The existence of voting rights for shareholders is justified by the fact that company law and corporate governance theory characterize all the shareholders as 'owners' of the corporation. On the legitimate objection that the characterization of the shareholder position does not correspond to the property in the legal sense, theory asserts that an economic perspective considers the equity investors as residual risk-bearers of the corporation. The shareholder is thus entitled to the economic proceeds of the business venture and can be understood as an economic 'owner'. Against this backdrop, corporate law theory concludes that the bearer of the economic risk is best suited to make informed decisions for the development of the company. Therefore, company law legislation grants shareholders in many situations a decision right that can be exercised collectively by the shareholders' meeting.

However, in corporate practice it is important to note that exercising voting rights is costly.[3] The shareholder must inform herself about the matter to be decided, where appropriate take advice, consult with other shareholders, and weigh various decision alternatives against each other. Under certain circumstances, it is advisable to also appoint a proxy. In small companies, where the investor is familiar with the everyday life of the company, this may still be relatively easy to deal with, since the information and monitoring problem is less severe for the interests of a small group of shareholders. In large public companies, by contrast, it is expensive for the individual shareholder to form a balanced opinion on business matters or to properly monitor the board. This results in the well-known phenomenon of 'rational apathy'.[4] Economically, it may make sense

[1] David Brooks, 'Depositary Trust Company and the Omnibus Proxy: Shareholder Voting in the Era of Share Immobilization' (2014) 56 South Texas Law Review 205, 214.

[2] Paul H Edelman, Randall S Thomas, and Robert B Thompson, 'Shareholder Voting in an Age of Intermediary Capitalism' (2014) 87 Southern California Law Review 1359.

[3] Frank H Easterbrook and Daniel R Fischel, 'Voting in Corporate Law' Ch. I n. 2.

[4] See the seminal work by Kenneth J Arrow, *The Limits of Organization* (Norton 1974). See also Mark J Roe, 'A Political Theory of American Corporate Finance' (1991) 91 Columbia Law Review 10; Bernard S Black, 'Shareholder Passivity Reexamined' (1990) 89 Michigan Law Review 520; Eddy Wymeersch, 'Shareholder(s) Matter(s)' in Stefan Grundmann and others (eds), *Festschrift für Klaus J. Hopt zum 70. Geburtstag am 24. August 2010: Unternehmen, Markt und Verantwortung* (De Gruyter 2010) 1571.

for shareholders *not* to exercise their right to vote—precisely because the costs that would be incurred by going to vote or by a proper preparation bear no relation to the expected benefits.[5] Even if it was possible to contribute to a positive change in the management's activity and to improve the company's returns by voting, a small shareholder would benefit from this only to the limited extent of his own interest in the company. Consequently, it is more consistent in such situations to support the proposals and actions of the administration or other (large) shareholders and to rely on their expertise ('free rider' behaviour). Alternatively, in the case of dissatisfaction with the company's management, there is always the possibility to sell—provided that a functioning capital market exists.[6] This choice is colloquially referred to as the 'Wall Street rule'.[7]

The assumption of rational restraint of the individual in the collective exercise of control presupposes that the shareholders have sufficiently congruent goals and interests. Put differently, a minority shareholder will not rely on the expertise of the majority shareholder if he cannot reliably assume that the common objectives of both investors are sufficiently homogeneous.[8] What is typically the case is that profit maximization is at the forefront of shareholders' interests in the Western capitalist regime. However, there may be situations in which the interests of the members diverge. For example, some shareholders may pursue a high-dividend policy and others may be more interested in the long-term value of the company shares that give lower pay-outs.[9] Shareholders may also be convinced that different strategic choices further the company's objectives better than others. Aside from the typical market movements by which like-minded shareholders are generally positioned in the market, led by shared beliefs, coming together for joint ventures, the objection of heterogeneous interests may be relativized by the fact that slightly different interests are often not financially sufficient to cause 'apathetic' minority shareholders to become active interventionists.[10]

[5] See Henry G Manne, 'Some Theoretical Aspects of Share Voting. An Essay in Honor of Adolf A. Berle' (1964) 64 Columbia Law Review 1427, 1441 f; Frank H Easterbrook and Daniel R Fischel, *The Economic Structure of Corporate Law* (Harvard University Press 1991) 66 f; Jesse H Choper, John C Coffee, and Ronald J Gilson, *Cases and Materials on Corporations* (8th edn, Wolters Kluwer Law & Business 2013) 532 ff.

[6] Albert O Hirschman, *Exit, Voice, and Loyalty: Responses to Decline in Firms, Organizations, and States* (Harvard University Press 1970); Jack Hirshleifer, 'The Private and Social Value of Information and the Reward to Inventive Activity' (1971) 61 The American Economic Review 561; Choper, Coffee, and Gilson (n. 5) 534; Theodor Baums, 'Germany' in Theodor Baums and Eddy Wymeersch (eds), *Shareholder Voting Rights and Practices in Europe and the United States* (Kluwer Law International 1999) 109, 11.

[7] Klaus J Hopt, 'Modern Company and Capital Market Problems: Improving European Corporate Governance After Enron' in John Armour and Joseph McCahery (eds), *After Enron: Improving Corporate Law and Modernising Securities Regulation in Europe and the US* (Hart Publishing 2006) 445, 451.

[8] Manne (n. 5) 1442. In Manne's view, this is the major difference to political voting, where the interests are less closely aligned.

[9] ibid. 1442.

[10] It should be noted that these problems do not arise to the same extent for large or even majority shareholders, or in small- or medium-sized enterprises (SMEs). This will be discussed later. See on this section II.B.

Rather strikingly, while they agree on the existing costs of the exercise of voting rights and the free rider problem previously described, scholars come to relatively different policy prescriptions. Parts of the literature from the United States consider it desirable that the management is given even greater independence from shareholders because of the often ill-informed and unqualified shareholder votes.[11] This view, particularly represented by Bainbridge, is based on the following argument: due to market forces, the management has an inherent incentive to create an optimal business organization. Since investors only invest in companies that offer them advantageous structures, they create a steady market pressure on management to care for good corporate governance. Mandating an increased influence of shareholders by legal intervention is therefore not required.[12] Moreover, it is cheaper for a company to transfer individual decisions to a professional board that is specially authorized and empowered than to convene shareholder meetings about every business decision.[13] According to this view, shareholder voting rights are just one of many mechanisms to monitor the management, and should only be used in exceptional cases.[14]

Others take the opposite view, and argue that shareholders must be given increased participation rights so that voting and participation in the corporate life becomes worthwhile for them.[15] The British system is often cited as a shining example, as this system has strong shareholder rights and has led to positive governance experiences. It is generally accepted that UK institutional investors in particular exert steady pressure for the highest standards of corporate governance.[16] In contrast, the American system, with its insulated board, is said to create increased potential for conflict between the interests of management and shareholders. Arguably, this goes so far that the management in a US corporation can de facto decide in which state the company incorporates—which provokes the well-known competition between the states with the effect of offering managers the most favourable legal system—to the detriment of shareholders.[17]

This academic dispute should not and cannot be explored in more detail or even decided here. Too much depends on ideological premises or on empirical findings.[18]

[11] Stephen M Bainbridge, 'Director Primacy and Shareholder Disempowerment' (2006) 119 Harvard Law Review 1735; Iman Anabtawi, 'Some Skepticism About Increasing Shareholder Power' (2006) 53 UCLA Law Review 561, 598; Lynn A Stout, 'The Mythical Benefits of Shareholder Control' (2007) 93 Virginia Law Review 789.

[12] Bainbridge (n. 11); Stephen Bainbridge, 'The Case for Limited Shareholder Voting Rights' (2006) 53 UCLA Law Review 601, 621 ff.

[13] Bainbridge (n. 11) 1746.

[14] ibid. 1750 f.

[15] In particular, Lucian A Bebchuk, 'The Case for Shareholder Access to the Ballot' (2003) 59 Business Lawyer 43; Lucian A Bebchuk, 'The Case for Increasing Shareholder Power' (2005) 118 Harvard Law Review 833; Lucian A Bebchuk, 'Letting Shareholders Set the Rules' (2006) 119 Harvard Law Review 1784, 1813. See also George W Dent Jr, 'The Essential Unity of Shareholders and the Myth of Investor Short-Termism' (2010) 35 Delaware Journal of Corporate Law 97.

[16] Bebchuk, 'The Case for Increasing Shareholder Power' (n. 15) 847 ff.

[17] ibid. 868 ff.

[18] The two protagonists of the debate, Bainbridge and Bebchuk, underpin their claims with different empirical studies, but come to different findings and conclusions.

For example, it is important to consider that the influence and power of institutional investors in the United Kingdom and the United States vary widely. Under US law, investment funds and similar institutional investors are restricted from acquiring larger blocks of shares that would allow them to have significant impact on the company.[19] Even for large British institutional investors, commitment is often de facto limited to more informal involvement, or involvement is very low, or there is no involvement at all.[20] This was evidenced by the introduction of a UK Stewardship Code with the implicitly recognized regulatory need to encourage more involvement.[21] The discussion presented can but clarify one thing, which is that the role of the shareholder in the company and the sustainability of their voting rights are not without controversy. The fundamental question of how useful it is for the shareholder to vote must be kept in mind in the following discussions. However, the controversy cannot be oversimplified—the role of shareholders will differ between jurisdictions, and the problem of low incentives and apathy cannot easily be transferred to jurisdictions with larger blockholders, where different problems prevail.

B. Blockholders

So far we have looked at the (low) incentives of dispersed shareholders in the typical Berle–Means corporation. It follows that the role of shareholders and their incentives change in two alternative scenarios. The equation will change first in the situation of concentrated ownership, where a large blockholder dominates the corporation, and secondly in the case of privately held corporations, which usually have few shareholders. On a positive note, in both scenarios it appears much more rational for both major shareholders in a public company and owners of small, privately held firms to exercise active influence on the company's strategic decisions.[22]

Two main reasons are mostly cited in the theoretical debate. First, such shareholders would have committed more assets in the firm (and are also

[19] Mark J Roe, *Strong Managers, Weak Owners: The Political Roots of American Corporate Finance* (Princeton University Press 1996).

[20] See Marco Becht and others, 'Returns to Shareholder Activism: Evidence from a Clinical Study of the Hermes UK Focus Fund' (2009) 22 Review of Financial Studies 3093.

[21] The Stewardship Code is available at <http://www.frc.org.uk/Our-Work/Codes-Standards/Corporate-governance.aspx>. For academic comment, see Brian R Cheffins, 'The Stewardship Code's Achilles' Heel' (2010) 73 The Modern Law Review 1004; Simon Wong, 'Why Stewardship Is Proving Elusive for Institutional Investors' (2010) 25 Butterworths Journal of International Banking and Financial Law 406; Iris H-Y Chiu, 'Turning Institutional Investors into "Stewards": Exploring the Meaning and Objectives of "Stewardship"' [2013] Current Legal Problems 443; Iris H-Y Chiu, 'Reviving Shareholder Stewardship: Critically Examining the Impact of Corporate Transparency Reforms in the UK' (2014) 38 Delaware Journal of Corporate Law 983.

[22] Andrei Shleifer and Robert W Vishny, 'Large Shareholders and Corporate Control' (1986) 94 Journal of Political Economy 461; Andrei Shleifer and Robert W Vishny, 'A Survey of Corporate Governance' (1997) 52 Journal of Finance 737, 753 ff.

usually not diversified in a comparable way), so that strong incentives exist to monitor the use of these invested assets.[23] Furthermore, shareholders in privately held companies as well as blockholders in public corporations typically cannot sell their shares that easily, as the capital market cannot readily absorb large blocks of shares. In family firms, selling restrictions in the firm's articles of association are also the rule. Furthermore, there is no liquid market for shares of private companies. Consequently, it is therefore more in the interests of large and family shareholders to exert stronger influence on the business policy of the company.[24]

These theoretical considerations are supported by a number of empirical studies. Two recent American studies have come to the conclusion that on receiving notice of the existence of a major shareholder, the company's share price increases significantly, as the market has positive expectations of the company's performance.[25] More specific investigations have shown that, for example, a positive correlation can be found between the existence of a major shareholder and more appropriate executive compensations[26] or increased vigilance by shareholders against restrictions against hostile takeover bids and management-friendly governance structures.[27] To be sure, the exact interests of the particular type of a major shareholder differ, and a growing literature deals with the differentiation in motivation depending on the different types of large shareholders.[28]

The fundamental question is therefore whether we can 'trust' the major shareholders' influence in the sense that they appropriately exercise their voting rights and thus overcome the apathy problem that we observed for retail investors.[29] Who are these major shareholders really? This depends largely on the jurisdiction

[23] Brian Cheffins, *Company Law: Theory, Structure and Operation* (Oxford University Press 1997) 63; Michael Rozeff, 'Growth, Beta and Agency Costs as Determinants of Dividend Payout Ratios' (1982) 5 Journal of Financial Research 249.

[24] Clifford Holderness and Dennis Sheehan, 'The Role of Majority Shareholders in Publicly Held Corporations: An Exploratory Analysis' (1988) 20 Journal of Financial Economics 317.

[25] Alon Brav, Wei Jian, Frank Partnoy, and Randall Thomas, 'Hedge Fund Activism, Corporate Governance, and Firm Performance' (2008) 63 Journal of Finance 1729; April Klein and Emanuel Zur, 'Entrepreneurial Shareholder Activism: Hedge Funds and Other Private Investors' (2009) 64 Journal of Finance 187.

[26] Marianne Bertrand and Sendhil Mullainathan, 'Are CEOs Rewarded for Luck? The Ones Without Principals Are' (2011) 116 The Quarterly Journal of Economics 901; Anup Agrawal and Tareque Nasser, 'Blockholders on Boards and CEO Compensation, Turnover and Firm Valuation', Working Paper 2012, available at <http://ssrn.com/abstract=1443431>.

[27] James Brickley, Ronald Lease, and Clifford Smith, 'Ownership Structure and Voting on Antitakeover Amendments' (1988) 20 Journal of Financial Economics 267; Anil Shivdasani, 'Board Composition, Ownership Structure, and Hostile Takeovers' (1993) 16 Journal of Accounting and Economics 167.

[28] See, for example, Michael J Barclay, Clifford Holderness, and Dennis Sheehan, 'Dividends and Corporate Shareholders' (2009) 22 Review of Financial Studies 2423, with further references; Ronald J Gilson, 'Controlling Shareholders and Corporate Governance: Complicating the Comparative Taxonomy' (2006) 119 Harvard Law Review 1641.

[29] On this fundamental question, see Bernard Black, 'Agents Watching Agents: The Promise of Institutional Investor Voice' (1992) 39 UCLA Law Review 811.

in question.[30] Roughly speaking, we can say that the dominant players in the US/UK context are mostly 'institutional investors', that is, pension funds, mutual funds and other investment companies, and hedge funds. The landscape in continental Europe differs starkly. In Germany, large blocks of shares are traditionally held by banks, families, or other industrial companies, often in cross-shareholdings.[31] Italy is known for its strong family ownership.[32] None of these major shareholder types remain free from their own conflicts of interest. Investment companies invest regularly in a wide variety of businesses and diversify their portfolio in this way. In consequence, they often suffer from motivational problems, because the blocks of shares they hold are often no bigger than 3–5 per cent of the company. Hedge funds in this respect are more of an exception, because they are, in spite of relatively small investments, often willing to exercise activist influence on company policy.[33] However, it is doubtful whether hedge funds can be appropriate 'guardians' of the management, especially since they are often driven by short-term earning horizons and might not always have long-term development in mind.[34]

In the German context, banks and other industrial companies are the centre of attention.[35] It is generally accepted that they can and do indeed monitor corporate policy and also exert active influence, but they are not free from problems of their own. Banks are often at the same time the main shareholder and creditor of a company, and thus biased in their risk incentives and interest alignment. Mutual entanglements in shareholdings and cross-participation used to be the core of the so-called 'Deutschland AG' and brought—besides some degree of macroeconomic stability—a number of disadvantages, especially conflicts of interest, mutual dependencies, and opaque and intransparent alliances. Germany, Inc. is now in the process of dissolution.[36] German blue-chip companies are increasingly in foreign hands, equity ownership is dispersing, and banks are scaling back their investments in corporate Germany.

As a result, both dispersed and concentrated ownership structures are fraught with problems in their own way when it comes to the effective exercise of shareholder voting rights. In both shareholder voting structures, shareholder influence can produce sub-optimal results. It is important to bear this point in mind during the following discussions and to build on it: only a theory of shareholder voting rights that takes the value (or lack of value) of the voting rights into consideration can live up to the realities of corporate ownership.

[30] See Gilson (n. 28).

[31] But the German patterns of concentrated ownership are slowly eroding. See Wolf-Georg Ringe, 'Changing Law and Ownership Patterns in Germany: Corporate Governance and the Erosion of Deutschland AG' (2015) 63 American Journal of Comparative Law 493.

[32] Alexander Aganin and Paolo Volpin, 'The History of Corporate Ownership in Italy' in Randall Morck (ed.), *A History of Corporate Governance around the World: Family Business Groups to Professional Managers* (University of Chicago Press 2005).

[33] Marcel Kahan and Edward Rock, 'Hedge Funds in Corporate Governance and Corporate Control' (2007) 155 University of Pennsylvania Law Review 1021. See section II.C.

[34] See section II.C. [35] See Ringe (n. 31). [36] ibid.

C. Activist Shareholders and Hedge Funds

One of the groups that seem to have overcome the apathy problem deserves further investigation. These are so-called 'activist shareholders', such as hedge funds and other institutional investors.[37] These investors play an important role in this book.

The advent of hedge funds, also described as 'alternative investment funds', presents one of the most pressing policy challenges of the past few years, as they masterfully exploit the traditional categories of corporate law, financial derivatives, and risk management.[38] Traditionally, hedge funds tended to trade predominantly in financial instruments.[39] This practice has changed in recent years, however. Benefiting from the development of information technology, futures markets, financial engineering, and the derivatives industry, a growing number of hedge funds discovered the potentials of equity markets. The ability to actively influence the strategy of target companies has become an attractive business model for them.[40] These hedge funds have chosen activism as part of their investment strategy: they invest in order to be active, not the reverse. The traditional literature characterizes this new strategy as 'offensive' activism, where activism is part of the investment plan, as opposed to 'defensive' activism, where shareholders with a pre-existing stake in a company are dissatisfied with the management and are hence lobbying for change.[41]

In short, while for cost reasons traditional institutional investors, such as pension funds, usually either abstained from voting altogether, voted with the management, or selected the 'Wall Street rule',[42] the past few years have seen the emergence of new types of investors and business models, which are designed by the financial industry and are built on active influence on strategic decisions of the target company. These are mainly the domain of activist hedge funds and private equity investors.[43]

[37] See, on the hope that they play an active role in corporate governance, John Plender, 'Activist Animals Sought for Governance Jungle' *Financial Times* (London, 8 June 2015) FTFm 13.

[38] On hedge funds generally, see David Stowell, *An Introduction to Investment Banks, Hedge Funds, and Private Equity: The New Paradigm* (Elsevier 2010); Peter Astleford and Dick Frase (eds), *Hedge Funds and the Law* (Sweet & Maxwell 2010).

[39] William W Bratton, 'Hedge Funds and Governance Targets' (2007) 95 Georgetown Law Journal 1375, 1378; Financial Services Authority (FSA), *Private Equity: A Discussion of Risk and Regulatory Engagement* 26, 30 (FSA Discussion Paper 06/6, 2006).

[40] Brian Cheffins and John Armour, 'The Past, Present and Future of Shareholder Activism by Hedge Funds' (2011) 37 Journal of Corporation Law 51; Eveline Hellebuyck, 'Activist Hedge Funds and Legal Strategy Devices' in Antoine Masson and Mary J Shariff (eds), *Legal Strategies* (Berlin/Heidelberg 2010) 277; Sean Geraghty and Harriet Smith, 'Shareholder Activism as a Strategy for Hedge Funds' in Astleford and Frase (n. 38) ch. 8; Dionysia Katelouzou, 'Worldwide Hedge Fund Activism: Dimensions and Legal Determinants' (2015) 17 University of Pennsylvania Journal of Business Law 789.

[41] See Iris H-Y Chiu, *The Foundations and Anatomy of Shareholder Activism* (Hart Publishing 2010).

[42] Hopt (n. 7) 451. On the 'Wall Street rule', see n. 7 and accompanying text.

[43] On this development, see Eddy Wymeersch, 'Shareholders in Action: Towards a New Company Paradigm?' (2007) 4 European Company Law 50; Kahan and Rock (n. 33); Matteo Erede, 'Governing Corporations with Concentrated Ownership Structure: An Empirical Analysis of Hedge Fund

While in a broader sense speculative hedge funds have long been known, the advent of hedge funds of the 'activist' type (which are of interest here) can be traced back to the 1990s in the United States. At that time, the decline of the big takeover wave of the 1980s left a vacuum for effective management control for many public companies.[44] Policy-makers at the time put great hopes on traditional institutional investors such as investment funds or pension funds. However, despite several regulatory reforms, they did not succeed in convincing these investors to substantially take over a meaningful monitoring role of management.[45] The financial incentives were too weak and the number of target or portfolio companies was too large to encourage greater engagement. It was precisely this power vacuum that the new breed of activist hedge funds stepped into. These were powerful investors who would recognize a weakness in the strategic direction of a potential target company and then invest in such company and influence the strategic direction of the company and its course, using innovative, often aggressive measures. We observe a wide range of activities that are used by such funds, from silent, internal pressure on public campaigns to actual engagement with the corporate strategy, for example by convening a general meeting for the purpose of voting on strategic decisions of the company or even the replacement of management.[46] What is special about this strategy is the size of the investment, as while hedge funds usually have slightly larger stakes than traditional, highly diversified institutional investors, the size of their stakes is normally much smaller than that of those who were at the forefront of the hostile takeover business during the 1980s. More recently, hedge funds have become increasingly active in Europe, too.[47]

Overall, these different funds specialize in identifying companies in the market that are underperforming due to inadequate or poor corporate governance or

Activism in Italy and Germany, and Its Evolution' [2013] European Company and Financial Law Review 328.

[44] Kahan and Rock (n. 33). On even earlier evidence from the first half of the twentieth century see John Armour and Brian Cheffins, 'Origins of "Offensive" Shareholder Activism in the United States' in Jonathan Koppell (ed.), *Origins of Shareholder Advocacy* (Basingstoke 2011) 253 ff.

[45] See, for an optimistic perspective from this time, Bernard Black 'Shareholder Passivity Re-examined' (1990) 89 Michigan Law Review 520; Mark Roe, 'A Political Theory of American Corporate Finance' (1991) 91 Columbia Law Review 10. An intriguing assessment from today's perspective is provided by Ronald J Gilson and Jeffrey N Gordon, 'The Agency Costs of Agency Capitalism: Activist Investors and the Revaluation of Governance Rights' (2013) 113 Columbia Law Review 863.

[46] See the list by Martin Lipton, 'Dealing with Activist Hedge Funds', The Harvard Law School Forum on Corporate Governance and Financial Regulation, 21 November 2013, available at <http://blogs.law.harvard.edu/corpgov/2013/11/21/dealing-with-activist-hedge-funds-2/>.

[47] Wolf-Georg Ringe, 'Shareholder Activism: A Renaissance' in Jeffrey N Gordon and Wolf-Georg Ringe (eds), *The Oxford Handbook of Corporate Law and Governance* (forthcoming, Oxford University Press 2016); Matteo Erede, 'Governing Corporations with Concentrated Ownership Structure: An Empirical Analysis of Hedge Fund Activism in Italy and Germany, and Its Evolution' [2013] European Company and Financial Law Review 328; Alexandros Seretakis, 'Hedge Fund Activism Coming to Europe: Lessons from the American Experience' (2014) 8 Brooklyn Journal of Corporate, Financial & Commercial Law 438.

strategy.[48] They invest and take active influence in the company in different ways and hope to make profit in a subsequent exit.[49] Whether these activities are to be considered beneficial for society as a whole is up for discussion. While some commentators, particularly in the German literature, are critical on the role of activist shareholders and highlight their contribution to market distortions,[50] others are convinced that activist shareholders play a positive role in monitoring the management and can contribute to the creation of market efficiency.[51]

Recent, particularly empirical, literature paints a more positive picture of activist hedge funds.[52] It says that, with their innovative orientation, they are overall very successful, as it appears that they succeed in generating profits in the companies that they invest in and influence. Recent empirical data from the United States and Europe also certify that hedge-fund activism brings benefits for the other shareholders. Thus, the entry of a hedge fund is usually associated with a significant increase in value of the stakes for the shareholders of the target company.[53] These increased returns are apparently a consequence of real improvements and reliable profits, and not a mere redistribution to the detriment of debtholders and other stakeholders.[54] Further, the holding periods of hedge funds are much longer than previously anticipated.[55] To be sure, such positive effects for the shareholders of a

[48] For some European evidence, see Ann-Kristin Achleitner, André Betzer, and Jasmin Gider, 'Do Corporate Governance Motives Drive Hedge Fund and Private Equity Fund Activities?' (2010) 16 European Financial Management 805.

[49] See in detail William W Bratton 'Hedge Funds and Governance Targets' (2007) 95 Georgetown Law Journal 1375; Thomas W Briggs, 'Corporate Governance and the New Hedge Fund Activism: An Empirical Analysis' (2007) 32 Journal of Corporation Law 681.

[50] For an overview, see Ulrich Seibert, 'Gute Aktionäre—schlechte Aktionäre—"Aktive Finanzinvestoren" und Stimmrecht' in Lutz Aderhold and others (eds), *Festschrift für Harm Peter Westermann zum 70. Geburtstag* (2008) 1505.

[51] See, for example, the position taken by former EU Commissioner Charlie McCreevy, 'Shifting up a gear—Transatlantic Cooperation in Financial Services' (Speech 07/125 at the US Chamber of Commerce, 2007):

> The evidence that hedge funds have increased the efficiency of our capital markets and increased liquidity is indisputable. That they are also keeping company managers on their toes is also indisputable. My suspicion is that much of the criticism levelled at hedge funds is based on the critics' view that management should be protected from shareholder activism, that they should be wrapped in cotton wool and have their diapers changed hourly. I do not share that point of view. On the contrary, we should go on strengthening the rights of shareholders and keep the managers under the spotlight: those who take the shilling must follow the drum!

[52] For an overview see Steven M Davidoff, 'A Standard Criticism of Activist Investors That No Longer Holds Up', *New York Times* (10 July 2013) B5.

[53] Alon Brav, Wei Jian, Frank Partnoy, and Randall Thomas, 'Hedge Fund Activism, Corporate Governance, and Firm Performance' (2008) 63 Journal of Finance 1729; April Klein and Emanuel Zur, 'Entrepreneurial Shareholder Activism: Hedge Funds and Other Private Investors' (2009) 64 Journal of Finance 187; Marco Becht Julian Franks, Colin Mayer, and Stefano Rossi, 'Returns to Shareholder Activism: Evidence from a Clinical Study of the Hermes UK Focus Fund' (2009) 22 Review of Financial Studies 3093; Lucian Bebchuk, Alon Brav, and Wei Jiang, 'The Long-Term Effects of Hedge Fund Activism' (2015) 115 Columbia Law Review 1085. See also Marco Becht, Julian Franks, and Jeremy Grant, 'Hedge Fund Activism in Europe', ECGI Finance Working Paper 283/2010; Marco Becht and others, 'The Returns to Hedge Fund Activism: An International Study', ECGI Finance Working Paper 402/2014.

[54] Brav and others (n. 53).

[55] Bidisha Chakrabarty, Pamela C Moulton, and Charles Trzcinka, 'Institutional Holding Periods', Working Paper 2013, available at <http://ssrn.com/abstract=2217588>.

company in which a hedge fund invests need to be distinguished from the question of whether a hedge fund brings profit for its own investors.[56] However, empirical evidence indicates that hedge funds make absolute returns from *c.* 5 to 7 per cent of the initial share price after commencing activism in the US, while further empirical evidence underlines that hedge funds make absolute returns of *c.* 12 per cent for the duration of a 2–3 year period following activist engagement.[57] Even though their performance during the years of the global financial crisis was much weaker, their popularity appears unaffected by this.[58]

An important and positive consequence of the occurrence of activist hedge funds was, at least in the US, that many of the traditionally rather passive investors were 'infected' by them. Some traditional funds gave up their former habit of usually voting passively with management, and followed the proposals made by activist hedge funds instead.[59] Considering this, the overall influence of hedge funds on the behaviour and the general role of shareholders should not be underestimated.[60] Conversely, the traditional investment funds may serve as a control institution. If hedge funds, in order to achieve their corporate strategy goals, are dependent on the support of other investors, and cannot pursue them alone, it can be assumed that the desired objectives bring overall benefit to shareholders as a whole. This is because the otherwise passive institutional investors can only be persuaded to lend their support to a measure which will serve all shareholders together, and not just hedge funds and other activist investors.[61] This symbiosis between activist hedge funds and passively participating mutual funds might thus contribute to an outcome in which private, idiosyncratic benefits for hedge funds are relatively constrained.

Nevertheless, caution is required. The pioneering role and power play of hedge funds and their resounding success must make market players vigilant. Hedge-fund activism has many problems of its own. In addition to relatively short-term investment horizons frequently associated with hedge funds, they pursue aggressive methods, often on the edge of legality, to arguably maximize their own immediate profit without taking into consideration the welfare of other investors. An example is the recently discussed strategy of seeking investment companies that have engaged in fraudulent or harmful business practices, but undetected and unknown to the market. After the discovery of such information, hedge funds short shares in these companies and then disclose the adverse information on them; hence the

[56] A body of scholarship is sceptical on this question: see in particular Simon Lack, *The Hedge Fund Mirage: The Illusion of Big Money and Why It's Too Good to Be True* (John Wiley 2012).

[57] Iris H-Y Chiu *The Foundations and Anatomy of Shareholder Activism* (Hart Publishing 2010) 75.

[58] Chris Flood, 'Hedge Funds Remain a Popular Choice' *Financial Times* (London, 8 June 2015) FTFm 12.

[59] Svea Herbst-Bayliss, 'Activist Investors Get More Respect amid Strong Returns', Thomson Reuters, 17 November 2013, <http://www.reuters.com/article/2013/11/18/us-investment-summit-activism-idUSBRE9AH02K20131118>. See also Gilson and Gordon (n. 45); Lipton (n. 46).

[60] Gilson and Gordon (n. 45).

[61] On this point, see Wolf-Georg Ringe 'Shareholder Activism: A Renaissance' in Jeffrey N Gordon and Wolf-Georg Ringe (eds), *The Oxford Handbook of Corporate Law and Governance* (forthcoming, Oxford University Press 2016), available at <http://www.oxfordhandbooks.com/>.

price falls and the hedge funds benefit.[62] In so acting, the business model of hedge funds is to pursue goals rather single-handedly, without seeking the support of larger partnering funds. A partial section of such activities is the subject of this book: the attempt, with economically risk-free positions, to influence the strategic direction of the firm, if necessary to the detriment of the company itself or the other shareholders. If this view is correct, then it is clear that hedge funds have limited utility in a beneficial function on the behaviour of other shareholders and can thus do more harm than good.

D. The Financial Crisis and Recent Developments

Regulation and legislation are dynamic processes that must continually adapt to new economic realities. In recent years, under the impact of the global financial crisis, our perspective on the role of shareholders in corporate governance and their voting rights has changed once again.

A general phenomenon is the ever-growing global importance of institutional investors. During the past years, most Western countries have experienced a dramatic increase in institutional ownership.[63] In the United Kingdom, for example, physical persons held 54 per cent of all publicly listed shares. This figure has dropped dramatically to under 11 per cent today.[64] The remainder is held by a broad variety of institutions, including pension funds, insurance companies, unit and investment trusts, banks, and other institutional investors, many of them residing abroad. Among the institutions that have grown in importance are also ownership entities that are associated with states, such as the controversial sovereign wealth funds.[65] In fact, the general growth of foreign ownership is the other important development: it has risen from 30.7 per cent in 1998 to 53.2 per cent today.[66]

It is this huge market share of institutional investors that has given rise to new problems, as it is the institutions that 'move the market', and yet, as we have seen,

[62] Tom Stabile, 'Fraud-chasing Profiteers Raise Questions' *Financial Times* (London, 14 May 2012) FTfm 11.

[63] Generally, see Serdar Çelik and Mats Isaksson, 'Institutional Investors and Ownership Engagement' [2013] OECD Journal: Financial Market Trends 93.

[64] Office for National Statistics, *Statistical Bulletin: Ownership of UK Quoted Shares* (2012), available at <http://www.ons.gov.uk/ons/dcp171778_327674.pdf>.

[65] On this issue, see Ronald J Gilson and Curtis Milhaupt, 'Sovereign Wealth Funds and Corporate Governance: A Minimalist Solution to the New Mercantilism' (2008) 60 Stanford Law Review 1345; Heike Schweitzer, 'Sovereign Wealth Funds—Market Investors or "Imperialist Capitalists"? The European Response to Direct Investments by Non-EU State-controlled Entities' in Ulf Bernitz and Wolf-Georg Ringe (eds), *Company Law and Economic Protectionism* (Oxford University Press 2010) 250; Mette Neville, 'Shareholder Activism: The Suspicious Shareholder' in Hanne Søndergaard Birkmose, Mette Neville, and Karsten Engsig Sørensen (eds), *The European Financial Market in Transition* (Alphen aan den Rijn 2012) 217.

[66] Office for National Statistics (n. 64).

have largely remained passive in their attitude to corporate strategy and their investment targets. Through free-riding on the decisions made by others, these institutions have grown steadily and left many public companies virtually 'ownerless'.

The larger the market share owned by institutional investors, the more the focus of regulatory attention has moved from the external relationship between institutional investors and target companies to the legal relationships *within* the institutions themselves. For example, it is often unclear who the decision-makers are within such investment companies, in whose interest they act, and which internal incentive structures and temporal perspectives exist. New research has coined the terminology of the 'agency costs of agency capitalism' to describe this phenomenon.[67]

One regulatory response is the development of incentive or 'stewardship' codes. The United Kingdom was at the forefront of this initiative. A few years ago, the Financial Reporting Council (FRC) evaluated the British corporate governance standards of the Combined Code on Corporate Governance to determine if they still met the current economic conditions in the United Kingdom. As a result of the consultation and subsequent reform, they adopted, inter alia, the so-called UK Stewardship Code, and renamed the Combined Code as the UK Corporate Governance Code.[68] The Stewardship Code explicitly establishes rules of conduct for institutional investors.[69] These include rules to monitor the portfolio companies, the tightening of rules for the protection or promotion of shareholder value, guidelines for collective activities with other investors, requirements for voting and voting policy and conflicts of interest, and finally public reporting requirements. The FRC urges all institutional investors to publicly declare whether and how they follow the recommendations of the Code. In addition, all Asset Management Funds authorized in the United Kingdom must issue a declaration (statement of commitment) or otherwise explain why compliance with the Code is not appropriate for their business model.[70] Market participants, however, are sceptical about whether the British advance has actually resulted in increased shareholder engagement.[71] Nevertheless, the concept of a Stewardship Code has

67 Ronald J Gilson and Jeffrey N Gordon 'The Agency Costs of Agency Capitalism: Activist Investors and the Revaluation of Governance Rights' (2013) 113 Columbia Law Review 863.

68 Both Codes are available at <http://www.frc.org.uk/Our-Work/Codes-Standards/Corporate-governance.aspx>.

69 For academic comment on the Stewardship Code, see Brian Cheffins 'The Stewardship Code's Achilles' Heel' (2010) 73 Modern Law Review 1004; Simon Wong 'Why Stewardship is Proving Elusive for Institutional Investors' (2010) 25 Butterworths Journal of International Banking and Financial Law 406; Iris H-Y Chiu, 'Turning Institutional Investors into "Stewards": Exploring the Meaning and Objectives in "Stewardship"' (2013) 66 Current Legal Problems 443; Iris H-Y Chiu, 'Reviving Shareholder Stewardship: Critically Examining the Impact of Corporate Transparency Reforms in the UK' [2014] Delaware Journal of Corporate Law 983.

70 Financial Services Authority (FSA), *Conduct of Business Sourcebook (Stewardship Code) Instrument 2010*, FSA 2010/57.

71 Pauline Skypala, 'Fund Managers Cannot Be Stewards' *Financial Times* (London, 19 March 2012) FTFm 6.

attracted attention elsewhere, and the European Union is currently discussing plans to introduce comparable EU-wide standards.[72]

Furthermore, the financial crisis of 2007/8 has thrown some of our traditional assumptions on the behaviour and role of shareholders in general into question, particularly with regard to their investment period and their investment goals. It has become obvious that the growing importance of global financial markets has created new incentives for shareholders on a different scale. In particular, they are accused of showing no interest in the long-term prospects of a company in which they invest. Instead, they are arguably only interested in short-term and fast profit, without any loyalty to the company in which they are investing. This issue has reached the mainstream political agenda; preliminary consultations are running and could result in corresponding legislative acts.[73] In particular, in the context of banks and other financial institutions, which are alleged to have taken excessive risks before and during the crisis, policy-makers claim that shareholders have promoted these risks in terms of their short or very short investment horizons, often amounting only to a few months.[74]

One of the perceived reasons for these incentives is the key principle of limited liability of shareholders, which allows them to benefit from positive upside, but to be only partly exposed to the risk of losses: their risk-exposure on the downside is limited.[75] In this context, the repeated attempts of the pre-crisis period to align the interests of the management with the interests of shareholders—for example, with performance-based compensation—may have contributed to an increase in the risk of companies. Arguably, this development has led to the well-known phenomenon of exorbitant executive pay, based on a short-term

[72] Some elements are found in ongoing reform of the Shareholder Rights Directive. European Commission, *Proposal for a Directive of the European Parliament and of the Council amending Directive 2007/36/EC as regards the Encouragement of Long-term Shareholder Engagement and Directive 2013/34/EU as regards Certain Elements of the Corporate Governance Statement*, COM(2014) 213 final. By way of background, see European Commission, *Communication from the Commission to the European Parliament, the Council, the European Economic and Social Committee and the Committee of the Regions, Action Plan: European Company Law and Corporate Governance—A Modern Legal Framework for More Engaged Shareholders and Sustainable Companies*, COM(2012) 740 final, para. 2.4; European Commission, *Green Paper—Corporate Governance in Financial Institutions and Remuneration Policies*, COM(2010) 284 final, question 5.2; European Commission, *Green Paper—The EU Corporate Governance Framework*, COM(2011) 164, para. 2.3.

[73] See on this topic for example the consultation by the UK Department for Business, Innovation & Skills (BIS): BIS, *A Long-Term Focus for Corporate Britain—A Call for Evidence* (URN 10/1225, 2010); European Commission, *Green Paper—Corporate Governance in Financial Institutions and Remuneration Policies*, COM(2010) 284 final, 8; European Commission, *Green Paper—The EU Corporate Governance Framework*, COM(2011) 164, 10. Furthermore, see the *Kay Review of UK Equity Markets and Long-Term Decision Making*, available at <https://www.gov.uk/government/consultations/the-kay-review-of-uk-equity-markets-and-long-term-decision-making>.

[74] See, for example, Rakesh Khurana and Andy Zelleke, 'You Can Cap the Pay, but the Greed Will Go On' *The Washington Post* (8 February 2009) B01.

[75] See European Commission, *Green Paper—The EU Corporate Governance Framework* (n. 72) 10 f. See also European Commission, *Corporate Governance in Financial Institutions: Lessons to be Drawn from the Current Financial Crisis, Best Practices* (Commission Staff Document SEC(2010) 669, 2010) 23.

perspective and targeting the goal of shareholder value as the sole performance measure.[76]

The topic examined in the present study is often associated with the currently perceived short-term orientation of investors. Risk-decoupling strategies, so the argument goes, make it possible to manipulate the influence on the company's interest and harm long-term oriented investors in particular.[77] In academic scholarship, scepticism over the perceived 'short-term' orientation and its negative effects prevails.[78]

Drawing these issues together, the European Commission considered action to be necessary. The two recent Green Papers on Corporate Governance[79] inter alia take stock of the role of shareholders in corporate governance and list, among others, the following points as relevant for future legislative activity:

- certain profitability models, based on possession of portfolios of different shares, lead to the abstraction, or even disappearance, of the concept of ownership normally associated with holding shares;
- the costs that institutional investors would face if they wanted to actively engage in governance of a company can dissuade them, particularly if their participation is minimal;
- intermediation of investments has increased, amplifying the importance of the agency relationship between long-term investors and their asset managers. It has been argued that the agency relationship actually contributes to short-termism on the market, which may also cause mispricing, herd behaviour, increased volatility, and lack of ownership of listed companies;
- conflicts of interest seem to be one of the reasons for a lack of shareholder engagement; they often arise where an institutional investor or asset manager, or its parent company, has a business interest in the investee company. An example of this can be found in financial groups where the asset management branch may not want to be seen to actively exercise its shareholder rights in a company to which its parent company provides services or in which it has a shareholding;
- the lack of effective rights allowing shareholders to exercise control (such as, for example, the lack of voting rights on director remuneration in certain jurisdictions), the maintenance of certain obstacles to the exercise of cross-border voting rights, uncertainty over certain legal concepts (for example that

[76] See already (pre-crisis) José-Miguel Gaspar, Massimo Massa, and Pedro Matos, 'Shareholder Investment Horizons and the Market for Corporate Control' (2005) 76 Journal of Financial Economics 135.

[77] See, for example, Hermes Equity Ownership Services, *Response to ESMA's Call for Evidence on Empty Voting*, 25 November 2011.

[78] See Mark J Roe, 'Corporate Short-Termism—In the Boardroom and in the Courtroom' (2013) 68 The Business Lawyer 977; Jesse M Fried, 'The Uneasy Case for Favoring Long-Term Shareholders' (2015) 124 Yale Law Journal 1554.

[79] See n. 72.

> of 'acting in concert'), and companies' disclosure to shareholders of information which is too complicated and unreadable, in particular with regard to risk, could all play a part, to varying degrees, in dissuading investors from playing an active role in the financial institutions in which they have invested.

The European Commission has analysed these problems first in the more specific context of corporate governance of banks and financial institutions, and subsequently also taken all listed companies into consideration.[80] Among the measures considered are initiatives to strengthen shareholder co-operation through the creation of discussion platforms, the publication of the voting decisions exercised by institutional investors, the above-mentioned rules of conduct for institutional investors (Stewardship Codes), the identification and publication of conflicts of interest of institutional investors, the disclosure of a remuneration policy of institutional investors for financial intermediaries, and an improvement in the level of information provided to investors about the risks associated with an investment.

At the end of 2012, the Commission presented an Action Plan, which transferred the theoretical framework into specific regulatory objectives for the coming years.[81] The Action Plan is based on the three main areas of improving transparency between the company and its investors, strengthening long-term commitment of shareholders, and improving the legal framework for cross-border functionality of firms.[82] As one of the first initiatives, the Commission proposed a revision of the Shareholder Rights Directive, which introduces some of the ideas that we discussed previously, such as the 'stewardship' idea. Further, the proposed revision would introduce tools to further the identification of shareholders, the facilitation of voting rights by the ultimate owners, and transparency of institutional investors.[83]

E. Shareholders and Risk-decoupling

Whatever one may think of shareholders as a group or individually, it is important for the ongoing debate to properly understand who these shareholders are and what their motives are. One key to understanding the proper place of equity in the governance of corporation is the *risk* that they hold. Every investment is a consequence of a risk assessment, and the legal framework plays an important part of that assessment. Every investment decision is based on a cost–benefit analysis of the risks involved, and every shareholder action, voting decision, or

[80] This is reflected in the two different Green Papers.

[81] European Commission, *Communication from the Commission to the European Parliament, the Council, the European Economic and Social Committee and the Committee of the Regions—Action Plan: European Company Law and Corporate Governance—A Modern Legal Framework for more Engaged Shareholders and Sustainable Companies*, COM(2012) 740 final.

[82] ibid. 5.

[83] The European Parliament adopted a number of amendments in July 2015. The legislative process is still ongoing.

shareholder campaign will take into account the financial risks involved. Thus, if regulators (and academics) are seeking ways to make sure that we can 'trust' shareholders and their influence, we must endeavour to ensure that risks and benefits are properly aligned.

It is precisely at this point that this study intervenes in the shareholder power debate. As we will see, one of the central points of this study is that the congruence between risk and share ownership is very much and increasingly questionable. In fact, due to commercial realities in equity ownership, today's capital markets, equity ownership, and commercial risk are no longer necessarily sure to be aligned.

This book thus contributes to the debate on shareholders in corporate governance by exploring the possibilities of severing the link between equity position (share ownership) and risk incurred. The present study is less interested in a detailed account of the mechanics of risk-decoupling, and more in the implications for both equity markets and regulators alike. I will show that various techniques exist to decouple risk from ownership, and which can potentially be used on a larger scale.

This intentional deconstruction of equity investment can take two forms. First, hedge funds may want to reduce the risk usually associated with an equity investment. They do this for obvious reasons: a shareholder with reduced risk exposure retains her voting power and her influence in the company, but she does not bear the risk of negative returns. This strategy is what we may call 'negative decoupling'. Second, activist investors can attempt to produce the opposite effect: they can acquire an economic stake in a company without gaining voting power. This may be particularly interesting during takeover situations because, under the circumstances, laws traditionally only require the disclosure of voting positions, not economic exposure.[84] Here the economic risk is higher than the voting power, and we may term this 'positive decoupling'.[85]

As a consequence of such decoupling activities, the legal framework governing our capital markets and corporate law must take this development into account. It is the objective of law and legal rules to respond to incidents of actual importance and to solve real-life problems. The law must thus remain adaptive and responsive to the constantly changing challenges of our society and our business life. The field of corporate law is no exception. The groundbreaking choices of modern corporate law are rooted in the needs of business life. For instance, consider the nineteenth-century ambition of encouraging investment in expensive projects, such as the construction of railways.[86] The decisions to grant companies separate

[84] This is under the EU Transparency Directive. See Directive 2004/109/EC of the European Parliament and of the Council of 15 December 2004 on the harmonisation of transparency requirements in relation to information about issuers whose securities are admitted to trading on a regulated market and amending Directive 2001/34/EC, [2004] OJ L390/38. The Directive has been modified several times.

[85] The American scholars Henry Hu and Bernard Black have coined the notions of 'empty voting' and 'hidden ownership' for these two situations. These terms are highly illustrative but can be a little misleading and imprecise. See Henry TC Hu and Bernard Black, 'The New Vote Buying: Empty Voting and Hidden (Morphable) Ownership' (2006) 79 Southern California Law Review 811.

[86] On separate legal personality, see Henry Hansmann, Reinier Kraakman, and Richard Squire, 'Law and the Rise of the Firm' (2006) 119 Harvard Law Review 1333; Henry Hansmann and Reinier

legal personalities and to introduce limited liability for their shareholders stem from this ambition. As a consequence of introducing the concepts of legal personality and limited liability, company law attempts to solve many ensuing problems, including the conflict between the shareholders and the creditors of a company.[87]

Many of the techniques analysed and discussed in this book are used by hedge funds. Internationally, law-makers and regulators are looking for ways to respond to the new, unusual players in the corporate landscape, who have emerged by questioning some of the cornerstones of corporate law. One of the many strategies of hedge funds, which have become the focus of regulators in recent years, is their intentional exploitation of loopholes in the legal system to break up the connection between risk and influence in shares of their portfolio companies, as described previously. That is, while a normal shareholder would always bear a certain economic risk that corresponds to the size of his stake in the company, hedge funds, by contrast, try to disconnect the relationship between equity and risk. When discussing these strategies, therefore, this book is also a contribution to the literature on the regulation of hedge funds and their activist initiatives in corporate ownership more generally.

This book addresses both forms of equity decoupling. It looks at the various forms of positive and negative risk-decoupling strategies and sheds light on their overall desirability. The main approach is functional–comparative in nature, focusing on law and economics, as well as traditional corporate and financial law scholarship. The jurisdictional focus will be on UK and US law, albeit with frequent discussions of various continental European jurisdictions. Particular emphasis will be placed on developing a legislative solution in the EU context.

Four distinct theoretical perspectives are used as an analytical framework to examine the vast challenges of risk-decoupling: (a) a classical agency cost approach; (b) an information cost perspective; (c) a corporate finance viewpoint; and (d) insights from the market for corporate control. We will see that shareholders with hedged risk exposure do not correspond to the traditional market expectations of shareholders. Corporate law is still widely based on the nineteenth-century assumption of optimal risk alignment and has not followed the pace of modern financial engineering opportunities. Risk-decoupling strategies create both agency and information costs for investors. Furthermore, they generate challenges for traditional categories of corporate finance, aiming to extract the 'best of both worlds'—that is, both debt and equity.

Kraakman, 'The Essential Role of Organizational Law' (2000) 110 Yale Law Journal 387. On limited liability, see Frank Easterbrook and Daniel Fischel, 'Limited Liability and the Corporation' (1985) 52 University of Chicago Law Review 89; Richard A Posner, 'The Rights of Creditors of Affiliated Corporations' (1976) 43 University of Chicago Law Review 499; see also Henry Hansmann and Reinier Kraakman, 'Toward Unlimited Shareholder Liability for Corporate Torts' (1991) 100 Yale Law Journal 1879.

[87] Reinier Kraakman and others, *The Anatomy of Corporate Law: A Comparative and Functional Approach* (2nd edn, Oxford University Press 2009) 35–7.

Based on the insights developed from these policy perspectives, I develop a number of regulatory reform proposals, particularly with regard to the EU context. Designing an adequate disclosure system is the appropriate and most effective remedy for the problems previously identified. In some exceptional situations, however, the regulator should be empowered to disenfranchise shareholders by imposing voting restrictions.

F. Conclusion

This section has provided the theoretical underpinnings for the economic and legal significance of shareholder voting rights. The right to vote is generally granted to equity investors as the residual owners of the corporation. Shareholders are assumed to have relatively homogeneous interests and seek to achieve the maximization of returns. It has become clear, however, that the exercising of voting rights by shareholders is often problem-burdened, as problems of collective action make it rational for individual shareholders generally to not exercise their voting rights. Exceptions may apply, however, for major shareholders and activist investors whose business models are dedicated to the pursuit of company strategy. The latter type of investor is the main focus of this study. We have, however, seen that the incentives of these institutional investors are not always optimal, and risk-decoupling is a prime example of a potentially pathological investment strategy.

III
Risk-Decoupling Strategies

The background explanations given so far allow us now to approach the specific topic of interest, which is decoupled risk in equity securities, in more detail. Risk-decoupling can be effectuated in a number of different ways. On the most granular level, we need to distinguish between risk increase and risk reduction.

A. Negative versus Positive Risk-decoupling

As a first step, a distinction must be made between shareholders who reduce the risk typically inherent in shares *below* the usual level, which will be referred to herein as 'negative risk-decoupling', and those shareholders who (as a mirror image) enter into a *higher* risk exposure than the normal state, which we may accordingly call 'positive risk-decoupling'. Although both phenomena appear to be related topics at first glance, they present problems of very different nature and intensity.

In *negative risk-decoupling situations*, the shareholder strives to retain a formal regular shareholder position, and to reduce or eliminate its risk exposure in terms of the share price development by means of different strategies. The holder of the share therefore seeks to keep their entitlement to all formal shareholder rights such as the right to vote, but attempts to exclude (or to limit) bearing the economic consequences of their actions. Such a situation may be brought about in various ways and will be illustrated by introducing separate categories in the following section. As a catchy label, scholars have introduced the notion of 'empty voting' to describe this situation.[1] This, however, only singles out one specific scenario, that of complete risk depletion, as a *pars pro toto* to describe a much larger problem, that of *reduced* risk. Thus, shareholder risk may only be partially reduced, not completely, or it may be over-reduced when the negative interest exceeds the positive exposure ('negative voting').[2] This book uses the term 'negative risk-decoupling' to encapsulate all of these different variants. Their different sub-categories are described later.

[1] Henry T C Hu and Bernard S Black, 'The New Vote Buying: Empty Voting and Hidden (Morphable) Ownership' (2006) 79 Southern California Law Review 811; Henry T C Hu and Bernard S Black, 'Empty Voting and Hidden (Morphable) Ownership: Taxonomy, Implications, and Reforms' (2006) 61 Business Lawyer 1011.

[2] On the latter, see for example Jonathan Cohen, 'Negative Voting: Why it Destroys Shareholder Value and a Proposal to Prevent It' (2008) 45 Harvard Journal on Legislation 237, 249 ff.

Positive risk-decoupling is the counterpart of negative risk-decoupling. In these situations, the economic risk exceeds the formal shareholder position. The market participant bears the typical risk in terms of the share price development of a particular company, but does not formally hold the position of a shareholder; in particular, he does not hold the corresponding shareholder voting rights. Such a construction is used primarily in takeover attempts. As we will see, the EU regulatory disclosure regime in capital markets usually uses the criterion of voting rights as a determining factor.[3] This allows for hidden stake-building through such derivatives and similar instruments that conceal the voting position. 'Hidden ownership' has become the prevailing term to describe these situations.[4] We will discuss 'positive risk-decoupling' in section III.C.

We will now turn to look at negative risk-decoupling in more detail. The following illustration is an attempt to create a taxonomy of different categories that occur in real business life. In the subsequent Chapter V, the discussion will turn to the legal and economic problems that arise in these different constellations.

Negative risk-decoupling can be implemented by market participants in various ways. Three main examples include the use of financial derivatives (category 1), share lending (category 2), and record-date capture (category 3). These activities can all be used either to reduce or to eliminate the inherent shareholder risk. Each strategy will be considered in turn.

B. Negative Risk-decoupling: More Influence than Risk

1. Category 1: Financial derivatives

The first example of a negative risk-decoupling strategy is the use of financial derivatives to reduce share risk.[5] The financial industry has developed a number of instruments that hedge shareholder exposure and shift the risk to another market participant.

At the most basic level, derivatives are financial instruments that allow a partial transfer of risk from the underlying reference values. Their price or value depends on a future price of trade goods (for example raw materials or food), assets (securities, such as shares or bonds), market-related reference variables (interest rates, indices), or specific events (such as the insolvency of a person or a state). Therefore, they are referred to as forward contracts in a broader sense. Their economic importance is enormous. They enable companies to hedge in international trade

[3] See text accompanying n. 198.

[4] Further, we can distinguish between 'hidden' and 'morphable' ownership. See Hu and Black, 'New Vote Buying' (n. 1).

[5] See Avner Kalay and Shagun Pant, 'Time Varying Voting Rights and the Private Benefits of Control', (Social Science Research Network 2009), available at <http://ssrn.com/abstract=1102832>.

against exchange rate, interest rate, and commodity price fluctuations. According to a recent survey by the International Swaps and Derivatives Association (ISDA), about 94 per cent of the world's 500 largest companies use derivatives to hedge against commercial and financial risks.[6] Foreign exchange derivatives and interest rate derivatives were most frequently used by these companies.[7]

In essence, derivatives are nothing more than contracts. Some of them are standardized and are traded on specific exchanges; some will be concluded individually, 'over the counter' (OTC).[8] Derivatives are risk transfer instruments the value of which depends on the changes in the value of an underlying reference asset. They can be structured in different forms and referenced to different types of assets.[9] Derivatives can be settled either physically or in cash. In the former case, a successful investment leads to the delivery of the physical reference asset, whereas in the latter case, the investor only receives in cash the net change in the value of the reference asset.[10] Well-known examples are options and warrants as well as forwards, futures, and swaps. They are of interest for the present study only insofar as they are referred to as equity or other shares, because they make it possible to transfer to another party the risk inherent in a share, without formally transferring the share itself.

To illustrate, we may consider the example of a simple trader who holds 100 shares of company X plc, trading at £50 per share. The simplest way to transfer the risk of this long position to another market participant would be for the trader to sell the shares, using a 'future' derivative. These instruments are standardized contracts between two parties to exchange a specified number of shares for a price agreed today to be delivered at a specified future date. This contract would free the trader from the risk of a price drop of X plc shares since he has already sold them. Nevertheless, he remains the shareholder, the 'owner' of the shares, until he has delivered them to the purchaser.

On a more sophisticated level, equity swap derivatives can transfer the entire risk of share price movements to the counterparty of a transaction.[11] Imagine two parties in a transaction, A and B, who agree to distribute the risk of the share price of X plc as follows: A has to reimburse B for any losses that the share price of X incurs over an agreed time period. Conversely, B has to pay A the equivalent of any

[6] International Swaps and Derivatives Association, *Derivatives Usage Survey*, Research Notes 2/2009, April 2009, available at <http://www.isda.org/researchnotes/pdf/ISDA-Research-Notes2.pdf>.

[7] The precise data are available at <http://www.isda.org/statistics/stat_nav.html>.

[8] For an overview, see Table III.1.

[9] Henry T C Hu, 'Hedging Expectations: "Derivative Reality" and the Law and Finance of the Corporate Objective' (1995) 73 Texas Law Review 985, 996; see also House of Lords European Union Committee, 10th Report of Session 2009–2010, 'The Future Regulation of Derivatives Markets: Is the EU on the Right Track?' dated 31 March 2010, available at <http://www.publications.parliament.uk/pa/ld200910/ldselect/ldeucom/93/93.pdf> accessed 9 March 2015, 8–12, which underlines the small size of equity derivatives in comparison to foreign exchange and interest rate derivatives.

[10] See Alastair Hudson, *The Law of Finance* (2nd edn, Sweet & Maxwell 2013) ch. 40.

[11] Henry T C Hu and Bernard S Black, 'Equity and Debt Decoupling and Empty Voting II: Importance and Extensions' (2008) 156 University of Pennsylvania Law Review 625, 640.

gains that the X shares make during the same time. Under this type of equity swap contract, A is called the 'long side', while B is called the 'short side', as A bears the same risk as if he held the agreed number of X shares, while B's interest is the exact opposite. For our purpose, the most interesting consequences emanate where B (the short side) is simultaneously a regular shareowner in X with the same amount of shares that are referenced under the swap agreement. If this is the case, B will be equally short as long as B's risk in the shares will be entirely eliminated. If the shares increase in value, B will have to reimburse the gains to A under the swap agreement, and if their value drops, B will be compensated by A for any losses. In other words, where a shareholder holds a corresponding short position pursuant to a derivative agreement, he may entirely lose his economic exposure to the shares and become indifferent as to the share price.[12]

Theoretically, most derivatives that shift risk onto another party can achieve a similar result.[13] For instance, a shareholder may use a short call—the sale of a right to purchase—or a long put—the purchase of a right to sell—to effectuate a similar result. Also, the shareholder could simply sell short an amount of shares corresponding to the long side in shares they hold. Short selling also creates a short position in shares.[14] Finally, it must be noted that the ratio between long and short positions can even be negative; namely, the holder of a block of shares may hold derivatives conferring a negative interest that exceeds the positive exposure.

Table III.1 Overview of derivatives and their use for risk-decoupling

Derivative	Short description	A	B
Forward, Future	Sale with performance in the future	Single stock future	
Call	Right to purchase	Short call (Sale of a right to purchase)	Long call (Purchase of a right to purchase)
Put	Right to sell	Long put (Purchase of a right to sell)	Short put (Sale of a right to sell)
Swap	Exchange of cash flows	Writer (short side)	Equity (long side)

(A = shareholder, B = bank)

[12] It should be noted that the long side of the swap agreement will usually also be interested in hedging its position. It can, for instance, short sell a corresponding share position to eliminate its risk from the derivative; ibid. 642.

[13] See, in detail, Kalay and Pant (n. 5) 2 ff.

[14] Henry T C Hu and Bernard S Black, 'Hedge Funds, Insiders, and the Decoupling of Economic and Voting Ownership: Empty Voting and Hidden (Morphable) Ownership' (2007) 13 Journal of Corporate Finance 343, 348; Roberta Karmel, 'Voting Power Without Responsibility or Risk: How Should Proxy Reform Address the Decoupling of Economic and Voting Rights?' (2010) 55 Villanova Law Review 93, 103. This situation became relevant in *Deephaven Risk Arb. Trading Ltd. v UnitedGlobalCom, Inc.*, No. Civ.A. 379-N, 2005 WL 1713067 (Del. Ch. July 13, 2005). Regarding this case, see Michael Lee, 'Empty Voting: Private Solutions to a Private Problem' [2007] Columbia Business Law Review 883, 886.

a) *The* Mylan–Perry *case*

The famous *Mylan–Perry* case, depicted in Figure III.1, illustrates this concept.[15] The case relates to an American takeover battle in 2004, in which Mylan Laboratories, Inc. sought to acquire King Pharmaceuticals, Inc. An American hedge fund, Perry Corp., had a significant ownership stake in King (the target) and stood to benefit from the takeover, which offered King's shareholders a 61 per cent premium.[16] However, it was unclear whether the takeover would benefit Mylan shareholders. In fact, some of the shareholders, including iconic hedge fund manager Carl Icahn, voiced strong concerns.[17] Since the takeover depended on an approving vote by the Mylan shareholders, Perry began its unusual strategy. It bought 10 per cent of Mylan's outstanding shares while intending to vote them in favour of the transaction. Perry proceeded to enter swap transactions that hedged risk from any potential drop in Mylan's share price. Technically speaking, Perry took the short side of a total return equity swap with third parties, essentially banks. These have been described previously.[18] As Perry referenced as many Mylan shares as it had previously bought on the stock market, it was indifferent as to the development of the share price. As a result, Perry could vote the Mylan shares in favour of the takeover, without fearing any potential economic downside (as other Mylan shareholders), in order to realize the value from the takeover as a King shareholder.[19]

The transaction was never consummated, for unrelated reasons.[20] In 2009, the Securities and Exchange Commission (SEC) announced a settlement agreement

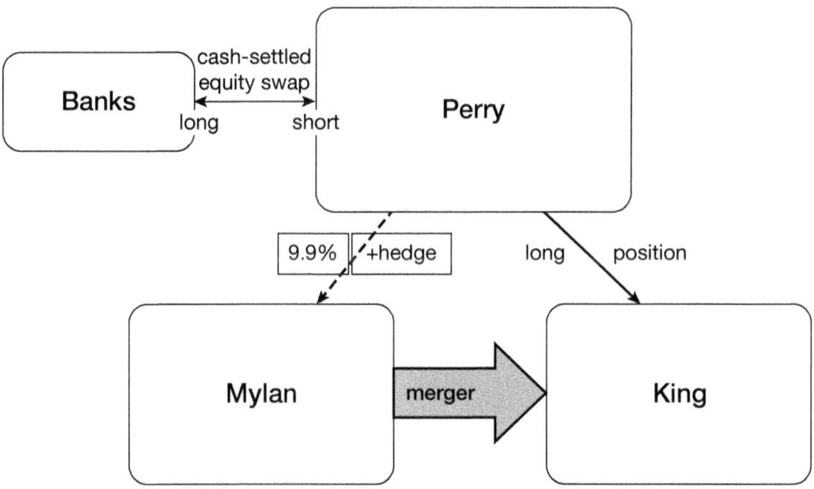

Figure III.1 The *Mylan–Perry* transaction

[15] See on this case the illustrations by Juan Ramirez, *Handbook of Corporate Equity Derivatives and Equity Capital Markets* (Wiley 2011) 242 ff.; see also Hu and Black, 'New Vote Buying' (n. 1) 816; Hu and Black, Taxonomy, Implications, and Reforms (n. 1) 1024.

[16] Hu and Black, 'New Vote Buying' (n. 1) 828.

[17] ibid.

[18] See text accompanying n. 10.

[19] Hu and Black, 'New Vote Buying' (n. 1) 828.

[20] ibid. 829.

with Perry over the question of whether the hedge fund correctly disclosed its accumulation of nearly 10 per cent in Mylan shares.[21] This settlement, however, only concerned the question of disclosure of the long position, and did not address the wider question of risk-decoupling. Pursuant to the settlement, Perry paid a $150,000 fine without admitting any wrongdoing.[22]

b) Other examples and implications

It should be noted that a total elimination of the risk, as in the *Mylan–Perry* case, is certainly an exceptional situation, and academic comment rightly emphasizes that comparable cases are certainly not frequent in real life. Another case that has become public and discussed by a wider audience is the *Stark/M-Flex* takeover bid, which cannot be discussed in detail here.[23]

A reliable comprehensive empirical study on the frequency of risk-decoupling situations does not exist.[24] Nevertheless, it should be noted that Professors Henry Hu and Bernard Black compiled an impressionistic overview of various risk-decoupling situations that have been reported by public media. Up until 2008, they collected a total of eighty-two incidences worldwide.[25] Hu is currently working on an update of this study and intends to publish the revised statistics soon.[26] Empirical findings are further discussed in section III.D.

When discussing the frequency of negative decoupling scenarios, a complete elimination of risk as in *Mylan–Perry* is likely to be an exception. But it does not seem implausible that derivatives are more often used by hedge funds to produce, at the very least, a *partial* reduction of the risk. The SEC's investigation into the *Mylan–Perry* case discussed 'merger arbitrage', a common behaviour of hedge funds during corporate takeovers.[27] It should be noted that the decoupling effect of derivatives may also be purely temporary in character.[28] Unlike traditional deviations from the 'one share, one vote' standard, such as multiple voting shares, derivative contracts allow hedge funds to construct economically similar results selectively in certain well-timed situations.[29]

[21] See *In the Matter of Perry Corp. Respondent*, Exchange Act Release Nos. 2907 & 60351, 2009 WL 2163550 (21 July 2009).

[22] Securities and Exchange Commission, Press Release 2009-165, *SEC Charges Perry Corp. with Disclosure Violations in Vote Buying Scheme* (21 July 2009), available at <http://www.sec.gov/news/press/2009/2009-165.htm>.

[23] On this story in more detail Hu and Black, 'Hedge Funds and Insiders' (n. 14) 349; Hu and Black, 'Empty Voting II' (n. 11) 634 f; Davies Ward Phillips & Vineberg LLP, *The Quality of the Shareholder Vote in Canada* (Discussion Paper, October 2010) 128 f., available at <http://www.dwpv.com/Sites/shareholdervoting/media/The-Quality-of-the-Shareholder-Vote-in-Canada.pdf>.

[24] See on various attempts to provide empirical evidence section III.D.

[25] Hu and Black, 'New Vote Buying' (n. 1) 861 ff.

[26] Henry T C Hu, 'Debt, "Debt Governance," and the Decoupling Framework: "Empty Creditors," "Hidden Non-Interests," and the Matter of Evidence', conference manuscript, June 2013.

[27] *In the Matter of Perry Corp. Respondent*, Exchange Act Release Nos. 2907 & 60351, 2009 WL 2163550, at *3 (21 July 2009).

[28] This is emphasized by Kalay and Pant (n. 5).

[29] See ibid.

A more typical activity for risk-eliminating or risk-reducing transactions is hedging transactions of management or other senior employees of the company. Using so-called 'collar transactions' or 'executive equity swaps', an investor can, for instance, sell a call option at a certain strike price and purchase a put option at a lower exercise price.[30] For a relatively low price, an investor can, in this way, limit the potential appreciation or depreciation of their long shares within a range (of a *collar*) between the two prices. Empirical studies have shown that management and senior personnel often use these structures to avoid or reduce the risk exposure of an equity stake they hold.[31] Thus, economically speaking, such transactions amount to a countermeasure against the multiple regulatory efforts over recent years to introduce variable components into executive remuneration. Stock option plans, employee share-based programmes, and other schemes have become popular to better align the interests of management and shareholders and to incentivize management to take on more risk.[32] Hedging these elements of variable pay may thus eliminate the incentives established by them.[33] This type of hedging transaction is particularly problematic when managers engage in the practice because they may possess insider information. The risk is that they can use the transaction, in addition to a hedge in their equity stake, to the detriment of shareholders.[34] The SEC has just recently initiated regulatory action on this topic, proposing to mandate disclosure of individual hedging arrangements.[35]

c) Short sales

So far, we have described how the economic risk of the share price can be reduced or eliminated using financial derivatives. A related technique, which is more expensive and therefore not as common in practice, is the use of *short selling*.[36]

30 See Paul Bolster, Don Chance, and Don Rich, 'Executive Equity Swaps and Corporate Insider Holdings' (1996) 25(2) Financial Management 14.

31 See J Carr Bettis, John M Bizjak, and Michael L Lemmon, 'Managerial Ownership, Incentive Contracting, and the Use of Zero-Cost Collars and Equity Swaps by Corporate Insiders' (2001) 36 Journal of Financial and Quantitative Analysis 345; Lucian Bebchuk and Jesse Fried, 'Executive Compensation as an Agency Problem' (2003) 17 Journal of Economic Perspectives 71; see also Securities and Exchange Commission, *Concept Release on the U.S. Proxy System* (Release Nos 34-62495, IA-3052, IC-29340; File No S7-14-10, 2010), (2010) 75 Federal Register 42981, 43018.

32 See Kevin J Murphy, 'Explaining Executive Compensation: Managerial Power versus the Perceived Cost of Stock Options' (2002) 69 University of Chicago Law Review 847.

33 Lucian Bebchuk and Jesse Fried, *Pay Without Performance. The Unfulfilled Promise of Executive Compensation* (Cambridge, MA, 2004) 176 f. More recently, Institutional Shareholder Services Inc. (ISS), *U.S. Corporate Governance Policy: 2013 Updates* (16 November 2012) 4, available at <http://www.issgovernance.com/file/files/2013USPolicyUpdates.pdf> accessed 17 August 2015.

34 Bebchuk and Fried, ibid. 61 ff.

35 Securities and Exchange Commission, *Disclosure of Hedging by Employees, Officers and Directors*, SEC Release No 339723 (9 February 2015), available at <https://www.sec.gov/rules/proposed/2015/33-9723.pdf> accessed 19 August 2015. See Commissioner Luis A Aguilar, 'Aligning the Interests of Company Executives and Directors with Shareholders' (9 February 2015), available at <http://www.sec.gov/news/statement/020915-ps-claa.html> accessed 19 August 2015.

36 Hu and Black, 'Hedge Funds and Insiders' (n. 14) 348.

Under certain conditions, short selling can create an equally hedged or even negative interest in the share price.

To begin with, a 'short sale' means nothing other than a sale of securities that the seller does not own. Usually, the seller borrows to-be-sold securities first ('covered' short sale)—after an ideally falling market price, the seller hopes to buy them cheaper in the market and then return them to the borrower.[37] The transaction can also occur without borrowing the shares initially, which is called a 'naked' or 'uncovered' short sale.[38]

A short position thus increases the interest in falling prices. Thus, if an investor holds regular shares (long) and also sells shares in the same company short, his positive interest from the long position is reduced, possibly even eliminated altogether. Where the short position exceeds the long position, the shareholder will even have an overall interest in a *negative* price performance.[39] The economic effect is thus quite similar to the derivatives described previously. Nevertheless, the use of short selling in order to decouple risk in practice is much more expensive and complex than the simple use of derivatives and remains less important in practice compared to derivatives. As a result of the new European Short Selling Regulation, the permissibility of naked short selling has now also been largely restricted.[40]

A recent case of this category even made it to the headlines of the press: the conflict between the Canadian telecommunications company Telus and US hedge fund Mason Capital, which kept Canadian courts busy throughout 2012.[41] Canada-based Telus Corporation has traditionally had a dual share structure composed of voting shares and non-voting shares, the former having historically traded at a premium of about 5 per cent as compared to the latter. In early 2012, Telus proposed to consolidate the two classes into one. When Telus announced this share consolidation plan, the market responded quickly, and the traditional market price difference between the two share classes narrowed. Mason Capital, however, pursued an alternative strategy. Over a long period, the fund invested in Telus voting-class shares and at the same time reduced the number of both voting and non-voting-class shares. Through this arbitrage strategy, Mason acquired almost 20 per cent ownership interest in Telus voting shares, though it had almost no economic interest in the company.[42] It hoped to be able to block the restructuring operation, which required a two-thirds majority. At the same time, Mason also brought forward its own proposal, which provided for a different exchange ratio,

[37] See, in detail, Chapter VI.C.5.

[38] Naked short sales were de facto banned by the 2012 EU Short Selling Regulation, article 12 (see Regulation (EU) No 236/2012 of the European Parliament and of the Council of 14 March 2012 on short selling and certain aspects of credit default swaps, [2012] OJ L86/1).

[39] Roberta Karmel 'Voting Power Without Responsibility or Risk: How Should Proxy Reform Address the Decoupling of Economic and Voting Rights?' (2010) 55 Villanova Law Review 93, 103.

[40] See n. 37.

[41] On this and the following, see Wolf-Georg Ringe, 'Empty Voting Revisited: The *Telus* Saga' (2013) 28 Butterworths Journal of International Banking and Financial Law 154.

[42] *TELUS Corp v CDS Clearing and Depository Services Inc* [2012] BCCA 403, [2012] BCJ No 2083 (QL), para. 15.

and would have provided Mason with a number of advantages over the remaining shareholders.

The case will not be discussed in any further detail here,[43] but it is remarkable in two ways: first, because this is the most important case in which risk-decoupling was effectuated using short selling as a technique, and second, because the case has involved several court decisions and triggered wide attention in the media.[44]

The complicated story involved (inter alia) two major court decisions. In the first one, the British Columbia Court of Appeal ruled on the validity of Mason's request for a shareholder meeting.[45] In essence, the Court upheld the request. Crucially, the Court held that Mason's risk exposure and its potential status as an 'empty voter' did not allow the Court to disregard the valid calling of the meeting. Two months later, the Supreme Court of British Columbia, in a separate procedure, approved the plan of arrangement as proposed by Telus. It ruled that the 'empty voting' situation was indeed one of the factors that had to be taken into account in assessing the *fairness* of the arrangement.[46] There are thus two diverging outcomes: the risk-decoupling situation was not considered relevant in the first case, but had an impact on the decision in the second. Both decisions are nevertheless not necessarily in conflict, but give a symptomatic picture of the difficulties of the judicial practice in appropriately handling such constellations. These decisions and their implications will be further discussed at a later stage.[47]

Another court decision should be briefly mentioned. In the US state of Delaware, a well-known case is one in which an overall risk-negative shareholder sought to enforce typical shareholder information rights against the company, relying on Delaware General Corporation Law (DGCL) § 220.[48] This raised the question of whether this particular shareholder, despite having emptied (and even negatively exceeded) its risk, still counted as a legal owner of the shares for the purposes of DGCL § 220. This was ultimately answered in the affirmative by the court.[49] Nevertheless, the court noted in an *obiter dictum* that they might have decided differently had this case concerned the exercise of shareholder voting rights.[50] This

[43] See, for more detail, Ringe (n. 41). See also Chapter VI.A.5.

[44] See, for example, Rita Trichur, 'Telus Looks to Regulator in Share-consolidation Spat' *The Globe and Mail* (27 April 2012), available at <http://www.theglobeandmail.com/globe-investor/telus-looks-to-regulator-in-share-consolidation-spat/article4102877/>; Boyd Erman, 'Fleshing Out Empty Voters' *The Globe and Mail* (16 October 2012) B2, available at <www.theglobeandmail.com/report-on-business/streetwise/telus-case-shows-more-disclosure-needed-for-empty-voting/article4614182>; Anita Anand, 'Telus Win Scores for Shareholders' *Financial Post* (17 October 2012), available at <http://business.financialpost.com/2012/10/17/telus-win-scores-for-%C2%ADshareholders/>; Julius Melnitzer, '"Empty Voting" Clouds Shareholder Rights Law' *Financial Post* (14 November 2012), available at <http://business.financialpost.com/2012/11/14/empty-voting-clouds-shareholder-rights-law/>.

[45] *TELUS Corporation v Mason Capital Management LLC* [2012] BCCA 403.

[46] *In re TELUS Corporation* [2012] BCSC 1919.

[47] See Chapter VI.A.5.

[48] *Deephaven Risk Arb. Trading Ltd. v UnitedGlobalCom, Inc.*, No. Civ.A. 379-N, 2005 WL 1713067 (Del. Ch. 2005).

[49] ibid. 15.

[50] ibid. 16. See on this Michael Lee, 'Empty Voting: Private Solutions to A Private Problem' [2007] Columbia Business Law Review 883, 886.

differentiation in assessment bears similarities to the two Canadian decisions mentioned previously.

Economically speaking, entering into a short position has very similar effects to the purchase of put options, the sale of call options and entering into a short position of single stock futures (discussed previously).[51] Smaller differences concern only the question of what amounts and income shall be reimbursed to the other party, but the economic effect is not affected by choosing one or the other.[52]

2. Category 2: Share lending

Besides using financial derivatives, another strategy is to use *share-lending* transactions to create risk-decoupled long positions. The notion of 'share lending' is slightly misleading, however, because it describes a transaction where securities are not simply 'lent' and then retransferred; rather, one party transfers the ownership of numerous securities to another and, at a later time, receives a corresponding number of (other) shares in return (though not necessarily the same shares).[53] The transaction can also be structured as a 'repurchase agreement', where shares are sold and later repurchased.[54] Both structures can be used for a variety of purposes, including hedging and speculation. Most commonly, borrowers use them to facilitate short selling, as borrowers are betting on falling share prices and sell shares that they do not own, hoping to obtain them later at a cheaper price. The International Corporate Governance Network (ICGN) emphasizes the beneficial role of share lending to the capital markets in its Code of Best Practice.[55] According to the guidelines, securities lending increases market liquidity, reduces the risk of failed transactions, and significantly increases the returns of investors.[56]

Overall, the volume of 'borrowed' securities rose sharply in global markets in the years just before the financial crisis. In 2007, the value of all borrowed securities on a single day worldwide amounted to about $1.6 trillion, according to Astec

[51] See also Hu and Black, 'Hedge Funds and Insiders' (n. 14) 348.

[52] ibid. 348, footnote 3.

[53] See International Securities Lending Association, *Global Master Securities Lending Agreement* (2010, with minor changes in 2012) para. 1.1: a transaction 'in which one party (Lender) will transfer to the other (Borrower) securities and financial instruments (Securities) against the transfer of Collateral [...] with a simultaneous agreement by Borrower to transfer to Lender Securities equivalent to such Securities on a fixed date or on demand against the transfer to Borrower by Lender of assets equivalent to such Collateral' (available at <http://www.isla.co.uk/wp-content/uploads/2015/08/GMSLA_2010_amendments_July_2012-1.pdf>). On the misnomer, see also Paul L Davies and Sarah Worthington, *Gower & Davies' Principles of Modern Company Law* (9th edn, Sweet & Maxwell 2012) para. 15-81.

[54] This will usually be based on the 'Global Master Repurchase Agreement' of International Capital Markets Association (ICMA), available in its most recent version at <http://www.icmagroup.org/assets/documents/Legal/GMRA-2011/GMRA-2011/GMRA%202011_2011.04.20 _formular.pdf>.

[55] The Securities Lending Code of Best Practice from 2007 is published in International Corporate Governance Network (ICGN), *Guidance on Securities Lending* (2015) 3, available at <https://www.icgn.org/file/599/download?token=Vu6g-24p>.

[56] ibid. 3.

Marketing Research.[57] In the years following 2008, however, we saw a significant decrease in such transactions. According to a *Financial Times* report, the income obtained from securities lending decreased from $14.3 billion in 2008 to $10.3 billion in 2011 (November).[58] More recently, the industry appears to have revived. Steven Maijoor, chairman of the European Securities and Markets Authority (ESMA), recently explained that securities lending in the EU in 2014 substantially exceeded 2013 figures ('securities issued on loan averaged 528 billion EUR [in the first half of 2014], compared to 485 billion EUR in the first half of 2013').[59]

a) *Share lending and risk-decoupling*

Securities lending can, however, also be used to effectuate risk-decoupling strategies. It is crucial to understand that the legal structure of a securities lending transaction necessarily implies a *transfer of ownership* between the lender and the borrower, as the borrower owns the shares during the time he borrows them. This transfer of ownership will typically correspond to the interests of the parties, as a securities lending transaction is intended to temporarily transfer the securities to the borrower while allowing him to use them commercially.

It follows that the borrower also acquires the voting right that is attached to the share.[60] This stands in stark contrast to the exposure felt from the consequences of the voting decision, which will affect the lender once the shares have been retransferred to him. The lender remains the 'beneficial' owner, that is, the person bearing the consequences of the share price development and the actor economically interested in the share. Thus, the borrower acquires temporary ownership in the shares but does not feel the economic consequences of this ownership. Strategic investors

[57] Kara Scannell, 'How Borrowed Shares Swing Company Votes—SEC and Others Fear Hedge-Fund Strategy May Subvert Elections' *Wall Street Journal* (26 January 2007) A1.

[58] See Paula Niall and Pauline Skypala, 'Regulatory Spotlight Turns on Lending Business' *Financial Times* (London, 23 January 2012) FTfm 8; see also Steve Johnson, 'Fidelity Eyes Stock Loans Exit' *Financial Times* (London, 8 April 2013) FTfm 1.

[59] Steven Maijoor, 'The ESA's role in financial consumer protection', speech at CNMV Conference, La Nueva Financiera Regulacion, Madrid, 15 October 2014, ESMA/2014/1265, available at <http://www.esma.europa.eu/system/files/2014-1265_keynote_speech_-_the_esas_role_in_financial_consumer_protection_cnmv_conference_madrid_-_steven_maijoor.pdf>.

[60] See Paolo Santella, Enrico Baffi, Carlo Drago, and Dino Lattuca, 'Legal Obstacles to Institutional Investor Activism in the EU and in the US' (2012) 23 European Business Law Review 257, 285; Mazars and Marccus Partners, *Transparency Directive Assessment Report—Prepared for the European Commission Internal Market and Services DG, Final Report* (December 2009) 124, available at <http://ec.europa.eu/internal_market/securities/docs/transparency/report-application_en.pdf>; Mark C Faulkner, *Securities Lending and Corporate Governance* (2005) 5, available at <http://www.bankofengland.co.uk/markets/Documents/gilts/slcgjun05.pdf>; European Securities Markets Expert Group (ESME), *First Report of ESME on the Transparency Directive ('TD')* (5 December 2007) 6, available at <http://ec.europa.eu/internal_market/securities/docs/esme/05122007_td_report_en.pdf>; Thomas Keijser, *Financial Collateral Arrangements: the European Collateral Directive Considered from a Property and Insolvency Law Perspective—An Academic Essay in Law* (Kluwer 2006) 148. See also Marcel Kahan and Edward B Rock, 'The Hanging Chads of Corporate Voting' (2008) 96 Georgetown Law Journal 1227, 1257.

have discovered and exploited this fact: some have used share borrowing to acquire temporary voting influence in a company or to temporarily cross a certain share threshold or quota. In particular, there is the danger that a borrower might vote the borrowed shares at a general meeting, whereas the lender will bear the economic consequences.

The problem may be illustrated by the following press quote:

> The insurers' and pension funds' trade bodies have underlined that next month's annual meeting of Mitchells & Butlers will be a cliffhanger, by urging members to call back lent stock and to refuse to lend it out. They fear borrowers may not vote the shares, or vote them in a way that the shareowners later regret.[61]

Consequently, the ICGN Code referred to previously also mentions the potential risks attached to a misuse of the voting right by the borrower.[62] In view of the potential abuse or misuse of voting rights following share lending, the ICGN Code states:

> [I]t is bad practice to borrow shares for the purpose of voting. Lenders and their agents, therefore, should make best endeavours to discourage such practice. Borrowers have every right to sell the shares they have acquired. Equally the subsequent purchaser has every right to exercise the vote. However, the exercise of a vote by a borrower who has, by private contract, only a temporary interest in the shares, can distort the result of general meetings, bring the governance process into disrepute and ultimately undermine confidence in the market.[63]

According to the ICGN, this situation can lead to cases of shares being voted by parties who have no equity capital at risk in the issuing company and thus no long-term interest in the company's welfare. The ICGN therefore calls for a clear lending policy for institutional investors.[64]

It is important to note that problematic securities lending does not necessarily happen with the objective of actually voting the shares themselves. Rather, lending transactions can also be used as an instrument in many other situations for risk-decoupling purposes, outside the general meeting. For example, the borrower may seek to fulfil certain quotas or thresholds—for example, for requesting an extraordinary general meeting or adding items to its agenda,[65] or for relying on shareholder information rights.[66] Another example would be the commencement of shareholder litigation. More important, however, is the indirect power that a borrower can obtain by temporarily owning an equity participation. Behind the scenes, a strong share block, even if only borrowed, translates into large bargaining

61 Andrew Hill, 'Neither a Borrower…' *Financial Times* (London, 18 December 2009) 18.

62 ICGN (n. 55) 3. 63 ibid. 5.

64 ibid. 6. See also ICGN, *Global Governance Principles* (2014) para. 17.5, available at <https://www.icgn.org/file/65/download?token=DY_GHtEO>.

65 This was harmonized across the EU by Directive 2007/36/EC of the European Parliament and of the Council of 11 July 2007 on the exercise of certain rights of shareholders in listed companies [2007] OJ L184/17 ('Shareholder Rights Directive'). Article 6 fixes a threshold of 5 per cent.

66 Shareholder Rights Directive, article 9.

power in negotiations with the management—of course, always with the threat of actually exercising the voting rights in a later meeting.

(i) Examples

In recent years, a number of strategies in securities lending have become known, and they have been used for the explicit purpose of achieving a risk reduction and corresponding indirect influence on the management. To illustrate these strategies, a few real-world examples will be discussed.[67]

In the *Lindner* case, 'borrowed' shares were used for the purpose of a 'squeeze-out' in a German partnership. Both the founder and general partner of a limited partnership, along with another shareholder, transferred, by way of a loan, their limited shares totalling 32.5 per cent to a shareholder who already held 62.59 per cent of the limited partnership. The loan agreements provided that an annual fee was to be paid and, during the term of the loan, the equivalent of all dividends would be reimbursed to the lenders. The borrower, whose stake had thus grown to 95 per cent, then demanded the implementation of a squeeze-out procedure in accordance with §§ 327a–f of the German Stock Corporation Act (*Aktiengesetz*).[68] The minority shareholders challenged the transaction on legal grounds.[69] However, their appeal was ultimately not successful; the German Federal Supreme Court held that the accumulation of a 95 per cent stake as required for the squeeze-out by way of a securities borrowing structure did not amount to an abusive or otherwise illegal procedure.[70] Therefore, the activity did not trigger legal nullity or voidability of the squeeze-out shareholder resolution.[71] From a conceptual perspective, this decision is based on a formal approach that focuses only on the legal ownership of the principal shareholder of the shares in question (and not the underlying deviating shareholder agreements).[72]

Another example in this context can be exhibited by the *British Land* case.[73] Shortly before the British real estate and investment company British Land held

[67] Another case which we will not be able to discuss in detail is the shareholder battle around Australian firm Coles Myer; see Stephen Bartholomeusz, 'Solly in Lieu of the True Share Owners', *The Age* (23 November 2002), available at <http://www.theage.com.au/articles/2002/11/22/1037697877160.html>.

[68] This requires 95 per cent of the shares.

[69] Bundesgerichtshof [BGH] [Federal Supreme Court], decision of 16 March 2009 (II ZR 302/06), Entscheidungen des Bundesgerichtshofes in Zivilsachen [BGHZ] 180, 154.

[70] ibid.

[71] ibid. The lower instance courts, by contrast, had held that the squeeze-out resolution was void. OLG München [Munich Court of Appeal], decision of 23 November 2006 (23 U 2306/06), [2007] Neue Zeitschrift für Gesellschaftsrecht [NZG] 192.

[72] For comments on the decision, see Mark S Rieder, 'Kein Rechtsmissbrauch beim Squeeze-out' [2009] Zeitschrift für Unternehmens- und Gesellschaftsrecht [ZGR] 981; Sebastian Goslar and Klaus von der Linden, 'Grenzen des Rechtsmissbrauchseinwands gegen Gestaltungen beim Aktienrechtlichen Squeeze out' [2009] Betriebs-Berater [BB] 1986. On the decision by the Munich Court of Appeal, see Christoph Kumpan and Martin Mittermeier, 'Risikoentleerte Stimmrechte—Auswirkungen von Wertpapierdarlehen im Gesellschaftsrecht' [2009] Zeitschrift für Wirtschaftsrecht [ZIP] 404.

[73] Juan Ramirez, *Handbook of Corporate Equity Derivatives and Equity Capital Markets* (Wiley 2011) 240; Norma Cohen, 'Laxey Partners Increases British Land Stake to 9%' *Financial Times* (London, 16 July 2002) 23.

its general meeting, the hedge fund Laxey Partners disclosed that it had more than tripled its equity stake from 2.9 per cent to 9.0 per cent within a few days. The general meeting was to, inter alia, decide on a proposed change in management and a share buyback programme.[74] As a consequence of the lending transaction, the general meeting ended in disagreement. While most other participants considered Laxey's strategy a violation of good corporate governance, Laxey's position was that it would act as an advocate for all shareholders and effectively control the company's management.[75] Ultimately, Laxey's position did not succeed, but the case nevertheless caused a stir and demonstrated the possible extent of voting manipulation by borrowed shares. Furthermore, the shift in Laxey's shares allowed the latter to significantly strengthen its position within the circle of shareholders, for instance by being given the option to convene an extraordinary general meeting.[76] The particular irony of the case was that prominent institutional investors, such as Hermes, were among the lenders, though Hermes knew nothing of its role in facilitating Laxey's rebellious action. Hermes, which is a leader and supporter of corporate governance standards, later apologised to British Land.[77]

The merger between the British cruise line P&O Princess Cruises plc and the American travel company Carnival Corporation later confirmed these fears. Discussions during the extraordinary general meeting of P&O Princess, which had to decide whether to accept the transaction, revealed that many shares were borrowed by activist shareholders and that the borrowers might vote against the wishes of the long-term investors.[78] There were also fears that some borrowers would tender their shares to Carnival as part of its partial takeover offer, again displacing the long-term investors.[79] This case led to considerable legal and political debate. Various reform proposals were considered, including a change in the content of standard borrowing agreements and the introduction of a prohibition on the borrowing of shares for the purpose of exercising the voting rights.[80] There was a fear, however, that these extensive changes would lead to market disruptions. Ultimately, the only successful consequence of the case was a modification of the voluntary Stock Borrowing and Lending Code of Guidance, a best practice code for securities lending. This code now states:

> C.7.4 A person could borrow shares in order to be able to exercise the voting rights and influence the voting decision at a particular meeting of the company concerned. There is a consensus, however, in the market that securities should not be borrowed solely for the

[74] Ramirez ibid.; Cohen ibid. [75] Hu and Black, 'New Vote Buying' (n. 1) 834.

[76] Cohen (n. 73).

[77] John Waples, 'Ritblat Hits at CSFB and Laxey for Vote "Conspiracy"' *Sunday Times* (London, 21 July 2002) 1; see also Hu and Black, 'New Vote Buying' (n. 1) 834.

[78] Stock Lending and Repo Committee, *Summary of Meeting Held at the Bank of England on 9 October 2002* (11 December 2002) para. 3, available at <http://www.bankofengland.co.uk/markets/Documents/gilts/slrcdec02.pdf>.

[79] Susan Christoffersen, Christopher Geczy, David Musto, and Adam Reed, 'Vote Trading and Information Aggregation' (2007) 62 Journal of Finance 2897, 2901.

[80] Stock Lending and Repo Committee (n. 78) para. 4.

purpose of exercising the voting rights at, for example, an AGM or EGM. Lenders should also consider their corporate governance responsibilities before lending stock over a period in which an AGM or an EGM is expected to be held. Beneficial owners need to ensure that any agents they have made responsible for voting and for securities lending act in [a] co-ordinated way.[81]

The Code is not binding law, but the reform was intended to send a strong signal to market participants that these practices would not be tolerated in the future.

(ii) Implications

The cases just described demonstrate that the strategic use of securities lending and borrowing transactions may affect the integrity of the voting process, because the lender does not regularly retain the right to vote with the shares that are lent out. The legal form of securities lending transactions results in the borrower becoming the temporary *owner* of the borrowed securities. This usually corresponds to the interests of the parties, as it is the goal of securities lending to grant the borrower full economic use of the securities—including their eventual sale.[82] As we noted previously, the transfer of ownership to the borrower in securities lending transactions implies that the borrower normally also acquires the right to vote the transferred shares.[83] This also follows on from considerations of legal certainty and from the principle of inseparability between voting rights and company share. The legal assessment thus seems clear: the legal title to the shares entitles the borrower to carry out all rights associated with them, including the right to vote.

The conflict that is of particular interest here, however, arises from the fact that the lender of securities must be considered as remaining the true beneficial owner or substantial risk-bearer of the risk inherent in the securities. In particular, the lender will retain the economic opportunities and risks attached to the shares, as he will at a certain point in the future receive equivalent shares, which will then have either appreciated or depreciated in value. The borrower thus de facto has only a temporary right to vote, as the economic consequences of the voting decision do not concern him. Thus, there is divergence between formal ownership (the borrower) and beneficial ownership (the lender). Looking only at this bilateral legal relationship, one could argue that the shift in risk does not do any harm, because it is voluntary and involves a deliberate abandonment of voting rights and the ownership position. However, as we will see later, these two actors are not alone in the game, and others will be affected by their decisions. In particular, the relationship between the borrower and the other shareholders of the company, as well as potential outside investors, is fraught with considerable problems.[84] The ICGN Code of Best Practice therefore denounces share borrowing for the purpose of voting.

[81] Bank of England, *Securities Borrowing and Lending Code of Guidance* (2009) 18, available at <http://www.bankofengland.co.uk/markets/Pages/gilts/slrc.aspx>; see also Stock Lending and Repo Committee (n. 78) para. 4.

[82] See text accompanying n. 60.

[83] See n. 60.

[84] See on this Chapter V.B.1.b.

A voter who has a mere temporary interest in the company's shares could distort the results of a shareholder resolution that affect the control of the company and ultimately undermine confidence in the markets.[85]

In the United Kingdom, former City Minister Lord Paul Myners pointed out the problem in his various reports on share voting from 2004 to 2007.[86] These documents highlight the need to demonstrate the consequences of share-lending transactions for the voting right for lenders. It becomes clear in this appeal that not all lenders are aware of the fact that they are lending not just the share but also their voting right.[87] Overall, Lord Myners advocated a necessary balance between the significant position of the voting right and the economically useful exchange of securities via lending transactions.[88]

The European Commission launched a consultation in 2007, which, inter alia, considered the problem of securities lending and voting.[89] The comments received on the consultation provided a colourful picture of proposals and reactions on the table and argued in principle for some form of regulatory intervention, without any agreement on the precise scope or method.[90] So far, the Commission has not followed up with any concrete legislative measures. In the changes to the Shareholder Rights Directive, as proposed in 2014, the only reference to this discussion is new article 3h(2), which provides that asset managers disclose to their investors on a semi-annual basis 'their policy on securities lending and the implementation thereof'.[91]

[85] ICGN (n. 55).

[86] Paul Myners, *Review of the Impediments to Voting UK Shares* (2004); Paul Myners, *Review of the Impediments to Voting UK Shares: An Update on Progress* (2005); Paul Myners, *Review of the Impediments to Voting UK Shares: An Update on Progress Three Years on* (2007) [hereinafter Myners, *Update Three Years On*].

[87] A 2010 information brochure on securities lending now makes the point unmistakably clear:

> You cannot vote if your securities are out on loan. However, your securities lending does not need to interfere with your corporate governance activity as shares may be recalled from loan if you wish to vote. You should consider under what circumstances you may wish to recall securities to vote (or prevent certain securities that you wish to vote on being lent in the first place) and ensure that all parties (such as your fund manager and agent) are aware of your policies. Normally securities can be recalled at any time but it is essential that timescales for recalls are understood and documented.

See *Securities Lending: An Introductory Guide* (September 2010) 6, available at <http://www.bankofengland.co.uk/markets/Documents/gilts/sl_intro_green_9_10.pdf>.

[88] Myners, *Update Three Years On* (n. 86) 9.

[89] European Commission, *Fostering an Appropriate Regime for Shareholders' Rights—Third Consultation Document of the Services of the Directorate General Internal Market and Services* (April 2007) part IV, available at <http://ec.europa.eu/internal_market/company/docs/shareholders/consultation3_en.pdf>.

[90] European Commission, *Synthesis of the Comments on the Third Consultation Document of the Internal Market and Services Directorate-General 'Fostering an Appropriate Regime for Shareholders' Rights'* (September 2007) 7 ff., available at <http://ec.europa.eu/internal_market/company/docs/shareholders/consultation3_report_en.pdf>.

[91] European Commission, *Proposal for a Directive of the European Parliament and of the Council amending Directive 2007/36/EC as regards the encouragement of long-term shareholder engagement and Directive 2013/34/EU as regards certain elements of the corporate governance statement*, COM(2014) 213 final (9 April 2014).

What, then, is the specific danger realized when voting with borrowed shares? It is necessary to distinguish between the bilateral relationship between the lender and the borrower on the one hand, and the multilateral relationship with other groups such as shareholders, investors, and other stakeholders on the other. Within the bilateral relationship, we could argue that the voting poses no problems that would require regulatory intervention. Ultimately, the impact of the voting decision only affects the lender who has voluntarily given up the right to vote in favour of the borrower.[92] Built on the Coase theorem, it is to be assumed that the parties will find a solution by private ordering. For example, this could be an agreement on granting the lender a proxy, the borrower's obligation to refrain from exercising the voting rights, or the right of the lender to recall the shares if he so wishes.[93]

But the case is different in a multilateral relationship. This is where the transaction can create externalities to the detriment of non-interested third parties. If two participants who are party to the transaction agree on the factual transfer of the voting right and thereby create costs for third parties, it is self-evident that this is an undue burden for the third party. The exact details of these costs and further discussion are reserved for a later section.[94]

(iii) Soft parking

The combination of securities lending and voting right can also be used in a manipulative way in yet another different constellation. It is possible to lend one's own shares to friendly or allied shareholders, and in this way avoid the voting prohibition for treasury shares.

The Second EU Company Law Directive in article 24(1)(a) states that a company is not entitled to vote its own shares.[95] This provision originates in German law, where a corresponding rule was adopted as early as in the 1930s.[96] Today, the policy reason is seen in the goal of avoiding 'capital-free corporate authority'.[97] In line with the broader context of this study, this refers to voting rights that are not underpinned by corresponding capital. More specifically, the provision also seeks to ensure that the board is prevented from exercising the voting rights on behalf of the company and thereby supporting itself, which is to the detriment of the

[92] In this sense, apparently, Charles Nathan, '"Empty Voting" and Other Fault Lines Undermining Shareholder Democracy: The New Hunting Ground for Hedge Funds' (2007) 15 The Corporate Governance Advisor 1, 6.

[93] See on solutions based on private ordering Chapter VI.A.

[94] See Chapter V.B.1.b.

[95] Directive 2012/30/EU of the European Parliament and of the Council of 25 October 2012 on coordination of safeguards which, for the protection of the interests of members and others, are required by Member States of companies within the meaning of the second paragraph of article 54 of the Treaty on the Functioning of the European Union, in respect of the formation of public limited liability companies and the maintenance and alteration of their capital, with a view to making such safeguards equivalent, [2012] OJ L315/74.

[96] For the historical background, see Jürgen Oechsler, § 71b, in Wulf Goette and others (eds), *Münchener Kommentar zum Aktiengesetz* (3rd edn, CH Beck 2008) para. 1. English law originally refused to accept the possibility that a company could hold its own shares altogether: *Trevor v Whitworth* (1887) 12 App Cas 409.

[97] See the seminal work by Ernst-Joachim Mestmäcker, *Verwaltung, Konzerngewalt und Rechte der Aktionäre* (CF Müller, 1958) 13.

shareholders' monitoring powers.[98] The ability to influence dividend policy and distribution rules is in this way also part of the reasoning.[99]

The strategy described here as 'soft parking' is basically a new attempt to circumvent this rule. If the management itself is not allowed to exercise the right to vote the company's own shares, the simple solution is to redirect them to others. Lending the shares to third parties who are favourably disposed to the administration achieves the effect that the voting rights are officially resurrected, because the shares are not formally 'own shares' anymore. Ultimately, this is about the problem of 'management entrenchment', that is, an inappropriate strengthening of the administration's position against shareholder monitoring. Here, too, the formal legal fact that the borrower becomes the full owner of the borrowed shares is of great importance, as it allows him to also exercise the voting rights of such shares.

Thus, this strategy can, for example, be used as a defence mechanism in takeover situations. Faced with a hostile takeover bid by its rival Sonaecom, Portugal Telecom (PT) transferred substantial blocks of shares to 'friendly' shareholders such as the British Barclays Bank and was thus able to successfully fend off the takeover attempt.[100] A similar situation occurred during the takeover attempt of the Hungarian energy company MOL by its Austrian competitor OMV. After OMV had increased its share in MOL from 10 per cent to 18.6 per cent and submitted a formal bid, MOL bought back nearly half of the shares freely available and immediately lent about 41 per cent of them to two Hungarian banks, in the clear expectation that they would support the MOL management.[101] Thereby, MOL circumvented Hungarian and European rules, according to which companies are not allowed to hold more than 10 per cent of their own shares.[102] Ultimately, however, MOL's defence strategy was successful (albeit mainly for reasons of competition law).[103]

b) Exacerbating the problem by perverse incentives in practice

The present discussion raises a variety of follow-up questions. In particular, it raises the question of how often the strategy of securities lending actually occurs in practice or is likely to occur. Second, and closely related, is the questionable role of the securities *lender* in this type of transaction. Intuitively, one might think that a lender who knows the intentions of the borrower, or anticipates them, will simply refrain from entering into the transaction or take precautions accordingly.[104] In

[98] Stefan Grundmann, *European Company Law—Organization, Finance and Capital Markets* (2nd edn, Intersentia 2012) 234.

[99] Oechsler (n. 96) para. 2.

[100] Hu and Black, 'Empty Voting II' (n. 11) 645 f; Jonathan Miller and Matthew DiRisio, 'The Potential Implications of Decoupling Shareholders' Economic and Voting Interests in Corporate Control Contests' [2008] International Corporate Governance Review 4, 7 f.

[101] Hu and Black, 'Empty Voting II' (n. 11) 645 f; Miller and DiRisio (n. 100) 7 f.

[102] Second Company Law Directive (n. 95), arts 21 and 22.

[103] 'Übernahme: MOL bekämpft OMV auf Pump' *Die Presse* (13 July 2007), <http://diepresse.com/home/wirtschaft/economist/316717/MOL-bekaempft-OMV-auf-Pump>.

[104] This does not apply to the specific situation of 'soft parking'.

short, questions relate to the significance of this approach at a practical level and the concrete interests of the parties involved.

(i) Constraints on using securities lending

The seemingly effortless use of securities lending transactions, as in the examples previously described, is subject to significant practical limitations when these transactions occur. In attempting to pursue such a strategy, a borrower faces the most obvious difficulty of a recall clause, which often appears in security lending agreements. Most of the popular framework agreements for lending securities include a standard clause for any type of early termination of the individual lending. In practice, the vast majority of international securities lending transactions are drafted on the basis of the Global Master Securities Lending Agreement (GMSLA).[105] This framework agreement is published by the industry group International Securities Lending Association (ISLA), and the current version dates from 2012.[106] Paragraph 8.1 of this document sets out the lender's right to terminate a loan of securities. Subject to any individual terms of the relevant loan, for example, where a fixed period has been agreed upon, the lender may terminate the agreement by giving notice equal to the standard settlement time for the securities concerned, and the borrower must redeliver the shares by the end of this period. As other master agreements contain similar clauses, most borrowing contracts in practice include a right of termination or a call-back option.[107] Whether such a right of revocation or termination is also realized, however, is another question. Practitioners point out that most borrowers are looking to avoid a recall of loaned securities. Frequent exercise of the recall option could accordingly render the lending business much less attractive for borrowers.[108] Meanwhile, market observers report that most securities are recalled only in exceptional circumstances, such as before a takeover or merger, whereas some lenders apparently never recall their shares due to cost concerns.[109]

[105] Kingsley T W Ong and Eugene Y C Yeung, 'Repos & Securities Lending: The Accounting Arbitrage and Their Role in the Global Financial Crisis' (2011) 6 Capital Markets Law Journal 92, 93.

[106] International Securities Lending Association (n. 53).

[107] Association Française de la Gestion financière, *Response to DG MARKT consultation on 'Fostering an appropriate regime for shareholders' rights'* (27 July 2007) 3.

[108] Mark Faulkner, *An Introduction to Securities Lending* (4th edn, London 2007) 49 ('Recalls are part and parcel of the securities lending business. However, borrowers seek to avoid recalls wherever possible and frequent recalls may discourage borrowers from accessing portfolios. In practice the lenders, or their agent, communicate the lender's position with regards to voting to the borrowers so as to avoid any surprises').

[109] Paolo Santella, Enrico Baffi, Carlo Drago, and Dino Lattuca, 'Legal Obstacles to Institutional Investor Activism in the EU and in the US' (2012) 23 European Business Law Review 257, 286–8; Mark C Faulkner, *Securities Lending and Corporate Governance* (2005) 6, available at <http://www.bankofengland.co.uk/markets/Documents/gilts/slcgjun05.pdf>; Hu and Black, 'New Vote Buying' (n. 1) 895 f.

In addition, a more frequent exercise of the right to recall lent shares would not even be desirable, as this could significantly reduce market liquidity. See European Securities Markets Expert Group (ESME), *First Report of ESME on the Transparency Directive ('TD')* (5 December 2007) 7, available at <http://ec.europa.eu/internal_market/securities/docs/esme/05122007_td_report_en.pdf>; Autorité des Marchés Financiers (AMF), *Rapport sur les opérations de prêt emprunt de titres en période d'assemblée générale d'actionnaires* (Groupe de place présidé par Yves Mansion 2008) 12.

Practitioners familiar with the market point out a second issue. It is often not easy to accumulate a large block of shares simply through borrowing shares.[110] This is especially true before general meetings, when important decisions are on the agenda, and in particular in decisions regarding reorganization or other transactions, as these plans often wake up other activist shareholders, arbitrageurs, and the 'true' owners, which reduces the availability of borrowable shares in the market.

A third consideration is the costs. Borrowing shares may indeed be possible at relatively low cost,[111] but in practice, substantial collateral has to be provided to the lender, who is naturally unwilling to bear the default risk of the borrower.[112] In the cases of *Laxey* and *British Land*, the collateral provided amounted to about 105 per cent of the market value of the shares and was therefore even above the actual share price.[113] The requirement to provide security at this level can thus be costly and pose a major obstacle for many potential borrowers of large blocks of shares.

Finally, both strategic marketing issues and the reputation of the borrower are to be considered. If such a borrowing strategy becomes known in the market, the credibility of the investor is jeopardized. Equally, their reputation and commitment to the welfare of the investment may be in doubt.[114] In a similar vein, sophisticated models of game theory or simply common sense suggest that lenders will not enter into similar lending transactions with the borrower a second time if they suffered from an abusive exercise of the voting right. Alternatively, lenders will at the very least take the risk into consideration and seek to negotiate a compensation for the potential loss of value of their investment.

(ii) The lender's interests

All of the discussed considerations are largely invalidated, however, when taking into account the motivations and incentives of the *lender*. Three factors seem to be particularly salient.

First, where the lender—as usual—is a sophisticated institutional investor,[115] she will usually balance the fees obtained from lending, on the one hand, with the cost of a recall and an informed exercise of their voting rights on the other.[116] On balance, an early recall of the shares will typically carry an overall additional cost in such a calculation. Furthermore, a lender who frequently recalls her shares may

[110] Ramirez (n. 73) 241 f. [111] See Christoffersen and others (n. 79).
[112] Ramirez (n. 73) 242. [113] ibid. 240. [114] ibid. 242.
[115] Hu and Black, 'New Vote Buying' (n. 1) 897.
[116] Florida State Board of Administration, *Corporate Governance—Annual Report 2006* (2007) 29:

> In consideration of recall, the SBA attempts to balance the cost of reduced securities lending income against the discernible benefits of recalling shares to exercise voting rights. In this context, the proportional SBA share ownership will be evaluated to determine an optimal amount, if any, of a company's loaned securities that need to be recalled

See also Millstein Center for Corporate Governance and Performance, Yale School of Management, *Voting Integrity: Practices for Investors and the Global Proxy Advisory Industry—Policy Briefing no 3* (2009) 11–12, available at <http://web.law.columbia.edu/sites/default/files/microsites/millstein-center/Voting%20Integrity%20Policy%20Briefing%20No%203%2002%2027%2009.pdf>.

be put at a disadvantage in relation to others, possibly even being forced out of business, having a reputation as an unreliable business partner.[117] This balancing exercise from the perspective of institutional lenders is well documented in the *Coles Myer* case, de facto ending up in a shoulder-shrugging decision in favour of a simple preference to lend rather than to vote.[118] Alternatively, the risk of abuse may seem so remote and abstract that it is not incorporated as a relevant factor in the cost consideration. One fund manager has described the conflict as follows: 'The problem is that the corporate governance implications cannot be easily costed, but lending can.'[119] Therefore, it is not surprising that, in practice, an overall recall of lent shares occurs very rarely.[120]

Second, a significant problem exists during the voting of important projects because many investors are not informed in time.[121] Particularly under US law, in the context of convening a general meeting, documentation and notice requirements appear at moments of unfavourable timing. Often, the lender does not have sufficient time to recall the shares.[122] But even where the timing is not an issue, it is uncertain whether the lender will actually call back the shares, due to internal structural problems of institutional investors. The lender will only do so if: (a) the factual decision-makers—those within the internal structure of the investment fund—become aware of the importance of the issue and the weight attached to the vote; and (b) these decision-makers convince other decision-makers involved in the same internal structure that a decision to recall the shares is necessary.[123] Moreover, existing remuneration incentives in the internal structure of the lending institutions may turn out to be problematic. For example, some funds pay their fund managers exclusively out of the fees that stem from securities lending transactions and provide no additional salary.[124] For these fund managers, their personal income depends on the fund's lending volume—thus the consequences of this arrangement do not require any further explanation.

[117] Marcel Kahan and Edward B Rock 'The Hanging Chads of Corporate Voting' (2008) 96 Georgetown Law Journal 1227, 1256 f.

[118] Stephen Bartholomeusz 'Solly in Lieu of the True Share Owners' *The Age* (23 November 2002), available at <http://www.theage.com.au/articles/2002/11/22/1037697877160.html>: 'The institutions he dealt with knew what he planned to do with the votes but were prepared to deal with him and accept the slightly enhanced returns. They valued the three or four cents a share more than they valued their ability to vote.'

[119] Chris Taylor, securities finance managing director for the UK and Europe at State Street, cited after Kit Bingham, 'Concern Grows over Borrowed Votes' *Financial News* (9 May 2005), <http://www.efinancialnews.com/story/2005-05-09/concern-grows-over-borrowed-votes>.

[120] Florida State Board of Administration (n. 116) ('Although the SBA shall reserve the right to recall the shares on a timely basis prior to the record date for the purpose of exercising voting rights for domestic, as well as international securities, the recall of loaned securities is likely to be infrequent.'); see also Myners, *Update Three Years On* (n. 86) 9 (discussing a study by the Investment Management Association); Simon Targett, 'Top Pension Funds Plan Securities Lending Code' *Financial Times* (London, 14 June 2004) 1 (discussing a study by Linstock).

[121] Millstein Center for Corporate Governance and Performance (n. 116) 12.

[122] Kahan and Rock (n. 117).

[123] Millstein Center for Corporate Governance and Performance (n. 116) 12.

[124] Simon Wong, 'Barriers to Effective Investor Engagement' *Financial Times* (London, 16 January 2012) 6.

The circumstances change, however, when the lender is a *small* investor or an *individual.* In these cases, the lender will almost never make the decision about a specific rental transaction himself. Rather, the preparation and execution of the contract is carried out in most cases by central depositors who bring together supply and demand on a case-by-case basis, but also automatically in accordance to standard contracts. Accordingly, retail investors often lack knowledge of their shares being lent out in the first place. Even where the investor is aware of the transaction, however, the problem of rational apathy of dispersed investors aggravates the conflict. As we know from the exercise of voting rights, the relationship between vote and benefit is often so unfavourable for retail investors that the rational investor will not seriously engage in calculating the value of his voting right and other rental options.[125] Instead, free-rider incentives will convince the investors that they had better keep the rental fee, since as long as the other shareholders do not lend out their shares, the possible abuse of their voting rights by the borrower is unlikely.[126] A potential worry about course-manipulating effects of potential short sales of borrowed shares is unfounded.[127] All this mirrors the basic collective action problem that we know from share voting—when it comes to lending shares, the same issue of free-riding can be observed.

Given all of these various incentives, it is not surprising that only a tiny fraction of the total shares on loan are being recalled. Empirical studies estimate the proportion of recalled shares to be no more than 2 per cent of all lent shares.[128]

(iii) Particular incentives within index funds

In addition to these basic problems, the incentives problems described previously are exacerbated by the structure of the modern fund industry. This becomes particularly acute for the so-called index funds—simple mutual funds that passively mimic a specific, representative index (such as the FTSE 100, Euro Stoxx, or Dow Jones) as accurately as possible. These funds are popular among investors because fees are usually quite low in comparison to actively managed funds, which charge extra management fees.[129] To achieve their aim, index funds invest in the securities underlying the index in the same proportion as the index. Other funds use derivatives (swaps) to bind the fund's performance to the index.[130] In 2012, about $3 trillion was invested in index funds.[131]

[125] See Hu and Black, 'Taxonomy, Implications, and Reforms' (n. 1).

[126] Hu and Black, 'New Vote Buying' (n. 1) 896. But see Reena Aggarwal, Pedro A C Saffi, and Jason Sturgess, 'The Role of Institutional Investors in Voting: Evidence from the Securities Lending Market' (2015) 70 Journal of Finance 2309.

[127] Steven N Kaplan, Tobias J Moskowitz, and Berk A Sensoy, 'The Effects of Stock Lending on Security Prices: An Experiment' (2013) 68 Journal of Finance 1891.

[128] Gene D'Avolio, 'The Market for Borrowing Stock' (2002) 66 Journal of Financial Economics 271, 273; see also the studies cited in n. 120.

[129] For a good overview, see Judith Evans and Jonathan Eley, 'A Changing, Passive Face of Modern Investment' *Financial Times* (31 January 2015) FTMoney 10.

[130] The so-called tracking error indicates how exact this replication is. The lower the tracking error, the closer the development of the fund is in comparison to the reference index.

[131] James Mackintosh, 'It's Easy to Only Just Beat a Poor Index' *Financial Times* (16 July 2012) 24.

The indexing of investment transposes findings from the efficient market hypothesis[132] and modern portfolio theory[133] into a simple investment strategy.[134] In its moderate form, the efficient market hypothesis holds that financial markets are efficient in the sense that, at the very least, all information publicly available is already priced in the securities.[135] With new information immediately and fully priced in, no one, except insiders, is able to achieve lasting above-market profits. Following this logic, investors should not try to systematically outperform the market, but rather should rely on a predefined index. On this basis, modern portfolio theory recommends that investors only need to solve a single optimization problem, which is to choose the market portfolio that best corresponds to their own maximization of preferences.[136] In practice, this is best represented by a predefined index, such as the Euro Stoxx.

In today's financial markets, the success of the indexing strategy is best illustrated by the rise of exchange-traded funds (ETFs).[137] These funds are themselves traded like securities on the stock market. Indeed, they imitate a particular index such as the FTSE 100 or the Dow Jones, and in more recent times they have also used bond or commodity indices. For investors, the low costs are of a particular advantage, because the management fee of index funds is usually less than 0.3 per

[132] See the seminal work by Eugene Fama, 'Efficient Capital Markets: A Review of Theory and Empirical Work' (1970) 25 Journal of Finance 383; for a good overview, see also Hendrik Houthakker and Peter Williamson, *The Economics of Financial Markets* (Oxford University Press 1996) 130.

[133] See William F Sharpe, 'Capital Asset Prices: A Theory of Market Equilibrium Under Conditions of Risk' (1964) 19 Journal of Finance 425; James Tobin, 'Liquidity Preference as Behavior Towards Risk' (1958) 25 Review of Economic Studies 65; see also Harry M Markowitz, 'Portfolio Selection' (1952) 7 Journal of Finance 77; Harry M Markowitz, *Portfolio Selection: Efficient Diversification of Investments* (2nd edn, Wiley 1991).

[134] Evans and Eley (n. 129).

[135] See the seminal work by Ronald J Gilson and Reinier Kraakman, 'The Mechanisms of Market Efficiency' (1984) 70 Virginia Law Review 549. More recently, for a perspective on the Global Financial Crisis of 2008, see Luigi Zingales, 'Learning to Live With Not-So-Efficient Markets' (2010) 139(4) Daedalus 31; Ronald J Gilson and Reinier Kraakman, 'Market Efficiency After the Fall: Where Do We Stand Following the Financial Crisis?' in Claire A Hill and Brett H McDonnell (eds), *Research Handbook On The Economics Of Corporate Law* (Edward Elgar 2012) 456; Ronald J Gilson and Reinier Kraakman, 'Market Efficiency After the Financial Crisis: It's Still a Matter of Information Costs' (2014) 100 Virginia Law Review 313.

[136] Tobin (n. 133).

[137] The ETF industry has grown over the past years by about 40 per cent per year and now administers total assets of over $3 trillion. Chris Flood, 'Dark Side of ETFs Erode Active Managers' Outperformance' *Financial Times* (London, 10 August 2015) FTfm 2. See also Ananth Madhavan, 'Exchange-Traded Funds: An Overview of Institutions, Trading, and Impacts' (2014) 6 Annual Review of Financial Economics 311, 312. Experts have repeatedly emphasized the systemic risks that may be created by ETFs. See Richard Milne, Michael Mackenzie, and Nicole Bullock, '"Push-button Perils" Investment: Exchange Traded Funds' *Financial Times* (London, 6 June 2011) 7; Chris Flood, 'Time to Re-examine the Entire ETF Ecosystem' *Financial Times* (London, 26 October 2015) FTfm 6; Financial Stability Board, *Potential Financial Stability Issues Arising from Recent Trends in Exchange-Traded Funds (ETFs)* (12 April 2011), available at <http://www.financialstabilityboard.org/wp-content/uploads/r_110412b.pdf>; Doron Israeli, Charles M C Lee, and Suhas Sridharan, 'Is There a Dark Side to Exchange Traded Funds (ETFs)? An Information Perspective' Working Paper 2015, available at <http://ssrn.com/abstract=2625975> accessed 20 August 2015. This critique has, however, in no way affected the funds' popularity. See Deutsche Bank Markets Research, *ETF Assets to Pass $3 Trillion Milestone in 2015*, ETF Annual Review & Outlook (26 January 2015), available at <https://

cent. For actively managed funds, the costs are almost always between 1.5 per cent and 3 per cent, sometimes even more. These higher fees may be understandable given the fund manager's efforts. For actively managed funds, the fund managers observe the markets and decide which securities are bought or sold. An index fund such as the ETF is passively managed, however. It only has to reflect the performance of the corresponding index. Changes must be made only if the index is adjusted or its contents are modified.[138]

The administrative costs of index funds can be further reduced where the fund temporarily lends out its portfolio securities to other market participants. This strategy is widely popular in practice.[139] Some funds allegedly make more profits with the fees they obtain from the loans than with the traditional fund fees.[140] As explained, many titles will be passively held in the portfolio for long periods of time without being traded. For these titles, funds are tempted to improve the return of their portfolio by lending them out instead of uselessly keeping them in their portfolio. Fund managers use the generated fees to further reduce the overall costs of the fund, and with that improve their competitive standing.[141]

It is important for the sake of the present study to note that the temporary transfer of these portfolio securities to other market players happens regularly without the option of retransferring for the general meeting.[142] Even if such an option existed, there is no incentive for fund managers to make use of it, as the strategic objective of the index fund is to reflect the underlying index as closely as possible—not to outperform or influence it. The fund therefore has no interest in exercising its voting rights, which in turn increases its willingness to temporarily let go of the securities—over and including the record date and the date of the annual general meeting. Where an investor borrows shares of a portfolio company against a fee in order to actively influence the strategy of the company, this will only be advantageous for the index fund. In this way, the index fund achieves a double advantage: it receives the rental fee and it benefits from the actions of the activist (borrower) shareholder, which, in the optimal case, have a positive influence on

www.altii.de/media/modelfield_files/fondsportal/pressrelease/pdf/Deutsche_Bank_Research_ETF_Market_Review_2014_Outlook_2015.pdf>. See David Ricketts, 'Traditional Index Funds Lose to ETFs' *Financial Times* (London, 6 February 2012) 9.

[138] See William M Humphries, 'Leveraged ETFs: The Trojan Horse Has Passed the Margin-Rule Gates' (2010) 34 Seattle University Law Review 299, 301 (discussing in detail the various characteristics of ETFs).

[139] Some funds lend out up to 25 per cent of their portfolio shares. See Niels Nauhauser, 'Index-ETFs bergen stets ein Kontrahentenrisiko', *Börse Online* (12 January 2010), available at <http://www.genios.de/presse-archiv/artikel/BONL/20101202/index-etfs-bergen-stets-ein-kontrah/A48508382.html>. In one study, researchers even found loan quotas of up to 100 per cent. SCM Private, 'SCM Private Research Reveals UK Retail Fund Managers Controlling over £241 Billion, Can Lend Out Up to 100% of Funds Yet Investors Are Kept in the Dark' (1 September 2011), <http://www.independentinvestor.info/PDF-Downloads/ETF-MUTUAL-FUNDS-WRAP-ACCOUNTS-FUNDS-08/doc.2133-%20SCM%202011%20UK%20fund%20stock%20lending.pdf>.

[140] Financial Stability Board (n. 137) 4–5. See also Ajay Makan, 'ETFs Under Fire over Revenues Generated by Securities Lending' *Financial Times* (10 May 2012) 33.

[141] On possible conflicts of interests, see Paula Niall and Pauline Skypala, 'Regulatory Spotlight Turns on Lending Business' *Financial Times* (23 January 2012) FTfm 8.

[142] International Corporate Governance Network, *Share Lending Vis-à-Vis Voting—a Report* (2004) 14.

the strategy of the management. This situation has important implications for the ability of third parties to borrow securities for the sole purpose of voting.

In other words, for a manager of an index fund, the performance of the target company is ultimately irrelevant, and all that counts is the exact mapping of the index. Given the choice of exercising voting rights in a particular company or passing them to other hands against a fee, the manager will always choose the latter option.

Studies have shown that predominantly large, passive institutional investors, whose investment targets are well-known publicly held companies, are the ones who lend out the most shares.[143] Given the reduced probability of a recall, borrowers prefer these types of investors as business partners, too.[144] Also, tax incentives increase the likelihood of passive funds in the lending business.[145]

Overall, the current market situation seems to virtually invite parties to borrow shares 'for free' and to use them for their own independent purposes. In any case, the lender usually has little or no motivation to control the exercise of its voting shares or the timing of recalling them.

(iv) Attempts to reform

A complete discussion of the subject matter of securities lending necessitates mentioning the first few attempts to reform the field. A number of specific responses have emerged in the recent years in policy discussion and in practice, and some states have already revised their legal framework to address the issue of voting rights and securities lending.

Noteworthy are, first, a number of self-regulatory attempts and best practice standards. These include the recommendations of the International Corporate Governance Network (ICGN) and the Stock Lending and Repo Committee of the Bank of England, which have both modified and adapted their regulations with regard to the subject matter. Even the revised version of the influential ICGN Global Governance Principles from 2014 now includes a section about stock lending.[146] We will discuss these instruments later, in the section that presents the problem analysis.[147]

Efforts in the United States have mainly aimed at providing help for self-help. Among other things, the introduction of a separate, early date for convening the annual general meeting has been proposed. That would allow the shareholders—especially institutional investors—to know early on what items should be discussed at the meeting, and would thus create greater incentives (and the possibility!) to call back their shares on time.[148] A counterexample is found in French law, which

143 See Gene D'Avolio, 'The Market for Borrowing Stock' (2002) 66 Journal of Financial Economics 271.
144 ibid. 145 ibid.
146 ICGN, *Global Governance Principles* (2014) para. 17.5, available at <https://www.icgn.org/file/65/download?token=DY_GHtEO>.
147 See Chapter VI.A.2–4.
148 See the discussion and proposals at Conference Board, *Hedge Fund Activism: Findings and Recommendations for Corporations and Investors* (2008) 42–3; Florida State Board of Administration, *Corporate Governance Annual Report 2006* (n. 116) 30; Shareowners.org, *Letter in Response to SEC Concept Release on the U.S. Proxy System*, File No. S7 1410 (20 October 2010) 2.

introduced a new legal framework based on a comprehensive reporting and disclosure system for borrowed securities in 2010, sanctioned with a potential loss of the voting right.[149] Further details will be discussed in the course of this study (in the problem discussion part). At this point, the aim is only to provide an overview of the range of potential regulatory responses.[150]

3. Category 3: Record-date capture

A third phenomenon of negative risk-decoupling is the strategy of 'record-date capture'. It is somewhat connected to securities lending, but it can be considered to be a separate category that includes distinct problems and implications. Many jurisdictions worldwide have introduced a system where there is a cut-off date for registering attendance for the general meeting. The date is some time before the meeting actually takes place. Certain shareholders may exploit the divergence between the record date and the date of the general meeting in order to produce a situation resembling a risk-decoupled shareholder.

The strategy is simple. The decisive day determines which shareholders are entitled to vote at the general meeting. Because there is necessarily a certain divergence between the record date and the date of the general meeting, the strategy allows for a situation in which the actual voters at the meeting are not necessarily also the current shareholders. This creates the possibility for shareholder decision-making and risk exposure to diverge. While smaller, unintentional deviations are to be accepted as inherent features of the system, larger deviations can deliberately be exploited and manipulated by knowledgeable market actors for their own purposes.

I proceed by first describing and explaining the record-date system, the individual configuration of which may differ widely between legal systems (section III.B.3.a). Subsequently, I proceed to discuss the potential exploitation of this system for the purpose of risk-decoupling, and possible regulatory responses (sections III.B.3.b and c).

a) The record-date system

The 'record date' refers to the date on which those shareholders are determined who are entitled to vote at the company's general meeting.[151] Most jurisdictions set such a specific date in advance of each shareholder meeting. This system is usually justified because it allows shareholders to make adequate preparations for the meeting. While the notion of a record date is fundamentally similar in most countries, the time span between the record date and the general meeting varies significantly between countries.

[149] See Chapter VI.C.2. [150] For further detail, see Chapter VI.C.2.

[151] European Commission, *Commission Proposal for a Directive of the European Parliament and of The Council on the Exercise of Voting Rights by Shareholders of Companies Having Their Registered Office in a Member State and Whose Shares are Admitted to Trading on a Regulated Market and Amending Directive 2004/109/EC*, COM(2005) 685 final (1 May 2006) 6.

In the United Kingdom, the period between the record date and the meeting is relatively short. As a starting point, the exact period is left to the articles of the company itself, and it can choose the period freely, though the date shall not be more than forty-eight hours before the meeting.[152] In practice, the vast majority of issuers choose a date as late as 6 p.m. on the day before the general meeting.[153]

At the other end of the spectrum, the laws of the United States (or, rather, Delaware), pursuant to § 213 of Delaware General Corporate Law, require a record date to be fixed prior to each meeting, which must occur within sixty days of the meeting and no less than ten days prior to the meeting.[154] A recent study found that the median value set by the companies is a period of about fifty-four days.[155] Those who are registered as shareholders on the record date are entitled to be informed of the meeting, to attend, and to vote at it.[156] Investors can indirectly find out the time period that any given company has set. While the company has no direct obligation to communicate this time period to individual investors, it is obliged to inform brokers, dealers, and other intermediaries about the details at least twenty trading days before the record date.[157] This information will therefore be widely known.

German law, in turn, provides a general statutory record date for all listed companies. The registration date for any voting entitlement is required to be twenty-one days before the general meeting.[158] However, this rule only applies to bearer shares.[159] It is a mandatory rule and cannot be changed by the company's articles of association. The government justifies the length of the period by stating that foreign shareholders in particular need a certain amount of time to prepare for their participation.[160]

[152] See CA 2006, s. 360B: 'A traded company must determine the right to vote at a general meeting of the company by reference to the register of members as at a time (determined by the company) that is not more than 48 hours before the time for the holding of the meeting.' See already The Uncertificated Securities Regulations 2001 (SI 2001/3755), reg. 41:

> For the purposes of determining which persons are entitled to attend or vote at a meeting, and how many votes such persons may cast, the participating issuer may specify in the notice of the meeting a time, not more than 48 hours before the time fixed for the meeting, by which a person must be entered on the relevant register of securities in order to have the right to attend or vote at the meeting.

[153] Institute of Chartered Secretaries and Administrators, ICSA Response to the Consultation on Modernisation of the Directive 2004/109/EC (Transparency Requirements for Listed Companies) (20 August 2010), available at <http://ec.europa.eu/finance/securities/transparency/index_en.htm>.

[154] Marcel Kahan and Edward Rock 'The Hanging Chads of Corporate Voting' (2008) 96 Georgetown Law Journal 1227, 1233.

[155] Susan Christoffersen, Christopher Geczy, David Musto, and Adam Reed, 'Vote Trading and Information Aggregation' (2007) 62 Journal of Finance 2897, 2900; Reena Aggarwal, Pedro A C Saffi and Jason Sturgess, 'The Role of Institutional Investors in Voting: Evidence from the Securities Lending Market' (2015) 70 Journal of Finance 2309, 2316–17.

[156] Delaware General Corporation Law § 219.

[157] Securities Exchange Act 1934, Rule 14c-7(a)(3).

[158] Aktiengesetz [AktG] [Stock Corporation Act], § 123(3).

[159] For registered shares, only those shareholders who have been entered into the official registry may invoke shareholder rights, AktG § 67(2). Only those registered may attend and vote at the general meeting. Many companies have also used the statutory option to determine a separate registration requirement for the general meeting. See AktG § 123(2).

[160] This is according to the official explanations of the Act. See Rechtsausschuss des Bundestages, *Beschlussempfehlung und Bericht zum Regierungsentwurf des UMAG*, BT-Drs 15/5693, at 17.

Throughout most of the European Union, the record-date system is a relatively recent concept supported by EU legislation. The Shareholder Rights Directive of 2007[161] made a record-date system mandatory for all EU Member States, and fixed thirty days as the maximum time span between the record date and the general meeting.[162] As we have seen, this large window of time has produced very different results in practice. Member States have chosen a range of time periods, from the above-mentioned two days in the United Kingdom (and Ireland or Cyprus) to thirty days in Malta.[163] In the recent past, UK policy-makers considered extending the period, as it was considered to be rather short.[164] These proposals have been withdrawn, however.[165] The Directive does not give further details of how the record-date system operates.

Despite these differences in the set record date, all systems experience similar legal effects. The entitlement to vote necessarily follows the ownership of shares on the record date. Put differently, shareholders who own the shares on the record date (or 'record moment', more precisely) do not lose their voting right if they sell their shares between the record date and the meeting. Conversely, those who acquire shares after the record date are not entitled to attend or vote at the meeting. The shareholding status quo on the record is 'frozen' for purposes of the general meeting. The usual justification for the system is that it enables shareholders (and the company) to adequately prepare for the meeting. Arguably, it takes a substantial amount of time for information and documents to be shipped in time for the general meeting.[166] Moreover, the record-date system is believed to alleviate concerns regarding any conflict in the voting process and to help determine the entitlement of voters.[167] Critical commentators point to the fact that in today's world of electronic trading and communication, the lengthy cut-off periods are no longer justified.[168]

[161] Directive 2007/36/EC of the European Parliament and of the Council of 11 July 2007 on the exercise of certain rights of shareholders in listed companies [2007] OJ L184/17 ('Shareholder Rights Directive'). See on this Arthur R Pinto, 'The European Union's Shareholder Voting Rights Directive from an American Perspective: Some Comparisons and Observations' (2009) 32 Fordham International Law Journal 587.

[162] See generally Hilde Laga and Floris Parrein, 'Corporate Governance in a European Perspective' in Koen Geens and Klaus J Hopt (eds), *The European Company Law Action Plan Revisited* (Leuven University Press 2010) 79, 97.

[163] European Commission, List of days provided for according to article 15 of Directive 2007/36/EC, [2010] OJ C285/1.

[164] Paul Myners, *Review of the Impediments to Voting UK Shares* (January 2004).

[165] Paul Myners, *Review of the Impediments to Voting UK Shares: An Update on Progress Three Years On* (2007).

[166] For the official explanations on the German law introducing the record-date system, see Bundesregierung, *Entwurf eines Gesetzes zur Unternehmensintegrität und Modernisierung des Anfechtungsrechts (UMAG) vom 7.1.2005*, BR-Drs 3/05, 25.

[167] Clearing and Settlement Advisory and Monitoring Experts' Group, *Solving the Industry Giovannini Barriers to Post-trading within the EU* (November 2008) 94, available at <http://ec.europa.eu/internal_market/financial-markets/docs/cesame/cesame_report_en.pdf>.

[168] Ronald Barusch, 'Dealpolitik: Dell Shines Spotlight on "Record Date" Anachronism' *Wall Street Journal* (1 August 2013), available at <http://blogs.wsj.com/moneybeat/2013/08/01/dealpolitik-dell-shines-spotlight-on-record-date-anachronism/> accessed 19 August 2015.

b) *Risk-decoupling and record-date capture*

Although the rules for setting a record date prior to the general meeting are specified in detail, one universal and critical feature is the inherent shift in risk and voting between the record date and the day of the meeting.[169] The record-date system favours legal certainty over commercial reality. Thus, the record date determines in advance which shareholders are entitled to vote and simultaneously accepts those who are entitled to vote and are allowed to sell their shares between the record date and the meeting. This implies that those voting are possibly no longer the economically interested shareholders and may no longer be affected by the economic consequences of the shareholders' decisions. Conversely, investors who purchase shares between the record date and the shareholders' meeting are not entitled to vote—their interests are therefore not relevant at the general meeting. There is a serious increase in the shift of risk as the period between record date and meeting gets larger.[170] For this reason, the European Commission sought to minimize the permissible time period when drafting the Shareholder Rights Directive.[171] This attempt to limit the period emerged at the end of the legislative process, however, and it was not possible to fully implement this ambitious goal.[172] Consequently, the longer period of thirty days was stipulated in the final Directive text.[173]

How, then, can certain investors strategically abuse this system? In a simple way, the record-date system can be combined with the strategy of securities lending, as described previously. A hedge fund may therefore borrow shares precisely over the record date, subsequently return them, and therefore acquire the right to vote at the general meeting. As an example, consider the aforementioned case of the hedge fund Laxey Partners, which briefly increased its stake in British Land to 9 per cent over the record period.[174] In a similar context, consider the 2010 general meeting of the restaurant chain Mitchells & Butlers.[175] In these two, as well as other

[169] Myners (n. 165) 7.

[170] Daniel E Wolf and others, 'Setting the Record (Date) Straight', Kirkland M&A Update, 17 April 2013, available at <http://www.kirkland.com/siteFiles/Publications/MAUpdate_041713.pdf>.

[171] European Commission, *Fostering an Appropriate Regime for Shareholders' Rights—Second Consultation by the Services of the Internal Market Directorate General* (2005) 12.

[172] See European Commission, *Proposal for a Directive of the European Parliament and of the Council on the Exercise of Voting Rights by Shareholders of Companies Having Their Registered Office in a Member State and Whose Shares are Admitted to Trading on a Regulated Market and Amending Directive 2004/109/EC*, COM(2005) 685, article 7.

[173] Overall, however, the EU-wide introduction of a record date has been a large step towards a more efficient European capital market. In fact, the legal systems of many Member States had previously subscribed to a system of 'share blocking'. This meant that, for example, trading of voting shares between registration date and general meeting was simply prohibited, or even that shares had to be deposited during this time. This practice considerably reduced the liquidity of securities markets in the days before the general meeting. Faced with the choice of either not being able to sell the shares or not voting at the meeting, institutional investors in particular often opted for the second alternative in such a framework. The share blocking system was thus also politically controversial, as policy-makers intended to increase the presence of all shareholders at general meetings. See Myners (n. 165) 7. For a practical example on the consequences, see Florida State Board of Administration, *Corporate Governance Annual Report 2006* (n. 116) 29: 'In order to protect full trading capabilities and ensure proper liquidity, the SBA may not execute proxy votes on securities when share blocking applies.'

[174] See text accompanying nn. 73–7.

[175] Andrew Hill, 'Neither a Borrower…' *Financial Times* (London, 18 December 2009) 18.

similar cases, a securities lending strategy was used to produce a short-term voting entitlement, and thus securities lending was made effective for its risk-decoupling function with regard to corporate voting.[176]

However, the strategy of record-date capture can also be used without the borrowing of shares. Ultimately, any transaction of shares between the record date and the general meeting is capable of bringing about a risk-decoupling situation. Every regular shareholder who sells any of his shares after the record date, but before the general meeting, may vote as a risk-free or risk-reduced shareholder at the general meeting. To be sure, buying will be more expensive than borrowing shares, and therefore probably less common.[177] Also, the parties close to this type of transaction will usually contractually agree over the exercise of the voting rights. Nevertheless, this consideration is another matter, and it is important here to determine the existing possibilities for risk-decoupling.

An additional constellation deserves mention, which has been notably pointed out by Professor Jaap Winter. Companies whose shares are traded on various stock markets can take advantage of different record-date arrangements for the purposes of manipulation of two different markets.[178] For example, if a European company is listed on both a European and an American stock exchange, it is conceivable that an investor may vote twice. First, he may obtain a voting entitlement according to the American record date, which is usually about sixty days before the annual general meeting.[179] If he then converts his American shares into European shares, he may possibly be entitled to vote, according to the European country's national system, a second time at the same meeting. Winter does not provide empirical evidence in support of this constellation, but he asserts that it does happen in practice.[180] The American clearing house DTC has recognized this risk, but so far it has not taken remedial action, especially because—due to generally low attendance rates at general meetings—there has never been an instance of 'over voting', where more votes are cast than actually exist.[181]

c) Regulatory reactions

The record-date problem has already provoked a set of first legislative responses in various jurisdictions. In the following section we shall briefly outline a few examples, namely the attempts to handle the issue in Portugal and in the US state

[176] As described above, securities lending transactions can also be instrumentalized in other situations, outside the voting process at the general meeting, for risk-decoupling purposes. Formal examples are the convening authority for an extraordinary general meeting, the use of information rights, or shareholder litigation. Additionally, however, indirect, informal influence over the management can be considered a constantly relevant field of application, even outside the annual general meeting.

[177] See on this n. 283 and accompanying text.

[178] Jaap Winter, 'The European Union's Involvement in Company Law and Corporate Governance', in Geens and Hopt (n. 162) 140.

[179] See text accompanying n. 155.

[180] Winter (n. 178).

[181] Author's private correspondence with Jaap Winter (October 2011).

of Delaware, as well as an initiative by the US SEC. None of these three initiatives, however, have fully achieved a solution to the problem at hand.

In Portugal, when the EU Shareholder Rights Directive[182] was implemented into national law, law-makers adopted an accompanying set of rules to address the record-date problem. According to these rules, each shareholder who sells his shares between the record date and the end of the general meeting is required to immediately inform the chairman of the general meeting, as well as the Portuguese financial markets regulator Comissão do Mercado de Valores Mobiliários (CMVM), of this.[183] The law gives no answer to the question of what happens with this information, nor whether it is published. In any case, the CMVM and the chairman will most likely monitor the voting behaviour of such a shareholder.[184] It is to be expected that the disclosure obligation exerts some deterrent effect. Overall, this is a step in the right direction of gathering some information about the problem and becoming aware of its extent.

Further, the law-makers in Delaware have approached the subject. With effect from August 2009, § 213 (a) Delaware General Corporation Law was amended so that it now allows the management to establish a separate, later record date for the exercise of voting rights in a general meeting, as distinct from the previous record date concerning the meeting registration.[185] Under the previous regime, the date for the entitlement to be invited to the meeting and the record date for determining the voting rights were both necessarily the same. This had led to the problems described, namely the possibility that—due to the long time frames in Delaware law—significant movements in shareholdings may take place between the record date and the general meeting. The new rule attempts to remedy this problem by offering an optional second date for the voting entitlement. The law provides for no time limit for the selection of the second record date, so that, theoretically, it could be placed as late as the day of the meeting itself.[186] However, this will not be possible for purely practical

182 See n. 161.

183 Comissão do Mercado de Valores Mobiliários, *Consultation on the Modernisation of the Transparency Directive* (August 2010) 10, available at <https://circabc.europa.eu/webdav/CircaBC/FISMA/markt_consultations/Library/company_law/transparency_requirement/public_authorities/CMVM_en.pdf>.

184 Artigo 23.º-C(7) Código dos Valores Mobiliários (*Participação e votação na assembleia geral*), adopted by Decreto-Lei n.º 49/2010, of 19 May 2010. The decisive part reads: 'Quem, nos termos do n.º 3, tenha declarado a intenção de participar em assembleia geral e transmita a titularidade de acções entre a data de registo referida no n.º1 e o fim da assembleia geral, deve comunicá-lo imediatamente ao presidente da mesa da assembleia geral e à CMVM.' 'Who, in accordance with paragraph 3, has declared his intention to participate at the general meeting, and transfers ownership of shares between the record date referred to in paragraph 1 and the end of the general meeting, shall immediately notify the President of the general meeting and the CMVM thereof.'

185 Daniel E Wolf and others, 'Setting the Record (Date) Straight', Kirkland M&A Update, 17 April 2013, available at <http://www.kirkland.com/siteFiles/Publications/MAUpdate_041713.pdf>.

186 Dean F Hanley, '2009 Updates to Delaware General Corporation Law—Part 2: Elimination of "Empty Voting"', Foley Hoag Business Alert, 29 April 2009, available at <http://www.foleyhoag.com/publications/alerts-and-updates/2009/april/2009-updates-to-delaware-general-corporation-law-part-2-elimination-of-empty-voting.

reasons, because the US proxy system requires a certain period of preparation before the meeting.[187] Nevertheless, here too this is a step in the right direction, since the smaller the time gap between the (second) record date and the general meeting, the higher the likelihood that share ownership on the (second) record date and continued economic interest on the day of the meeting coincide. To be sure, this new provision will only capture involuntary voting right shifts. It cannot prevent market participants who intend to manipulate the meeting from deliberately circumventing the system.

In addition to this state-law solution, the federal SEC has addressed the issue. In a concept paper from 2010, the SEC similarly proposed a separation of the dates of the right to vote and meeting registration.[188] However, the SEC also mentioned several technical problems with the introduction of two separate record dates, so that for the time being, the concept paper limits itself to the collection of opinions from interested parties. So far, the SEC has not changed its rules in this respect, and commentators have so far treated the proposal rather cautiously.[189]

C. Positive Risk-decoupling: More Risk than Influence

The discussion so far has focused on situations in which a shareholder enjoys, compared to the economic risk, a disproportionate influence on the voting behaviour of a company. Since this situation is characterized by a risk that is reduced vis-à-vis the corresponding voting power, we have used the term 'negative risk-decoupling' for this scenario.

The mirror-image side includes situations in which the shareholder carries *more* risk than actual voting rights. These situations are referred to here as 'positive risk-decoupling'. Again, there is no congruence between the shareholder's influence in the company due to her voting rights and her risk exposure, but this time the voting rights are lower than the risk exposure. Unlike the rich variety of techniques for negative decoupling, there is essentially only one way of effectuating positive risk-decoupling, and that is by using financial derivatives. In particular, a derivative called 'Contract for Difference' has gained particular prominence in this context. It allows the shareholder to acquire de facto economic interest in the shares of a company without becoming their formal owner, and thus avoiding voting right reporting obligations.

[187] Hanley ibid. See also Securities and Exchange Commission, *Concept Release on the U.S. Proxy System* (Release Nos 34-62495, IA-3052, IC-29340; File No S7-14-10, 2010), (2010) 75 Federal Register 42981, 43015.

[188] SEC ibid. 43015 f. See on this Katayun I Jaffari and Whitney W Deeney, 'One Share, One Vote? Not Necessarily: Manipulation of the SEC Proxy System to Effect Empty Voting' *Legal Intelligencer* (25 February 2011) 7; Jay W Eisenhofer and Michael J Barry, *Shareholder Activism Handbook* (looseleaf, as per supplement 2013) para. 9-9.

[189] For example Bonnie Roe, 'When the Voting Is "Empty": No Quick Fix is Seen in Record Date Reform Proposals' *New York Law Journal* (29 November 2010) 9.

1. Contracts for Difference

The Contract for Difference (CfD) is a financial derivative instrument that was first developed in the City of London in the early 1990s to work around the UK stamp duty. The stamp duty is a tax that is levied on every stock transaction on the London Stock Exchange in the amount of 0.5 per cent of the share value.[190] The construction of the CfD makes it possible, through an off-market transaction, to achieve an economically identical effect to trading the stock directly, and thus avoids triggering the stamp duty obligation.[191]

Technically speaking, the CfD is an agreement on a cash settlement of the difference between the buying and selling price of a financial instrument. The CfD thus reflects the exact performance of the underlying base value, without it having to be acquired through an equivalent use of capital. In contrast to most other derivatives, contracts for difference are not futures, as they have no maturity, and the holding period is unlimited. CfDs allow investors to speculate on both the rising prices (long position) and the falling prices (short position) of the underlying asset. The transaction does not envisage the effective delivery of shares, but is typically settled by a cash payment.

In the case of shares, the typical transaction operates as follows. The CfD agreement[192] is concluded between a party holding a long position and a party going short, usually a bank.[193] The parties bet on the change in value of a reference share. The long party is interested in the increase in the target share price, whereas the short party bets for the decrease in the reference price. If the share price increases, the long party is entitled to gain the difference, as well as any distributions made by the target company from the short party.[194] In the case of a decrease in value, the short party gains the net change accordingly. In addition, the long party is usually obligated to pay the short party interest equal, for example, to LIBOR, and an arrangement fee.[195]

It thus becomes clear that the long party overtakes the economic exposure corresponding to that of an actual shareholder who has financed the share acquisition with debt.[196] A CfD investment costs the long party the sum of the interest and

[190] Finance Act 1986, ss. 66 ff.

[191] CfDs are also referred to as total return swaps in the US literature.

[192] CfDs are usually operated under the standardized ISDA Master Agreement; see further in Alastair Hudson, *The Law of Finance* (2nd edn, Sweet & Maxwell 2013) ch. 41.

[193] See Paul L Davies and Sarah Worthington, *Gower and Davies' Principles of Modern Company Law* (9th edn, Sweet & Maxwell 2012) para. 28-45.

[194] For fraudulent attempts to utilize CfD contracts to profit from underlying heding transactions, see *7722656 Canada Inc (formerly carrying on business as Swift Trade Inc) and Peter Beck v Financial Conduct Authority* [2013] EWCA Civ 1662. On the importance of this decision, see Simon Goldstone, 'Will Genuine CFD Trading Be Caught by the EU Market Abuse Regulation?' (2015) 30 Butterworths Journal of International Banking and Financial Law 550.

[195] Dirk Zetzsche, 'Hidden Ownership in Europe: BAFin's Decision in Schaeffler v. Continental' (2009) 10 EBOR 115, 120–1.

[196] Davies and Worthington (n. 193); Kay-Michael Schanz and Christoph Schalast (eds), 'Schaeffler KG/Continental AG im Lichte der CSX Corp.-Entscheidung des US District Court for the Southern District of New York' (Frankfurt School of Finance and Management—Working Paper Series, Working Paper No. 100, July 2008) 13 <http://www.frankfurt-school.de/clicnetclm/

the fee as well as a possible payment in case of loss in the target value. Yet, crucially, the long party does not need to invest the entire value of the underlying asset in order to receive the upside or downside corresponding to that of the shareholder. Therefore, the capital tied to CfDs is much smaller than in the case of a direct investment to the reference share, but can deliver the same economic benefit.[197]

The bone of contention in the policy debate was situations in which such CfDs were used to build large economic influence in a company without acquiring the relevant shares. In this way, the corresponding reporting requirements in securities law could be avoided, and the market was unaware of large-style acquisitions of economic interest in public companies. For example, in Europe, the Transparency Directive requires disclosure of significant equity positions in the following way:

> [W]here a shareholder acquires or disposes of shares of an issuer whose shares are admitted to trading on a regulated market and to which voting rights are attached, such shareholder notifies the issuer of the proportion of voting rights of the issuer held by the shareholder as a result of the acquisition or disposal where that proportion reaches, exceeds or falls below the thresholds of 5%, 10%, 15%, 20%, 25%, 30%, 50% and 75%.[198]

The starting point for EU disclosure obligations is thus the acquisition (or disposal) of shares and the corresponding voting rights. By contrast, economic-only positions and mere risk exposure do not fall under the original system of the Transparency Directive.[199] This precisely is the loophole that hedge funds and other sophisticated investors have been exploiting.

This constellation became known to the European public through several spectacular transactions: the attempted takeover of Volkswagen by Porsche and the successful acquisition of Conti by Schaeffler are two prominent examples from Germany.[200] There were also other high-profile cases in Switzerland (Unaxis, Sour, SIG, and Sulzer[201]),

fileDownload.do?goid=000000227192AB4>. See also Daniel Bertaccini, 'To Disclose or Not to Disclose? *CSX CORP.*, Total Return Swaps, and Their Implications for Schedule 13D Filing Purposes' (2009) 31 Cardozo Law Review 267, 275–6.

197 Henry T C Hu and Bernard Black, 'Hedge Funds, Insiders, and the Decoupling of Economic and Voting Ownership: Empty Voting and Hidden (Morphable) Ownership' (2007) 13 Journal of Corporate Finance 343, 345; Theodor Baums and Maike Sauter, 'Anschleichen an Übernahmeziele mit Hilfe von Aktienderivaten' (2009) 173 Zeitschrift für das gesamte Handelsrecht und Wirtschaftsrecht (ZHR) 454, 459–61; Financial Services Authority, *Disclosure of Contracts for Difference, Consultation and draft Handbook text, CP 07/20* (November 2007) 11–12 <http://www.fsa.gov.uk/pubs/cp/cp07_20.pdf>.

198 Article 9(1) of Directive 2004/109/EC of the European Parliament and of the Council of 15 December 2004 on the harmonisation of transparency requirements in relation to information about issuers whose securities are admitted to trading on a regulated market and amending Directive 2001/34/EC, [2004] OJ L390/38 (as amended).

199 The same is true for many other countries and jurisdictions worldwide.

200 See, for example, Zetzsche (n. 195).

201 For an overview, see Susan Emmenegger, 'Creeping Takeovers in Deutschland und in der Schweiz' in Stefan Grundmann and others (eds), *Unternehmen, Markt und Verantwortung—Festschrift für Klaus J. Hopt zum 70. Geburtstag am 24. August 2010* (de Gruyter 2010) 1763; Peter V Kunz, 'Kapitalmarktrechtliche Beteiligungstransparenz im Lichte moderner Finanzinstrumente—Perspektive der Schweiz', in Holger Fleischer, Susanne Kalss, and Hans-Ueli Vogt (eds), *Konvergenzen und Divergenzen im deutschen, österreichischen und schweizerischen Gesellschafts- und Kapitalmarktrecht* (Mohr Siebeck 2011) 181; Hans Caspar von der Crone, Eva Bilek, and Matthias Hirschle, 'Neuerungen

France,[202] and other countries.[203] Many other cases are discussed in a global context, such as the conflict between the hedge fund The Children's Investment Fund (TCI) and the railway company CSX in the United States.[204] More recently, Australia has seen a number of undisclosed attempts to effectuate hostile takeovers with the help of equity derivatives.[205]

Despite the increased interest among the EU and its Member States, most countries responded very slowly to the problem.[206] However, a number of EU Member States, beginning with the United Kingdom, imposed both general disclosure and takeover-specific regulation to limit the abuse of CfDs.[207] In 2013, the EU Transparency Directive was modified to impose far-reaching disclosure obligations for CfDs.[208] All of these instruments take the economic interest as decisive in determining legal disclosure obligations.[209] On the all-or-nothing spectrum, it can be argued that the EU regime is at the 'all' end of the spectrum, as it imposes an obligation to the entire CfD market and gives little credit to the beneficial and acceptable purposes for which CfDs are used.

US disclosure regulation is essentially similar to the European regime.[210] It does not include an explicit obligation to disclose CfDs, but recent case law has shown that

im Offenlegungsrecht', Schweizerische Zeitschrift für Wirtschafts- und Finanzmarktrecht (SZW/RSDA) 2008, 1; Jacques Iffland and Nadia Gilliard, 'Les nouvelles règles en matière de publicité des participations importantes', [2007] Zeitschrift für Gesellschafts- und Kapitalmarktrecht (GesKR) 365; see also Samuel Stadelmann and Noël Bieri, 'Die Offenlegung von Finanzinstrumenten nach Art. 20 Börsengesetz' [2010] GesKR 310.

[202] Alan Mason, Gabriel Flandin, and Sophie Bauquis, 'Des récentes affaires impliquant l'usage des dérivés actions' [2011] Revue Trimestrielle de Droit Financier 36.

[203] For further cases, see European Securities Markets Expert Group (ESME), *Views on the Issue of Transparency of Holdings of Cash Settled Derivatives* (November 2009) 4 ff., available at <http://ec.europa.eu/internal_market/securities/docs/esme/tdcash_en.pdf>.

[204] *CSX Corporation v the Children's Investment Fund Management (UK) LLP*, 562 F Supp 2d 511 (SDNY 2008), 12 June 2008, 08 CV 02764; see Brian T Sullivan, 'CSX Corp. v. Children's Investment Fund Management and the Need for SEC Expansion of Beneficial Ownership' (2009) 87 North Carolina Law Review 1300; Bertaccini (n. 196).

[205] Jonathan Shapiro and Gretchen Friemann, 'How Deutsche Bank's Name Sparks Fear' *The Australian Financial Review* (21 June 2014) 36.

[206] Committee of European Securities Regulators (CESR), *CESR Proposal to Extend Major Shareholding Notifications to Instruments of Similar Economic Effect to Holding Shares and Entitlements to Acquire Shares*, CESR/09-1215b (January 2010) 3 <http://www.esma.europa.eu/system/files/09_1215b.pdf> accessed 9 August 2015; see also ESME (n. 203) 6.

[207] DTR 5.3 and Takeover Code, rules 8.3, 9.1, and 9.5. For Germany, see Chapter V nn. 166 and 177.

[208] Directive 2013/50/EU of the European Parliament and of the Council of 22 October 2013 amending Directive 2004/109/EC of the European Parliament and of the Council on the harmonisation of transparency requirements in relation to information about issuers whose securities are admitted to trading on a regulated market, Directive 2003/71/EC of the European Parliament and of the Council on the prospectus to be published when securities are offered to the public or admitted to trading and Commission Directive 2007/14/EC laying down detailed rules for the implementation of certain provisions of Directive 2004/109/EC, [2013] OJ L294/13.

[209] See, e.g., Takeover Code, Definitions—Interests in securities.

[210] See Securities Exchange Act 1934, section 13(d). On recent evidence and reform plans, see Lucian A Bebchuk, Alon Brav, Robert J Jackson, Jr, and Wei Jiang, 'Pre-Disclosure Accumulations by Activist Investors: Evidence and Policy' (2013) 39 Journal of Corporation Law 1; David A Katz and Laura A McIntosh, '13(d) Reporting Inadequacies in an Era of Speed and Innovation' *New York Law Journal*, 24 September 2015.

it can be interpreted to include a similar type of reporting obligation.[211] The 2010 Dodd–Frank Act was a step back, as it put the decision on whether economic interests in securities are to be disclosed as 'beneficial ownership' under section 13(d), which is essentially placing it in the hands of the SEC.[212] In the absence of action by the latter, this means that the *CSX* decision has de facto been reversed. Thus, at present, CfDs (or equity swaps) would not have to be disclosed under the US legal framework.[213]

2. CfD investments and their abuse

To understand the background of the policy problem, it is important to note that CfDs are mainly used for purposes not related to corporate control, and that abusive practices are rare, even if they can have severe effects on the market. CfDs and other derivatives are not novelties, but rather commercially important parts of the financial markets, and their news value has been greatly increased by the recent financial crisis.[214] The functions of derivatives vary depending on their reference asset. Despite these differences, derivatives, including CfDs, are commonly used for two purposes: hedging and speculation.[215] When derivatives are most commonly used for hedging, that is for preventing losses when the value of a target asset decreases, an investment is made in the opposite movement of the value of the target asset, similar to insurance. Speculation, on the other hand, is a more classical investment technique, as it is used for gaining profits on the basis of fluctuations in the price of a target asset.[216]

It should be noted that the building of CfD positions for either of these purposes does not in itself indicate control-seeking behaviour.[217] The intentional building of stakes or toeholds could be described as a separate, and therefore the third, function of CfDs.[218] Yet, in comparison to the CfD industry as a whole, this function is rare, though potentially destructive.[219]

[211] See the *CSX* case (section III.C.3.a).

[212] Section 766(e) of the Dodd–Frank Act added a new paragraph (o) to section 13 Securities Exchange Act 1934. This now reads as follows:

> BENEFICIAL OWNERSHIP.—For purposes of this section and section 16, a person shall be deemed to acquire beneficial ownership of an equity security based on the purchase or sale of a security-based swap, *only to the extent that the Commission, by rule, determines* after consultation with the prudential regulators and the Secretary of the Treasury, that the purchase or sale of the security-based swap, or class of security-based swap, provides incidents of ownership comparable to direct ownership of the equity security, and that it is necessary to achieve the purposes of this section that the purchase or sale of the security-based swaps, or class of security-based swap, be deemed the acquisition of beneficial ownership of the equity security (emphasis added).

[213] See Henry T C Hu, 'Financial Innovation and Governance Mechanisms: The Evolution of Decoupling and Transparency' (2015) 70 Business Lawyer 347, 367.

[214] Henry T C Hu, 'Hedging Expectations: "Derivative Reality" and the Law and Finance of the Corporate Objective' (1995) 73 Texas Law Review 985, 988; House of Lords European Union Committee, 10th Report of Session 2009–2010, 'The Future Regulation of Derivatives Markets: Is the EU on the Right Track?' dated 31 March 2010 <http://www.publications.parliament.uk/pa/ld200910/ldselect/ldeucom/93/93.pdf> accessed 9 March 2015, 7, 19–21.

[215] Hudson (n. 192) paras 40-06 ff.; see also ESME (n. 203) 7–8; Hu (n. 9) 998.

[216] See FSA, CP 07/20 (n. 197) 12.

[217] Baums and Sauter (n. 197) 471.

[218] FSA, CP 07/20 (n. 197) 7.

[219] See, e.g., CESR, Proposal 09-1215b (n. 206) 3; ESME (n. 203) 12; and Hu (n. 214) 990.

In contrast to the described use of CfDs for purely financial interests, the present study is obviously more interested in the problematic aspects of this financial instrument, which is the use of CfDs for strategic or control-related purposes. This is referred to as 'CfD abuse'. A CfD abuse makes use of normal CfDs, and does not entitle their holder to receive underlying reference shares or related voting rights.[220] Therefore, CfD holdings are seemingly useless from the perspective of an investor seeking to obtain control in a target company. Nevertheless, CfDs turn out to be a powerful tool for acquiring control of voting rights in a target company with a small capital investment in comparison to the acquisition of actual shares.[221] They enable the CfD holder to comfortably secure a block of shares (a toehold), which can be expected to be tendered in a takeover bid with a price premium or even when the CfDs are unwound in the normal course of business.[222] Furthermore, the acquisition of the toehold in these situations can be made at a price that does not reflect the market's reaction to the acquisition, thus allocating the gains to the acquirer instead of the target shareholders or other market participants much in the manner supported in early US disclosure regulation.[223] This structure, which is based on market practice and illustrated for instance in the takeover bid by Schaeffler KG for the shares of Continental AG in 2008, operates as follows.[224]

Investment banks, counterparties to CfDs, are not in the speculative business, and they tend to hedge their short positions against the risk of positive change in the value of a target share, that is, their payment obligation. This can be done either by investing in further CfDs or other derivatives referenced to the same underlying shares, thus possibly spreading the risk to several other financial institutions, or directly by acquiring the underlying shares, that is, with a natural hedge.[225] If

[220] The following discussion focuses on CfD takeovers, but the presented structure applies also to other forms of abuse of control.

[221] This structure has been described as 'hidden (morphable) ownership' in Henry T C Hu and Bernard S Black, 'Empty Voting and Hidden (Morphable) Ownership: Taxonomy, Implications, and Reforms' (2006) 61 Business Lawyer 1011, 1014; see also Tom Siebens and Melissa Gambol, 'Who's Hiding Behind the Hedges? Developments in the USA and UK May Limit the Use of Total Return Swaps to Conceal Equity Stakes in Public Companies' (2009) 4 Capital Markets Law Journal 172, 174; Baums and Sauter (n. 197) 459–60. See also *CSX Corporation v the Children's Investment Fund Management (UK) LLP*, 562 F Supp 2d 511 (SDNY 2008), 12 June 2008, 08 CV 02764, 12; Dirk Zetzsche, 'Challenging Wolf Packs: Thoughts on Efficient Enforcement of Shareholder Transparency Rules', Center for Business and Corporate Law Research Paper Series 0044 (2/2010) 15–20, available at <http://papers.ssrn.com/sol3/papers.cfm?abstract_id=1428899> accessed 23 August 2015; and Bertaccini (n. 196).

[222] Regarding toeholds, see Mike Burkart, 'Economics of Takeover Regulation' (Stockholm School of Economics, CEPR, December 1999) 19–22, available at <http://www2.hhs.se/personal/MikeBurkart/papers/w_p5.pdf> accessed 15 April 2015.

[223] See Jonathan R Macey and Jeffry M Netter, 'Regulation 13D and the Regulatory Process' (1987) 65 Washington University Law Quarterly 131, 139–40 and, regarding the disclosure regulation's possible negative effects on value-enhancing takeover activity, 142–5.

[224] See a description of the *Schaeffler/Continental* takeover in Dirk Zetzsche, 'Hidden Ownership in Europe: BAFin's Decision in Schaeffler v. Continental' (2009) 10 European Business Organization Law Review (EBOR) 115.

[225] Zetzsche ibid. 121–4.

losing the bet, the short party can either unwind its derivatives or sell the hedging shares back to the market.[226] This structure effectively abolishes the counterparty risk dreaded in connection with derivatives in general. It increases the other general risk of derivatives markets, however, which is the lack of transparency, as it enables short parties to help in the creation of large, indirect long exposures to the target shares without those exposures having effect on short parties' own business.[227]

In this structure, there are two noteworthy aspects.[228] First, target shares are often locked into the CfD structure. Even though it is not obligated to any—let alone to a certain—form of hedging, the short party hedges its position in most cases, which means that either it or some further hedging party purchases the reference shares from the market. This is due to the fact that a natural hedge is often operationally and administratively the simplest form of hedging CfDs.[229] The voting rights carried by these hedge shares are held by a party in the CfD chain which has no economic exposure to the target company and thus also no interest in the voting rights carried by the target shares.[230] The bank as a short party is, however, interested in maintaining its client relationships and may be willing (although not obligated) to use its voting rights in the manner preferred by the long party, even in the absence of any agreement.[231]

The second and most important aspect of a CfD abuse concerns a long party's access to the target shares via its CfD position. If the CfD holder decides to announce a takeover offer or otherwise exercise influence in the target company, it can unwind the CfDs. It is convenient and common for the short party to then tender the hedging shares with a premium in the offer to cover its payment obligations if the share price has increased during the CfD contract period. In the absence of a bid, the short party can simply sell the block of shares to the long party instead of the market, as a large equity position can be difficult to dispose of in public trading.[232] Yet the short party has neither an obligation to hedge its position

[226] FSA, CP 07/20 (n. 197) 11–12; Zetzsche (n. 224) 121; Baums and Sauter (n. 197) 460; *CSX Corporation v the Children's Investment Fund Management (UK) LLP*, 562 F Supp 2d 511 (SDNY 2008), 12 June 2008, 08 CV 02764, 10; Schaeffler KG, 'Angebotsunterlage, Freiwilliges öffentliches Übernahmeangebot (Barangebot) der Schaeffler KG an die Aktionäre der Continental Aktiengesellschaft' [Formal Voluntary Takeover Bid] (30 July 2008) 16, available at <http://www.bafin.de/SharedDocs/Downloads/DE/Angebotsunterlage/schaeffler.pdf?__blob=publicationFile&v=5> accessed 10 August 2015.

[227] House of Lords European Union Committee Report (n. 214) 18.

[228] Michael C Schouten, 'The Case for Mandatory Ownership Disclosure' (2009) 15 Stanford Journal of Law, Business and Finance 127, 160; *Perry Corporation v Ithaca (Custodians) Ltd* [2004] 1 NZLR 731 para. 59.

[229] See Paul L Davies and Sarah Worthington, *Gower and Davies' Principles of Modern Company Law* (9th edn, Sweet & Maxwell 2012) para. 28-45; Baums and Sauter (n. 197) 460.

[230] Kay-Michael Schanz and Christoph Schalast (eds), 'Schaeffler KG/Continental AG im Lichte der CSX Corp.-Entscheidung des US District Court for the Southern District of New York' (Frankfurt School of Finance and Management—Working Paper Series, Working Paper No. 100, July 2008) 23 <http://www.frankfurt-school.de/clicnetclm/fileDownload.do?goid=000000227192AB4>.

[231] Davies and Worthington (n. 229) para. 28-45; Baums and Sauter (n. 197) 462; Hu and Black (n. 197) 351; Bertaccini (n. 196) 277; *Perry Corporation v Ithaca (Custodians) Ltd* [2004] 1 NZLR 731 para. 63.

[232] FSA, CP 07/20 (n. 197) 21; Offer document of Schaeffler KG (n. 226) 16, *Perry Corporation v Ithaca (Custodians) Ltd* [2004] 1 NZLR 731 para. 66.

with physical shares nor one to sell them to the long party in a subsequent offer or otherwise.[233] Nevertheless, the use of CfDs, especially in connection with a tender offer, bears little risk of loss to the CfD holder, as the price of the underlying shares typically increases after the announcement of an offer.[234] Therefore, a CfD holder is often making a bet that cannot be lost. It can do this merely with the help of the market practice and, most importantly, without the need to conclude an agreement or form an understanding with the short party.

Even though this may sound ingenious, the assumptions on which the described market practice is based have been strongly and rightly criticized by market participants, including ISDA and the SEC. The criticism claims that standard CfD agreements do not confer any voting rights to a long party, that 'as a general matter, a person that does nothing more than enter into an equity swap should not be found to have engaged in an evasion of the reporting requirements', and that this conclusion is not affected by possible economic or business incentives that the long party may have.[235] Therefore, CfD transactions should not fall under disclosure obligations merely on the basis of the existing, and admittedly accommodating, market practice that allows the long party to assume that the underlying securities will be easily available for it to purchase.[236] In addition, professional short parties generally manage hedge positions not on a transactional basis, but rather in portfolios, and they also often have guidelines and internal policies that limit voting with hedge shares.[237]

Even if the short position was hedged with matching shares of the target company, the market practice is not foolproof in catering for the needs of the long party. The short party holding the hedge shares can generate additional revenue by using these shares for stock lending purposes, for internal trading, or as collateral in other transactions. In all these cases, the hedge shares would not be immediately available to be acquired by the long party when unwinding the CfDs.[238] Also, the policies of investment banks regulate the unwinding of hedge positions with the aim of causing no or only limited market effects.[239] These practices and policies do

[233] Baums and Sauter (n. 197) 461–2, 465–6; Offer document of Schaeffler KG (n. 226) 16.

[234] Baums and Sauter (n. 197) 459.

[235] Brief of Amicus Curiae by the Securities and Exchange Commission in the matter CSX Corp. v. The Children's Inv. Fund Mgmt., L.L.P., et al., 08-Civ. 2764 (4 June 2008) 2, 4, available at <http://www.chadbourne.com/files/Publication/ce4995ec-b733-4eef-89e5-d5574a182080/Preview/PublicationAttachment/ed741d95-84e9-4fb9-b0a6-c196c813e5bf/SECBrehenyLetter.pdf>, accessed 19 August 2015.

[236] See *Perry Corporation v Ithaca (Custodians) Ltd* [2004] 1 NZLR 731 paras 73 and 78 as discussed previously.

[237] See *CSX Corporation v the Children's Investment Fund Management (UK) LLP*, 562 F Supp 2d 511 (SDNY 2008), 12 June 2008, 08 CV 02764, 11; Siebens and Gambol (n. 221) 174; Schanz and Schalast (n. 230) 18.

[238] *Perry Corporation v Ithaca (Custodians) Ltd* [2004] 1 NZLR 731 para. 61.

[239] Brief of Amici Curiae by International Swaps and Derivatives Association, Inc. and Securities Industry and Financial Markets Association in the matter CSX Corp. v. The Children's Inv. Fund Mgmt., LLP, et al., 08-Civ. 2764 (2 June 2008) 11–15, available at <http://www.sifma.org/WorkArea/DownloadAsset.aspx?id=1708> accessed 15 April 2015; FSA, CP 07/20 (n. 197) 22, 33–4; see also Hu and Black (n. 197) 351–2.

not, however, necessarily eliminate the impact on the voting structure of the target company or the possibility of abuse created by the hedging structure, because they are not legally binding.

3. Case studies

The practice of CfD abuse has severe effects but is scarce in numbers. This type of abuse is well documented in the following cases.

a) CSX

First, CfDs were deemed as a device with the purpose of divesting beneficial ownership, thus constituting a breach of the US disclosure requirements under Rule 13d-3, in the controversial decision of the US District Court for the Southern District of New York in *CSX Corporation v The Children's Investment Fund (UK) LLP*.[240] In this case, two activist hedge funds built a 14 per cent stake in the railway company CSX Corporation with the help of CfDs, or 'total return equity swaps', as the instruments are called in US literature.[241] Both the SEC, the US authority responsible for disclosure regulation, and ISDA,[242] an interest group representative of participants in the privately negotiated derivatives industry, opposed the court's reasoning, though without success. The judgment in *CSX v TCI* has been criticized, not only due to its outcome, but also on the basis of its rather far-reaching interpretation of the wording of the regulation and the rules of evidence.[243] Even more dissatisfying is the subsequently adopted appeals decision, handed down by the Second Circuit Court of Appeals on 18 July 2011.[244] The Second Circuit's majority opinion did not resolve the question of whether the CfDs in question gave the hedge funds beneficial ownership of the CSX shares, noting instead that there was 'disagreement within the panel'. Nonetheless, in his separate opinion, Judge Winter carefully elaborated on the question and concluded that the hedge funds did *not* have beneficial ownership of the underlying shares. The majority opinion neither criticized nor commented on this analysis.

[240] *CSX Corporation v the Children's Investment Fund Management (UK) LLP*, 562 F Supp 2d 511 (SDNY 2008), 12 June 2008, 08 CV 02764, 64; see Brian T Sullivan, 'CSX Corp. v. Children's Investment Fund Management and the Need for SEC Expansion of Beneficial Ownership' (2009) 87 North Carolina Law Review 1300, 1306; Daniel Bertaccini, 'To Disclose or Not to Disclose? *CSX CORP.*, Total Return Swaps, and Their Implications for Schedule 13D Filing Purposes' (2009) 31 Cardozo Law Review 267, 282–4; further on the US disclosure regulation, see Chapter V.E.1.

[241] For a general description of the case and the transaction structure, see Bertaccini (n. 240) 279–81.

[242] International Swaps and Derivatives Association, Inc.

[243] SEC Brief of Amicus Curiae (n. 235) 2–3; ISDA & Sifma Brief of Amici Curiae (n. 239) 5; Sullivan (n. 240) 1302, 1308–9, 1313, 1316, and 1319; Siebens and Gambol (n. 221) 174.

[244] *CSX Corp v The Children's Investment Fund Management*, No. 08-2899-cv, slip op. (2d Cir. July 18, 2011).

b) Perry v Ithaca

Second, a different path was chosen in the New Zealand case *Perry Corporation v Ithaca (Custodians) Ltd*,[245] a case very similar to *CSX*. New Zealand disclosure regulation largely corresponds to that of the United States. The main difference between these regulations is that an arrangement with the effect of circumventing the disclosure regime does not lead to beneficial ownership and disclosure requirements in New Zealand, whereas it does so in the United States.[246] The court in *Perry v Ithaca* discussed in detail the market practice of short parties hedging their position, which conveniently brings the target shares within reach though not under the control of the long party. The court held that such market practice did not establish an arrangement or understanding between the CfD counterparties and therefore did not lead to Perry Corporation being under a disclosure obligation.[247]

c) Schaeffler v Conti

Finally, a European example worth discussing in some detail is the case between *Schaeffler* and *Continental*, set in the traditional German car industry. Schaeffler KG, a medium-sized automotive supplier, had by 2008 built up a share of 2.97 per cent of the voting rights of the larger competitor Continental AG ('Conti'), which deliberately remained under the first-time disclosure obligation threshold of 3 per cent.[248] On 15 July 2008, the company disclosed the size of the shareholding, at the same time providing the information that they held swap positions with physical delivery for 4.95 per cent of the voting rights with the Royal Bank of Scotland and other swaps with cash settlement equal to approximately 28 per cent of the voting rights in Conti with investment bank Merrill Lynch.[249] These swaps put Schaeffler in an economic situation identical to that of a direct shareholder, as the company would be rewarded for share price increases, but had to correspondingly compensate its contractual partners for any losses.[250] Formally, however, Schaeffler did not become a formal holder of the shares, and legally Schaeffler had no right to receive shares of Conti.

However, as counterparties of the CfDs, Merrill Lynch and the other banks under their guidance hedged their own positions—as usual—by acquiring corresponding long positions in Conti shares. This created the typical

[245] *Perry Corporation v Ithaca (Custodians) Ltd* [2004] 1 NZLR 731.

[246] See sections 20–36 of the Securities Markets Act 1988 No 234.

[247] *Perry Corporation v Ithaca (Custodians) Ltd* [2004] 1 NZLR 731 [73] and [78].

[248] Wertpapierhandelsgesetz (WpHG) [Securities Trading Act] § 21 fixes the first-time obligation at 3 per cent, lower than the European standard, which is 5 per cent.

[249] Schaeffler KG, 'Angebotsunterlage: Freiwilliges Öffentliches Übernahmeangebot (Barangebot) an die Aktionäre der Continental Aktiengesellschaft' [Formal Voluntary Takeover Bid] (30 July 2008), available at <http://www.bafin.de/SharedDocs/Downloads/DE/Angebotsunterlage/schaeffler.pdf?__blob=publicationFile&v=5>.

[250] See on the operation of CfDs section III.C.1.

economic situation in which the holder of the CfD (Schaeffler) officially has no access to the underlying shares, but a cancellation of the contract 'may' lead to a tender of the shares—since an investment bank itself usually has no strategic interest in the investment object.[251] Presumably there was even a gentleman's agreement between the two parties to proceed in this way, and Jürgen Geißinger, the CEO of Schaeffler, even said that this was 'implicitly agreed upon'.[252] In fact, it happened as expected: the bank consortium under the leadership of Merrill Lynch later offered all the shares they had acquired for hedging purposes to Schaeffler, after Schaeffler had cancelled the swap agreement.[253]

The subsequent legal debate discussed whether Schaeffler had violated any disclosure laws with this unexpected transaction structure, or whether they had even been under an obligation to launch a mandatory bid for Conti. In particular, the question arose of whether the voting rights of the shares held by the banks would have had to be attributed to Schaeffler, since the latter had at least indirect influence over the shares. Under the law at the time, a number of additional rules existed that sought to avoid any circumvention of disclosure laws. For example, a disclosure obligation existed where a person or legal entity did not hold the shares personally, but where they were 'held by a third party in its own name on behalf of that [first] person or entity'.[254] Alternatively, the notification requirements also applied to a natural person or legal entity who 'holds, directly or indirectly, financial instruments that result in an entitlement to acquire, on such holder's own initiative alone, under a formal agreement, shares to which voting rights are attached, already issued, of an issuer whose shares are admitted to trading on a regulated market'.[255] Finally, the disclosure obligation applied also to the situation of 'acting in concert'—triggering the obligation of a person or legal entity where the 'voting rights [are] held by a third party with whom that person or entity has concluded an agreement, which obliges them to adopt, by concerted exercise of the voting rights they hold, a

[251] See Schaeffler, Formal Voluntary Takeover Bid (n. 249) 16: 'Die Bieterin wird das Swap-Geschäft während der Annahmefrist kündigen. [...] Nach der Kündigung muss Merrill Lynch International die unter dem Swap-Geschäft aufgebaute Position in Continental-Aktien in wirtschaftlich sinnvoller Weise (*commercially reasonably manner*) auflösen. Welche Maßnahmen Merrill Lynch International dann vornehmen wird, ist der Bieterin nicht bekannt.' 'The Bidder will terminate the swap transaction during the acceptance period. [...] After the termination, Merrill Lynch International must unwind the position established under the swap transaction in Continental shares "*in a commercially reasonable manner*". The bidder does not know which measures Merrill Lynch International will then take' (author's translation).

[252] Jürgen Geißinger, CEO of Schaeffler, said that this was 'implicitly agreed'. See 'Die Anschleichtaktik' *Financial Times Deutschland* (Hamburg, 17 July 2008) 1.

[253] Emmenegger (n. 201) 1768.

[254] Transparency Directive 2004/109/EC, article 10(g). In German law, this corresponded to WpHG § 22(1) no 2. The equivalent rule for takeovers was Wertpapiererwerbs- und Übernahmegesetz (WpÜG) [Takeover Act] § 30(1) no 2.

[255] Transparency Directive 2004/109/EC, article 13(1). In German law, this corresponded to WpHG § 22(1) no 5; the equivalent rule for takeovers was WpÜG § 30(1) no 5.

lasting common policy towards the management of the issuer in question'.[256] None of these scenarios, however, fit fully the scenario discussed here. The legal uncertainty was considerable.

For these reasons, the German market supervisor BaFin initiated a formal investigation into the matter, but in August 2008 reached the conclusion that Schaeffler had *not* violated any reporting requirements.[257] BaFin stated that it was unable to establish that there had been any relevant agreements between the parties, or that other notification requirements had been violated.[258] For example, they

> had not been able to establish that Merrill Lynch had been acting as coordinator of swap agreements for Schaeffler or that shares acquired as cover were to have been delivered in any subsequent takeover bid. Nor had the swap agreement created any reporting requirement for Schaeffler in respect of holding other financial instruments (section 25 (1) WpHG), since the cash-settled total return equity swap conveyed no claim to delivery of Continental shares. The only financial instruments which were reportable for the purposes of the Act were those which entitled the holder of the financial instrument to unilaterally acquire shares with voting rights attached that had already been issued.[259]

From this analysis, it appears that the reporting obligations for major shareholdings are to be applied rather literally. The original system was built on voting rights alone, and the separation of risk and influence was not considered to be possible or relevant. The literal application of the WpHG provisions is understandable given the far-reaching consequences from a disclosure obligation and its violation. It is for these reasons that the German market watchdog saw no legal ground to intervene.

4. Conclusion

Overall, positive risk-decoupling is conceptually the opposite of negative risk-decoupling, and therefore a related strategy using similar techniques. As we have seen, however, the setting and the potential policy concerns are of a very different nature.

CfDs are an unquestionably useful instrument with many legitimate fields of application. In a nutshell, it may become a source of regulatory concern where positive decoupling is all about 'hiding' from disclosure regulation, thus amounting to a 'CfD abuse'. To distinguish the one from the other is the main challenge that every regulator faces.

We will revisit this problem in the problem analysis in Chapter V.E. Before this, however, we shall explore some empirical evidence.

[256] Transparency Directive 2004/109/EC, article 10(a). In German law, this corresponded to WpHG § 22(2); the equivalent rule for takeovers was WpÜG § 30(2).

[257] BaFin, 'No Breach of Reporting Requirements Identified in Continental AG Takeover Procedure' (21 August 2008), available at <http://www.bafin.de/SharedDocs/Veroeffentlichungen/EN/Pressemitteilung/2008/pm_080821_conti.html>.

[258] BaFin ibid. [259] BaFin ibid.

D. Empirical Evidence

The different constellations and categories in both negative and positive risk-decoupling described above are all in need of empirical support. To what extent are these strategies actually used in practice? What is, in other words, their empirical reality?

To date, there is no conclusive empirical analysis that demonstrates the pervasiveness of these strategies in real life, though we know of a number of cases that have become known to the broader public via the media or through court procedures.[260] Beyond these high-profile cases, however, it is difficult to assess whether we have exposed only the tip of the iceberg. This is mostly due to the hidden nature of the strategies employed. Given that there is no obligation of transparency, there is no requirement to disclose negative interests in shares, and until very recently there was no obligation to disclose positive interest either.[261] No notice of borrowed shares is required; nor is there a requirement that the wider public be informed of record-date strategies. Usually, the risk-decoupler—typically, a hedge fund—pursues this business strategy for the very reason that there is no existing obligation of disclosure. Indeed, hedge funds pursue many activist strategies behind the scenes—that is, with little or no publicity.[262] It is this uncertainty over the frequency of risk-decoupling strategies that caused the European market supervisor, ESMA,[263] to launch a 'call for evidence' on empty voting in September 2011 in order to assess whether regulatory intervention was necessary.[264] Much of the evidence lacked concrete figures or statistics, which, as confirmed by their sources, can be explained by the hidden nature of the activities in question.[265]

Academic literature nevertheless attempts to shed some light on the issue and to provide evidence on how negative risk-decoupling strategies play out in practice.

For example, Professors Henry Hu and Bernard Black compiled and documented a number of worldwide incidences of risk-decoupling. Their most recent paper counts eighty-two instances.[266] This compilation allows for a prima facie understanding of the problem. We have to bear in mind, however, that these two

[260] For example, see the cases discussed in sections III.B and III.C. A few cases, such as the *Telus* story (section III.B.1.c a), have been thoroughly discussed by a broader public.

[261] This has now changed—see Chapter V.E.1.

[262] Thomas W Briggs, 'Corporate Governance and the New Hedge Fund Activism: An Empirical Analysis' (2007) 32 Journal of Corporation Law 681, 708.

[263] ESMA is the acronym for the European Securities and Markets Authority.

[264] European Securities and Markets Authority (ESMA), *Call for Evidence—Empty Voting* (ESMA/2011/288, 14 September 2011), available at <http://www.esma.europa.eu/system/files/2011_288.pdf>.

[265] The responses are published at <http://www.esma.europa.eu/consultation/Call-evidence-Empty-voting#responses> (last visited on 9 March 2015). There is also an official feedback statement: ESMA, *Feedback Statement—Call for Evidence on Empty Voting* (ESMA/2012/415, 29 June 2012), available at <http://www.esma.europa.eu/system/files/2012-415.pdf>.

[266] Henry T C Hu and Bernard S Black, 'Equity and Debt Decoupling and Empty Voting II: Importance And Extensions' (2008) 156 University of Pennsylvania Law Review 625, 661 ff.

academics draw their information from publicly available sources only.[267] With this understanding, the study must be considered as a first impressionistic overview. More recently, one of them provided some updated empirical findings, but did not go into comparable detail.[268] For the related phenomenon of 'empty creditors', that is, risk-decoupling by debt-holders,[269] Hu and Black are working on a separate update, which contains many new examples.[270]

In an ambitious and innovative study, Susan Christoffersen and co-authors examined the market for securities lending.[271] Their main finding is that the borrowing of securities significantly increases around the record date.[272] This finding supports the conclusion that there is an active market for voting rights. The authors show that the volume of borrowed shares spikes on the record date in such a way that, on average, 0.1 per cent more shares are borrowed on these days than on regular days.[273] At first glance, this does not seem like a dramatic increase, but an average increase of this magnitude can mean a big increase in an individual case.[274] Second, the study found that borrowing costs are generally extremely low.[275] This finding may, however, be questionable, as the low price may be due to the fact that the authors' data include all types of meetings, including votes on issues of relatively low importance. However, the price is known to increase significantly for important measures such as restructuring decisions.[276] Also, this finding may simply confirm the claim that lenders of securities often have no information, or at least no timely information, on when an important vote is scheduled.[277] In contrast to the Christoffersen study, other research does demonstrate that there is indeed an increase in borrowing costs for votes in the run-up to a general meeting.[278]

[267] ibid.

[268] Henry T C Hu, 'Financial Innovation and Governance Mechanisms: The Evolution of Decoupling and Transparency' (2015) 70 Business Lawyer 347, 363 ff. The most prominent new addition is the *Telus* case, see section III.B.1.c.

[269] See on this section III.E.1.

[270] Henry T C Hu, 'Debt, "Debt Governance," and the Decoupling Framework: "Empty Creditors," "Hidden Non-Interests," and the Matter of Evidence', conference manuscript, June 2013.

[271] Susan Christoffersen, Christopher Geczy, David Musto, and Adam Reed, 'Vote Trading and Information Aggregation' (2007) 62 Journal of Finance 2897.

[272] ibid. 2910. [273] ibid.

[274] But contrast this with the study by Aggarwal, Saffi, and Sturgess (n. 126), who find a relatively small increase in demand around the record date.

[275] Christoffersen and others (n. 271) 2912.

[276] David Yermack, 'Shareholder Voting and Corporate Governance' (2010) 2 Annual Review of Financial Economics 103, 113. But see the report about the *Coles-Myer* battle (on this, above n. 66) by Stephen Bartholomeusz, 'Solly in Lieu of the True Share Owners' *The Age* (23 November 2002), available at <http://www.theage.com.au/articles/2002/11/22/1037697877160.html>, according to which the voting rights in this situation were available 'for a few cents'.

[277] Florida State Board of Administration, *Corporate Governance Annual Report 2006* (2007) 31; see also Council of Institutional Investors, *Everything You Always Wanted to Know About Securities Lending, but Were Afraid to Ask* (2006) 4.

[278] Reena Aggarwal, Pedro A C Saffi, and Jason Sturgess, 'The Role of Institutional Investors in Voting: Evidence from the Securities Lending Market' (2015) 70 Journal of Finance 2309; Avner Kalay, Oğuzhan Karakaş, and Shagun Pant, 'The Market Value of Corporate Votes: Theory and Evidence from Option Prices' (2014) 69 Journal of Finance 1235.

In any case, the study emphasizes the potential importance of borrowing transactions for the voting process.[279] Participants of a practitioners' roundtable workshop at Yale School of Management echoed this theory.[280] Other market participants have confirmed this assessment. For instance, the Florida State Board of Administration (SBA), one of the largest pension funds in the United States, recently examined its lending volume for general meetings with important voting issues.[281] The SBA found that there indeed was an unusually high volume of borrowed shares in the context of controversial or important general meetings.[282]

The informative value of these studies reporting on the tendencies of the market for *borrowed securities* will depend on whether similar movements (before and after the record date) can equally be observed on the *regular stock market*. Hypothetically, each and every investor clearly could buy regular shares in order to gain additional voting power with respect to a particular voting date.[283] This is why Christoffersen and her co-authors compared the activities around the record date of borrowing and purchase markets.[284] The study did not find any comparable increase of regular trading around the record date that could correspond to the borrowing volume.[285] The authors concluded that the regular and legal process of 'vote buying through share buying' only occurs on a rare basis, and that the temporary borrowing of shares is more advantageous for activist investors.[286]

There is an absence of meaningful data on the use of *derivatives* to effectuate risk-decoupling. This lack of data is particularly due to the fact that, at least until recently, trading of OTC derivatives was possible without any registration or supervision.[287] This means that data for the past is difficult, or even impossible, to obtain. Nevertheless, the British Investment Management Association estimates that negative risk-decoupling strategies in the variant of the use of derivatives occur more frequently in practice than share borrowing or record-date capture.[288]

In this context, the only reliable figures are from the specific context of 'collar transactions', which were discussed previously.[289] In particular, management uses

[279] Christoffersen and others (n. 271) 2904.

[280] Millstein Center for Corporate Governance and Performance, Yale School of Management, *Voting Integrity: Practices for Investors and the Global Proxy Advisory Industry—Policy Briefing no 3* (2009) 11, available at <http://web.law.columbia.edu/sites/default/files/microsites/millstein-center/Voting%20Integrity%20Policy%20Briefing%20No%203%2002%2027%2009.pdf>.

[281] Letter from Ashbel C Williams, Executive Director, State Board of Administration of Florida, to Elizabeth M Murphy, Secretary, Securities and Exchange Commission (20 October 2010), available at <http://www.sec.gov/comments/s7-14-10/s71410-180.pdf>.

[282] ibid. 5.

[283] See, for example, the French state using this practice to prevent an opt-out from the controversial Loi Florange: Michael Stothard, 'French Companies Fight Back against Share Legislation' *Financial Times* (London, 17 April 2015) 19.

[284] Christoffersen and others (n. 271) 2908–9.

[285] Christoffersen and others (n. 271) 2908.

[286] ibid.

[287] This is now changing thanks to new post-crisis regulation, which introduces new reporting requirements for most OTC derivatives. See Regulation (EU) No 648/2012 of the European Parliament and of the Council of 4 July 2012 on OTC derivatives, central counterparties and trade repositories [2012] OJ L201/1.

[288] Ellen Kelleher, 'Enquiry Starting into Empty Voting' *Financial Times* (London, 25 September 2011) 3.

[289] See section III.B.1.b.

these transactions in an attempt to reduce dependence on the stock price.[290] In other words, management seeks to counteract the results intended by stock option programmes and share-based remuneration agreements, which attempt to bind remuneration to stock performance. Empirical studies have shown that management and executive staff use these instruments frequently and expressly to avoid the risk exposure of their shares.[291]

Finally, a general study by Yair Listokin on the stock price development of listed companies deserves mention. Listokin examined the contrary valuations of shares by both shareholders and the market to show that both groups reach different conclusions at narrow and contentious general meetings.[292] For example, when shareholders vote in favour of a management proposal by a close majority, the market evaluates this negatively, and vice versa. From this result, Listokin believes that conclusions can be drawn on the existence of risk-decoupling strategies in the company.[293] This concerns at least the special constellation where the management profits itself from a risk-decoupling situation. If this situation is the case, the empirical results of Listokin's study are consistent with the theoretical expectations. In both constellations, the voting process is distorted, which leads to a divergence between voting result and market valuation.

Drawing these different accounts together, there is some significant and important evidence of the presence of negative risk-decoupling in the market. Of course, most of it falls more into the category of anecdotal evidence, and we do not have a thorough, comprehensive account that would exhaustively depict the market realities. We know of many cases where the occurrence of empty voting strategies is strongly suspected, but cannot be fully verified. Due to the lack of comprehensive disclosure rules in the market, this should not surprise us. On the contrary, this would support calls for the introduction of transparency requirements to get a clearer idea of the actual occurrence of negative risk-decoupling.[294]

Ultimately, however, a sophisticated and fully satisfying evaluation of risk-decoupling occurrences is only of minor importance for the main argument of this book. This is due to the fact that for many of the examined problem areas and conflict situations (see Chapter V), the mere abstract possibility that a risk-decoupling has been carried out, or that risk-decoupling is possible at all, is sufficient. In anticipation of the problem perspectives to be discussed later, many of the monitoring and information costs created by risk-decoupling at the disadvantage of shareholders and investors will increase simply because of a mere

[290] ibid.

[291] See J Carr Bettis, John M Bizjak, and Michael L Lemmon, 'Managerial Ownership, Incentive Contracting, and the Use of Zero-Cost Collars and Equity Swaps by Corporate Insiders' (2001) 36 Journal of Financial and Quantitative Analysis 345; Lucian Bebchuk and Jesse Fried, 'Executive Compensation as an Agency Problem' (2003) 17 Journal of Economic Perspectives 71; see also Securities and Exchange Commission *Concept Release on the U.S. Proxy System* (Release Nos 34-62495, IA-3052, IC-29340; File No S7-14-10, 2010), (2010) 75 Federal Register 42981, 43018.

[292] Yair Listokin, 'Corporate Voting versus Market Price Setting' (2009) 11 American Law & Economics Review 608.

[293] ibid. 632.

[294] See Chapter VI.C.

possibility of risk-decoupling in a given company. Risk-decoupling has the potential of unsettling the market and of undermining market confidence and trust in the legal institution. For this general distrust to awaken, it only takes a few high-profile cases that catch the attention of the media, become known to the general public, and undermine confidence in the integrity of the market.[295] This loss of market confidence translates into damage to the functionality of markets, and will increase firms' costs of capital.

For the further development of the discussion in this book, all of this means that the actual problems created by risk-decoupling (which we are yet to fully develop) exist irrespective of how many quantifiable cases we count each year. We have seen that there is some robust support for the real occurrence of such behaviour, and this is reinforced by the possibility of using such strategies. Against this backdrop, the legal and practical feasibility of such strategies make risk-decoupling an urgent policy concern—and the many attempts already undertaken by legislatures and regulators worldwide bear witness to the seriousness of these apprehensions.[296]

E. Related Situations Not Covered in This Book

The topic covered in the present study touches upon several different related problem areas that are not directly subject of the investigation. These areas are delineated briefly in the following.

1. Related risk-decoupling strategies

The present work deliberately does not cover the broad category of risk-decoupling for *debt-holders*, and explicitly deals with risk-decoupling for equity only.

Various accounts have described processes in which holders of corporate bonds sought to separate risk from the bond itself in a similar way as described here for shares. Mirroring the notion of 'empty voting', scholars have coined the term 'empty creditor' to describe this phenomenon.[297] Instead of shareholders

[295] On the perspective of system distrust and market integrity, see Chapter V.E.1.

[296] See, for example, Securities and Exchange Commission, *Concept Release on the U.S. Proxy System* (Release Nos 34-62495, IA-3052, IC-29340; File No S7-14-10, 2010), (2010) 75 Federal Register 42981; European Securities and Markets Authority (ESMA), *Call for Evidence—Empty Voting* (ESMA/2011/288, 14 September 2011), available at <http://www.esma.europa.eu/system/files/2011_288.pdf>; ESMA, *Feedback Statement—Call for Evidence on Empty Voting* (ESMA/2012/415, 29 June 2012), available at <http://www.esma.europa.eu/system/files/2012-415.pdf>. See in detail Chapter VI.

[297] In particular, Henry T C Hu, '"Empty Creditors" and the Crisis' *Wall Street Journal* (New York, 10 April 2009) A13; see also Pablo Triana and Mari Subrahmanyam, 'Another Troublesome Feature of CDS Usage' *Financial Times* (London, 9 April 2012) 11; Dante A Marinucci, 'Empty Creditor Syndrome and Vivisepulture: Preventing Credit-Default-Swap Holders from Pushing Companies into Premature Graves by Refusing to Negotiate Restructurings' (2012) 62 Case Western Reserve Law Review 1285; Mark Roe and Federico Venezze, 'A Capital Market, Corporate Law Approach To Creditor Conduct' (2013) 112 Michigan Law Review 59; Patrick Bolton and Martin Oehmke, 'Credit Default Swaps and the Empty Creditor Problem' (2011) 24 Review of Financial Studies 2617.

(equity-holders), here it is the creditors of the company who hedge their bonds against the company by using similar derivatives structures as described in category 1 previously.[298] This may lead to the consequence that certain bond-holders, for example during a meeting of the creditors, have similarly distorted incentives to support initiatives that are contrary to all regular creditors' interests. In extreme cases, they could even benefit from situations where the company has to file for insolvency.[299]

In continuation of this logic, risk-decoupling strategies are even conceivable as 'hybrid' forms, which combine decoupling elements from both debt and equity.[300] For example, a long position can be generated by equity, but combined with a short position in corporate bonds, and vice versa. There are multiple combination possibilities.[301]

However, neither the aspects of hybrid nor creditor risk-decoupling are part of the present study. Many of the concepts and problem-solving approaches presented and developed here come to legal assessments and proposals that can be applied in some way to these two additional subjects. To avoid a boundless expansion of the subject, however, the present investigation is limited to the clearest and most relevant field of application of risk-decoupling scenarios, which is that of equity.

2. 'One share, one vote'

The present study has multiple points of contact with the classic discussion of the legal principle of 'one share, one vote' (OSOV).[302] This ideal of shareholder democracy postulates the absolute synchronization of voting rights and share ownership, and is therefore also referred to as the 'proportionality principle'. In particular, this principle challenges any deviations from proportionality, as they may exist for example in multiple voting rights, preferential voting arrangements, or voting right ceilings, commonly referred to as 'control-enhancing mechanisms' (CEMs).

It has to be said that the proportionality principle is very controversial, and no jurisdiction subscribes to it to a full degree. In some EU countries, such as Germany, legal rules at least partly require an OSOV standard (mainly due to the 1998 KontraG reform[303]), while in others, like the United Kingdom, market

298 See section III.B.1.

299 Henry T C Hu and Bernard S Black, 'Equity and Debt Decoupling and Empty Voting II: Importance And Extensions' (2008) 156 University of Pennsylvania Law Review 625, 728 ff.; Henry T C Hu and Bernard Black, 'Debt, Equity and Hybrid Decoupling: Governance and Systemic Risk Implications' (2008) 14 European Financial Management 663, 679 ff.; Henry T C Hu 'Debt, "Debt Governance," and the Decoupling Framework: "Empty Creditors," "Hidden Non-Interests," and the Matter of Evidence' conference manuscript, June 2013. For a critical perspective, see International Swaps and Derivatives Association (ISDA), 'The Empty Creditor Hypothesis', Research Notes 3/2009, 17 December 2009.

300 Hu and Black, 'Hybrid Decoupling' (n. 299) 688 ff.

301 Hu (n. 299).

302 See, for a number of points where the topics overlap, Chapters V.B.1.a and VI.B.1.

303 This reform de facto abolished multiple voting rights in Germany. Gesetz zur Kontrolle und Transparenz im Unternehmensbereich (KonTraG), 27 April 1998, Bundesgesetzblatt I 1998, 786.

pressure by institutional investors de facto guarantees an OSOV standard.[304] Other jurisdictions, however, allow CEMs and deviations from the principle to a larger extent.[305] Recently, the topic has regained a certain prominence in the policy discussion due to plans to grant additional 'loyalty' shares to long-term shareholders in France and in Italy, with the objective of combating short-term attitudes in capital markets.[306]

What is the difference between OSOV and the topic of this book? Unlike the traditional deviations from the proportionality principle—the so-called CEMs, such as multiple voting rights—the present study is devoted to internal, hidden deviations that affect the motivation of shareholders. In this, they deviate from open CEMs, which are typically known in the market and are rooted in the structure of corporate law itself. Instead of elaborating on the pros and cons of the admissibility of CEMs that openly grant the shareholder multiple voting rights, the present study relates to the interests of a shareholder who gives to the outside world the impression of being a regular shareholder with a properly aligned risk exposure—and yet, due to internal arrangements (such as derivatives), is oriented towards a distorted interest. Another difference is that negative risk-decoupling in the way studied here—and unlike traditional CEMs—does not just allow for partial risk reduction, but even permits a complete risk elimination and—in extreme cases—even the creation of negative interest (which exceeds the positive interest). Therefore, both issues differ significantly in their effects.

Nevertheless, in several respects, the proportionality principle manifests some parallels to the problem area of interest here, which we shall address throughout the present study. The theoretical discussion on OSOV relies at times on related arguments and thinking patterns. The relatedness of the question thus permits partial recourse to the theoretical arguments of the OSOV debate, even if the admissibility of traditional deviations from proportionality (CEMs) is not the direct subject of this work. Fundamental aspects of the OSOV debate will therefore only be included in the following sections to the extent that they are relevant to the specific question at stake.[307]

3. Proxy advisors

Thematically a little further away, but also somewhat related to the topic of this book, is the problem of proxy advisors. These are commercial entities who offer

304 For a comparative discussion, see Wolf-Georg Ringe, 'Deviations from Ownership-Control Proportionality—Economic Protectionism Revisited' in Ulf Bernitz and Wolf-Georg Ringe (eds), *Company Law and Economic Protectionism* (Oxford University Press 2010) 209.

305 Shearman & Sterling LLP, ISS, and ECGI, *Proportionality between Ownership and Control in EU Listed Companies: Comparative Legal Study* (May 2007).

306 Rachel Sanderson, 'Italy Makes U-turn on Loyalty Shares' *Financial Times* (FT.com, 5 February 2015); Steve Johnson, '"Protectionist" French Law Alarms Investors' *Financial Times* (FT.com, 22 February 2015).

307 For example, see Chapters V.B.1.a and VI.B.1.

professional advice to shareholders on how to exercise their voting rights. The costs of making an informed decision and apathy considerations drive the need for such advice. The flipside is that proxy advisors have become very powerful in recent years, in particular when they advise a large group of (institutional) investors. The market is essentially an oligopoly, and the market leader, Institutional Shareholder Services Inc. (ISS), counts as one of the most powerful influencers in US corporate governance. Many shareholders, and in particular institutional investors, de facto follow their advice without question. Thus, we can essentially consider the powerful position of proxy advisors as a type of separation between influence and risk—in a way related to the theme under consideration here.[308]

This and other aspects (such as potential conflicts of interest) have produced significant public pressure on the industry of proxy advisors and compelled ISS to adopt its own code of best practice.[309] Nevertheless, the topic has come into the focus of legislative activity and is subject to position papers from both the US SEC[310] and the European Commission,[311] and the proposed changes to the Shareholder Rights Directive seek to improve the transparency of the proxy advisory industry.[312]

Nevertheless, the issue of proxy advisors is not part of this study, because the differences in detail compared to the subject of interest are too large. It is true that proxy advisors exercise de facto a considerable influence on the voting practices in many public companies, but they are—contrary to the activist shareholders and hedge funds of interest here—typically not invested in these companies themselves, and therefore do not pursue their own strategic interests. In contrast to the scenarios investigated here, proxy advisors are not themselves interested in the company's strategy and do not purport to gain influence to derive their own financial benefits. Further, voting advisors are in a contractual relationship with the shareholders they advise, and these shareholders will turn away from them in

[308] See on the policy debate generally, Paul Rose, 'The Corporate Governance Industry' (2007) 32 Journal of Corporation Law 887; Stephen J Choi, Jill E Fisch, and Marcel Kahan, 'The Power of Proxy Advisors: Myth or Reality?' (2010) 59 Emory Law Journal 869; Paul Rose, 'On the Role and Regulation of Proxy Advisors' (2011) 109 Michigan Law Review First Impressions 62; Holger Fleischer, 'Proxy Advisors in Europe: Reform Proposals and Regulatory Strategies' (2012) 9 European Company Law 12; Lars Klöhn and Philip Schwarz, 'The Regulation of Proxy Advisors' (2013) 8 Capital Markets Law Journal 90.

[309] See ISS, *Best Practice Principles for Providers of Shareholder Voting Research & Analysis—ISS Compliance Statement* (10 June 2014), available at <http://www.issgovernance.com/file/duediligence/BPP-ISS-ComplianceStatement-1406010.pdf>.

[310] Securities and Exchange Commission, *Concept Release on the U.S. Proxy System* (Release Nos 34-62495, IA-3052, IC-29340; File No S7-14-10, 2010), (2010) 75 Federal Register 42981, 43009, 43011 ff.

[311] European Commission, *Green Paper: The EU Corporate Governance Framework*, COM(2011) 164 final (5 April 2011) section 2.5 and question 18; see also ESMA, *Discussion Paper: An Overview of the Proxy Advisory Industry. Considerations on Possible Policy Options*, ESMA/2012/212 (22 March 2012).

[312] European Commission, *Proposal for a Directive of the European Parliament and of the Council amending Directive 2007/36/EC as regards the encouragement of long-term shareholder engagement and Directive 2013/34/EU as regards certain elements of the corporate governance statement*, COM(2014) 213 final (9 April 2014).

the case that they perform disappointingly.[313] Finally, it must be said that voting advisors do not become the owner of the shares and do not vote themselves, but only provide recommendations to their clients, who are at all times free to reject the advice and vote in their own interest. Thus, although some practical similarities are noted, the legal structure and economic incentives differ significantly between the two problems. This justifies an independent, separate treatment of this problem.

4. Limited liability

Finally, it should be emphasized that from an abstract point of view, a risk-decoupling scenario in the broader sense already exists by virtue of the basic corporate law principle of 'limited liability'. According to this principle, shareholders in a company remain only liable up to the amount of their required contributions, and towards the creditors, only the company's assets are liable.

This principle is a cornerstone of corporate law and has been subject to intensive assessments and economic analysis.[314] Its advantages are no longer questioned today (even if excesses may be addressed by various legal mechanisms, such as the principle of exceptionally 'piercing the corporate veil'[315]). In the legal policy debate at the time of its initial introduction in the nineteenth century, however, the topic was a matter of controversial debate.[316] Academics of the twentieth century also occasionally criticized the principle. Constitutional economists like Walter Eucken and Franz Böhm argued for a full alignment of liability and risk, thus a fundamental principle of *un*limited liability for debts of a company, in order to ensure free competition and to allow the best possible allocation of resources.[317] In recent years—with regard to the problems of the global financial crisis of 2007–9—both academic literature and legislative initiatives have again questioned whether an unrestricted application of shareholders' limited liability is always appropriate, given the arguably exaggerated risk-taking levels of some firms prior to 2007.[318]

[313] This is, of course, somehow challenged by the existence of the oligopoly (or even almost a monopoly).

[314] For example, Frank Easterbrook and Daniel Fischel, 'Limited Liability and the Corporation' (1985) 52 University of Chicago Law Review 89; Richard A Posner, 'The Rights of Creditors of Affiliated Corporations' (1976) 43 University of Chicago Law Review 499; Henry Hansmann and Reinier Kraakman, 'Toward Unlimited Shareholder Liability for Corporate Torts' (1991) 100 Yale Law Journal 1879.

[315] Details vary depending on the jurisdiction. For a comparative assessment on veil-piercing, see Marco Ventoruzzo and others, *Comparative Corporate Law* (West Academic Publishing 2015) 144 ff.

[316] The leading English case *Salomon v Salomon* [1897] AC 22 was one of the most controversial cases of English law.

[317] Walter Eucken, *Grundsätze der Wirtschaftspolitik* (1952) 254, 279 ff.; Franz Böhm, *Die Ordnung der Wirtschaft als geschichtliche Aufgabe und rechtsschöpferische Leistung* (Kohlhammer, 1937) 37, 126.

[318] See, for example, Hans-Werner Sinn, *Casino Capitalism—How the Financial Crisis Came About and What Needs to Be Done Now* (Oxford University Press 2010) 71 ff.; European Commission, *Green Paper: The EU Corporate Governance Framework*, COM(2011) 164 final (5 April 2011) 12; Steven L Schwarcz, 'The Governance Structure of Shadow Banking: Rethinking Assumptions about Limited Liability' (2014) 90 Notre Dame Law Review 1.

These criticisms may have some valid points, though they suffer, in my opinion, from only relying on the disadvantages of the limited liability principle, and lacking a comprehensive cost–benefit analysis. The topic cannot be discussed in any more detail here, as it is outside the scope of this study. The present investigation is interested in the deliberate and concealed decoupling of the risk against the choices made by the legislature (as in risk-decoupling), rather than exploring the shifting of commercial risk as a consequence of an express legislative consideration (as in limited liability). The principle of limited liability may also lead to a certain distortion of incentives. However, these are deliberately chosen by the legislature—and, incidentally, third parties are aware of them.

F. Summary

For the purposes of this study, the detailed technical procedures and the extent of separation of voting and risk are less important than the fact that such risk-decoupling scenarios are actually possible, and—in view of the growing importance of derivatives and securities lending markets—much easier and more cost-effective than in the past. The partial or complete decoupling of risk and influence is thus an important factor in our capital markets, and law-makers, judges, and regulators should be aware of the phenomenon, take it into account in their assessments and regulatory processes, and find adequate responses. The examples that were mentioned were only used to illustrate what already happens and can happen in many other ways.

Chapter IV provides an account of how traditional categories of law approach the modern phenomenon of risk-decoupling. Subsequently, Chapter V aims to develop a thorough problem discussion, followed by the development of concrete solutions in the subsequent Chapter VI.

IV
The Failure of Traditional Categories of Law

Traditional categories of law have failed to properly address the issues of risk-decoupling. As the problem at the heart of the present study touches upon areas of corporate and securities law, but also more generally on hedge fund regulation, we will consider these different areas in turn.

A. Corporate and Securities Law

Both corporate and securities law usually take for granted the alignment between share ownership and risk exposure. In doing so, the law neglects the effects of the true risk exposure of shareholders and non-shareholders. This is evidenced by many instances in both areas of law.

For example, on the most basic level, *corporate law* rules throughout all legal systems give voting rights to 'shareholders'. The person owning the share is entitled to vote (and exercise other shareholder rights, including dividends), irrespective of their risk exposure. Certainly, there may be different classes of shares, including non-voting (preference) shares or multiple voting rights, but these varying degrees of risk exposure are publicly known and addressed by rules on different 'classes' of shares.[1] The ordinary shareholder, however, whenever he or she is mentioned in the company law statute of any jurisdiction, is assumed to be exposed to a commercial risk that corresponds to their voting power. Thus, the various rights that shareholders enjoy—voting, appointment of the board, dividends, litigation—are all dependent simply on the shareholder's formal ownership of a share.[2] Maybe the clearest example is the choice of most legal systems to establish a 'record date' prior to a shareholder meeting, at which the entitlement to vote at the meeting is determined.[3] The record date will usually be a few days

[1] See, for example, CA 2006 ss. 629 ff.

[2] As an example, see the rules in British law: appointment of the board: SI 2008/3229 Schedule 4 article 20; removal rights: CA 2006 ss. 168–9; derivative claims: CA 2006 s. 260 ('proceedings [...] by a member of a company'); distribution of profits: CA 2006 s. 829 ('distribution of a company's assets to its members').

[3] See Directive 2007/36/EC, article 7(2): '[...] the rights of a shareholder to participate in a general meeting and to vote in respect of his shares shall be determined with respect to the shares held by that shareholder on a specified date prior to the general meeting (the record date).' In the UK, see CA 2006, s. 360B: 'A traded company must determine the right to vote at a general meeting of the company by reference to the register of members as at a time (determined by the company) that is not

before the meeting actually takes place.[4] This system deliberately accepts a certain divergence between those registered on the record date and thereby accepts that the shareholder body may change between the record date and the general meeting.[5] This embodies the principle on which corporate law is built, which is that of the formal entitlement to a share, whereas the economic interest is not the regulatory target. This choice of form over interest is understandable, since the law assumes that both are in congruence anyhow; and it is much easier to prescribe entitlements or obligations by referring to a clear and formal list of persons rather than to varying economic interests.

Another bedrock of most corporate law systems is the ban on separating voting rights from the underlying shares. According to this understanding, the 'share' encapsulates a bundle of rights and duties which cannot be artificially split and unbundled. The most pronounced treatment of this principle is in German law, which attaches high importance to this so-called *Abspaltungsverbot* ('separation ban').[6] While less prominent, this ban is recognized elsewhere too. For example, the International Corporate Governance Network, an international organization with members from over fifty different jurisdictions, notes in its best practice codes as an almost universal dogma that '[t]he voting right is normally inseparable from the share in which it inheres'.[7] In the United States, the issue is debated under the heading of whether 'vote buying' should be permitted. Whereas traditional doctrine does not allow voting rights to be transferred to third parties without corresponding economic exposure,[8] recent Delaware case law has introduced a

more than 48 hours before the time for the holding of the meeting.' See The Uncertificated Securities Regulations 2001 (SI 2001/3755), reg 41:

> For the purposes of determining which persons are entitled to attend or vote at a meeting, and how many votes such persons may cast, the participating issuer may specify in the notice of the meeting a time, not more than 48 hours before the time fixed for the meeting, by which a person must be entered on the relevant register of securities in order to have the right to attend or vote at the meeting.

[4] For more detail, see Chapter III.B.3.a. [5] See Chapter III.B.3.a.

[6] See on this principle the seminal analyses by Matthias Habersack, *Die Mitgliedschaft—subjektives und 'sonstiges' Recht* (Munich 1996) 78 ff.; Harm P Westermann, *Vertragsfreiheit und Typengesetzlichkeit im Recht der Personengesellschaften* (Berlin and Heidelberg 1970); Herbert Wiedemann, *Die Übertragung und Vererbung von Mitgliedschaftsrechten bei Handelsgesellschaften* (Munich 1965) 274 ff. See also Karsten Schmidt, *Gesellschaftsrecht* (4th edn 2002) 557. For a recent account of Greek law, see Panagiotis Kon. Panagiotou, 'The Disruption of the Principle of Indivisibility of the Share and the Assignment of Autonomous Voting Rights' (2015) 36 Company Lawyer 67.

[7] International Corporate Governance Network (ICGN), *Guidance on Securities Lending* (2015) appendix II, para. 1.1 (available at <https://www.icgn.org/file/599/download?token=Vu6g-24p>).

[8] See, for example, *Chew v Inverness Mgmt. Corp.*, 352 A.2d 426 (Del. Ch. 1976); *Stott v Stott*, 242 N.W. 747 (Mich. 1932). This follows from general public policy. See *Macht v Merchs. Mortgage & Credit Co.*, 194 A. 19, 22 (Del. Ch. 1937). In some states, such as New York, the prohibition on vote buying is even enshrined in legislation. See § 609(e) New York Business Corporation Law:

> A shareholder shall not sell his vote or issue a proxy to vote to any person for any sum of money or anything of value, except as authorized in this section and section 620 (Agreements as to voting; provision in certificate of incorporation as to control of directors); provided, however, that this paragraph shall not apply to votes, proxies or consents given by holders of preferred shares in connection with a proxy or consent solicitation made available on identical terms to all holders of shares of the same class or series and remaining open for acceptance for at least twenty business days.

few limited relaxations to the strict ban.[9] The prohibition of separating voting rights from shares is also recognized in the UK and other common law countries as 'self-evident'.[10]

This principle may be thought to be in conflict with risk-decoupling strategies, when in fact it is not. All scholarship, case law, and legislation concerning the separation ban apply to situations in which the right to vote or other administrative rights are separated from the share. By contrast, in the situations under consideration here, things are different. In both categories, that is, negative and positive risk-decoupling, the share as an institution remains intact. The right to vote is neither sold nor granted to a third party. The shareholder always remains entitled to vote. Instead, the policy concern stems from the fact that the underlying risk exposure is transferred to another party. Most commentators even in German scholarship (where the bundling principle is considered as sacrosanct) therefore conclude that the separation ban is not formally violated by modern risk-decoupling strategies.[11]

To be sure, the economic outcome of risk-decoupled shareholders bears some strong similarities to the situations incriminated by traditional legal doctrine, but it is not covered under the law as it currently stands. Building an analogy, as considered by some, should not come easily.[12] It would only make sense where the purpose of the traditional no-separation rule requires the same legal solution to be

For comments from the academic literature, see Michael D Schmitz, 'Shareholder Vote Buying—A Rebuttable Presumption of Illegality' [1968] Wisconsin Law Review 927; Robert C Clark, 'Vote Buying and Corporate Law' (1979) 29 Case Western Reserve Law Review 776. For the older doctrine see Rainer Kulms, 'A Shareholder's Freedom of Contract in Close Corporations—Shareholder Agreements in the USA and Germany' (2001) 2 European Business Organization Law Review 685, 687.

[9] The leading case is *Schreiber v Carney*, 447 A.2d 17 (Del. Ch. 1982). More recent case law is *Weinberger v Bankston*, No. Civ.A. 6336, 1987 WL 20182 (Del. Ch. Nov. 19, 1987); *Crawford v Cincinnati Bell, Inc. (In re IXC Communications, Inc. Shareholders Litigation)* No. C.A. 17324, 1999 WL 1009174 (Del. Ch. Oct. 27, 1999); *Hewlett v Hewlett Packard Co.* No. Civ.A. 19513-NC, 2002 WL 549137 (Del. Ch. Apr. 8, 2002); *Crown EMAK Partners, LLC v Kurz*, 992 A.2d 377 (Del. 2010). For a detailed discussion, see Michael Lee, 'Empty Voting: Private Solutions to A Private Problem' [2007] Columbia Business Law Review 883, 887 ff.

[10] For Australia, see *Shears v Phosphate Co-operative Company of Australia Ltd* (1988) 14 ACLR 747; *Amalgamated Pest Control Property Ltd v McCarron* (1994) 31 ACSR 42. Cf Roman Tomasic, Stephen Bottomley, and Rob McQueen, *Corporations Law in Australia* (2nd edn, Sydney 2002) para. 13.9.4; Pamela Hanrahan, Ian Ramsay, and Geof Stapledon, *Commercial Applications of Company Law 2011* (12th edn, North Ryde 2011) para. 7-420. For Singapore, see Victor Yeo and others, *Commercial Applications of Company Law in Singapore* (3rd edn, North Ryde 2008) para. 8-420; for English law, see Derek French, Stephen W Mayson, and Christopher Ryan, *Mayson, French & Ryan on Company Law* (32nd edn, Oxford University Press 2015) para. 14.10.1.6.

[11] As a starting point, see Holger Fleischer, 'Finanzinvestoren im ordnungspolitischen Gesamtgefüge von Aktien-, Bankaufsichts—und Kapitalmarktrecht' [2008] Zeitschrift für Gesellschafts—und Unternehmensrecht (ZGR) 185, 216; Christoph Seibt, 'Verbandssouveränität und Abspaltungsverbot im Aktien—und Kapitalmarktrecht—Revisited: Hidden Ownership, Empty Voting und andere Kleinigkeiten' [2010] ZGR 795, 814 f. See also Ingo Theusinger and Daniel Möritz, 'Empty Voting als moderner Stimmenkauf?' [2010] Neue Zeitschrift für Gesellschaftsrecht (NZG) 607, 609.

[12] All those cited in n. 11 ultimately believe that risk-decoupling violates the 'spirit' or 'gist' of the no separation rule. Conceptual differences exist.

applied to today's problems. We will examine this question in more detail in the problem analysis section to come.[13]

Moving on to the field of *securities law*, European and national pieces of legislation specify disclosure obligations for holders of shares. All of them are equally based on formal share ownership, without taking into account the shareholder's economic exposure. The basic rule is article 9(1) of the Transparency Directive, which holds that

> [...] where a shareholder acquires or disposes of shares of an issuer [...], such shareholder notifies the issuer of the proportion of voting rights of the issuer held by the shareholder as a result of the acquisition or disposal where that proportion reaches, exceeds or falls below the thresholds of 5%, 10%, 15%, 20%, 25%, 30%, 50% and 75%.[14]

This rule has been amended over time, but it becomes clear that, as a starting point, the disclosure system of EU securities law is based on voting rights alone.[15] A corresponding rule is the takeover-related mandatory bid rule where a shareholder acquiring control in a target company is required to make an equivalent bid to all outstanding shareholders.[16] While the term 'control' is not defined in the Directive, it becomes clear from its general context that 'control' refers to voting control, and thus to a certain ownership in voting rights. Accordingly, Member States have typically implemented this provision by fixing a specific voting rights threshold, most commonly 30 per cent.[17]

In both corporate law and securities law, the legislative design has the consequence of the rules being both over- and under-inclusive. First, the law might empower 'shareholders' or regulate holders of 'voting rights' which are formally in such a position, but have hedged their economic position or reduced their risk exposure. They will also catch temporary 'shareholders' or 'voting rights' holders, who have borrowed shares for a certain time with the obligation to return them in the future.[18] Second, and conversely, the law *does not catch* those who are economically exposed to the company, like a shareholder, but fall short of being formal owners of the share. This latter consequence has been addressed by various legislative amendments over recent years.[19]

In consequence, these legal fields fail to adequately address the potential for risk-decoupling. Disclosure mandated under EU securities law will give investors the formal picture of holders of voting rights, but not of those necessarily interested in the company. Corporate law grants powers to shareholders in the same way. These areas therefore fall short of adequately capturing the problem at stake in the present study.

[13] See Chapter VI. [14] Directive 2004/109/EC, as amended.

[15] For subsequent qualifications, see Chapter V.E.1.

[16] See Directive 2004/25/EC of the European Parliament and of the Council of 21 April 2004 on takeover bids [2004] OJ L142/12, article 5.

[17] European Commission, *Report on the Implementation of the Directive on Takeover Bids*, SEC(2007) 268 (21 February 2007) 12–13.

[18] 'Borrowed' shares make the 'borrower' the full owner of the shares, temporarily, and thus imply full benefits and obligations just like long-term shareholders. See in detail Chapter III.B.2.a.

[19] See Chapter V.E.1.

B. Hedge Fund Regulation

We now turn to another field of regulation. The European Union first regulated hedge funds extensively with the Alternative Investment Fund Managers Directive (AIFM Directive), which was adopted in 2011.[20] This Directive has harmonized the supervisory approach to hedge fund regulation across the EU Member States. It introduced a comprehensive transparency and admission regime, detailing, inter alia, capital requirements, a maximum of leverage, and an independent asset valuation.[21]

The subject matter at the heart of the present study is, however, unaffected by the AIFM Directive. As has become clear, negative risk-decoupling particularly exemplifies great implications of hedge fund activity for the functioning of traditional corporate governance mechanisms. It is clear that hedge funds' sophistication in exploiting the traditional categories and tools of corporate governance poses significant challenges for regulators and law-makers. However, hedge fund regulation like the AIFM Directive does not address any of the problems discussed here, as it does not purport to address any direct activity undertaken by hedge funds. Instead, it establishes a general framework for their supervision.

Indeed, it is a shortcoming of the AIFM Directive that it remains completely silent on almost all aspects of hedge fund activity. The AIFM Directive limits itself to rules on the supervision of hedge fund managers; *it does not pursue an activities-based approach.*[22] In a comparable context, the Treasury Committee of the UK House of Commons came to the following conclusion: 'A fundamental problem with the [AIFM Directive] is that it focuses on issues relating to macro-prudential risk, but does not address the risks to the real economy caused by the operation of private equity and hedge funds.'[23] This limitation is surprising for two reasons. First, it has traditionally been difficult to find a convincing definition of a 'hedge fund', such that every legal rule applicable to a hedge fund raises questions of legal scope and raises arbitrage opportunities.[24] Second, and more importantly, in numerous situations regulatory intervention is made not in accordance with the existence of a given hedge fund, but rather with the concrete market or investment strategy it pursues. Like empty voting, risk-decoupling strategies may be pursued

[20] Directive 2011/61/EU of the European Parliament and of the Council of 8 June 2011 on Alternative Investment Fund Managers and amending Directives 2003/41/EC and 2009/65/EC and Regulations (EC) No 1060/2009 and (EU) No 1095/2010, [2011] OJ L174/1.

[21] Eilís Ferran, 'After the Crisis: The Regulation of Hedge Funds and Private Equity in the EU' (2011) 12 European Business Organization Law Review 379, 399; Daniel Awrey, 'The Limits of EU Hedge Fund Regulation' [2011] Law and Financial Markets Review 119.

[22] There are just a few such abstract provisions, in particular, on risk and liquidity management. See AIFM Directive (n. 20), article 12.

[23] House of Commons Treasury Committee, *Banking Crisis: International Dimensions, 2008–9*, HC 615, at Ev 90, available at <http://www.publications.parliament.uk/pa/cm200809/cmselect/cmtreasy/615/615.pdf> accessed 9 March 2015.

[24] See for instance the definition of an 'alternative investment fund' in the AIFM Directive (n. 20), article 4.

by any sophisticated market actor, not only a hedge fund. One example concerns the conflict between car-makers Porsche and Volkswagen in 2008, where Porsche attempted to take over Volkswagen with an opaque strategy using derivatives and options. According to the press, Porsche acted 'very much like a hedge fund'.[25]

It is obvious that the supervisory approach pursued by the AIFM Directive fails to take into account specific activities that hedge funds pursue, among them the decoupling of equity risk that is of interest for the present study. For this reason, the present investigation adopts an approach that is distinguishable from the AIFM Directive, rather taking an activity-based perspective and analysing the implications of risk-decoupling for corporate governance. It proposes a regulatory approach that is not limited to hedge funds, but generalizes all market actors who engage in this strategy. It should be noted that risk-decoupling is only one of many different legal strategies that hedge funds pursue which might warrant further study.[26] It nevertheless merits a detailed discussion because of its salient features and the particular challenges it poses for corporate scholarship.

[25] See Richard Chang, 'Porsche: A "Hedge Fund With a Carmaker Attached"', *New York Times* (23 January 2009), <http://wheels.blogs.nytimes.com/2009/01/23/porsche-a-hedge-fund-with-a-carmaker-attached>; Susanne Preuss, 'Ein Hedge-Fonds namens Porsche' ['A Hedge Fund called Porsche'], *Frankfurter Allgemeine Zeitung* (29 October 2008), <http://www.faz.net/aktuell/wirtschaft/unternehmen/vw-aktien-ein-hedge-fonds-namens-porsche-1711580.html>; Dietmar Hawranek, 'Kafka und die Cash-Optionen' [Kafka and the Cash Options], *Der Spiegel*, (3 November 2008) 82, available at <http://www.spiegel.de/spiegel/print/d-61822082.html>. See on the Porsche/VW case also Chapter V.E.1.

[26] See, e.g., Marcel Kahan and Edward Rock, 'Hedge Funds in Corporate Governance and Corporate Control' (2007) 155 University of Pennsylvania Law Review 1021.

V

Problem Perspectives

The analysis so far has shown that risk-decoupling strategies are legally feasible, and that savvy investors are indeed ready to use them in pursuing their goals. While a certain uneasiness about the use of these strategies is immediately conceivable, a thorough analysis is required to justify any legislative intervention. If no case is made for the existence of a market failure, the phenomenon could equally be understood as quite the opposite; we could endorse it as a market-efficient choice by specific actors.[1]

In order to examine the deeper implications of risk-decoupling strategies and to illuminate the economic problems underpinning the phenomenon, four different problem perspectives may be selected. After initially presenting the relevance of the problem, I will use a classic principal-agent approach (section V.B), a perspective from information cost and transaction cost theory (section V.C), and a view from corporate finance (section V.D). Finally, elements of positive risk-decoupling will be considered in the context of the market for corporate control (section V.E).

A. Outline and Relevance of the Problem

No problem analysis may limit itself to simply identifying the problem and then looking for solutions. Crucially, it must first dedicate some thought to the question of how serious the conflict situation is and whether there is a legally relevant

[1] For instance, this could be underpinned by contract-based corporate theories and by elements of the efficient market hypothesis. See on this first, Frank Easterbrook and Daniel Fischel, *The Economic Structure of Corporate Law* (Harvard University Press 1991); see also Brian Cheffins, *Company Law: Theory, Structure, and Operation* (Oxford University Press 1996); on the latter Eugene Fama, 'Efficient Capital Markets: A Review of Theory and Empirical Work' (1970) 25 Journal of Finance 383; see also Hendrik Houthakker and Peter Williamson, The Economics of Financial Markets (1996) 130; Ronald J Gilson and Reinier Kraakman, 'The Mechanisms of Market Efficiency' (1984) 70 Virginia Law Review 549. More recently, with regard to the financial crisis of 2008, see Luigi Zingales, 'Learning to Live With Not-So-Efficient Markets' (2010) 139(4) Daedalus 31; Ronald J Gilson and Reinier Kraakman, 'Market Efficiency after the Financial Crisis: It's Still a Matter of Information Costs' (2014) 100 Virginia Law Review 313.

problem situation that cannot be regulated by the market itself, but requires regulatory intervention.

The previous considerations have shown that risk-decoupling is actually possible and that it is happening on a large scale.[2] It has also become clear that it obviously contradicts some basic assumptions of our traditional corporate law—at least in spirit—and in particular the legal concept of bundling voting right and risk in a share and the concept of proportionality, as discussed previously.[3]

However, the question remains whether this conflict between economic reality and traditional principles and legal rules actually represents a relevant problem, as this can in no way be readily assumed. Depending on the theoretical perspective taken, the phenomenon of risk elimination could also easily be understood as an unproblematic exercise of the freedom of contract. Contractually oriented corporate law theories are based on the assumption that the objective of corporate law should only be the reproduction, in statutory law, of what structure the parties to an economic enterprise would have agreed upon or designed in the first place.[4]

Consequently, according to this view, the objective of corporate law is limited to reducing any transaction costs for business creation and management. Accordingly, it is merely understood as an 'offer' to the economic actors and should contain mainly default rules and little to no mandatory law.[5] Such a view of the economy could classify all of the risk-decoupling strategies described here as a market-efficient opt-out from the (default) rules, as proposed by the legal system. In other words, the parties to the corporate enterprise should be free to design their own system for the efficient exercise of their business, including the individual risk distribution or elimination.

This approach could be accompanied by ideas of the efficient market hypothesis. This important assumption of capital market theory is represented in three variants—strong, semi-strong, and weak—and states, in its most common semi-strong form, that the efficiency of financial markets ensures that at least all public information has already been priced indirectly in the prices of goods.[6] This

[2] See Chapter III.D. [3] See Chapter IV.A.

[4] Classic proponents of this view are, for example, Frank H Easterbrook and Daniel R Fischel, *The Economic Structure of Corporate Law* (Harvard University Press 1991); Brian Cheffins, *Company Law: Theory, Structure, and Operation* (Oxford University Press 1997). See also Michael Klausner, 'The Contractarian Theory of Corporate Law: A Generation Later' (2006) 31 Journal of Corporation Law 779.

[5] See Klausner ibid.

[6] See the seminal work by Eugene Fama, 'Efficient Capital Markets: A Review of Theory and Empirical Work' (1970) 25 Journal of Finance 383. For perspectives from legal scholarship, see Ronald J Gilson and Reinier Kraakman, 'The Mechanisms of Market Efficiency' (1984) 70 Virginia Law Review 549. More recently, for a perspective on the global financial crisis of 2008, see Luigi Zingales, 'Learning to Live With Not-So-Efficient Markets' (2010) 139(4) Daedalus 31; Ronald J Gilson and Reinier Kraakman, 'Market Efficiency After the Fall: Where Do We Stand Following the Financial Crisis?' in Claire A Hill and Brett H McDonnell (eds), *Research Handbook On The Economics Of Corporate Law* (Edward Elgar 2012) 456; Ronald J Gilson and Reinier Kraakman, 'Market Efficiency After the Financial Crisis: It's Still a Matter of Information Costs' (2014) 100 Virginia Law Review 313. For a good overview, see also Hendrik Houthakker and Peter Williamson, *The Economics of Financial Markets* (Oxford University Press 1996) 130.

impounding of the price happens without a delay, so no one—except insiders—is able to deliver consistent above-market profits. If this hypothesis is correct, it could be argued that the market will itself be able to address the challenges and problems linked to risk-decoupling, vote buying, and vote trading.[7] A much-cited example is the non-voting preference share, which is known to be traded on the capital markets with a generally significant discount to the price of the regular shares.[8] Similarly, a market could be imagined in which voting rights would be traded separately from the shares, and where the market itself would provide for an adequate and reasonable price development. If such a market is conceivable, then this thought must also apply to the development of structures that achieve similar or identical effects, such as trading equity derivatives and securities lending.[9] What is interesting about this thought experiment is that such markets actually do exist. Derivatives on equity securities are traded on a large scale on private markets, and the global securities lending market, especially among institutional investors, is immensely large.[10] Relying on the efficient market hypothesis, we may then expect that the information on traded derivatives and loans is impounded into the performance of the relevant shares and that they are therefore adequately priced. From this perspective, the market could be said to find its own answer to the problems described here. Of course, we should already point out that the transactions under consideration here are mostly characterized by a specific lack of transparency, and thus stand in sharp contrast to the characteristics of non-voting preference shares, as discussed previously.[11]

A third consideration may be added, which is that the general idea of hedging and insuring risk is pervasive in our legal and economic system and is not generally viewed as problematic. Insurance fulfils a positive function in our economy as a risk management tool based on the idea of pooling various risks together and over time. The risk presented by any given insured person is thus assumed collectively by the community of insured entities. The law of large numbers means that the credibility of the data increases with the size of the sample pool available: the larger the sample size of insured persons, the greater the probability that loss will correspond to the expected loss experience.[12] To be sure, the availability of insurance creates the risks of moral hazard and adverse selection,[13] but the welfare-enhancing function of insurance is undisputed. As the settlement and insurance of risk is not

[7] For such a view, see for example Charles Nathan, '"Empty Voting" and Other Fault Lines Undermining Shareholder Democracy: The New Hunting Ground for Hedge Funds' (2007) 15 The Corporate Governance Advisor 1, 6.

[8] Luigi Zingales, 'The Value of the Voting Right: A Study of the Milan Stock Exchange Experience' (1994) 7 Review of Financial Studies 125; Luigi Zingales, 'What Determines the Value of Corporate Votes?' (1995) 110 Quarterly Journal of Economics 1047; Shmuel Hauser and Beni Lauterbach, 'The Value of Voting Rights to Majority Shareholders: Evidence from Dual Class Stock Unifications' (2004) 17 Review of Financial Studies 1167.

[9] Nathan (n. 7). [10] See Chapters III.B.1. and III.B.2. [11] See Chapter IV.A.

[12] Alfred Manes, 'Insurance: Principles and History' in Edwin Seligman and Alvin Johnson (eds), *Encyclopaedia of the Social Sciences*, volume VIII (New York 1932) 95.

[13] See the seminal work by George A Akerlof, 'The Market for "Lemons": Quality Uncertainty and the Market Mechanism' (1970) 84 Quarterly Journal of Economics 488.

only permissible but even economically desirable, this fact could be put forward as an argument in favour of supporting risk-decoupling scenarios.[14] In particular, the situation of negative decoupling by use of derivatives could provoke the discussion of why the economic risk of an asset, a currency, or a security may be legally insured, but a company's share cannot. This question will be discussed separately at a later stage.[15] At this point, the problem will only be raised as a matter of principle.

On the other hand, we have seen above that risk-decoupling scenarios are not currently caught by the traditional categories of corporate law or securities. Nevertheless, certain tensions with the law exist.[16] In particular, the rule of 'no separation' between risk and voice, and the bundling character of a share are *formally* left untouched; in *substance*, however, their underlying principles are clearly affected. These principles aim at protecting third parties, as risk-decoupling activities may create negative externalities for them.

This fundamental tension will determine the following in-depth considerations, with private autonomy and private ordering on one side and an abstract protection of shareholders and outside investors on the other. However, this tension cannot and should not be resolved at this point. Nonetheless, the mere existence of this basic conflict illustrates the complications of the problem. Further, it demonstrates that the simple reference to self-regulating market forces does not do justice to the issue.[17] Put differently, the conceptual starting point shows that simply rejecting the need for regulatory action constitutes an oversimplification and is probably inappropriate, and that the case for legislative intervention in any case cannot be dismissed without further analysis. This tension will be the compass for the following problem analysis.[18]

B. Principal-agent Perspective

The first problem perspective for analysing the problem of risk-decoupling is a classical view stemming from principal-agent theory, which is well established in corporate law and governance.[19] Traditional theory holds that agents

[14] In this sense, Charles Nathan, '"Empty Voting" and Other Fault Lines Undermining Shareholder Democracy: The New Hunting Ground for Hedge Funds' (2007) 15 The Corporate Governance Advisor 1, 6; Christine Osterloh-Konrad, 'Gefährdet "Empty Voting" die Willensbildung in der Aktiengesellschaft? Überlegungen zur Proportionalität zwischen Stimmrechtseinfluss und wirtschaftlicher Betroffenheit der Aktionäre' [2012] Zeitschrift für Unternehmens- und Gesellschaftsrecht (ZGR) 35.

[15] See n. 52 and accompanying text. [16] See Chapter IV.

[17] On this in more detail Chapter VI.A.

[18] The following builds in parts on Wolf-Georg Ringe, 'Hedge Funds and Risk-Decoupling—The Empty Voting Problem in the European Union' (2013) 36 Seattle University Law Review 1027.

[19] See Michael C Jensen and William H Meckling, 'Theory of the Firm: Managerial Behavior, Agency Costs and Ownership Structure' (1976) 3 Journal of Financial Economics 305. For an overview, see John Armour, Henry Hansmann, and Reinier Kraakman, 'Agency Problems and Legal Strategies' in Reinier Kraakman and others, *The Anatomy of Corporate Law: A Comparative and Functional Approach* (2nd edn, Oxford University Press 2009) ch. 2.

who make decisions that affect the position of others may create agency costs by deviating from the interests of the principal. In the context discussed here, the claim will be that a risk-decoupled shareholder, as a new and unexpected actor with a different risk profile, creates new and additional agency costs for investors.[20]

1. Risk-decoupling and agency costs

Agency conflicts are ubiquitous in corporate governance and corporate law.[21] Traditional theory distinguishes mostly three different types of these conflicts: they are said to exist between management and shareholder (managerial agency costs), between shareholders (in particular, between majority and minority shareholders), and, less prominently, between the shareholders (or the company as a whole) and other stakeholders (such as employees, creditors, or customers).[22] In the following section, I will show how risk-decoupled shareholders create additional agency costs that exceed the assumptions of our regular corporate sector. I will discuss first the types of costs that are created, and second, in which relationships they are prevalent.

a) Types of costs

Negatively risk-decoupled shareholders create agency costs essentially on two fronts. First, they have distorted incentives, which may influence their power in the firm, and second, they may seek additional private benefits.

(i) Distorted incentives

A risk-decoupled shareholder has a different risk profile than a regular shareholder and will therefore exercise voting power either in a more or a less risk-averse way than the average shareholder, depending on the situation. Economic theory and empirical studies have shown that some shareholders who have voting power that exceeds their relative economic exposure tend to show non-justifiable, risk-averse behaviour.[23] This finding has important implications for the community of shareholders as they share a joint enterprise and a common interest. Institutions such as shareholder voting and majority rule derive their authority implicitly from the assumed fact that shareholders will vote in an optimal relationship to the capital invested. This is the basis for the development of the proportionality principle applicable to risk and influence, which leads, in its strictest form, to the principle

[20] See generally Jill E Fisch, 'Securities Intermediaries and the Separation of Ownership from Control' (2010) 33 Seattle University Law Review 877; Andrew Lumsden and Saul Fridman, 'Proxy Voting and Vote Selling' (2009) 61 Keeping Good Companies 332, 333, 337.

[21] See the references provided in n. 19.

[22] Armour, Hansmann, and Kraakman (n. 19).

[23] Ronald J Gilson and Bernard Black, *The Law and Finance of Corporate Acquisitions* (2nd edn, Foundation Press 1995) 249.

of 'one share, one vote'.[24] As a principle of legal policy, the normative claim of 'one share, one vote' holds that one should ensure a proportionate allocation of share ownership and control in a company. 'Ownership' can in this context be equated with 'cash flow rights'. The principle implies that any shareholder should own the same fraction of cash flow rights and voting rights, thus attributing an amount of control to a shareholder that is proportionate to her shareholding. Inherent in the principle is the proscription of deviations from a proportionate allocation of ownership and control via so-called 'control-enhancing mechanisms' (CEMs).[25] While it is academically debated, many perceive proportionality as being rationally compelling, based first on the observation that shareholders—as the company's residual claimants—have the strongest interest in maximizing firm value, and second on the belief that voting power should match economic incentives alone. Additionally, recent public debates about proportionality have assumed an emotional dimension; the idea that each share entitles the owners to equal influence has intuitive appeal. It has led to slogans such as 'shareholder democracy', based on assumed parallels between societal and corporate governance.[26] The ultimate objective of establishing a 'one share, one vote' principle in the EU has been pursued on two levels, with diverging methods and aims. Based on the recommendations of an academic expert group, the European Commission has pondered whether to introduce mandatory legislation, while the Court of Justice of the European Union has indirectly been working on a case law-based approach over the past years.[27]

Easterbrook and Fischel authored the quintessential 'one share, one vote'-supporting paper in 1983. The article emphasizes that deviations from equal voting rights in a company will create agency costs of management.[28] This essential assertion is based on two instances. First, and fundamentally, the two scholars argue that shareholders in possession of disproportionate voting rights will not make optimal decisions for the company.[29] Where a shareholder bears a higher

[24] On this subject, see Jonathan Rickford, 'Invisible Hand or Dead Hand?—Reflections on the EU "One Share One Vote"' in European Policy Forum (ed.), *One Share One Vote? Tomorrow's Companies: One Universal Model or Tailored Equity Structures?* (London 2006) 67; Mike Burkart and Samuel Lee, 'One Share—One Vote: the Theory' (2008) 12 Review of Finance 1; Renée Adams and Daniel Ferreira, 'One Share—One Vote: The Empirical Evidence' (2008) 12 Review of Finance 51; Wolf-Georg Ringe, 'Deviations from Ownership-Control Proportionality—Economic Protectionism Revisited' in Ulf Bernitz and Wolf-Georg Ringe (eds), *Company Law and Economic Protectionism* (Oxford University Press 2010) 209; Koen Geens and Carl Clottens, 'One Share One Vote: Fairness, Efficiency and EU Harmonisation Revisited' in Koen Geens and Klaus J Hopt (eds), *The European Company Law Action Plan Revisited* (Leuven University Press 2010) 145.

[25] Possible CEMs are, for instance, multiple voting rights, voting ceilings, non-voting (preference) shares, etc.

[26] The term 'shareholder democracy' is imprecise, as modern democracy would imply proportionality between influence and the number, rather than investments, of shareholders.

[27] For more detail, see Ringe (n. 24).

[28] Frank H Easterbrook and Daniel R Fischel, 'Voting in Corporate Law' (1983) 26 Journal of Law and Economics 395, 409.

[29] ibid. See also Armen A Alchian and Harold Demsetz, 'Production, Information Costs, and Economic Organization' (1972) 62 American Economic Review 777, 783; Daniel R Fischel, 'Organized Exchanges and the Regulation of Dual Class Common Stock' (1987) 54 University of Chicago Law Review 119, 135.

economic risk than is reflected in his voting right,[30] his incentives to vote may be distorted. This is because he might be more willing to accept risk when his financial interest is lower than his actual influence in the company. Conversely, if his financial exposure is greater than his equity share, he might not be in a position where his voice is heard in the same way that corresponds to his interests.

Second, the paper claims that disproportionate ownership structures impede corporate takeovers or changes of control, thereby strengthening managers' position over shareholders.[31] Disproportionate voting rights can thus lead to an insulated management position, especially when the management is supported by, or connected with, the shareholder who enjoys special voting rights.[32] This is relevant on three levels. First, differentiated voting rights facilitate control by an economic minority stake and make a takeover extremely difficult without a break-through rule, which sets them aside during the period of a takeover bid. Second, means of circumventing 'one share, one vote', such as voting agreements, may increase managerial discretion and discourage potentially value-increasing takeovers.[33] Third, voting restrictions such as voting caps can represent important anti-takeover devices that discourage potential bidders from making an offer.[34] Moreover, many recognize that deviations from 'one share, one vote' permit an overrepresentation of minority interests in the company's governance, leading to the possibility that there will be diverging preferences among the members of the board. Thus, schemes such as these expose the firm to an uncompensated risk of making inconsistent or illogical decisions.[35]

The above-mentioned arguments certainly cannot all be easily transferred to the problem of risk-decoupling. However, the strongest claim—that there are distorted incentives for the exercise of voting rights—also remains an essential feature of risk-decoupled shareholders. A shareholder who eliminates his risk exposure will vote for different reasons than someone who has responsibility for his financial position. Even if it is only a gradual reduction in risk, decisions and votes are already to some extent distorted.

This is mainly a problem in negative risk-decoupling scenarios (where the risk is reduced). In positive decoupling situations, the shareholder is risk-exposed, but does not have the corresponding voting power. To be sure, such a shareholder will typically have distorted incentives too, but the low voting power will normally suggest that there is no voting or governance problem, simply because the 'potential' shareholder

[30] Or vice versa—his voting rights are greater than his economic risk.

[31] See Easterbrook and Fischel (n. 28). This point is emphasized by a dissenting opinion in the Jenkins Report. See Board of Trade, *Report of the Company Law Committee*, Cmnd 1749 (June 1962) 207-10, available at <http://www.takeovers.gov.au/content/Resources/other_resources/downloads/jenkins_committee_v2.pdf>.

[32] Marc Goergen, Marina Martynova, and Luc Renneboog, 'Corporate Governance Convergence: Evidence from Takeover Regulation Reforms in Europe' (2005) 21 Oxford Review of Economic Policy 243, 253.

[33] See Rafel Crespi and Luc Renneboog, 'United we Stand: Corporate Monitoring by Shareholder Coalitions in the UK' (CentER Discussion Paper No 2000-18, 2000), available at <https://pure.uvt.nl/portal/files/534699/18.pdf>.

[34] Goergen and others (n. 32).

[35] See Easterbrook and Fischel (n. 28).

cannot (yet) vote. And even if we assume, as in some situations, that the temporary holders of the shares will comply with the risk-exposed shareholder (even without any formal agreement), this would only lead to a reconciliation between risk and voice.

Overall, we can summarize that negative risk-decoupling can lead to increased agency costs, in particular because of distorted incentives for voting. A shareholder who eliminates or reduces his risk exposure will decide and act based on different considerations than someone who has full responsibility for his financial position. The present line of thought is mostly relevant for the variant of *negative risk-decoupling*, as it presupposes that someone has a certain voting power that they can use. For this category, it follows that, according to principal-agent theory, a negatively risk-decoupled partner will be *more risk-friendly* than a regular shareholder with properly aligned interests. Since he will not meet the economic consequences in the same way as the regular shareholder, the decoupler will use his vote to pursue riskier purposes than normal. This divergence and distortion of incentives alone produces costs, as the regular shareholder is directly affected in his financial position. If he wants to avoid this, he must increase his monitoring strategy or take other measures to limit the resulting disadvantages for him.

(ii) Private benefits

Aside from the mere distortion of incentives, the second point to be mentioned is the so-called idiosyncratic, 'private' benefits of control that a risk-decoupled shareholder may pursue.

The concept of special benefits (private benefits of control) stems from finance scholarship and is a relatively new discovery. The traditional literature has assumed that all shares are homogeneous, that they exist equally, and that shareholders therefore generate returns on the same scale. Over the past thirty years, however, a different view has slowly gained support. According to this new view, a controlling shareholder can reach a number of advantages which other shareholders cannot obtain. Originating in a simple model from 1980,[36] the concept of 'private benefits' has become central in explaining the relationship between different groups of shareholders. Empirical studies have shown that the level of private benefits gained by controlling shareholders diverges significantly, and depends on the legal system in question.[37] These levels of private benefits are also used as universal indicators of the principal-agent conflict—the degree of severity between majority and minority shareholders in a jurisdiction.[38]

[36] See Sanford J Grossman and Oliver D Hart, 'Takeover Bids, the Free-Rider Problem, and the Theory of Corporation' (1980) 11 Bell Journal of Economics 42.

[37] Tatiana Nenova, 'The Value of Corporate Voting Rights and Control: A Cross-Country Analysis' (2003) 68 Journal of Financial Economics 325, 336; Alexander Dyck and Luigi Zingales, 'Private Benefits of Control: An International Comparison' (2004) 59 Journal of Finance 537, 551; see also Michael J Barclay and Clifford G Holderness, 'Private Benefits from Control of Public Corporations' (1989) 25 Journal of Financial Economics 371; Lucian A Bebchuk, 'Efficient and Inefficient Sales of Corporate Control' (1994) 109 Quarterly Journal of Economics 957.

[38] Luca Enriques, Henry Hansmann, and Reinier Kraakman, 'The Basic Governance Structure: Minority Shareholders and Non-Shareholder Constituencies' in Kraakman and others (n. 19) 89, 107.

These private benefits can arise in many different shapes and constellations.[39] How, then, do they accompany risk-decoupled shareholders? A shareholder whose risk falls short of his voting influence can profit from disproportionate benefits compared to the other shareholders. The *Mylan–Perry* case described previously[40] serves as an extreme example, as the hedge fund Perry became involved with Mylan without bearing any commercial risk. The company could thereby enjoy the additional, and private, benefit in the form of its involvement with the competitor King. More precisely, in such an extreme situation, the shareholder resolution in favour of the takeover is beneficial for one shareholder in particular (Perry), but it does not bring the same benefits for all other shareholders. The same result can be observed also on a less dramatic level. The fact that the risk profile of one shareholder is distinct from that of other shareholders means that, in transactions with the company, an investment decision or a specific management strategy for the company as a whole (including the minority shareholders) may be both detrimental and beneficial for the risk-decoupled shareholder.

In addition to the distorted voting incentives, these special benefits represent an additional and distinct cost factor. As argued previously, the distortion of voting interests means that the risk-decoupled investor enters into either 'too much' or 'too little' risk, in comparison with a regular shareholder who enters with proper risk alignment. The pursuit of private benefits is distinguishable from this, as it allows the voting shareholders to pursue separate advantages due to their increased voting power. For instance, if a hedge fund, H, holds 5 per cent of the shares of company X, but temporarily acquires an additional 5 per cent by means of securities borrowing transactions over the record date, certain aspects have to be distinguished. On the one hand, there is the danger that H will vote in a more risk-friendly way than it would as a regular shareholder because H bears a reduced risk exposure compared with other shareholders. The other shareholders are thus affected by H's increased appetite for risk because, unlike regular shareholders, H does not fully encounter the consequences of its decisions.[41] An additional and separate risk stems from the possible variety of private benefits: H may use its voting power of 10 per cent of the votes in such a way that the company enters into transactions that are advantageous only for H, either directly or via a third party.[42] In extreme cases, as with *Mylan–Perry*, H can cause X to enter into inherently harmful measures from which H itself will, however, benefit because of the interest in a competitor or takeover target.

[39] See Ronald J Gilson, 'Controlling Shareholders and Corporate Governance: Complicating the Comparative Taxonomy' (2006) 119 Harvard Law Review 1641.

[40] See Chapter III.B.1.a. [41] See Chapter V.B.1.a.i.

[42] The figure of 10 per cent was only chosen as an example—in jurisdictions with dispersed ownership structures, it can be sufficient to influence or to decide voting outcomes. In a concentrated ownership environment, a higher share would be required.

b) Relevant agency relationships

So far, we have only explored the different costs that may arise or occur in the context of the above-mentioned principal-agent conflict. They are due to the modified risk profile of the risk-decoupled shareholders as 'agents' and their realizable private benefits. But who is the 'principal' in this relationship? In what follows, we will discuss who actually bears the costs and to whose disadvantage the modified risk profile of decoupled shareholders has a negative effect. In this context, several groups should be considered.

First, it is noteworthy that such a cost does certainly *not* occur *within* the relationship in which the risk is shifted. This is true for the 'securities lending' set of cases for instance (category 2), as between 'lender' and 'borrower'.[43] In this bilateral relationship, the potentially negative impact of the voting decision only affects the lender, who has voluntarily given up the right to vote in favour of the borrower.[44] The same applies to the legal relationship between the parties to a financial derivative contract referenced to shares, in the sense of the above-described derivatives strategy (category 1).[45] On the basis of the Coase theorem, it can be expected that these parties will find a private solution, for example an agreement of a proxy in favour of the lender, or an agreement on the borrower's obligation to refrain from exercising the voting rights.[46]

However, this two-party situation needs to be distinguished from the multilateral relationship between the risk-decoupler and *other constituencies in the company*, such as shareholders, creditors, and other stakeholders. These groups, who are not involved in the risk-shifting agreement, encounter involuntary *negative externalities*. Where two parties to a share lending transaction agree to shift the voting rights to a non-economically interested party and thereby cause costs to others (who cannot avoid or influence the transaction), there is a direct, adverse interference with the interests of such third parties. In addition, the transaction can also have a negative overall impact on the market, which in turn would lead to a decline in investor confidence as a result. This aspect is further treated later.[47] At this point, the relationships between the different groups within the company are of primary interest.

More specifically, there will be a conflict *between risk-decoupled and regular shareholders*. This became evident in the H/X example given previously.[48] The regular shareholder is affected by a co-shareholder's risk modification by the creation of additional agency costs. In analogy to the above-mentioned classical conflict between minority and majority shareholders, shareholders with a diverging risk profile also pursue idiosyncratic goals that disadvantage the weaker principal.

43 See in detail Chapter III.B.2.

44 In this sense, apparently, we have to understand the contributions by both Nathan (n. 14) and Osterloh-Konrad (n. 14).

45 See Chapter III.B.1.

46 On private ordering solutions, see Chapter VI.A.2.

47 See Chapters III.A., III.B.1.c, and E.2, and section V.B.2.

48 See text accompanying n. 41.

Furthermore, a principal-agent relationship may exist between the risk-decoupled shareholder and *outside, potential investors*. If investors make their investment decisions for shares of a company that suffers from risk-decoupling, they entrust their capital to a not optimally incentivized, but risk-reduced, agent. In the absence of any specific information, investors would normally assume a regular congruence between risk and influence in the company. Risk-decoupling thus creates higher information and contracting costs.

Finally, such a principal-agent conflict may even exist *in relation to the management*. The administration is normally obliged to act in the 'best interests of the company' (which, depending on the jurisdiction, may have the label of 'shareholder value', 'enlightened shareholder value', or the 'interests of the enterprise')—with varying shades, this essentially means the interests of the *shareholders*. Even if—as especially in German law—the importance of the interests of other groups such as employees, creditors, and customers are emphasized ('stakeholder approach'),[49] there is an agreement that the management acts as a kind of trustee, at least for the assets of the shareholders.[50] The correct and proper fulfilment of this task requires that the company's shareholders are a sufficiently homogeneous group who pursue reasonably similar goals (especially profit maximization). Only if this is the case will it be possible for management to adequately perform its task. The occurrence of risk-decoupled shareholders complicates this process.[51] If the shareholders have different (financial) interests and have diverging risk profiles, it will be almost impossible for the management to reconcile these different needs and to satisfy all shareholders simultaneously.

It should be clear that we are dealing with a multi-person problem, the impact of which on investors and third parties in general is of particular importance. The objection raised above, for example, that insuring risks is in principle a legitimate concern,[52] is thus relativized in its importance. It is precisely not just a two-party relationship between policy-holder and insurer whose contractual relationship is, without doubt, a completely legitimate and efficient exchange of risks. Rather, the incentives and externalities of insured persons in relation to third parties are centre stage—and not only in relation to the anonymous third party investor, but also to other shareholders who are supposed to pursue a common economic goal together with shareholders with a different risk exposure. In addition, legitimate expectations of third parties do not include any insured or hedged risk exposure in the

[49] The German Corporate Governance Code (4.1.1) states that 'The Management Board is responsible for independently managing the enterprise in the interest of the enterprise, thus taking into account the interests of the shareholders, its employees and other stakeholders, with the objective of sustainable creation of value'. This restates the case law: BGH, decision of 21 April 1997 (II ZR 175/95), NJW 1997, 1926, 1928 (*ARAG/Garmenbeck*); OLG Frankfurt, decision of 17 August 2011 (13 U 100/10) ZIP 2011, 2008.

[50] See, for example, Markus Weber, in Wolfgang Hölters (ed.), *Aktiengesetz—Kommentar* (2nd edn, Munich 2014) § 76 para. 19. British law is more straightforward; see CA 2006 s. 172.

[51] Jill E Fisch, 'Securities Intermediaries and the Separation of Ownership from Control' (2010) 33 Seattle University Law Review 877, 878.

[52] See text accompanying nn. 12 ff.

context of interest here. Instead, due to the necessary free transferability of shares, standardization seems appropriate. This aspect is explored further later on, in the section on transaction and information costs.[53]

c) *Further considerations*

The economic analysis of law adds an important dimension to the principal-agent problem. The risk of opportunistic behaviour by the agent has repercussions for the principal's willingness to entrust his goods to the agent in the first place. In the context of the firm, this means that if there is a risk that the manager or major shareholder (as agent) engages for example in self-serving behaviour, which can be detrimental to the company as a whole and to the minority shareholders, the latter will be less willing to invest in the company from the outset.[54]

The inefficiencies occurring *ex post* thus have an *ex ante* impact on the investment decisions of market participants and can lead to inefficiencies as early as at this stage. It is therefore in the interest of the respective agent—either a manager or a major shareholder—to signal that the possibility of opportunistic behaviour is subject to legal restrictions, by using legally binding rules. The various elements of corporate governance and corporate law can thus be understood as an *ex ante* self-commitment of each agent (management or major shareholder) to allow reliable investment decisions and to establish *ex post* efficiency.[55]

Applied to the facts of interest here, this means that the occurrence of risk-decoupling situations can lead to a general decline in the willingness to invest. The agency costs, which occur *ex post* in any particular case, can thus have an additional *ex ante* impact on the investment appetite of investors in general. This can lead to increasing loss of confidence in the functioning of the capital markets and overall rising capital costs.[56]

2. Possible reduction of agency costs?

In contrast to the discussion thus far, some commentators argue that risk-decoupling structures do not exacerbate agency costs, but can rather reduce them.[57] This claim is based on the following reasoning: one of the main problems of shareholder

[53] See section V.C.

[54] Oliver Williamson, *The Economic Institutions of Capitalism* (Free Press 1985) 47 ff.; Sanford J Grossman and Oliver D Hart, 'The Costs and Benefits of Ownership: A Theory of Vertical and Lateral Integration' (1986) 94 Journal of Political Economy 691, 716.

[55] Andrei Shleifer and Robert W Vishny, 'A Survey of Corporate Governance' (1997) 52 Journal of Finance 737, 743.

[56] See also section V.C.

[57] Susan Christoffersen, Christopher Geczy, David Musto, and Adam Reed, 'Vote Trading and Information Aggregation' (2007) 62 Journal of Finance 2897, 2904 f; Peter Esö, Stephen Hansen, and Lucy White, 'A Theory of Vote-Trading and Information Aggregation', Working Paper 2014, available at <http://www.econ.upf.edu/~shansen/votetrading.pdf>; see also Mike Burkart and Samuel Lee, 'Signaling to Dispersed Shareholders and Corporate Control' (2015) 82 Review of Economic Studies 922, 940; Jordan M Barry, John William Hatfield, and Scott Duke Kominers, 'On Derivatives Markets and Social Welfare: A Theory of Empty Voting and Hidden Ownership' (2013) 99 Virginia

voting rests on the fact that small shareholders generally do not exercise their voting rights. This finding is the well-known phenomenon of 'rational apathy' of (small) shareholders.[58] The argument then deduces that these apathetic shareholders could transfer their voting rights to other shareholders. The collective action problem could be overcome in this way—shareholders who take an active interest in the strategic direction of the company could accumulate a stronger voting position in order to effectively control the management, and thus reduce managerial agency costs.[59] Especially in an environment characterized by high dispersion of shares, medium-sized shareholders could become effective and important controllers of management.[60] This process would alleviate the above-described collective action problem among atomic shareholders.

As previously mentioned, this argument was advanced as the central justification for hedge fund Laxey Partners as part of the initiative around British Land.[61] As shown, Laxey justified its actions to try to influence a strategic decision with the use of borrowed shares with the argument of monitoring the management in the interest of all shareholders. Furthermore, it is sometimes argued that risk-decoupling strategies can also be used to overcome opportunistic obstructions in corporate restructuring transactions, as was recently demonstrated in an impressive example concerning US company Emmis Communications.[62]

Law Review 1103, 1124 ff.; Paul Ali, Ian Ramsay, and Benjamin Saunders, 'Securities Lending, Empty Voting and Corporate Governance' [2014] Law and Financial Markets Review 326, 328.

[58] See Kenneth J Arrow, *The Limits of Organization* (Norton, 1974); Mark Roe, 'A Political Theory of American Corporate Finance' (1991) 91 Columbia Law Review 10; Bernard S Black, 'Shareholder Passivity Reexamined' (1990) 89 Michigan Law Review 520; Eddy Wymeersch, 'Shareholder(s) Matter(s)', in Stefan Grundmann and others (eds), *Unternehmen, Markt und Verantwortung—Festschrift für Klaus J. Hopt zum 70. Geburtstag am 24. August 2010* (de Gruyter, Berlin 2010) 1565, 1571.

[59] Katayun I Jaffari and Whitney W Deeney, 'One Share, One Vote? Not Necessarily: Manipulation of the SEC Proxy System to Effect Empty Voting' *Legal Intelligencer* (25 February 2011) 7:

> However, some have observed that strategic traders and those savvy to the financial markets have access to unique information regarding a corporate decision or the impact of a decision on the corporation's value, and can more quickly and efficiently gather such information. Thus, some argue that allowing these well-informed traders and investors access to a corporation's vote, whether they have an economic interest or not, increases efficiency and that these investors will make the 'right' decision, positively influencing the corporation. In other words, informed shareholders should be permitted to acquire a large voting position from less informed shareholders, to improve efficiency in the voting process, increase accuracy in electoral outcomes and enhance shareholder value.

[60] See Henry T C Hu and Bernard S Black, 'The New Vote Buying: Empty Voting and Hidden (Morphable) Ownership' (2006) 79 Southern California Law Review 811, 820, 852; see also Securities and Exchange Commission, *Concept Release on the U.S. Proxy System* (Release Nos 34-62495, IA-3052, IC-29340; File No S7-14-10, 2010), (2010) 75 Federal Register 42981, 43017; Consob, *Position Paper on the Disclosure of Cash-Settled Derivatives* (8 October 2009) 13, available at <http://www.consob.it/mainen/legal_framework/consultations/dp_cash_derivatives_20091008.pdf> accessed 15 August 2015. For a more differentiated view, see Alon Brav and Richmond Mathews, 'Empty Voting and the Efficiency of Corporate Governance' (2011) 99 Journal of Financial Economics 289.

[61] See text accompanying n. 73 in Chapter III.

[62] *Emnis* made use of total return swaps to overcome the rights of preference shareholders. See Kimberly Gladman and Beth M Young, 'The Dangers of Dual Share Classes', Harvard Law School Forum on Corporate Governance and Financial Regulation (21 May 2012), available at <http://blogs.law.harvard.edu/corpgov/2012/05/21/the-dangers-of-dual-share-classes/>. See also

This claim is an old argument in disguise. In the literature on isolated vote trading and vote buying, when investigating whether it could produce value-enhancing situations, proponents argued that such an approach could help overcome the problem of investors' passivity.[63] This argument was primarily made in the context of takeovers and acquisitions, to enable the bidder to acquire additional voting rights and thus replace the management of the target company.[64] Opponents have pointed out that this theory is based on two conditions, which are not always met: first, that the proposed acquisition was actually in the interests of the shareholders, and second, that the purchaser used the right to vote in a way that is actually in the interests of all shareholders.[65]

These objections also prove viable in the context at issue here. In particular, the second argument is an important consideration: it says that all different structures of risk-decoupling demonstrate vividly that the risk-decoupled voter usually pursues objectives that are precisely not in the interest of the wider community of shareholders, but rather uses her idiosyncratic position deliberately for the purpose of achieving her own benefits and for disadvantaging other investors. Accordingly, we are talking about two very different issues here that need to be properly distinguished. First, in corporate takeovers, the management of the target company often acts out of self-interest (usually the risk of losing their position). Second, and in contrast, the voting buyer in risk-decoupling situations threatens to consciously undermine or manipulate the voting process, due to the absence of own risk or because of reduced risk. This will often be disadvantageous to third parties. Whether one adopts this traditional argumentation or not, it fails to make a convincing claim in the context of interest here.[66] An informed decision of the voting rights acquirer cannot be equated with a decision that aggregates the preferences of all shareholders.[67]

Additionally, it is worth noting that in special cases, risk-decoupling structures may not only be used to reduce or eliminate risk, but can even serve to create a situation where the negative interest *exceeds* the positive interest entirely.[68] When

Steven M Davidoff, 'Taking the Preferences Out of Preferred Stock', *New York Times Dealbook* (13 September 2012).

[63] See, e.g., Henry G Manne, 'Some Theoretical Aspects of Share Voting: An Essay in Honor of Adolf A. Berle' (1964) 64 Columbia Law Review 1427, 1436; Bruce Kobayashi and Larry Ribstein, 'Outsider Trading as an Incentive Device' (2006) 40 UC Davis Law Review 21, 39; more recently Burkart and Lee (n. 57).

[64] Thomas J André, Jr, 'A Preliminary Inquiry into the Utility of Vote Buying in the Market for Corporate Control' (1990) 63 Southern California Law Review 533, 587.

[65] Robert Thompson and Paul Edelman, 'Corporate Voting' (2009) 62 Vanderbilt Law Review 129, 162 (referring on both points to André (n. 64) 587; Richard Hasen, 'Vote Buying' (2000) 88 California Law Review 1323, 1354; Saul Levmore, 'Voting with Intensity' (2000) 53 Stanford Law Review 111, 137.

[66] Equally sceptical are Thompson and Edelman (n. 65) 163; Michael Schouten, 'The Case for Mandatory Ownership Disclosure' (2009) 15 Stanford Journal of Law, Business and Finance 127, 171 f.

[67] Borrowing the terminology from Christoffersen and others (n. 57).

[68] See discussion in Chapters III.A, III.B.1.c, and E.2.

a short position, created with derivatives, exceeds the value of the long position, it is in the immediate interest of the shareholder to support value-reducing activities that damage the company's business. An effective control of the administration to the benefit of all shareholders seems rather implausible in such a scenario. This point also highlights its main difference from the traditional 'one share, one vote' debate, as deviations from 'one share, one vote' surely disturb the proportionality between ownership and voting rights.[69] For example, multiple voting rights are distortions of the influence of the voting shareholders, but unlike risk-decoupling structures, they do not permit the complete elimination of risk, or even the *creation of a negative interest*, which exceeds the positive interest. Both issues are treated similarly in the literature, but their fundamental difference is often ignored.

All of this should not undermine the possibility that risk-decoupling strategies may indeed help overcome the principal-agent conflict in individual cases. For instance, in the case of British Land, the hedge fund Laxey's borrowing of shares can be interpreted as an attempt to monitor management more efficiently, in the interests of all shareholders.[70] Fundamental scepticism remains, as there is no guarantee that the voting rights borrowed by Laxey will not be used for its own private advantages, instead of for the interests of other shareholders. Already the theoretical possibility of being able to pursue such special benefits exacerbates the conflict between the various members or groups of shareholders.[71] The alleged claim that risk-decoupling structures are useful is not convincing as a whole, though in individual situations opinions may differ. This observation will be revisited in the next section when we turn to developing a concrete regulatory response.[72]

3. Objection

An additional counter-argument beyond the potentially improved monitoring might be that conflicts similar to risk-decoupled equity situations do often occur and have been unregulated so far. For example, institutional investors often hold shares in a large number of portfolio companies. This means that in particular circumstances, they may hold the shares of two direct competitors. Institutional investors will then determine their voting decision by pure arithmetic—where do they stand to win most?[73] This may mean that an institutional investor, A, is forced (by its individual portfolio composition) to exercise its voting power in a portfolio company, B, to the detriment of B's share price because A holds a much higher share in portfolio company C, a competitor of B, and will thus secure a net profit over both positions. A similar situation would occur if company C was a takeover

[69] For more detail, see Wolf-Georg Ringe, 'Deviations from Ownership-Control Proportionality—Economic Protectionism Revisited' in Ulf Bernitz and Wolf-Georg Ringe (eds), *Company Law and Economic Protectionism* (Oxford University Press 2010) 209.

[70] Laxey indeed claimed this. See text accompanying n. 73 in Chapter III.

[71] See Jaffari and Deeney (n. 59) 7.

[72] See Chapter VI.

[73] Thompson and Edelman (n. 65) 155.

target of company B.[74] It could thus be argued that similar conflicts of interest can occur without risk-decoupling structures or elegantly devised elaborate strategies, solely through the holding of shares in different companies.[75]

While this objection is powerful, there are several reasons why it must ultimately be rejected. First, it can be assumed with great probability that, insofar as these conflict situations exist for institutional investors, they are for the most part caused by fortuity, and are not planned deliberately. This means that in a random distribution of these situations in the market, the effects can cancel each other out due to the multitude of individual investors and their contrary risk-alignments. Hence, a potentially and individually arising conflict can be offset by a market diversification.[76]

Second, the conflict situation imagined here would have an entirely different quality than the one created by a risk-decoupling structure. This can be demonstrated in two ways. First, it is obvious (using the example just given) that investor A meets the full economic risk on both sides of the equation in both portfolio companies. Its position is not hedged by derivatives, and it is not based only on temporary, borrowed shares. The interests thus differ significantly from that of a risk-decoupled position, and the probability of A manipulating the voting process is much lower. Moreover, the resulting agency costs will be significantly lower than in a risk-decoupling situation. In the cost calculation conducted previously, we distinguished between costs due to a distortion of the voting incentives from those due to the pursuit of private benefits.[77] While a risk-decoupled shareholder creates both components, A is biased only by possible private benefits. This is because A's influence and risk in portfolio company B are entirely proportionate. Only because of its stake in C does the opportunity arise to improve A's overall position. In other words, A's incentives are not distorted because of an increased risk friendliness per se, but solely because of a conflict situation, based on A's portfolio structure. This structure allows the extraction of a number of private benefits. These benefits may simply be the well-known related party transactions, or other conflicts of interest, which are being controlled by traditional corporate law.[78] Overall, one can conclude that a conflict situation that exists solely on the basis of random fractional ownership in two or more competing firms shows a fundamentally different quality than deliberately induced risk-decoupling, like the scenario described here.

[74] This would correspond to the *Mylan—Perry* scenario (see Chapter III.B.1.a). See also SEC (n. 60) 43018.

[75] Thompson and Edelman (n. 65).

[76] In this sense, Marcel Kahan and Edward Rock, 'Hedge Funds in Corporate Governance and Corporate Control' (2007) 155 University of Pennsylvania Law Review 1021, 1075; Thompson and Edelman (n. 65) 155. On the phenomenon of random biases that will cancel one another out, see generally Ronald J Gilson and Reinier Kraakman, 'The Mechanisms of Market Efficiency' (1984) 70 Virginia Law Review 549, 581.

[77] See section V.B.1.a.

[78] Luca Enriques, Gérard Hertig, and Hideki Kanda, 'Related Party Transactions' in Reinier Kraakman and others, *The Anatomy of Corporate Law: A Comparative and Functional Approach* (2nd edn, Oxford University Press 2009) 153.

4. Implications

The analysis thus far shows that risk-decoupling can create a principal-agent problem, which will impose significant costs on the company. There are costs that take the form of both distortion of voting incentives as well as private benefits for the decoupled shareholder, both with possible adverse consequences for the minority shareholders and actual, or potential, investors. This finding is later brought up again for the development of concrete regulatory solutions.[79]

The meat of the previous section lies in the fact that it has become clear who is affected and is the 'principal' of risk-decoupling agency costs. Both (co-)shareholders and outside investors are faced with agency costs. This finding is important for the regulatory proposals to be developed in the further course of this study (Chapter VI), as it identifies potentially vulnerable groups. By contrast, we have not gained any insight yet on the possible selection of an appropriate regulatory instrument, as the principal-agent model does not specify the regulatory tool that would be best suited to deal with it. Agency problems can be addressed with a variety of legal instruments.[80] To gain a better understanding of how to select an appropriate legal instrument, other problem perspectives will be discussed later, and especially the perspective of information and transaction costs (section V.C) and the theory of corporate finance (section V.D) will be highlighted.

C. Information Costs

The second perspective considers the problem of risk-decoupling as an issue of information and transaction costs. The claim here is that all risk-decoupling strategies have the effect of imposing additional information costs for investors and shareholders, which ultimately create higher costs of capital for the company.

This argument is developed in two steps. First, we have to understand a few basic aspects of the concept of information and transaction costs, and how instruments of corporate law traditionally contribute to their reduction. Second, we demonstrate how the topic under consideration here, risk-decoupling, runs contrary to this objective.

1. Information and transaction cost theory

Information and transaction cost theory is a fundamental part of New Institutional Economics, a research area that has contributed greatly to the economic understanding of the law. Based on the existence of property rights—and different from classical economics—the New Institutional Economics School explicitly

[79] See Chapter VI.

[80] For example, the authors' team of the *Anatomy of Corporate Law* (n. 78) distinguishes a number of different 'regulatory strategies' and 'governance strategies'. ibid. 37 ff.

emphasizes, inter alia, the existence of transaction costs, the lack of complete information, bounded rationality, and limited self-interest of human activity.[81] Transaction cost economics and information economics are correspondingly important branches of New Institutional Economics. Transaction cost economics analyses the costs incurred by maintaining the value and the use of property rights, as allocated by the legal system. The basic statement of the discipline is that the state can reduce these costs substantially by optimally designing the legal rules (that is, by producing 'institutions' such as those of company law in the broader sense) and by creating or optimizing organizations to enforce these rules. Specifically, company law is primarily conceived as a tool used to reduce transaction costs for firms and in this way increase the number of desired transactions.[82] Ultimately, legal institutions should facilitate access to any entrepreneurial activity as efficiently as possible and maximize the economic participation in this activity for investors and consumers. Where legal rules threaten to obstruct an economic activity due to prohibitively high transaction costs, this school of thought would advocate for a corporate law framework that prefers default rules that are subject to individual bargaining. Following the work of Calabresi and Melamed, so-called 'liability rules' would in this case be superior to 'property rules'.[83] Scholars subscribing to information economics are looking for solutions to the problems arising from asymmetric information between two or more (potential) contract or corporate partners.

Many supporters concede that the transaction cost approach in particular uses a one-dimensional approach as to how to facilitate market transactions, and thereby neglects constitutional or cultural–political aspects that should definitely be taken into account in the design of corporate law. Nevertheless, the New Institutional Economics concept with transaction cost economics and information economics can be viewed as a helpful starting point for the economic–theoretical explanation of company law.

Information costs are considered in law and economics literature as a category of market transaction costs.[84] For example, if market participants consider entering

[81] On New Institutional Economics, see Eirik G Furubotn, 'The New Institutional Economics and the Theory of the Firm' (2001) 45 Journal of Economic Behavior & Organization 133; Oliver E Williamson, 'The New Institutional Economics: Taking Stock, Looking Ahead' (2000) 38 Journal of Economic Literature 595. See also Christine Jolls, Cass Sunstein, and Richard Thaler, 'A Behavioral Approach to Law and Economics' (1998) 50 Stanford Law Review 1471, 1476 ff.

[82] Furubotn (n. 81).

[83] Guido Calabresi and Douglas Melamed, 'Property Rules, Liability Rules, and Inalienability: One View of the Cathedral' (1972) 85 Harvard Law Review 1089; in the context of corporate law Zohar Goshen, 'The Efficiency of Controlling Corporate Self-Dealing: Theory Meets Reality' (2003) 91 California Law Review 393. In the case of a 'property rule', a resource can only be used if the owner of the property right agrees. The user fee is specified *ex ante*, determined by the subjective ideas of the property right holder. A liability rule by contrast allows the use of the resource without prior approval of the property right holder. The user must pay a compensation fee to be determined by a third party (e.g. by a court or the legislature).

[84] Furubotn (n. 81); Williamson (n. 81).

into a particular transaction, they have to find a suitable contract partner, as well as information about the nature of the product to be sold, including its quality and price. Through this process of information gathering and verifying, the market participants incur costs.[85]

The concept of information costs as costs of the initiation of a contract emerged during the second half of the twentieth century as part of the broader concept of transaction costs. In contrast to theories of neoclassical microeconomics (positing a market of perfect information), Ronald Coase, in his seminal essay 'The Nature of the Firm', early on described the phenomenon that information costs can occur in markets by virtue of price co-ordination.[86] Today, the concept of information costs is recognized as an integral part of transaction costs.[87]

Accordingly, the reduction of information costs is generally a priority objective of the law in any jurisdiction. One conclusion of the Coase theorem is that transaction and information costs can lead to market distortions.[88] Because these costs are regularly non-negotiable, the original specification and allocation of property rights is important for the expected transaction costs.

Specifically, corporate law attempts to reduce the information costs and transaction costs of organizing economic activities in firms. Two of these methods are important for the present analysis: the legal nature of shares as property rights, and the corporate *numerus clausus*.

First, consider the legal classification of a share as a *property right*, as opposed to a contractual position. A shareholder does not merely acquire a contractual, personal claim against the corporation, but rather acquires a right *in* the corporation.[89] This organization of the share as a property-type bundle of rights is of paramount importance for corporate governance and capital markets. First, it facilitates the continued existence of the corporation and avoids the problems involved with the exit of one business partner that are well known in partnership law (and some private firms). This in turn increases the liquidity of investments and allows shareholders to efficiently diversify their funds.[90] As a consequence, the firms' capital costs should be lower. Finally, free transferability of shares also indirectly supports

[85] In theory, questions of search and information costs are treated in the specialized field of information economics. See George Stigler, 'The Economics of Information' (1961) 69 Journal of Political Economy 213; see also Jack Hirshleifer, 'Exchange Theory: The Missing Chapter' (1973) 11 Economic Inquiry 129; Jack Hirshleifer and John G Riley, 'The Analytics of Uncertainty and Information—An Expository Survey' (1979) 17 Journal of Economic Literature 1375.

[86] Ronald Coase, 'The Nature of the Firm' (1937) 4 Economica 386.

[87] Eirik G Furubotn and Rudolf Richter, *Economics, Cognition, and Society: Institutions and Economic Theory—The Contribution of the New Institutional Economics* (2nd edn, University of Michigan Press 2010) 48.

[88] Ronald H Coase, *The Firm, the Market, and the Law* (University of Chicago Press 1990); Ronald H Coase, 'The Problem of Social Cost' (1960) 3 Journal of Law and Economics 1.

[89] This distinction is true in most if not all legal systems. For example, see the leading case in the United Kingdom, *Borland's Trustee v Steel Bros & Co* [1901] 1 Ch 279, 288.

[90] John Armour, Henry Hansmann, and Reinier Kraakman, 'What Is Corporate Law?' in Reinier Kraakman and others (eds), *The Anatomy of Corporate Law: A Comparative and Functional Approach* (2nd edn, Oxford University Press 2009) 1, 11.

a stronger control of management and thus contributes to the accountability of the management from the perspective of the firm's owners.[91] However, the most important contribution of the share as a property right is its transferability and tradability on modern capital markets as a 'standardized' product, which reduces investors' information costs. Share acquirers must not investigate the specific characteristics of the shares they purchase every time they do so, because, by virtue of the legal framework, they can expect to acquire a bundle of the usual characteristics (without which large-scale trades would be unthinkable). They can assume they will obtain a more or less standardized security, so that it is sufficient for their trade to simply specify the type and quantity of the shares they want to acquire.

Thus, the creation of property rights overcomes some of the weaknesses of contract law and the principle of relativity. The economic consequences cannot be overstated. Property rights are said to 'create markets', as they allow the continuous exchange of goods—in this case, shares in companies—on markets in a global dimension, thus overcoming the fatal problem of lack of information on and the diversity of legal systems.[92]

The property law side of corporate law goes hand-in-hand with the principle of *numerus clausus*.[93] Corporate law offers a limited number of legal forms for firms to choose from, including private limited or public limited companies, partnerships, and others. In the second instance, within the corporate form chosen, the law allows for a limited number of types of shares to be created, although the law is more generous here in permitting a certain variation of their features. Where shares differ in their features, they are usually grouped in separate classes of shares and are being made transparent.

The legal tool of *numerus clausus* is a controversial element of property law, but is recognized as a way of mitigating third party externalities.[94] In a similar, but distinct, direction, it can be understood as addressing an information problem.[95] Third parties seeking to acquire a property right can be relieved from their information

[91] Frank H Easterbrook and Daniel R Fischel, 'Limited Liability and the Corporation' (1985) 52 The University of Chicago Law Review 89, 95.

[92] Tamar Frankel, 'The Legal Infrastructure of Markets: The Role of Contract and Property Law' (1993) 73 Boston University Law Review 389; Tamar Frankel, 'The New Financial Assets: Separating Ownership from Control' (2010) 33 Seattle University Law Review 931, 934.

[93] John Armour and Michael J Whincop, 'The Proprietary Foundations of Corporate Law' (2007) 27 Oxford Journal of Legal Studies 429, 444.

[94] On the *numerus clausus* discussion, see Ben McFarlane, 'The Numerus Clausus Principle and Covenants Relating to Land' in Susan Bright (ed.), *Modern Studies in Property Law*, vol. 6 (Hart 2011) 311; Bernard Rudden, 'Economic Theory v. Property Law: The Numerus Clausus Problem' in John Eekelaar and John Bell (eds), *Oxford Essays in Jurisprudence: Third Series 1987* (Clarendon Press 1987) 239; see also Reinier H Kraakman and Henry Hansmann, 'Property, Contract, and Verification: The Numerus Clausus Problem and the Divisibility of Rights' (2002) 31 The Journal of Legal Studies S373; Michael A Heller, 'The Boundaries of Private Property' (1998) 108 Yale Law Journal 1163; Thomas W Merrill and Henry E Smith, 'Optimal Standardization in the Law of Property: The Numerus Clausus Principle' (2000) 110 Yale Law Journal 1. For an overview, see Bram Akkermans, *The Principle of 'Numerus Clausus' in European Property Law* (Intersentia [et al.] 2008); Nestor M Davidson, 'Standardization and Pluralism in Property Law' (2008) 61 Vanderbilt Law Review 1597.

[95] Merrill and Smith (n. 94).

costs in terms of potential encumbrance of the right. If a legal system were to recognize the creation of any property rights, this would lead to negative information externalities. The agreement of each new right *in rem* would thereby increase the cost of information. Market participants would have to inquire whether the right to be acquired is encumbered with one or more different unknown rights. The limitation of the rights recognized by the legislature therefore reduces the need for additional information, since the purchaser must examine only the existence of a limited number of issues. This feature is believed to be a pre-condition for trading shares on liquid capital markets.[96]

As a result, through this type of standardization, the principle of *numerus clausus* also aims to reduce information costs for market participants. Firms that must choose from a catalogue of permissible corporate forms and shares are thus prevented from creating opaque and non-transparent arrangements, which would be burdensome for third parties trying to evaluate them.

2. Risk-decoupling and information costs

After revisiting the traditional approach that corporate law takes towards reducing information costs, we can now turn our attention to the ways in which risk-decoupling activities interfere with the general objectives previously outlined. The key point here is that risk-decoupling strategies, which are strategically used by market participants (in particular, hedge funds), undermine the main regulatory goals previously described. Instead of striving to reduce information and transaction costs, these strategies create additional costs for market participants.

a) Consequences for investors

Distortions in the risk exposure of certain shareholders increase the information and transaction costs of other market participants. This primarily applies to investors who wish to acquire shares in the company. Under normal circumstances, they would benefit from the standards previously described because a limited number of legal forms and a limited number of share types would normally mean that an investor could assess the rights and properties that they receive in a reliable manner. The 'standard product' they purchase is the traditional bundle of rights, consisting of the well-known management and property rights that accrue to the shareholders according to the paradigm of corporate law. The acquirer can therefore make a relatively simple purchasing decision, and is not obliged to conduct extensive research in evaluating the individual aspects of his shareholder position or the potentially modified parts of the legal status to be acquired, or even to engage external consultants. Should the characteristics of shares be modified in a particular case, the investor can, under the traditional system, trust that significant

[96] Stefan Grundmann, *European Company Law: Organization, Finance and Capital Markets* (2nd edn, Intersentia 2012) 253f, 282 f.

changes are disclosed. For example, as stated previously, different classes of shares are required to be specified in the company's articles of association, and are therefore made transparent to the outside world. The investor can view the specific arrangements for each company through accessing the articles of association from a particular public register.[97]

As a general rule, the law creates a standardized bundle of rights and obligations, including the right to vote, and the corresponding economic risk exposure. Risk-decoupling strategies undermine this legislative choice to bundle together influence and risk. It is, in other words, *an attempt to split the legislative bundle by way of private autonomy*. It is the attempt to use contract law to undo what has been bundled together by property law. If, as we said above, property law is preferable over contract law in creating and supporting markets,[98] a reintroduction of the latter causes problems for the former. In our context, the presence of risk-modified shares among the usual shares of the company requires investors to take precautions, make investigations, and possibly even engage external advice on the specific characteristics of the shares they are contemplating buying.[99] In particular, the investor can no longer be sure that the normal combination of risk and influence is followed.[100] The problem is exacerbated by the fact that the mere technical and abstract possibility of risk-decoupling is sufficient to cause severe disruption for the entire trade of the company's shares, regardless of whether they actually occur in the company. This is because once the investors are aware that the earlier assumption of there being a link between influence and risk can no longer be generally trusted, additional investigation costs are unavoidable.

The following example illustrates this problem. Let us say that hedge fund H holds 10 per cent of the shares in X plc, whose risk it eliminated by using derivative transactions as described previously (category 1).[101] The remaining shares are held by other medium-to-small investors. Pension fund P is considering purchasing shares of X plc. Under normal circumstances, P could assume that the *numerus clausus* principle and the property characteristics of the shares to a certain extent relieve him from an extensive previous examination of the relationships and circumstances within the company. He could have assumed that all shareholders—in the absence of separate classes of shares—have equal rights and obligations, which are bundled together in the shares by the legislative authority. With regard to these points, obtaining legal advice, due diligence and other verification steps would therefore not have been necessary. But the situation changes where

1. P learns through market rumours that H has entered into hedging transactions with respect to its shareholding in X plc with several banks;

[97] The articles of association of a company need to be disclosed Europe-wide, according to article 2 of the First Company Law Directive 2009/101/EC.

[98] See n. 92.

[99] More precisely, the very shares an investor purchases won't be directly affected by risk-decoupling strategies because contracts have only relative effect. But the presence of *other* risk-decoupled shares in the company will trigger higher information costs for any new investor.

[100] Armour and Whincop (n. 93) 444.

[101] See Chapter III.B.1.

2. P learns that H has contracted similar agreements to hedge its shares in other companies in the past;
3. P has had similar bad experiences with risk-decoupled hedge funds in another investment target and therefore wants to ensure that this time there is no risk-decoupling present in the shareholder structure of X plc;
4. P has only just learned that risk-decoupling is technically possible, and that it sometimes occurs in reality, especially when hedge funds are involved.

In all four situations, before investing, P will seek to initiate examinations to investigate the concrete extent of H's risk exposure in X plc. The dramatic effects of this development can be seen by the fact that constellation 4 is practically always satisfied when the market participants and investors are theoretically aware of the problems discussed here and they consider them as relevant for their investment decisions. The result is a general insecurity and mistrust of the market that will expand with increasing frequency of occurrence of risk-decoupling situations—up to the complete loss of confidence in the legal framework.[102]

Overall, we can therefore say that information costs for investors such as P will in general rise with the appearance of risk-decoupling mechanisms, and thus ultimately the cost of capital for companies.

b) *Consequences for existing shareholders*

To take it a step further, the information cost problem described here not only acts to the disadvantage of outside investors, but also impacts the relationship between the existing shareholders. Standardization, property rights, and the *numerus clausus* principle also reduce the ongoing costs for monitoring once an investment has been made.[103] The risk elimination in H's shares therefore creates information costs not only for outside investors, but also for the other shareholders of X plc. Under normal circumstances, these latter shareholders would benefit from the *numerus clausus* and property right character, as they would not encounter any substantial monitoring costs after they had made their investment choice. At least, the monitoring costs would be greatly reduced.[104]

The founding shareholders, as well as any subsequent shareholders, should be able to rely on the basic terms and conditions that hold at the time of their entry,

[102] See on the importance of trust in institutions the seminal work by Ludwig Raiser, 'Vertragsfunktion und Vertragsfreiheit' in Ernst v. Caemmerer (Hrsg.), *Hundert Jahre Deutsches Rechtsleben, Festschrift zum 100jährigen Bestehen des Deutschen Juristentages 1860-1960*, (CF Müller 1960) vol. 1, 101; Niklas Luhmann, *Vertrauen: Ein Mechanismus zur Reduktion sozialer Komplexität* (4th edn, Lucius & Lucius 2000).

[103] Armour and Whincop (n. 93): 'internal monitoring costs are greatly reduced.'

[104] A similar effect is usually attributed to the principle of limited liability; see Easterbrook and Fischel, 'Limited Liability and the Corporation' (n. 91) 95; Paul Halpern, Michael Trebilcock, and Stuart Turnbull, 'An Economic Analysis of Limited Liability in Corporation Law' (1980) 30 The University of Toronto Law Journal 117. See section V.E.4.

and it should not be possible to have these subsequently and unilaterally changed by a sophisticated financial expert to their own advantage. However, the occurrence of risk-decoupling situations will give rise to additional monitoring and control efforts by the co-shareholders. Again, the mere occurrence of such events in the market will create a gradual increase in the monitoring relevance generally, without the specific company having to be affected.

In an attempt to generalize this issue, we can state the problem as follows: both the property rights character of shares and the *numerus clausus* principle of features attached to shares have the objective of reducing transaction and information costs. This cost reduction comes to the benefit of both potential investors[105] and other existing shareholders.[106] *Risk-decoupling strategies undermine this statutory objective by significantly increasing the cost of information and ongoing monitoring for both groups.* The legislative objective of reducing information costs before, and monitoring costs after, the share acquisitions is thus thwarted. Consequently, it is legitimate to expect that the cost of capital will rise inefficiently.

3. Summary and implications

a) *Risk-decoupling as an information problem*

Confronting the risk-decoupling problem in this section from a different angle, we see it as an information and transaction cost problem. In anticipation of a more detailed discussion to come, this examination yields a number of valuable insights for the required regulatory intervention or response (see Chapter VI): an information problem is most effectively encountered with the imposition of information and disclosure requirements.[107] This should thus be seriously considered in the risk-decoupling scenarios under examination here.

In substance, we have developed two different aspects of the problem. The first is to *protect investors* through market information. The lack of transparency discussed previously leads to the market having no clarity about who has what influence in the company, and which incentives the various actors have. This is the 'investor perspective': legal information obligations in favour of potential investors facilitate their investment decisions, as they can more easily estimate the distribution of interests in the target company.

The second issue is the *protection of minorities*. Existing shareholders are forced by risk-decoupling incidents to monitor and reassess the risk structure in their own company. Here, the objective is to reduce the need for steady and overly burdensome monitoring. Regulatory intervention would thereby strengthen the investment in the capital market as a whole.

The present section complements the previous analysis of the principal-agent conflict in two important ways. First, the information and transaction costs theory

[105] Frankel, 'The New Financial Assets' (n. 92).

[106] Armour and Whincop (n. 93) 444.

[107] See specifically Chapter VI.C.

confirms the previously identified vulnerable target groups. As with the principal-agent theory, we show that, in particular, shareholders and outside investors are affected.

Second, our understanding of the deeper problem is much improved and goes further than merely looking at it from a principal-agent theory, since information and transaction theory gives a first indication of a functional selection of possible legal instruments. After what has been said, a disclosure and information framework must, in principle, appear as suitable to address the problem and must thus be considered as a regulatory tool of first choice.[108]

b) Relevance especially for publicly traded companies

The above considerations have led indirectly to an additional insight that has not yet been noted. The above analysis makes it clear that the problem under consideration here is specifically relevant to one particular area of corporate law. The phenomenon of risk-decoupling will be most salient for large, listed companies that rely on capital markets for financing. The problem of information cost will be most relevant in these companies, and investors must rely most heavily on the standardized aspects of securities. The importance of a liquid market for the purposes of corporate governance was explained previously.[109] We mentioned the continuity of operations despite changes in the ownership structure, diversification, and the creation of a market for corporate control, which has a disciplinary effect on the activity of the management.[110] All of these aspects are particularly important for public companies. By contrast, small, private companies are usually governed by stronger personal relationships. This means that personal information can facilitate overcoming the problem of anonymity described previously. Additionally, private companies will usually have different arrangements of conflict resolution and overall governance.[111] To pre-empt the discussion on the different regulatory choices, any regulatory intervention should therefore focus primarily on the market segment of only publicly listed companies. In an effort to minimize any regulation and government intervention in the market, this would be a proportionate and reasonable limitation.

D. Corporate Finance

Thus far we have approached the analytical discussion from the vantage point of two perspectives: the principal-agent conflict and information costs. An additional perspective looks at the phenomenon of risk-decoupling from the view of

[108] ibid. [109] See section V.C.1. [110] See sections V.C.1 and V.C.2.

[111] See in particular Gregor Bachmann and others (eds), *Regulating the Closed Corporation* (de Gruyter 2014); Joseph A McCahery and Erik P M Vermeulen, *Corporate Governance of Non-Listed Companies* (Oxford University Press 2008).

corporate finance and provides far-reaching insights into the financial law aspects of risk-decoupling, in addition to the legal characteristics of shares.

1. Debt versus equity

The starting point of the enquiry is the traditional distinction between debt and equity. This distinction is fundamental to the structuring of corporate finance, and is important, among other things, in the areas of tax,[112] accounting,[113] insolvency,[114] and corporate law and governance.[115]

Crucial to the discussion is the corporate law side of this differentiation. Shareholders provide equity to the company, thereby enabling the shareholders to become part-owners of the company. External parties provide borrowing and act as separate entities because they only conclude a regular loan contract with the company. It follows that equity investors have rights *in* the company, and creditors have rights *against* the company. This distinction is significant, for example, when it comes to questions of control and the strategic direction of the company. On both points, only the equity investor has influence, whereas the external creditor only has contractual claims based on his loan agreement.

What justifies this dramatic differentiation? The most important distinction between debt and equity capital is the *risk* entered into by the respective provider of capital.[116] Without discussing the details, equity investment is perceived as being much riskier than debt financing because equity-holders' profit expectations are more closely attuned to the economic perspectives of the company than to the position of the lenders. Lenders usually get a steady return on interest, usually a fixed rate per year, and at the end of the term they receive a repayment of the original loan amount. Equity investors, however, must bear a double burden of risk, as the capital provided to finance the company will only bear interest if and when a profit has been generated, and ultimately it will only be refunded if liquidation proceeds cover the liabilities. The expected 'interest', in the form of a dividend, is formally only in the hands of the management, and there is no direct entitlement for the shareholders to demand payment.[117]

[112] Wolfgang Schön and others, 'Debt and Equity in Domestic and International Tax Law—A Comparative Policy Analysis' [2014] British Tax Review 146.

[113] European Financial Reporting Advisory Group (EFRAG), 'Distinguishing between Debt and Equity—Discussion Paper' (2008) <http://www.iasplus.com/en/binary/efrag/0801liabequitydp.pdf>.

[114] Royston Miles Goode, *Principles of Corporate Insolvency Law* (4th edn, Sweet & Maxwell 2011) para. 1-04.

[115] Andrei Shleifer and Robert W Vishny, 'A Survey of Corporate Governance' (1997) 52 Journal of Finance 737, 761.

[116] Eilís Ferran and Look Chan Ho, *Principles of Corporate Finance Law* (2nd edn, Oxford University Press 2014) 19 f.

[117] The claim to dividend payments is subject to managerial discretion. See *Bond v Barrow Haematite Steel Co* [1902] 1 Ch 353. For more detail, see Ferran and Ho (n. 116) 207; see also Louise Gullifer and Jennifer Payne, *Corporate Finance Law Principles and Policy* (Hart Publishing, Oxford 2011) 13.

As always, incurring a high level of risk can also be rewarded. If the company is successful, shareholders will generate above-average returns in the form of increased dividends, whereas the outsider creditors still only achieve their originally agreed fixed rate of interest. It turns out that equity investment carries a higher volatility and a higher risk, both in the positive and negative sense, while debt financing promises a steady but relatively low-risk cash return expectation.

This basic distinction allows us to understand the economic justification for granting voting rights to shareholders. Voting or control rights can be simultaneously understood as a type of compensation for the risk entered into and as an incentive to invest. By virtue of the fact that providing equity capital is risky, the equity-holders will receive a control device, a tool to at least partially influence the fate of the company and their own funds.[118]

This is not to deny that debt financing also carries a risk. As the recent financial crisis has clearly demonstrated, even and especially this kind of financing is burdened with many uncertainties. The extent of risk faced by debt-holders, however, remains below the risk of equity-holders, which is reflected in the insolvency law ranking in favour of creditors. In addition, powerful creditors are, in practice, in the position to insist on strong contractual rights by virtue of their bargaining power, which gives them quasi-control rights in their favour. In particular, banks and other major creditors generally insist on so-called covenants, that is, contractual clauses that allow them under certain conditions a considerable influence on the business policy and strategic direction of the company.[119] In this way, creditors seek access to the strategic direction of their debtor in a similar manner to shareholders. The agreement of such clauses can be understood as a private emulation of the statutory voting rights of shareholders. While the legal system grants shareholders such control rights *ab initio* because of their higher risk exposure, debt-holders who are comparatively low-risk-exposed are limited to the general contractual protection mechanisms—which means that they may seek such influence by contractual means. More recently, the sometimes rather strong effect of outside creditors on the internal corporate governance structure of the company has provoked more academic attention.[120]

[118] See Andrei Shleifer and Robert W Vishny, 'A Survey of Corporate Governance' (1997) 52 Journal of Finance 737, 761.

[119] Shleifer and Vishny ibid. 761 ff.; Ferran and Ho (n. 116) 270 f.; Gullifer and Payne (n. 117) 155 ff.

[120] For example, see George G Triantis and Ronald J Daniels, 'The Role of Debt in Interactive Corporate Governance' (1995) 83 California Law Review 1073; Frederick Tung, 'Leverage in the Board Room: The Unsung Influence of Private Lenders in Corporate Governance' (2009) 57 UCLA Law Review 115; Charles K Whitehead, 'The Evolution of Debt: Covenants, the Credit Market, and Corporate Governance' (2009) 34 Journal of Corporation Law 641; William W Bratton, 'Bond Covenants and Creditor Protection: Economics and Law, Theory and Practice, Substance and Process' (2006) 7 European Business Organization Law Review (EBOR) 39. For an overview, see Gullifer and Payne (n. 117) 81 ff.

2. Risk-decoupling between debt and equity

It is now possible for us to understand the impact of risk-decoupling activities on the financing structure of the company. Negative risk-decoupled shareholders can be described as shareholders who reduce the inherent risk of equity financing and, ideally, eliminate it completely. They want the 'best of both worlds'. On the one hand, they want to be equity investors with ownership of the company's shares and control rights. On the other, they want the risk profile of an external debt investor without giving up their control rights, which are not provided for by the statutory system. In an extreme situation, a fully risk-decoupled shareholder can even reach the 'best of three worlds' when they—in their position as shareholder and with the risk profile of a debt-holder—seek to attract additional private benefits, for example by holding a stake in a competing firm (as in the *Mylan–Perry* example[121]).[122]

This situation results in a contradiction between core values. Economically, according to the above principles, a negatively risk-decoupled share is more akin to debt than equity. However, from a legal perspective, a risk-decoupler remains a shareholder (of an empty shell) and retains the share's voting right. In other words, the shareholder attempts to strip off the risk associated with an equity investment, while formally remaining a shareholder. Herein lies the problem: according to the principles discussed previously, shareholders are given the right to vote simply by virtue of the fact that they carry a distinctive economic risk. If this risk is eliminated, the justification for the assignment of voting rights disappears. For risk-decoupled shareholders, the legitimacy of exercising voting rights no longer exists.

Against the reasoning developed thus far, one may object that the line between equity and debt is rather thin, as hybrid financial instruments can often be very difficult to associate to the one or the other category.[123] In addition, one might argue that both debt and equity providers constantly seek to achieve the best conditions for themselves, and to overcome the traditional barriers between the two means of financing. With the insistence on covenants, as already mentioned, creditors for instance intend to achieve a similar level of control to the one held by shareholders, that is, a low-risk investment paired with strategic influence. Vice versa, shareholders always strive for the elimination of risk, such as with non-voting preferred shares, which are much more in line with the risk structure of a debt instrument than an equity share.[124] These apparent counter-arguments lose much of their

[121] See Chapter III.B.1.a.

[122] Cf. European Parliament, *The Use of Shareholder Voting Rights During the General Assembly of Company Shareholders—Study IP/A/ECON/2008-32* (December 2009) 9, available at <http://www.europarl.europa.eu/RegData/etudes/etudes/join/2009/429978/IPOL-ECON_ET%282009%29429978_EN.pdf> accessed 13 August 2015.

[123] See Roger McCormick and Harriet Creamer, *Hybrid Corporate Securities: International Legal Aspects* (Sweet & Maxwell 1987); Wolfgang Schön, 'The Distinct Equity of the Debt-Equity Distinction' (2012) 66 Bulletin for International Taxation (IBFD Bulletin) 490, 495.

[124] Murray A Pickering, 'The Problem of the Preference Share' (1963) 26 Modern Law Review 499. See also Ferran and Ho (n. 116) 133.

persuasive power when we remember the difference of the risk-decoupling strategies of interest here. The radical difference is transparency. For instance, preferred shares are not formed in silence without publicity, but must be made known as a separate class of shares.[125] They are recognized by the market as such, and are usually traded at a significant discount compared to ordinary shares.[126]

In addition, the presented techniques of risk-decoupling, such as using derivatives, can create a disconnection between influence and risk which is of a significantly different quality compared to conventional mechanisms. In particular, they allow for a short, temporary risk transfer, which notably differs from the introduction of non-voting preference shares or multiple voting shares. The short-term, goal-oriented risk distortion stands in stark contrast to these traditional methods.[127]

3. Shareholders as residual risk-bearers

These reflections can be supported by one of the fundamental assumptions of corporate governance. Viewed in the broader context, scholars have long argued that shareholders bear the residual risk of the firm.[128] That is, if the enterprise fails, shareholders only have a claim to the assets that remain after all other constituencies have been satisfied. This position of residual risk-bearer provides shareholders with, relatively speaking, the best incentives to make the company profitable for their own interest. It also justifies granting them the right to make strategic decisions for the benefit of both the company and the economy as a whole.[129]

This insight supports the point made here, that if their risk exposure is the real justification for shareholders being entitled to vote, this justification disappears when the shareholder is able to eliminate that risk. A risk-free shareholder cannot fulfil the function of the vote, which is to express the best possible decision for the strategic direction of the company. A risk-free shareholder will always exercise his voting rights for purely selfish intentions, which can potentially have detrimental social outcomes. The right to vote, from this perspective, loses its positive function, while a rational actor would exercise it in the spirit of the firm's community. It potentially becomes an instrument prone to abuse, merely leading to idiosyncratic benefits for the risk-free shareholder.

125 Ferran and Ho (n. 116) ch. 6.

126 Fabio Braggion and Mariassunta Giannetti, 'Public Debate and Stock Prices: Evidence from the Voting Premium' (Social Science Research Network 2014) SSRN Scholarly Paper ID 2138949 <http://papers.ssrn.com/abstract=2138949> accessed 13 April 2015.

127 Avner Kalay and Shagun Pant, 'Time Varying Voting Rights and the Private Benefits of Control' (Social Science Research Network 2009) SSRN Scholarly Paper ID 1102832 <http://papers.ssrn.com/abstract=1102832> accessed 13 April 2015.

128 Frank H Easterbrook and Daniel R Fischel, *The Economic Structure of Corporate Law* (Harvard University Press 1991) 68; Armen A Alchian and Harold Demsetz, 'Production, Information Costs, and Economic Organization' (1972) 62 American Economic Review 777.

129 See the sources cited in n. 128.

4. Implications

It follows from the previous discussion that risk-decoupling situations have the potential to jeopardize the distinction between debt and equity. In substance, a risk-free shareholder resembles a debt-holder rather than an equity-holder. As policy reasons suggest, the law assigns the voting right to equity shareholders largely due to their specific risk profile, thus eliminating the justification for such assignment in the presence of risk elimination.

Based on this analysis, one immediate conclusion may seem to follow: if risk-decoupled shareholders lack the internal legitimacy for the exercise of voting rights, it could be argued that one should simply *strip those shareholders' entitlement to vote.*[130] From the perspective of corporate finance, a risk-decoupled shareholder only formally resembles an equity-holder, while in substance he fits much more into the category of debt-holder. Against this background, law-makers should deny them the right to vote.

Thus, the discussion around potential legal responses to the phenomenon of risk-decoupling has been enriched by another variant. In section V.C, the problem was viewed as an information cost problem, and thus to be corrected by an information or disclosure regime. The analysis carried out here, which is based on the perspective of corporate finance, brings into play another aspect, which is a potential loss of the voting rights for risk-decoupled shareholders.

We will deal with the precise regulatory responses at a later stage, as at this point we are only interested in the various facets of the problem and the regulatory foundations.[131] The two arguments presented here clearly demonstrate that risk-decoupled shareholders lack the inner legitimacy to exercise their right to vote. A voting decision exercised in such a situation would be deprived of its proper justification. This core idea is supported by the various examples presented in the following.

A similar argumentation pattern was used in the decision of the Delaware Court of Chancery in the case *Parfi Holding AB* as early as 2008.[132] This case concerned the right to launch a shareholder (derivative) lawsuit, which was ultimately denied. In support of the decision, the court explained that the plaintiff had, by entering into various transactions since the initiation of the action, lost its economic interest in bringing an action. According to the court, there is an unwritten requirement for bringing a derivative suit, namely that it has to be for the benefit of the company. Therefore, the claimant is required to be exposed to an economic risk that corresponds to that of the company, and to have the overall objective of pursuing welfare gains for the company as a whole.[133] The

[130] In this direction, see Ronald J Gilson and Charles K Whitehead, 'Deconstructing Equity: Public Ownership, Agency Costs, and Complete Capital Markets' (2008) 108 Columbia Law Review 231, 251 ff.; Frankel, 'The New Financial Assets' (n. 92) 950.

[131] See on the regulatory responses Chapter VI.

[132] *Parfi Holding AB v Mirror Image Internet, Inc* 954 A2d 911 (Delaware Court of Chancery).

[133] ibid. 939. See *Alabama By-Products Corporation v Cede & Co* 657 A2d 254, 265-66 (Supreme Court of Delaware); *Schilling v Belcher* 582 F2d 995, 1002.

court held that this inherent prerequisite was not fulfilled in the specific situation. Instead, it described the claimant as an 'empty plaintiff', in reference to the term 'empty voting', as coined by Professors Hu and Black.[134] In such a situation, the Court of Chancery explained, 'form (i.e., ownership of shares) does not trump substance (i.e., lack of any economic interest whatsoever in the recovery pursued for the corporation)'.[135] Therefore, the conclusion was that the claimant lacked legal standing, notwithstanding the fact that the applicant had formally retained ownership of a share.[136] This corresponds exactly to the assessment reached previously, that the shareholder loses his legitimacy to exercise a particular right—either the initiation of legal action or the right to vote—when the actual inner justification has disappeared because of a lack of corresponding risk exposure.

The second example comes from a completely different direction. Instructive material can be expected from the English restructuring mechanism called 'scheme of arrangement', which is governed by Companies Act 2006, sections 895 ff.[137] It is a tool that, with the approval of a court, allows a variety of company restructurings, both within a company structure as well as outside of it. It can therefore for instance serve as a basis for a corporate merger or division, or for settlements of the company with its creditors. The special feature of interest here concerns the shareholders' authorization to vote on the implementation of a scheme. The agreement requires a 75 per cent majority in value and a 50 per cent majority in the number of the shareholders (or creditors) present or represented.[138] An important detail follows, however, from the case law: the English courts hold that only parties that have an economic interest in the particular transaction are entitled to vote on its ratification. In *Re Bluebrook* it was decided that the company does not have to consult those creditors who are not affected by the scheme, as they have no economic interest in the company.[139] For support, the court relied on a precedent from 1903, *In re Tea Corporation Ltd*.[140] The latter case involved the winding up of a company, in which separate meetings of creditors, preferred shareholders, and ordinary shareholders were held, but the ordinary shareholders opposed the winding-up plan. The Court of Appeal denied them legal standing because they no longer carried an economic interest in the company under the circumstances, as they did not stand to expect any payment due to the economic situation of the

[134] *Parfi Holding AB v Mirror Image Internet, Inc* (n. 132) 940, with reference to Hu and Black (as well as Martin and Partnoy) in footnote 108.

[135] ibid.

[136] See on this aspect of the case Roberta S Karmel, 'Voting Power without Responsibility or Risk: How Should Proxy Reform Address the Decoupling of Economic and Voting Rights' (2010) 55 Villanova Law Review 93, 103; Davies Ward Phillips & Vineberg LLP, *The Quality of the Shareholder Vote in Canada—Discussion Paper* (2010) 124 ff.

[137] See in detail Gullifer and Payne (n. 117) 619 ff.; Jennifer Payne, *Schemes of Arrangement: Theory, Structure and Operation* (Cambridge University Press 2014).

[138] See CA 2006 s. 899. On the problems concerning proxies see *Re Abbey National plc* [2004] EWHC 2776.

[139] *Re Bluebrook Ltd* [2009] EWHC 2114.

[140] *In re Tea Corporation Ltd* [1904] Ch 12.

company. Both cases are based on the idea that a person forfeits the exercise of a right, in whose favour it can no longer be invoked.[141]

These two illustrations are of interest for the present discussion because they support the broader argument that only the economically interested should be legitimate holders of a right. Such a fundamental principle of law can be found in many other examples and in various contexts. One objection might be that this argument does not apply in all situations. It works when the share is completely risk-eliminated, but not when only a partial risk-decoupling has occurred. On the basis of this tension, the discussion to come concerns the question of whether risk-decoupled shareholders should lose their right to vote.[142]

E. The Market for Corporate Control

Most of the problem analysis undertaken so far has been limited to negative risk-decoupling situations. The problem perspectives developed previously do not apply with the same force to positive-decoupling scenarios. The reason is that negative risk-decoupling is concerned with shareholders' distorted incentives, which might result in using their voting power to pursue improper purposes. Hence the discussion of intra-shareholder agency costs, information costs, and more. When considering positive risk-decoupling,[143] however, the conceptual contrast is that the risk-decoupler usually does not have any significant voting power. In fact, the opposite really seems to be the problem—the risk-decoupler seeks to avoid being entitled to vote, as holding voting rights may trigger disclosure obligations that the risk-decoupler wants to circumvent. The agent in this situation does not have any significant voting power to impose costs on the principal.

Inspiration must thus come from another context. In the following section, positive risk-decoupling is portrayed largely as a problem of market manipulation and takeover regulation, and the problem is placed in the context of the market for corporate control.

1. Harmful market impacts of CfD dealings

A previous section described what contracts for difference (CfDs) are, how they are normally used, and how they can be used in order to gain unjustified benefits.[144] To reiterate, the term 'CfD abuse' denotes a transaction where CfDs are bought by an investor with the ultimate goal (although no legal entitlement) of acquiring the underlying shares in a target company. The short party ultimately offers him these shares to compensate for share price increases during the reference period.[145] This transaction allows the long party to accumulate a large block of shares at a

[141] See Gullifer and Payne (n. 117) 639.
[142] See, in particular, Chapter VI.D.
[143] For a description, see Chapter III.C.
[144] See Chapter III.C.
[145] See Chapter III.C.2.

low price and may permit the purchaser to ultimately seize control of the target company without disclosing this to the market.

This section discusses the effects of such CfD abuse. Three of these effects—those on market integrity, on the valuation of individual investments, and on takeover activity—focus on the investment market, whereas the fourth concerns the corporate governance of target companies.[146]

The first issue raised by CfDs concerns the information efficiency and asymmetry, as well as the integrity and transparency, of the markets.[147] Share prices are deemed to reflect market information, and, be it more or less efficiently, it is agreed that this information matters.[148] It can be related to the control of a target company, as in connection to major shareholder notifications, but it can also be related to several other factors affecting the share prices.[149]

Information related to CfDs can influence the market in the same way as information on shareholdings if the disclosure implies a control-seeking intention. In addition, as CfDs usually give rise to hedging positions, they can lead to hidden ownership patterns, exceptional block trades, and distortions of free-float. These problems can affect the liquidity and price formation on the market and eventually increase the costs of capital of listed companies.[150] An example of this kind of market disturbance took place in 2008 when Porsche disclosed its 30 per cent

[146] See also Financial Services Authority, *Disclosure of Contracts for Difference, Consultation and Draft Handbook Text, CP 07/20* (November 2007) 5 <http://www.fsa.gov.uk/pubs/cp/cp07_20.pdf>, identifying inefficient price formation, distorted market for takeovers, and diminished market confidence as market failures of the non-disclosure of CfDs; and Committee of European Securities Regulators (CESR), *CESR proposal to extend major shareholding notifications to instruments of similar economic effect to holding shares and entitlements to acquire shares*, CESR/09-1215b (January 2010) 6 <http://www.esma.europa.eu/system/files/09_1215b.pdf> accessed 9 August 2015, in which CESR respectively listed inefficient price formation, lack of transparency and circumvention of mandatory bid rules with equitable price leading to distortion of the exit possibility of minority shareholder.

[147] See Michael C Schouten, 'The Case for Mandatory Ownership Disclosure' (2009) 15 Stanford Journal of Law, Business and Finance 127, 167; Henry T C Hu and Bernard S Black, 'Empty Voting and Hidden (Morphable) Ownership: Taxonomy, Implications, and Reforms' (2006) 61 Business Lawyer 1011, 1048; Paul L Davies and Sarah Worthington, *Gower and Davies' Principles of Modern Company Law* (9th edn, Sweet & Maxwell 2012) para. 26-23.

[148] Eugene Fama, 'Efficient Capital Markets: A Review of Theory and Empirical Work' (1970) 25 Journal of Finance 383; Ronald J Gilson and Reinier Kraakman, 'The Mechanisms of Market Efficiency' (1984) 70 Virginia Law Review 549; Eilís Ferran, *Principles of Corporate Finance Law* (2nd edn, Oxford University Press 2008) 75–7; Frank H Easterbrook and Daniel R Fischel, 'Mandatory Disclosure and the Protection of Investors' (1984) 70 Virginia Law Review 669, 673. See also Troy Paredes, 'Blinded by the Light: Information Overload and Its Consequences for Securities Regulation' (2003) 81 Washington University Law Quarterly 417. See criticism in Susanna K Ripken, 'The Dangers and Drawbacks of the Disclosure Antidote: Toward a More Substantive Approach to Securities Regulation' (2006) 58 Baylor Law Review 139, 176–84. See also High Level Group of Company Law Experts, *Final Report on a Modern Regulatory Framework for Company Law in Europe* (4 November 2002) 34 <http://ec.europa.eu/internal_market/company/docs/modern/report_en.pdf> accessed 19 April 2015; and FSA, CP 07/20 (n. 146) Annex 2, 1-3.

[149] Wayne H Mikkelson and Richard S Ruback, 'An Empirical Analysis of the Interfirm Equity Investment Process' (1985) 14 Journal of Financial Economics 523, 552; see also DTR 2 and DTR 5.

[150] Henry T C Hu and Bernard S Black, 'Hedge Funds, Insiders, and the Decoupling of Economic and Voting Ownership: Empty Voting and Hidden (Morphable) Ownership' (2007) 13 Journal of Corporate Finance 343, 356; FSA, CP 07/20 (n. 146) 6, 20–1.

hidden position in Volkswagen.[151] This led to speculative short sellers racing to acquire sufficient shares to cover their positions under share lending arrangements, which were estimated to amount to some 13 per cent of Volkswagen's shares against the factual free-float of approximately 6 per cent.[152] The Volkswagen share price responded by increasing from approximately EUR 200 to over EUR 1,000, making it the most valuable company in the world based on market capitalization for a short period of time, ultimately forcing the operator of the Frankfurt stock exchange (*Deutsche Börse AG*) to adjust its DAX index.[153] This example illustrates how, under this category of CfD market effects, the need for regulatory protection comes from the need to secure market integrity and transparency.

Second, CfDs can affect the valuations of individual investments. Capital market regulation does not aim at protecting investors from losses, as markets are inherently risky. However, it does, and should, provide protection for sound and informed decision-making.[154] CfDs can disturb this basis for investor decisions *ex ante* if they are indirectly used for obtaining control over the target company or its share price, or if the CfD trading reflects information that has not been disclosed to the market. In the latter case, equity investors cannot fully inform themselves of the control structures of the target companies, and therefore do not know what kind of companies they are actually investing in. Similarly, the creation of hidden CfD positions can also effectively limit liquidity and the exit opportunities of the existing shareholders *ex post*, that is, after they have already invested in a particular target company.[155] Here the protected interest is the informed decision-making of outside investors.[156]

[151] See on the Porsche/VW saga Chapter IV.B.

[152] A landmark decision was delivered on 15 August 2014 by the US Court of Appeals for the Second Circuit in *Parkcentral Global Hub Limited v Porsche Automobile Holdings, SE*, 11-397-CV (2d Cir. N.Y. Aug. 15, 2014), rejecting US jurisdiction. See Kevin M LaCroix, 'Second Circuit Affirms Porsche Securities Suit Dismissal; Domestic Transaction Necessary But Not Sufficient to Invoke U.S. Securities Laws' D&O Diary, 18 August 2014, available at <http://www.dandodiary.com/2014/08/articles/securities-litigation/second-circuit-affirms-porsche-securities-suit-dismissal-domestic-transaction-necessary-but-not-sufficient-to-invoke-u-s-securities-laws/>; Herbert Smith Freehills, 'US Federal Appeals Court Limits Extraterritorial Application of Anti-Fraud Provisions of the U.S. Federal Securities Laws' 2 September 2014, available at <http://www.herbertsmithfreehills.com/-/media/Files/ebulletins/2014/20140902%20-%20Alert%20re%20Second%20Amendment%20Circuit%20Porsche%20decision.htm>.

[153] Deutsche Börse AG, 'Deutsche Börse Extraordinarily Adjusts DAX Weightings' (29 October 2008), available at <http://deutsche-boerse.com/dbg/dispatch/en/notescontent/dbg_nav/press/10_Latest_Press_Releases/10_All/INTEGRATE/mr_pressreleases?notesDoc=FBC308516A591080C12574F000795B04> accessed 19 August 2015; Rachel Nolan, 'VW Stock Price Anomaly "Must Not Be Allowed"' (*Der Spiegel*, 29 October 2008), available at <http://www.spiegel.de/international/the-world-from-berlin-vw-stock-price-anomaly-must-not-be-allowed-a-587293.html> accessed 19 August 2015.

[154] Final Report of the High Level Group of Company Law Experts on a Modern Regulatory Framework for Company Law in Europe (n. 148) 34; Alastair Hudson, *The Law of Finance* (2nd edn, Sweet & Maxwell 2013) paras 3-10, 35-03.

[155] This *ex post* factor has been cited as the central motive for the US disclosure regulation; see Daniel Bertaccini, 'To Disclose or Not to Disclose? *CSX CORP.*, Total Return Swaps, and Their Implications for Schedule 13D Filing Purposes' (2009) 31 Cardozo Law Review 267, 288.

[156] See Michael C Schouten, 'The Case for Mandatory Ownership Disclosure' (2009) 15 Stanford Journal of Law, Business and Finance 127, 135 f.

A third, and quite dramatic, way in which CfDs can influence investments in capital markets is a 'CfD takeover'. A block acquisition, or a secured position in the form of hedge shares, increases the share price due to a higher demand for particular target shares on the market. As this price increase does not include information on a CfD holder working towards a large position, the offer price can be lower than in the case of full information disclosure of the CfD holder's intentions. Accordingly, the offer premium can be artificially low and invite shareholders to tender on an uninformed basis.[157]

Also, a CfD holder making a tender offer typically discloses a CfD arrangement in the offer document, and thereby effectively announces a secured block of shares to be tendered. This can force the remaining shareholders to tender even on unfavourable terms, as they most often do not want to end up as minority holders in a company under changed control. This pressure to tender exerted indirectly by CfDs operates in a way similar to old-fashioned share toeholds.[158] In addition to the shareholder perspective, toehold stakes may also discourage competitive bidders who would drive bid prices up and with that benefit target shareholders.[159] In this scenario, the regulation is directed to enable shareholders to exit for a fair price.

The fourth impact of abusive CfD trading concerns the governance of traded companies, rather than the investment market.[160] Because CfDs can be used for obtaining more or less formal control of voting rights, they can, in certain situations, be compared to real shareholdings. On this basis, CfD holders may sometimes claim to interfere with the management of a target company. If CfD positions are not disclosed, the target management may be unable to verify the power of the CfD holder's arguments and judge whether the CfD holder has a power over the voting rights in the company.[161] This impact on governance is illustrated in *CSX v TCI,* where two hedge funds with CfD positions communicated with the target board explicitly in their capacity as de facto shareholders.[162] CfD positions can also distort the disciplining effect of the market for corporate control from the perspective of other potential bidders, major shareholders, and the board

[157] See Theodor Baums and Maike Sauter, 'Anschleichen an Übernahmeziele mit Hilfe von Aktienderivaten' (2009) 173 Zeitschrift für das gesamte Handelsrecht und Wirtschaftsrecht (ZHR) 454, 460.

[158] Lucian Bebchuk, 'Toward Undistorted Choice and Equal Treatment in Corporate Takeovers' (1985) 98 Harvard Law Review 1695, 1722.

[159] FSA, CP 07/20 (n. 146) 25, in which, interestingly, the FSA did not discuss the distortion of the exit price of old shareholders. See also John C Coffee Jr, 'Regulating the Market for Corporate Control: A Critical Assessment of the Tender Offer's Role in Corporate Governance' (1984) 84 Columbia Law Review 1145, 1174.

[160] See Schouten (n. 156) 148, 168; Dirk Zetzsche, 'Against Mandatory Disclosure of Economic-only Positions referenced to Shares of European Issuers—Twenty Arguments against the CESR Proposal' (2010) 11 EBOR 231, where hidden voting based on CfD is considered as a mere corporate governance issue; see also Reinier H Kraakman and others (eds), *The Anatomy of Corporate Law: A Comparative and Functional Approach* (2nd edn, Oxford University Press 2009) 81.

[161] FSA, CP 07/20 (n. 146) 21.

[162] See *CSX Corporation v the Children's Investment Fund Management (UK) LLP*, 562 F Supp 2d 511 (SDNY 2008), 12 June 2008, 08 CV 02764, 72, 25–6; and Bertaccini (n. 155).

of directors.[163] In the context of corporate governance, regulation is directed to benefit shareholders rather than investors, and its purpose is to protect effective governance structures and shareholders' rights in the target companies.[164]

a) Current CfD regulation

The United Kingdom was one of the forerunners in preventing CfD abuse. Early on, France, Switzerland, and Hong Kong also adopted specific CfD disclosure regulations,[165] and Germany followed suit a little later.[166] More recently, the EU has adopted legal requirements for CfD disclosure. After the publication of a seminal consultation paper[167] by the former Committee of European Securities Regulators (CESR),[168] a lengthy legislation process began, which concluded with a revision of the EU Transparency Directive concerning major shareholdings.[169] The EU reform largely reflected what several Member States had already implemented. Academics had predicted larger convergence of CfD disclosure along the lines of the UK regime.[170]

The most comprehensive framework is still in place in the United Kingdom. As early as 2005, the Takeover Panel amended the Takeover Code to include economic

[163] See Davies and Worthington (n. 147) paras 26-22, 26-23, and 28-45; and Kraakman and others (n. 160) 236.

[164] See Davies and Worthington (n. 147) paras 26-22 and 26-23.

[165] Overview at Eugenio de Nardis and Matteo Tonello, 'Know Your Shareholders: The Use of Cash-Settled Equity Derivatives to Hide Corporate Ownership Interests' The Conference Board no DN-009 (July 2010) 4–6.

[166] The *Gesetz zur Stärkung des Anlegerschutzes und Verbesserung der Funktionsfähigkeit des Kapitalmarkts (Anlegerschutz- und Funktionsverbesserungsgesetz)*, adopted on 5 April 2011, [2011] Bundesgesetzblatt I 538 ('Act on strengthening investor protection and improving the functionality of capital markets'), introduced new section § 25a into the WpHG. This provision mandates disclosure of 'other instruments' which 'facilitate' the acquisition of shares in listed companies.

[167] CESR, Consultation Document 09-1215b (n. 146); see also European Securities Markets Expert Group (ESME), *Views on the Issue of Transparency of Holdings of Cash Settled Derivatives* (November 2009) 13–15, available at <http://ec.europa.eu/internal_market/securities/docs/esme/tdcash_en.pdf>; Schouten (n. 156) 176. For criticism, see Zetzsche (n. 160) 19.

[168] With effect from 1 January 2011, CESR was replaced by ESMA, the European Securities and Markets Authority. See <http://www.esma.europa.eu/>.

[169] Directive 2013/50/EU of the European Parliament and of the Council of 22 October 2013 amending Directive 2004/109/EC of the European Parliament and of the Council on the harmonisation of transparency requirements in relation to information about issuers whose securities are admitted to trading on a regulated market, Directive 2003/71/EC of the European Parliament and of the Council on the prospectus to be published when securities are offered to the public or admitted to trading and Commission Directive 2007/14/EC laying down detailed rules for the implementation of certain provisions of Directive 2004/109/EC, [2013] OJ L294/13. For comment, see Rüdiger Veil, 'The Reform of the Transparency Regime in European Capital Markets Laws' [2013] European Company and Financial Law Review 18, 33 ff.; Luca Enriques and Matteo Gatti, 'Creeping Acquisitions in Europe: Enabling Companies to be Better Safe than Sorry' (2015) 15 Journal of Corporate Law Studies 55, 73 ff.

[170] See Tom Siebens and Melissa Gambol, 'Who's Hiding Behind the Hedges? Developments in the USA and UK May Limit the Use of Total Return Swaps to Conceal Equity Stakes in Public Companies' (2009) 4 Capital Markets Law Journal 172, 178; Brian T Sullivan, 'CSX Corp. v. Children's Investment Fund Management and the Need for SEC Expansion of Beneficial Ownership' (2009) 87 North Carolina Law Review 1300, 1319.

positions when calculating the threshold for triggering the mandatory bid obligation, as well as to require disclosure of CfD positions of 1 per cent or more in both the target and the bidder company during an offer period.[171] Subsequently, the Disclosure and Transparency Rules (DTR) under the (former) FSA Handbook were amended in 2009 to require the disclosure of financial instruments that create long positions to the economic performance of shares in listed companies. This regulation applies independent of whether these instruments are settled physically or in cash.[172] In the United Kingdom, the regulation restricting CfD abuse is thus part of both law on takeovers and law on disclosure of major shareholder notifications. Both of these regulations aim at handling the same market problem, but takeover law operates mostly *ex post*, whereas disclosure regulation has its effect *ex ante*.

Disclosure rules under the Takeover Code serve the information needs of shareholders and market participants in the event of a takeover, that is, when the control structures of a company are most vulnerable. Therefore, takeover-related disclosure is well measured and effective even if it is based on economic interests, as it is by definition always connected to situations affecting corporate control. However, the focus of the following analysis is on the disclosure requirements under the DTR.

Originally, the FSA had suggested two alternatives for the regulation on CfD disclosure under the DTR: a broad general disclosure regulation, and a narrower safe harbour regulation.[173] The consultation showed mixed opinions in the market, but eventually the FSA adopted the general disclosure obligation to be triggered by economic exposure.[174] Although the regulation was extensively prepared with several consultation papers, the FSA's reasons for preferring the general disclosure obligation are unclear and contradictory. According to the FSA, the aim of the CfD disclosure was mainly to increase information on persons or entities having significant influence in target companies, that is, control-related information. Emphasizing the threats of excessive disclosure, the FSA specifically stated that increased transparency of CfD positions, irrespective of any link to voting rights, could not justify CfD disclosure.[175]

These arguments seem to point in the direction of a more narrow and control-oriented disclosure regulation. Nevertheless, the FSA opted for the general disclosure obligation triggered by CfD positions of 3 per cent or higher.[176] The

[171] Rules 8.3 and 9.1 of the Takeover Code.

[172] FSA 2009/13: Disclosure and transparency rules (disclosure of contracts for differences) instrument 2009 amending the Disclosure Rules and Transparency Rules sourcebook (DTR); DTR 5.3.

[173] FSA, CP 07/20 (n. 146) 8–9; see also another regulatory alternative in Dirk Zetzsche, 'Hidden Ownership in Europe: BAFin's Decision in Schaeffler v. Continental' (2009) 10 European Business Organization Law Review (EBOR) 115, 132. See also, for example, the discussion in Italy, Consob, *Position Paper on the Disclosure of Cash-Settled Derivatives* (8 October 2009), available at <http://www.consob.it/mainen/legal_framework/consultations/dp_cash_derivatives_20091008.pdf> accessed 15 August 2015.

[174] Financial Services Authority, *Disclosure of Contracts for Difference: Feedback and policy statement on CP07/20, and further technical consultation, CP 08/17* (October 2008) 5 <http://www.fsa.gov.uk/pubs/cp/cp08_17.pdf> accessed 19 August 2015; see also CESR/09-1215b (n. 146) 3, Baums and Sauter (n. 157) 493–501 and Hu and Black (n. 147) 1049, 1052.

[175] FSA, CP 08/17 (n. 174) 5, 9.

[176] DTR 5.1.2 and 5.3.

counter-arguments in favour of the safe harbour alternative are discussed in more detail in section V.E.2.c. Here, it suffices to note that the justifications for the CfD disclosure rules seem to lie more in the objections against the alternative proposal than in its own merits.[177]

The EU Transparency Directive is the equivalent instrument on the EU level. The original version of this Directive did not contain any reference to CfDs or other economic-only positions. The EU Commission initiated a recent review of the Directive after a number of loopholes became apparent. After commissioning an external study,[178] it launched a consultation paper on a possible revision of the Directive in 2010.[179] The Commission also adopted a report on the operation of the directive and a related staff working document on emerging issues.[180] One of the issues to be considered was whether a revised version of the Directive should include disclosure obligations for holdings of cash-settled derivatives, in particular CfDs. The consultation drew explicit parallels to the UK regime under consideration here, as well as to the Swiss regulation.[181]

At the end of 2010, the Commission presented the results of the consultation.[182] The vast majority of respondents to the consultation had considered that the disclosure of holdings of cash-settled derivatives would be beneficial to the market with a view to avoid hidden ownership.[183] Nevertheless, it seems that the responses were not unanimous, and that divergences persisted. Most respondents favoured a well-targeted and proportionate disclosure system, avoiding the provision of useless or irrelevant information and reducing the number of notifications; and there were calls for clear exceptions.[184] Nevertheless, some respondents highlighted the alleged positive experience with the UK disclosure system of CfDs.[185]

Essentially, however, the final version of the revised EU Transparency Directive[186] for the most part follows the UK's lead and requires disclosure of major holdings of all financial instruments that could be used to acquire economic interest in listed

[177] It should be noted that the newly adopted legislation in Germany (n. 166) follows the same direction: new § 25a WpHG introduces a full disclosure regime for all CfD type derivative positions from an initial 5 per cent threshold. See on this conceptual choice Holger Fleischer and Klaus-Ulrich Schmolke, 'Zum beabsichtigten Ausbau der kapitalmarktrechtlichen Beteiligungstransparenz bei modernen Finanzinstrumenten' [2010] Neue Zeitschrift für Gesellschaftsrecht (NZG) 846, 853.

[178] Mazars and Marccus Partners, *Transparency Directive Assessment Report—Prepared for the European Commission Internal Market and Services DG, Final Report* (December 2009), available at <http://ec.europa.eu/internal_market/securities/docs/transparency/report-application_en.pdf>.

[179] See European Commission, *Consultation document on the modernisation of the Directive 2004/109/EC on the harmonisation of transparency requirements in relation to information about issuers whose securities are admitted to trading on a regulated market*, 27 May 2010.

[180] European Commission, *Report to the Council, the European Parliament, the European Social and Economic Committee and the Committee of the Regions on the Operation of Directive 2004/109/EC on the harmonisation of transparency requirements in relation to information about issuers whose securities are admitted to trading on a regulated market*, COM(2010) 243.

[181] Consultation document (n. 179) questions 11 and 12.

[182] European Commission, *Feedback Statement Summary of Responses to the Consultation by DG Internal Market and Services on the Modernisation of the Transparency Directive (2004/109/EC)*, 17 December 2010.

[183] ibid. 20 ff. [184] ibid. 20 f. [185] ibid. 21. [186] See n. 169.

companies and that have the same effect as equity holdings.[187] Since the reform came into effect, article 13(1) of the Transparency Directive[188] requires disclosure, inter alia, of

(a) financial instruments that, on maturity, give the holder, under a formal agreement, either the unconditional right to acquire or the discretion as to his right to acquire, shares to which voting rights are attached, already issued, of an issuer whose shares are admitted to trading on a regulated market;
(b) financial instruments which are not included in point (a) but which are referenced to shares referred to in that point and with economic effect similar to that of the financial instruments referred to in that point, whether or not they confer a right to a physical settlement.

Article 13(1b) then even explicitly mentions contracts for difference as one example of instruments which potentially fall within the scope of paragraph (1).[189] The revised Directive is currently being implemented by the EU Member States. As it largely reflects the United Kingdom's existing approach, the British government will not have to significantly alter its current DTR rules.[190]

Consequently, both the United Kingdom and the EU (and ultimately all EU Member States) chose to adopt the 'big solution', as a comprehensive disclosure of CfD positions is required at all times. The 'small solution', as contemplated initially by the United Kingdom (which would have provided for some safe harbour exceptions), was accordingly rejected.

In comparison, the US disclosure regulation on shareholdings under section 13(d) of the Securities Exchange Act of 1934, also known as the Williams Act,[191] is based on the concept of beneficial ownership.[192] According to SEC Rule 13d-3(a), beneficial ownership refers to 'any person who, directly or indirectly, through any contract, arrangement, understanding, relationship or otherwise has or shares' either voting power[193] or investment power.[194] Also a person who uses an arrangement to prevent 'the vesting of such beneficial ownership as part of a plan or scheme to evade the reporting requirements' is deemed the beneficial owner of the target securities.[195] Thus, the US regulation sanctions the circumvention of

187 For details, see ESMA, *Final Report on Draft Regulatory Technical Standards on major shareholdings and an indicative list of financial instruments subject to notification requirements under the revised Transparency Directive*, ESMA/2014/1187 (29 September 2014) paras 138 ff. For a critical view, see Veil (n. 169).

188 Directive 2004/109/EC, as amended.

189 See article 13(1b)(f).

190 Financial Conduct Authority (FCA), *Implementation of the Transparency Directive Amending Directive (2013/50/EU) and other Disclosure Rule and Transparency Rule Changes—Consultation Paper CP 15/11* (March 2015), para. 3.4. For comment, see Henry T C Hu, 'Financial Innovation and Governance Mechanisms: The Evolution of Decoupling and Transparency' (2015) 70 Business Lawyer 347, 369.

191 Act of July 29, 1968, Pub. L. No. 90-439, § 2, 82 Stat. 454 (1968) (the Williams Act) as part of the Securities Exchange Act of 1934 as amended through P.L. 111-257, approved 5 Oct. 2010.

192 As for the legislative background see Jonathan R Macey and Jeffry M Netter, 'Regulation 13D and the Regulatory Process' (1987) 65 Washington University Law Quarterly 131.

193 The power to vote, or to direct the voting.

194 The power to dispose, or to direct the disposition.

195 Rule 13d-3(b).

the disclosure rules by, inter alia, CfD-type arrangements, even though there is no obligation to disclose CfDs as such.

We saw that the leading case *CSX v TCI* affirmed that CfDs can be used to evade disclosure requirements and that CfD holdings can therefore lead to beneficial ownership of the underlying securities for the purposes of the disclosure regulation.[196] However, the judgment in *CSX v TCI* did not rule on the question whether a CfD instrument directly amounts to an understanding under which a CfD holder has indirect voting or investment power, and therefore triggers a disclosure obligation. However, the court indicated that the power to influence the disposition or voting of the hedge shares was sufficient to constitute beneficial ownership.[197] This latter question has been discussed in the New Zealand case *Perry v Ithaca,* in which it was held that 'an arrangement or understanding did not exist merely with the knowledge and expectation that, because of market reality, there would be an ability to repurchase the shares [under the CfD contracts]'.[198]

The US disclosure rules, even if not directly applicable to CfDs, set a higher level of detail for the information to be disclosed than the corresponding UK regulation. As opposed to just disclosing the targeted number of voting rights, the exercise period and maturity of the financial instruments, and the identity of the holder under the UK regulation,[199] the US rules also require, for instance, disclosure of the background and nature of the beneficial ownership, and details regarding the intention to acquire control in the target company under Schedule D.[200]

The US disclosure rules include exceptions for certain types of investors. They allow first, passive investment firms (under SEC Rule 13d-1(b)), and second, other entities that have not acquired the securities with control purpose and hold less than a 20 per cent interest (under SEC Rule 13d-1(c)), to make a short-form statement of their holdings according to Schedule G, which broadly equals the UK disclosure requirements (here referred to as the 'passive investor exemption').[201] Passive investment firms are allowed to make aggregate disclosures within forty-five days of the end of the calendar year in which the obligation arose, whereas other entities with no controlling intentions still need to make the short-form disclosure within ten days of the acquisition. Further, the exemption for passive investment firms only applies to acquisitions made in the ordinary course of business by specific types of companies, such as banks, insurance companies, and brokers, which act without the purpose or the effect of changing or influencing the control of the relevant issuer.

[196] *CSX Corporation v the Children's Investment Fund Management (UK) LLP*, 562 F Supp 2d 511 (SDNY 2008), 12 June 2008, 08 CV 02764, 72; see, for a thorough discussion, generally Sullivan (n. 170) and Siebens and Gambol (n. 170) 175.

[197] *CSX Corporation v the Children's Investment Fund Management (UK) LLP*, 562 F Supp 2d 511 (SDNY 2008), 12 June 2008, 08 CV 02764, 60; Siebens and Gambol (n. 170) 175; Sullivan (n. 170) 1306 and 1309.

[198] *Perry Corporation v Ithaca (Custodians) Ltd* [2004] 1 NZLR 731 para. 78.

[199] DTR 5.8.

[200] SEC Rule 13d-101.

[201] SEC Rule 13d-102; compare with DTR 5.8.2.

In response to the financial crisis, the US Dodd–Frank Act[202] has partly reformed the system. While granting the SEC broad authority to determine under which circumstances security-based swaps confer beneficial ownership, section 766 of the Act provides that such swaps do not generally confer beneficial ownership, except to the extent that the SEC affirmatively adopts rules providing otherwise. The SEC has proposed to readopt the original rules, thereby preserving the *status quo ante*—pending completion of a separate project being undertaken by its staff to develop proposals for reforming section 13(d) and (g) reporting.[203]

A comparison of the different systems draws attention to two factors. First, the US criterion for disclosure obligation is 'beneficial ownership', that is, direct or indirect voting, investment power, or an arrangement used to divest[204] the investor in question of the beneficial ownership. The US disclosure obligation is therefore not triggered by the mere existence of a CfD position. Second, under both US and New Zealand case law, the market practice described in Chapter III.C.3 could trigger a disclosure obligation only in connection with either a consensus or communication concerning the use of voting or investment power,[205] or an arrangement to circumvent the disclosure obligation with 'an accumulation of securities with a potential shift of corporate control'.[206] Thus, importantly, neither the US nor the New Zealand regulation imposes a disclosure obligation merely due to a CfD position; rather, it is only in connection with control-related intentions. By contrast, the current UK and EU legislation requires general disclosure of CfD positions, as described previously.

2. What is wrong with a general CfD disclosure obligation?

The EU approach[207] is, to a large extent, based on the assumption that potential problems caused by CfDs would disappear if these instruments were subject to an all-embracing disclosure obligation.[208] Other jurisdictions find different solutions. This section seeks to identify the problems caused by CfD abuse in order to assess different regulatory approaches. To this end, the focus will be on identifying what CfD-related information is important to the market and on whether threats of market disturbance do in fact require full disclosure.

Neither market regulation in general, nor disclosure in particular, is of value in itself, and they should only be used when the overall benefits outweigh the costs.[209]

[202] Dodd–Frank Wall Street Reform and Consumer Protection Act, HR 4173.
[203] Securities and Exchange Commission Release No. 34-64087, File no S7-10-11, 17 March 2011.
[204] This latter qualification is not included in the New Zealand regulation.
[205] *Perry Corporation v Ithaca (Custodians) Ltd* [2004] 1 NZLR 731 para. 78.
[206] *CSX Corporation v the Children's Investment Fund Management (UK) LLP*, 562 F Supp 2d 511 (SDNY 2008), 12 June 2008, 08 CV 02764, 71.
[207] See text accompanying n. 187.
[208] See Frank H Easterbrook and Daniel R Fischel, 'Mandatory Disclosure and the Protection of Investors' (1984) 70 Virginia Law Review 669, 692–6, 700; Zetzsche (n. 160) 22.
[209] Baums and Sauter (n. 157) 472.

On this ground, it will be argued that, between the two alternatives identified by the FSA, a safe harbour option would have been more suitable and would have led to greater overall benefits on the market than the current general disclosure regime.[210] This view is based on the fact that the market disturbance by the CfDs is not created by the economic positions, but by the structural link between the instruments and the voting rights carried by hedge shares.

Most importantly, the market needs to know about large CfD positions only if they are used as a surrogate for shareholdings in order to gain corporate control instead of, or in addition to, financial investment purposes.[211] Therefore, a general disclosure requirement creates an overly far-reaching obligation, both incurring unnecessary costs to the CfD market and confusing equity investors with an overload of information. As noted in *Perry v Ithaca*, '[CfD disclosure regulation] is conceptually directed at voting rights rather than economic interests'.[212]

a) What does the market need to know?

Securities law, including CfD disclosure regulation, aims to facilitate informed investor decision-making and to control possible dishonest behaviour of corporate managers and other market participants.[213] Both of these aims enhance market transparency and efficiency, increase investment activity, decrease the cost of capital and investment risk, and strengthen investor confidence.[214]

Generally, CfD disclosure regulation is part of the disclosure of major shareholdings. This subset of mandatory disclosure law can promote the market for corporate control as it allows the market to monitor directors by indicating accumulations of share positions, and therefore the threat of a (hostile) takeover.[215] Furthermore, major shareholder notifications enhance shareholder decision-making by revealing who holds actual or potential control in the company, as well as who is active on the market and to what extent.[216] This information enables the market to adjust the share price to the expected impacts that may result from the conduct of a large shareholder.[217]

[210] See contradictorily in FSA, CP 08/17 (n. 174) 9 where it is argued, in favour of the general disclosure regulation, that '[the] purpose of the disclosures required by the DTRs is to inform the market of who has a significant influence in a company—. Disclosure of investors' economic positions is a by-product of the legislation, not its purpose'.

[211] FSA, CP 07/20 (n. 146) 6, 32, 43–4; see Baums and Sauter (n. 157) 473.

[212] *Perry Corporation v Ithaca (Custodians) Ltd* [2004] 1 NZLR 731 para. 76.

[213] Final Report of the High Level Group of Company Law Experts on a Modern Regulatory Framework for Company Law in Europe (n. 148) 38; Easterbrook and Fischel (n. 208) 699.

[214] Susanna K Ripken, 'The Dangers and Drawbacks of the Disclosure Antidote: Toward a More Substantive Approach to Securities Regulation' (2006) 58 Baylor Law Review 139, 151–5.

[215] FSA, CP 07/20 (n. 146) Annex 2, 4–5.

[216] Davies and Worthington (n. 147) para. 26-18; FSA, CP 07/20 (n. 146) Annex 2, 6-7.

[217] John Armour and Jeffrey N Gordon, 'The Berle–Means Corporation in the 21st Century' 22 (unpublished draft, on file with the author).

(i) Information carried by CfD positions

Shareholder disclosure produces information regarding the distribution of voting rights and control in the target company.[218] In the case of concrete shareholdings, this is clear because ordinary shares carry voting rights, whereas for CfD investments there is technically no connection between CfD holdings and corporate control. Nevertheless, there are three types of information connected to CfD positions that can influence the market in a similar way to actual shareholder notifications. These include information on a CfD holder that influences the use of voting rights, information on the identity of the CfD investor and the size of investment position, and information on the trading activity based on the hedging practices by CfD short parties.

Influence on voting rights. As discussed in Chapter III.C.3, market realities can frequently enable CfD holders to influence the use of voting rights carried by the hedge shares. When this structure is utilized, the information on CfD holdings essentially becomes the same information as that disclosed in shareholder notifications, that is, information on the control of the target company. Therefore, the justification for disclosure of this type of information is generally acknowledged.[219]

Under the revised EU disclosure system, this connection between CfDs and voting power is taken for granted, as CfD positions are required to be disclosed precisely like holdings of shares, and are even aggregated. In this regard, the assumption of CfDs conveying voting power is taken too far. The US disclosure regulation, however, is not explicitly applicable to CfDs. In order to fall under the disclosure obligation, a CfD position should give the holder at least indirect voting or investment power, or be arranged under a construction that aims to divest such power. Therefore, the wording of the US regulation considers this first type of information, which concerns the influence on voting, as being the basis of the disclosure regulation. However, this conclusion can be questioned in the light of *CSX v TCI*, in which the court concluded that the economic position of the long party, under which it was able to influence the short party's decisions, led to beneficial ownership of the underlying shares.[220] This judgment was passed despite the fact that, for example, the SEC clearly asserted that 'economic and business incentives [...] are not sufficient to create beneficial ownership under Rule 13d-3'.[221]

Investor identity and size of the economic position. Independent of its influence on voting rights, the identity of the CfD holder could be argued to have an effect

[218] See article 9(1) of the Transparency Directive 2004/109/EC.

[219] FSA, CP 07/20 (n. 146) 20, 23 and Annex 2, 3–4; see also e.g. Davies and Worthington (n. 147) para. 26-23; Mikkelson and Ruback (n. 149) 551–2.

[220] *CSX Corporation v the Children's Investment Fund Management (UK) LLP*, 562 F Supp 2d 511 (SDNY 2008), 12 June 2008, 08 CV 02764, 60.

[221] Brief of Amicus Curiae by the Securities and Exchange Commission in the matter CSX Corp. v. The Children's Inv. Fund Mgmt., L.L.P., et al., 08-Civ. 2764 (4 June 2008) 2, available at <http://www.chadbourne.com/files/Publication/ce4995ec-b733-4eef-89e5-d5574a182080/Preview/PublicationAttachment/ed741d95-84e9-4fb9-b0a6-c196c813e5bf/SECBrehenyLetter.pdf>, accessed 19 August 2015; Sullivan (n. 170) 1309.

on the share price, thereby requiring the position to be disclosed.[222] According to this argument, mere large economic exposures can have a market effect and would therefore justify disclosure.[223] This price effect could either arise if the CfD holder had, due to pure economic interest, influence on the target company (although these types of interests are generally bordered by market abuse regulation), or if the market would otherwise use this particular information for pricing the target shares. According to FSA research, there is no empirical evidence of market effects based on pure economic positions apart from the context of insider trading.[224] Even if the identity of an investor can have a price effect, this is based on the market anticipating often control-related intentions, in which case the need for disclosure is not connected to the investor's identity as such, but to the intentions of that investor.[225] Moreover, it should be noted that capital markets are inherently anonymous. Part of their functionality is based on the fact that investors are not, and should not be, by virtue of their economic investment, known to the rest of the market.[226]

Furthermore, the assumption concerning the efficiency of the capital markets in generating other information from the identity of an investor does not take into account the costs of analysing this information (and further disclosure costs) which the market needs to incur before the new information can be used. From this perspective, it would be more efficient to allocate the costs of generating the useful information to the party that can do that most cheaply, that is, the investor in question.[227] Thus, merely the fact that a particular person has an economic interest in a target company should not justify a disclosure obligation.

In spite of these arguments, the revised EU disclosure regulation for CfDs takes the economic position as its starting point. In comparison, the US disclosure regulation of beneficial ownership, which is generally also applicable to holdings in derivative instruments, is based on voting or investment power, and does not consider economic interest to be a decisive factor that triggers the obligations. However, the judgment in *CSX v TCI* narrows this distinction by linking the definition of a scheme to evade disclosure to the economic interest and market structure. Yet, the US disclosure regulation generally allows even notable positions not to be disclosed when these positions are held by passive and professional investors who do not aim to influence the control of the target company.[228]

Trading information. The effect on trading volume which can result from a short party's need to acquire hedge shares could be seen to justify a disclosure requirement.[229] In this context, the disclosure obligation could be imposed either on the shareholder,

[222] Macey and Netter (n. 192) 146–7.
[223] FSA, CP 07/20 (n. 146) 23–4; and FSA, CP 08/17 (n. 174) 5.
[224] FSA, CP 07/20 (n. 146) 23–4, 30–2 and Annex 2, 3–4; compare to Macey and Netter (n. 192) 148–9.
[225] Compare to Macey and Netter (n. 192) 146–9.
[226] FSA, CP 07/20 (n. 146) 24.
[227] This is based on the standard law and economics insight known as the 'cheapest cost avoider'. See the seminal work by Guido Calabresi, *The Costs of Accidents: A Legal and Economic Analysis* (Yale University Press 1970); Guido Calabresi and Jon T Hirschoff, 'Toward a Test for Strict Liability in Torts' (1972) 81 Yale Law Journal 1055.
[228] SEC Rule 13d-1(c).
[229] FSA, CP 07/20 (n. 146) 24; Schouten (n. 156) 141.

that is, the short party, under the current major shareholder notification regulation or, alternatively, on the long party due to the benefit it indirectly gets from the hedging acquisition. However, this information on specific and large hedging investments is already reflected on the market as the share prices correspond to demand and supply. Even if CfD trading does not have a direct impact on the underlying share price through changes in trading volumes, acquisitions of hedging positions do. Therefore, this information does not require a specific disclosure.[230]

The current rules in the United States do not require specific disclosure of short positions taken merely for hedging purposes. However, it should be noted that the EU has adopted another legal instrument, the Short Selling Regulation, which regulates the disclosure of net short positions and volumes of short sales. This indirectly increases market information on long positions and related trading activities.[231]

In addition, in order for traders to price markets efficiently, at least some of them need to be informed of the reasons underlying the price fluctuations.[232] In CfD-related trades, this pricing information concerns either the intentions of the long parties or the size of the economic exposure. Thus, information on trading is not independent from the other two types of information discussed previously.

(ii) Connections between CfD information and market impacts caused by CfD abuse

The previous discussion analysed which kind of information on CfDs should be disclosed on the basis of the price effect the information could give rise to. In comparison, section V.E.1 discussed the market impact of CfD transactions. These included the distortion of, first, general market efficiency; investment decisions both *ex ante* as second and *ex post* as third; and, fourth, corporate governance. Efficient disclosure regulation should counter these instances of market failure. Moreover, it should do this by requiring the disclosure of price-affecting CfD information, thus focusing on *what* the market actually needs to know.

As discussed, CfD information giving rise to a price effect can crudely be divided into control-related information and information for purely economic interests. Currently, all holders of economic long positions are under a disclosure obligation. In this context, it will now be assessed which type of information would be needed for remedying detrimental market impacts.

General market efficiency. It could be argued that the protection of market integrity and liquidity, including market confidence and sufficient free-float, would justify disclosure regulation of all economic long positions, and not only positions based on control-related intentions. This concern is reflected in the example of Porsche's long position in Volkswagen, which was discussed in section V.E.1.

[230] Zetzsche (n. 160) 15.

[231] Regulation (EU) No 236/2012 of the European Parliament and of the Council of 14 March 2012 on short selling and certain aspects of credit default swaps, [2012] OJ L86/1. See on this framework in more detail Chapter VI.C.5.

[232] Easterbrook and Fischel (n. 208) 694–5.

However, it should be noted that under current UK takeover law—a body of regulation complementing disclosure law for situations of control shifts—CfD positions also trigger a mandatory bid obligation at the 30 per cent threshold.[233] This takeover regulation generally prevents CfD abuse, as only substantial CfD positions can have damaging impacts on the whole market.[234] This reflects the view that it is only control-relevant CfD trading positions that might have an impact on liquidity and market integrity, and therefore need to be regulated.[235] Note that the EU Takeover Directive does not require such an approach. According to the Directive, the mandatory bid obligation is triggered when somebody acquires 'control' in a target company, and the details of such control acquisition are left for the Member States to work out when implementing the Directive.[236]

Ex ante *investment protection.* There is a vast, although newly sceptical, literature on the decision-making processes of investors and on the role of mandatory disclosure in guiding investors' choices.[237] Nevertheless, it is at least clear that changes in corporate control can lead to changes in, for example, business operations and dividend strategies, as well as in the treatment of minority shareholders. Control-related information could therefore be of interest to both prospective investors and current shareholders, and should therefore be disclosed when the control-related intentions are backed with CfD positions.[238]

Additionally, pure economic positions seem to have an impact on investment decision-making as either rational or irrational, often reputation-based, herd behaviour by less informed investors, resulting in them following the investment or divestment decisions of other investors without having their own strategic reasons.[239] Even if only partially true, it does not mean that disclosure regulation should encourage or protect herd behaviour. In fact, it has been explicitly stated that disclosure regulation aims at protecting *informed* decision-making.[240] Gossip

[233] Rule 9.1 of the Takeover Code. See the definition of 'interests in securities' at p C10-11 of the Code:

> A person who has long economic exposure, whether absolute or conditional, to changes in the price of securities will be treated as interested in those securities [...], in particular, if [...] (4) he is party to any derivative: (a) whose value is determined by reference to their price; and (b) which results, or may result, in his having a long position in them.

[234] Interestingly, the US regulation does not contain rules on mandatory takeover bids but relies only on ongoing disclosure which, for the part of ownership disclosure, is based on disclosing detailed information on the acquirer's control-related intentions.

[235] This discussion from the perspective of market efficiency should not be confused with the following discussion concerning the *ex ante* investment protection.

[236] Takeover Directive, article 5(1).

[237] See e.g. Troy Paredes, 'Blinded by the Light: Information Overload and Its Consequences for Securities Regulation' (2003) 81 Washington University Law Quarterly 417; also Ripken (n. 214).

[238] See Henry T C Hu and Bernard S Black, 'Empty Voting and Hidden (Morphable) Ownership: Taxonomy, Implications, and Reforms' (2006) 61 Business Lawyer 1011, 1048.

[239] David Hirshleifer and Siew Hong Teoh, 'Herd Behaviour and Cascading in Capital Markets: a Review and Synthesis' (2003) 9 European Financial Management 25, 56; see also Michael C Schouten, 'The Case for Mandatory Ownership Disclosure' (2009) 15 Stanford Journal of Law, Business and Finance 127, 141.

[240] See e.g. Final Report of the High Level Group of Company Law Experts on a Modern Regulatory Framework for Company Law in Europe (n. 148) 34; Alastair Hudson, *The Law of Finance* (2nd edn, Sweet & Maxwell 2013) paras 3-10, 35-03.

and rumours of investment decisions are inevitably part of capital markets but disclosure of this information would not correct any market failure and should therefore not be protected by regulation.[241]

Ex post *investor protection.* It is obvious that, when CfD positions are used for initiating takeovers, they cause market disturbance by interfering with the public voting power structures. As passive economic positions do not carry control rights, investors cannot use them alone for takeover preparation. It could, however, be argued that a large investor with a reputation on the market could have a de facto effect or even control the share price, and thus limit the informed exit of other shareholders.[242] Yet, instead of a damaging effect, large investments generally have a positive impact on the share price as they increase market demand, independent of the identity of the investor. Thus, disclosure of pure economic interests does not add value to the protection of fair market exits, whereas disclosure of control-related holdings does.

Corporate governance. Lastly, CfD disclosure could reveal information about de facto owners of the target company and therefore be useful to other shareholders and to the management. Although this corporate governance relationship is more a concern of company law than capital markets law, it is related to corporate control and, thus, CfD disclosure could be used to remedy corporate governance problems (though only when limited to control-related positions).[243]

It can still be questioned whether investors with pure economic interests can influence the management of their target companies and cause governance disturbance.[244] Managers arguably interact with market participants and the business community and can exchange ideas with both equity and debt investors. If this is in the interest of the company, it most probably favours the shareholders and therefore does not cause any problem. In the case where the company and its share price are negatively affected, directors' behaviour can amount to a breach of their fiduciary duties, and should as such be handled by company law and not by disclosure regulation.[245]

b) *Costs of CfD disclosure*

Securities regulation is commonly based on the assumption that the more information, the better. Instead of prohibiting potentially harmful market activity or expecting voluntary disclosure, capital markets are largely covered by mandatory disclosure obligations.[246] Yet, disclosure is not a value on its own, but is used

[241] FSA, CP 07/20 (n. 146) 24. [242] Ripken (n. 214) 180. [243] Zetzsche (n. 160) 17.

[244] See FSA, CP 07/20 (n. 146) 23, in which the FSA raises the question without elaborating on the answer.

[245] See e.g. Companies Act 2006, sections 172 and 173.

[246] Reinier H Kraakman and others (eds), *The Anatomy of Corporate Law: A Comparative and Functional Approach* (2nd edn, Oxford University Press 2009) 277–9; Paredes (n. 237) 417, 463, quoting Louis Brandeis according to whom, famously, 'Sunlight is said to be the best of disinfectants'; see also Final Report of the High Level Group of Company Law Experts on a Modern Regulatory Framework for Company Law in Europe (n. 148) 37–8.

either for facilitating informed investment decisions or for preventing or revealing prohibited activity.[247] As the potential market abuse discussed in the present study is at least partly based on the very *non*-disclosure of investment positions, more information on CfD positions would indeed seem to be better.[248] However, mere disclosure never offers a comprehensive solution. The market must be able to make efficient use of the disclosed information.[249]

The availability of too much information can disable the market from recognizing the usefulness of unrelated or commonplace information. This phenomenon of information overload has been extensively discussed in the literature.[250] If investors do not recognize valuable disclosure, or if abusive activity can hide behind irrelevant information, regulation cannot achieve its goals.[251] This concern has been raised particularly in relation to CfD disclosure, as too much information could lead to market confusion and false feelings of 'potential' shareholdings.[252] Thus, too much disclosure could lead to similar results as incorrect disclosure. According to the conclusion reached previously, this information overload is currently produced by disclosure of pure economic CfD positions.[253]

A counter-argument could point to the existence of sophisticated market experts who filter useful data from complex and lengthy disclosure statements.[254] It should be noted, however, that the overload of CfD disclosure under the current regulation stems not from the length or complexity of the disclosure, but from the volume and the indeterminacy. This is because disclosure does not need to include information on the purpose for which the CfDs are used.[255] Though costly, experts could manage large amounts of disclosure, but they would not be any better positioned to investigate whether the disclosed positions are purely financial or whether they are control-related, as this knowledge rests with the CfD holders alone.

Irrespective of the potential overload, disclosure creates both direct and indirect costs.[256] First, disclosed information must be prepared according to legal specifications, disseminated to the market, and analysed by the recipients. Although

[247] See e.g. Kraakman and others (n. 246) 280; Paredes (n. 237) 431; and already Frank H Easterbrook and Daniel R Fischel, 'Mandatory Disclosure and the Protection of Investors' (1984) 70 Virginia Law Review 669, 696.

[248] Henry T C Hu and Bernard Black, 'Hedge Funds, Insiders, and the Decoupling of Economic and Voting Ownership: Empty Voting and Hidden (Morphable) Ownership' (2007) 13 Journal of Corporate Finance 343, 359, 363.

[249] Paredes (n. 237) 432.

[250] See e.g. Paredes (n. 237); Ripken (n. 214); Final Report of the High Level Group of Company Law Experts on a Modern Regulatory Framework for Company Law in Europe (n. 148) 34; and European Securities Markets Expert Group (ESME), *Views on the Issue of Transparency of Holdings of Cash Settled Derivatives* (November 2009) 10, available at <http://ec.europa.eu/internal_market/securities/docs/esme/tdcash_en.pdf>.

[251] Final Report of the High Level Group of Company Law Experts on a Modern Regulatory Framework for Company Law in Europe (n. 148) 38; Paul L Davies and Sarah Worthington, *Gower and Davies' Principles of Modern Company Law* (9th edn, Sweet & Maxwell 2012) 922–3; Kraakman and others (n. 246) 250.

[252] FSA, CP 07/20 (n. 146) 22; and FSA, CP 08/17 (n. 174) 9; Baums and Sauter (n. 157) 502.

[253] See section V.E.2.a. Cf. Zetzsche (n. 160) 13–14.

[254] See Paredes (n. 237) 452.

[255] See DTR 5.8.1.

[256] See Gilson and Kraakman (n. 148) 592; Zetzsche (n. 160) 20; and Ripken (n. 214) 188.

the drafting of a CfD notification is by far not as time-consuming as the preparation of, for example, a prospectus, notifications under these rules are produced in volumes.[257] Also, interpretation costs can, as discussed previously, be substantial if investors make an effort to identify control-related disclosure.

In addition to costs typical of all disclosure obligations, CfD disclosure also leads to specific costs. High disclosure standards for CfD instruments can lead to unnecessary duplication of disclosure: two market players—a shareholder and a CfD holder—may have to provide disclosure in respect of the same shares. Another cost specific to CfD disclosure arises if CfD holders and short parties decide to limit trading or value-enhancing takeover activity because they do not want to disclose their strategies or incur costs of compliance. This can lead to a loss of market liquidity and, ultimately, an increase in the cost of capital, as well as inefficient use of resources.[258] In addition to the general equity markets, these impacts could be reflected in the CfD market, threatening the entire business model.[259] The possible effects of extended CfD disclosure obligations have been considered in the United States, where the law regarding CfD disclosure is, to say the least, unclear. In *CSX v TCI*, institutions like ISDA, SIFMA, and also, interestingly, the SEC, have all noted that broadened disclosure regulation would create significant uncertainties for investors who use equity swaps in accordance with market practice.[260]

In comparison to the EU, the combination of disclosure regulation and takeover law imposes a particular cost on acquirers in the United States, because there the target board of directors can take defensive measures much more freely than in Europe. As potential acquirers have to reveal their strategies within ten days of reaching the initial threshold, target boards get an advance warning and can take defensive measures at an early stage, instead of letting the shareholders decide the fate of the CfD acquirer. This can lead to both a waste of the target company's resources in defence of a beneficial takeover and a decrease in the number of value-enhancing takeovers in general.[261] However, it is important to note that these costs do not normally arise in the context of an EU takeover due to the principle of no frustration under the Takeover Directive.[262]

In spite of the foregoing, the hindrances imposed by disclosure regulation on market activity should not be exaggerated. The new EU disclosure obligation for

[257] Cf. Daniel Bertaccini, 'To Disclose or Not to Disclose? *CSX CORP.*, Total Return Swaps, and Their Implications for Schedule 13D Filing Purposes' (2009) 31 Cardozo Law Review 267, 289.

[258] Jonathan R Macey and Jeffry M Netter, 'Regulation 13D and the Regulatory Process' (1987) 65 Washington University Law Quarterly 131, 142–5.

[259] FSA, CP 07/20 (n. 146) Annex 2, 3, see also Macey and Netter (n. 258) 144–5; Bertaccini (n. 257) 289, especially n. 131.

[260] Brief of Amici Curiae by International Swaps and Derivatives Association, Inc. and Securities Industry and Financial Markets Association in the matter CSX Corp. v. The Children's Inv. Fund Mgmt., LLP, et al., 08-Civ. 2764 (2 June 2008) 17, available at <http://www.sifma.org/WorkArea/DownloadAsset.aspx?id=1708> accessed 15 April 2015; Brief of Amicus Curiae by the SEC (n. 221) 4; concerning the US discussion, see Brian T Sullivan, 'CSX Corp. v. Children's Investment Fund Management and the Need for SEC Expansion of Beneficial Ownership' (2009) 87 North Carolina Law Review 1300.

[261] Macey and Netter (n. 258) 150–3.

[262] Takeover Directive 2004/25/EC, art. 9, which is, however, optional in this part for the Member States.

CfDs, like the traditional shareholdings disclosure, does not concern most investors, as only a marginal part of all CfD positions exceeds the notification thresholds.[263] Furthermore, Judge Kaplan, in *CSX v TCI*, replied to the above-mentioned concerns with reference to the UK disclosure regulation by noting that 'there is no reason to believe that the sky has fallen, or is likely to fall, in London'.[264] Nevertheless, the question here is not whether the market will cope under strict regulation or not—as Judge Kaplan insightfully observes, the market will cope—but whether the burdens of the current regulation are justified. The present investigation argues that the burdens of the revised EU disclosure system are *not* justified.[265] It is therefore inappropriate to argue, as the EU Commission does, that we should take comfort from the British experience, where it 'has not witnessed a dramatic increase in announcements and the market has adapted efficiently to the additional obligations placed on them'.[266]

Finally, when assessing the costs of additional disclosure requirements, any additional onus may have a chilling effect on various forms of shareholder activism. In particular, given that institutional investors quite frequently interact with management of their portfolio companies, one might anticipate that the proposal made here might deter such dialogue, to the potential detriment of the monitoring role played by institutional investors.

c) *The FSA safe harbour alternative*

During the drafting and consultation process of the UK CfD disclosure rules, the former FSA prepared two alternatives: a 'full disclosure' regulation and a more nuanced 'safe harbour' regime. In the early consultation stage, the FSA itself was inclined to adopt the safe harbour alternative, but it eventually opted for the current regime that requires full disclosure.[267] When the European Commission initiated the revision of the Transparency Directive, it also discussed a 'safe harbour' rule as a possibility, but ultimately rejected it as unworkable.[268]

The alternative regulatory structure, which was not adopted in either case, focused on the *intentions* of the CfD investor. It required the disclosure of CfD positions when they were above the specified threshold, unless certain safe harbour conditions were applicable. These conditions were the following.[269] First, a CfD

[263] See also Tom Siebens and Melissa Gambol, 'Who's Hiding Behind the Hedges? Developments in the USA and UK May Limit the Use of Total Return Swaps to Conceal Equity Stakes in Public Companies' (2009) 4 Capital Markets Law Journal 172, 177.

[264] *CSX Corporation v the Children's Investment Fund Management (UK) LLP*, 562 F Supp 2d 511 (SDNY 2008), 12 June 2008, 08 CV 02764, 63.

[265] Cf. Bertaccini (n. 257) 289.

[266] European Commission, *Commission Staff Working Paper—Impact Assessment accompanying the document proposal for a Directive of the European Parliament and of the Council amending Directive 2004/109/EC on the harmonisation of transparency requirements in relation to information about issuers whose securities are admitted to trading on a regulated market*, SEC(2011) 1279 final (25 October 2011) 66, quoting the FSA.

[267] FSA, CP 07/20 (n. 146) 60, 65; and FSA, CP 08/17 (n. 174) 5.

[268] European Commission, *Impact Assessment* (n. 266) 69.

[269] ibid.

agreement needed to prevent a CfD holder from exerting influence over the short party's hedge shares. Second, the CfD agreement had to exclude arrangements or understandings related to the potential sale of the hedge shares after the instruments are unwound.[270] Third, the CfD holder needed to give a written declaration to the CfD writer, that is, the short party, saying that it did not have any intention to acquire or obtain access to the hedge shares. This intention was required to be genuine and to remain accurate during the term of the CfD agreement. If the intention changed, the safe harbour would have ceased to be available, thus triggering the disclosure obligation. In addition, the target company would under certain conditions have the right to request information from particularly suspicious investors.[271]

This alternative disclosure regime resembles the passive investor exemption in the United States, discussed previously in section V.E.1. This passive investor exemption from the full disclosure requirement can be granted to investors when they invest without the purpose or the effect of changing or influencing the control of the target company.[272] Investment firms, as defined by the SEC, are more or less fully exempted, as they only have to file a short-form statement on an annual basis concerning their positions if their holdings do not reach the 10 per cent threshold. Other passive investors, however, are still required to make disclosure within ten days of the acquisition, but can use the same shorter form provided that their positions do not reach 20 per cent.

The passive investor exemption reduces the substantive disclosure requirements. For example, information on the source and amount of consideration for the acquisition, the purpose of the transaction, and, in the case of multiple parties, the description of the agreements concerning the holdings, does not have to be disclosed.[273]

The requirements under the US passive investor exemption broadly correspond to the general disclosure requirements in the EU, though they are not triggered by a purely financial investment. Instead, the relevant criterion is direct or beneficial share ownership, and disclosure by groups of passive investment firms is required only on an annual basis.[274] Furthermore, a formal comparison between the two regimes may not necessarily be appropriate, as the US exemption is closer to the EU regulation than to the general US rules. Nevertheless, it underlines the fact that US law treats passive investment positions more leniently than potentially control-related positions.

Similarly to the FSA safe harbour proposal, the US passive investor exemption requires the investors to make use of a short-form disclosure to

> certify that, to the best of [their] knowledge and belief, the securities [in question] were not acquired and are not held for the purpose of or with the effect of changing or influencing

[270] FSA, CP 07/20 (n. 146) 49–50. [271] FSA, CP 07/20 (n. 146) 49–50.
[272] Rule 13d-1(b) and (c). [273] See Rule 13d-101 and Rule 13d-102.
[274] DTR 5.8.2; Rule 13d-3.

the control of the issuer of the securities and were not acquired and are not held in connection with or as a participant in any transaction having that purpose or effect.[275]

However, importantly, the FSA safe harbour would not have provided, and the US passive investor regulation does not provide, the relevant investors[276] with a full exemption from disclosure obligations.

The FSA/EU safe harbour alternative was initially favoured due to its targeted and cost-effective approach to the identified concerns.[277] Yet, this regulatory structure was rejected because the FSA and the European Commission were concerned that it still would allow hidden stake-building, that it was too complex, and that it would have been too difficult to enforce.[278] These problems will be discussed in more detail in Chapter VI.G. The following discussion will, instead, focus on whether a person's intention can be used to trigger a disclosure obligation.

The present study takes the view that the potential of CfD abuse is not to be seen in the CfDs themselves. CfDs are not harmful instruments as they do not carry the voting rights needed for exercising control, and holdings in CfDs are therefore not an indication of abusive behaviour. CfDs should primarily be viewed as economic investment instruments and, as such, CfD holdings resemble share positions held by investment firms for purely economic purposes. These positions are granted an exemption from disclosure obligation under US law. Moreover, the origin of the few, but notable, problems caused by CfDs is in the market-driven hedging structure. Therefore, the link between CfDs and hedge shares—not the pure existence of a CfD position—should be in focus of the disclosure regulation. Plainly, the rejected safe harbour alternative would have achieved exactly that, that is, it would have exposed only control-related CfD trades to the market.

It is worth noting that there is nothing wrong with using CfDs in obtaining corporate control *if* this intention is disclosed.[279] An intention-based regulation would have allowed CfD holders to use these instruments for gaining control, but it would have also held them responsible for their intentions. Most CfD holders would have happily adjusted their deal documentation to comply with the safe harbour requirements, an assumption also voiced by the FSA. The safe harbour alternative would only have exposed the potentially dangerous investors to the market. It is worth noting that this rationale of revealing control-related intentions was not criticized in itself during the FSA consultation process. Instead, the respondents' criticisms were directed to enforcement difficulties as well as to problems with distinguishing genuine changes in investors' intentions from dishonest ones.[280]

[275] Rule 13d-102; the cited certification concerns Rule 13d-1(c) situations whereas the language slightly differs for Rule 13d-1(b) situations.

[276] The broadest exemption concerning passive investment firms still requires disclosure on annual basis. Furthermore, positions held by other entities which do not aim at influencing the control of the target company still need to be disclosed in real time, within the US scope of ten days. Also, the information to be disclosed by both groups under the exemption corresponds broadly to the UK disclosure requirements.

[277] FSA, CP 07/20 (n. 146) 60.

[278] FSA, CP 08/17 (n. 174) 13.

[279] FSA, CP 07/20 (n. 146) 50, 65 (emphasis added).

[280] FSA, CP 08/17 (n. 174) 13.

Intention-based regulation is not a novelty either in EU law in general or in capital markets law in particular. A number of examples from adjacent fields bear witness to this. Closest to the topic of this study, a number of EU Member States, for example Germany, require the disclosure of intentions where the holder of a significant block of shares crosses a specified threshold in a publicly traded company.[281] In a different context, client-serving intermediaries are exempt from the obligation to disclose holdings in financial instruments when they can, inter alia, certify to the market supervisor that they are not using the held instruments for intervening in, or exerting influence on, the target management.[282] The US Hart–Scott–Rodino Act of 1976 requires notification of share blocks only when they are held with an 'active' purpose: this de facto also requires the purchaser to self-assess its intentions, and only passive acquisitions are exempt from the notification requirement.[283] Furthermore, the UK Takeover Panel recently clarified its interpretation on the mandatory bid rule in connection with shareholder activism. According to the Panel's statement, the triggering of the bid obligation would, as a prerequisite, require that activist shareholders were inviting 'a general meeting to consider a "board control-seeking" resolution'.[284] In addition, competition law employs an intention-based regulatory technique as it allows private parties to assess whether their undertakings fall under the block exemption provisions in TFEU article 101(3) and Regulation 1/2003.[285] The same approach is applied by the 'Chapter I' cartel prohibition under the UK Competition Act 1998.[286] Interestingly, the early legislative history of US disclosure regulation under the Williams Act includes a proposal of an intentions-based exception for the disclosure

[281] WpHG § 27a, according to which

> Any party subject to the notification requirement within the meaning of sections 21 and 22 whose shareholding reaches or exceeds the threshold of 10 percent, or a higher threshold, of voting rights attached to shares must, within 20 trading days after reaching or exceeding the threshold, inform the issuer [...] of the aims underlying the purchase of the voting rights [...]. [More specifically,] the party subject to the notification requirement shall notify whether
> 1. the investment is aimed at implementing strategic objectives or at generating a trading profit;
> 2. it plans to acquire further voting rights within the next twelve months by means of a purchase or by any other means;
> 3. it intends to exert an influence on the appointment or removal of members of the issuer's administrative, managing and supervisory bodies and
> 4. it intends to achieve a material change in the company's capital structure, in particular as regards the ratio between own funds and external funds and the dividend policy
>
> (unofficial translation by BaFin).

[282] DTR 5.3.1(3)(c).

[283] For a recent controversy concerning Third Point's acquisition of Yahoo shares, see Federal Trade Commission, *Statement of the Federal Trade Commission In the Matter of Third Point*, File No. 121-0019, 24 August 2015, available at <https://www.ftc.gov/system/files/documents/public_statements/777341/150824thirdpointcommstmt.pdf>.

[284] The Takeover Panel, *Practice Statement No. 26: Shareholder Activism* (9 September 2009) 1, available at <http://www.thetakeoverpanel.org.uk/wp-content/uploads/2008/11/PS26.pdf> accessed 19 August 2015.

[285] See Richard Whish, *Competition Law* (6th edn, Oxford University Press 2009) 162; Valentine Korah, *An Introductory Guide to EC Competition Law and Practice* (9th edn, Hart, Oxford 2007) 95.

[286] Competition Act 1998 s. 9; Whish (n. 285) 350 ff.

requirements based on the SEC's discretion in cases where the acquisition was made purely for investment reasons.[287]

3. CfDs and the market for corporate control

Ultimately, then, the sole justification pattern for a disclosure requirement can emerge from a takeover context.

This line of argumentation is based on the following four points.

1. Unsolicited takeovers are an important building block of (external) corporate governance of listed companies. The pressure of the capital market and the permanent threat of a hostile takeover (which is usually followed by replacement of the management) are regarded by traditional scholarship as an effective way to discipline the management and to encourage behaviour that maximizes firm value and that is beneficial for the stock price.[288]
2. The acquisition of economic interest in a listed company without corresponding voting rights may represent an attempt to circumvent reporting requirements and in this way perform a surprising takeover attempt. Inter alia, this may entail bypassing legitimate protection concerns of minority shareholders, avoiding price increases, and undermining exit opportunities.[289]
3. On the other hand, a mandatory disclosure requirement for contracts for difference and similar instruments will have a chilling effect on corporate takeovers altogether by making them more expensive. In the absence of a disclosure rule, a potential bidder can acquire a toehold of shares on a large scale, unnoticed by the capital market, that is, avoiding the usual price increase. In so doing, the bidder could avoid paying at least parts of the normally payable takeover premium. In addition, an earlier disclosure requirement at the same time allows the administration an earlier initiation of defensive measures (where they are allowed), which in turn makes the entire takeover plan more cumbersome or can thwart it altogether.[290]
4. Finally, the issue boils down to a problem of *distribution*: Who should be entitled to the takeover premium?[291] Should the bidder be rewarded for their pre-bid efforts—by being granted the possibility of getting a 'foot in the door' at a cheap price, and exempting such situations from disclosure? Or are the interests of the other shareholders (and the management) more

[287] See Macey and Netter (n. 258) 134.

[288] See the seminal work by Henry G Manne, 'Mergers and the Market for Corporate Control' (1965) 73 Journal of Political Economy 110; Frank H Easterbrook and Daniel R Fischel, *The Economic Structure of Corporate Law* (Harvard University Press 1991) 112 ff.

[289] European Securities Markets Expert Group (ESME), *Views on the Issue of Transparency of Holdings of Cash Settled Derivatives* (November 2009) 7, available at <http://ec.europa.eu/internal_market/securities/docs/esme/tdcash_en.pdf>

[290] Macey and Netter (n. 258) 144.

[291] ESME (n. 289) 7: 'avoidance of the launch of a mandatory bid at an equitable price; no take over premium and no real exit for minority shareholders.'

> important, so that they should be informed about the entry of a new major shareholder—which would usually lead to an immediate increase in the share price and would effectively assign an extended takeover premium to the minority shareholders?

To a large extent, the answer will depend on which legal policy side you take concerning the role of corporate takeovers, in general. Those who believe in unsolicited takeovers' disciplining effect should endeavour to facilitate them, and therefore not support the call for extensive disclosure requirements. By contrast, those who are sceptical as to their value-enhancing role should make use of every possibility to drive up their costs, by mandating early disclosure, even of economic-only positions.

The continental European legal culture has traditionally always had more followers in the latter camp. Persistent doubts over the board neutrality rule and the permissibility of defensive measures are symptomatic. European law-makers found no majority for these requirements, and so the decisive parts of the Takeover Directive famously remain optional for the Member States.[292] The majority view in the United Kingdom is quite the opposite—the UK Takeover Code is one of the most takeover-friendly systems in the world, and it was, and is, shaped by the market power of British institutional investors.

Whichever view you take on these questions, and whichever legal policy positions you have concerning hostile takeovers, the present analysis shows that the question of a disclosure requirement for contracts for difference is part of the context of takeovers, and should therefore be discussed here. We will return to the specific details in Chapter VI, which is devoted to discussion of the concrete regulatory responses.[293]

[292] See Paul L Davies and Klaus J Hopt, 'Control Transactions' in Reinier H Kraakman and others (eds), *The Anatomy of Corporate Law: A Comparative and Functional Approach* (2nd edn, Oxford University Press 2009) ch. 8.

[293] See Chapter VI.G.

VI

Solutions

Law-makers and regulators have been looking for solutions ever since risk-decoupling strategies became known to the wider public and generally increased in significance. In 2007, then Securities and Exchange Commission (SEC) chairman Christopher Cox indicated that the various risk-decoupling strategies are 'almost certainly going to force further regulatory response to ensure that investors' interests are protected. This is already a serious issue and it is showing all signs of growing.'[1]

A number of jurisdictions, including the European Union, have addressed the issue of positive risk-decoupling by mandating the disclosure of risk exposure similar to long positions in shares by revising the EU Transparency Directive.[2] By contrast, negative risk-decoupling has not been comprehensively regulated to date. Some jurisdictions took initial steps, but did not follow up with a comprehensive solution. For example, the SEC conducted a public consultation on negative decoupling in 2010 in order to anticipate eventual regulation.[3] Likewise, the new European market authority, the European Securities and Markets Authority (ESMA), launched a consultation that assesses the case for regulatory intervention.[4] Since then, the European Commission has considered the issue in various discussion papers.[5] Since the *Telus* case unsettled the Canadian stock market, regulators there have also been assessing the case for regulation.[6]

[1] Kara Scannell, 'How Borrowed Shares Swing Company Votes—SEC and Others Fear Hedge-Fund Strategy May Subvert Elections' *Wall Street Journal* (26 January 2007) A1.

[2] See text accompanying Chapter V n. 187.

[3] Securities and Exchange Commission, 'Concept Release on the U.S. Proxy System (Release Nos 34-62495, IA-3052, IC-29340; File No S7-14-10, 2010)' (2010) 75 Federal Register 42981, 43019.

[4] European Securities and Markets Authority (ESMA), *Call for Evidence—Empty Voting* (ESMA/2011/288, 14 September 2011), available at <http://www.esma.europa.eu/system/files/2011_288.pdf>; ESMA, *Feedback Statement: Call for Evidence on Empty Voting* (ESMA/2012/415, 29 June 2012), available at <http://www.esma.europa.eu/system/files/2012-415.pdf> accessed 15 August 2015.

[5] European Commission, *Proposal for a Directive of the European Parliament and of the Council Amending Directive 2004/109/EC on the Harmonisation of Transparency Requirements in Relation to Information about Issuers Whose Securities Are Admitted to Trading on a Regulated Market and Commission Directive 2007/14/EC* COM(2011) 683; as well as the accompanying impact assessment: European Commission, *Commission Staff Working Paper: Impact Assessment* SEC(2011) 1279 final 19 f., 124 f.; European Commission, *Green Paper: Corporate Governance in Financial Institutions and Remuneration Policies* (2010) COM(2010) 284, question 5.3; European Commission, *Feedback Statement: Summary Of Responses to Commission Green Paper on Corporate Governance in Financial Institutions* (2010) 17 f.

[6] Jay Hoffman and Melissa Ghislanzoni, 'Empty Voting—Waiting for a Regulatory Response' *Miller Thomson Securities Practice Note* (2012), available at <http://www.millerthomson.com/en/

For several years, regulators in various jurisdictions have attempted to find answers to the multifaceted problems and conflicts. The following analysis does not discuss these attempts directly, but rather proceeds to examine the problem from the vantage point of each particular regulatory technique. All possible regulatory models are structured, assessed, and compared. They will be seen in the specific legal context of the European Union. The goal is to ultimately develop the most desirable regulatory response for EU institutions.

The lion's share of the discussion is devoted to negative decoupling, as this is the most uncertain and controversial part of the picture. While several strategies discussed in practice are rejected, I will demonstrate that, in particular, a transparency regime (section VI.C) and—under certain conditions—a disenfranchisement of the risk-decoupler (section VI.D) are promising solutions. An additional element could be fiduciary duties of shareholders or other flexible corporate remedies (section VI.E). In this context, I will develop a concrete legislative proposal for dealing with negative decoupling, designing an integrated disclosure regime (section VI.C.6).

Positive decoupling is largely discussed in the context of disclosure regulation—and most jurisdictions have adopted such requirements. Section VI.G develops an alternative, intentions-based disclosure paradigm.

The final question to address is whether regulation for both scenarios should take place on the EU or on the national level. This will be the subject of Chapter VII.

A. Doing Nothing

Any discussion of regulatory intervention begins with the option of doing nothing. It has become the standard in modern legislative 'impact assessments' to discuss policy considerations in the context of 'no action', or 'to do nothing'.[7] Considering this option is a helpful exercise, as it allows the regulator to assess what happens if no regulatory action is taken, and prevents policy-makers from directly jumping into the various interventionist approaches without reflecting on whether the problem is actually in need of any regulatory intervention in the first place. This forces regulators to justify their final choices.

The option of 'doing nothing' brings up a number of issues. First, we have to consider what 'no action' would mean for the market of voting rights (section VI.A.1). Subsequently, this will lead us to assess the possibility of private ordering by self-regulation of market participants (sections VI.A.2, 3, and 4). Finally, we will examine whether the current regulatory framework already provides sufficient legal tools that can tackle the problem at hand (section VI.A.5).

publications/newsletters/securities-practice-notes/fall-2012/empty-voting-waiting-for-a-regulatory>. On the *Telus* case, see Chapter III.B.1.c and section VI.A.5.

[7] See for instance the famous impact assessment by the European Commission, 'Impact Assessment on the Directive on the Cross-Border Transfer of Registered Office' SEC(2007) 1707, para. 3.5.

1. Persisting decoupling of voting rights

In connection with the subject matter under consideration here, doing nothing would ultimately mean 'non-regulation' of the various risk-decoupling constellations. Consequently, shareholders and investors could, as before, freely dispose over voting rights and economic risk. A few radical commentators in the literature seem to be pointing in that direction. For example, the eminent American academic Henry G Manne argued over fifty years ago that the free exchange of voting rights would benefit shareholders in much the same way as the exchange of goods brings welfare gains to other areas of the economy.[8] In a similar vein, Robert Clark advocated in 1979 that the free trade of votes in a company should be permitted.[9] According to Clark, the advantage of such an approach lies in its possibility to overcome the free-rider problem—an unrestricted accumulation of voting rights would allow shareholders to gain greater influence in the company and to exert stronger influence over management. Diversified, passive retail investors who are not interested in exercising control over management could thus forgo their voting rights and clear the way for others. In this way, the apathy problem resulting from dispersed shareholder ownership could be overcome.[10]

Even more extreme is a recent suggestion from economics scholars to separate voting right and dividend entitlement completely.[11] According to this view, some shares should carry a voting entitlement, some should carry dividend rights, and some both; and investors should be free to choose between them. This is in substance nothing else than an abolition of the traditional rule that risk and voting right should be bundled in the share.

In the United Kingdom, former City Minister Lord Paul Myners made policy recommendations in favour of readjusting the relationship between voting rights and share ownership.[12] In a number of reports, Lord Myners emphasized the need for a differentiated weighting of shares in order to encourage institutional investors to take up their ownership role more seriously.[13] He argued that additional voting rights for long-term shareholders could create a more sustainable investment culture and that this would have remedied the perceived short-term orientation of investors during the global financial crisis. Lord Myners stigmatized the

[8] Henry G Manne, 'Some Theoretical Aspects of Share Voting. An Essay in Honor of Adolf A. Berle' (1964) 64 Columbia Law Review 1427, 1428.

[9] Robert Charles Clark, 'Vote Buying and Corporate Law' (1979) 29 Case Western Reserve Law Review 776.

[10] ibid. 793.

[11] Dan Palmon and Fred Sudit, 'Empowering Democracy in Corporate Governance by Unbundling Shareholders' Voting Rights from Their Return on Investment Rights' (2008) 5 International Journal of Disclosure and Governance 93; see also Dan Palmon and Ephraim F Sudit, 'Shareholders Groups, Unbundled Rights, and Corporate Democracy: A Commentary' (2011) 20 Group Decision and Negotiation 133; Kin-Wai Lee, 'Corporate Voluntary Disclosure and the Separation of Cash Flow Rights from Control Rights' (2007) 28 Review of Quantitative Finance and Accounting 393.

[12] At the time, the 'City Minister' was a Financial Services Secretary to the Treasury, thus a UK government official responsible for the City of London.

[13] 'Leading Questions: Interview of Lord Paul Myners', BBC television broadcast (1 August 2009).

current situation with the notion of the 'ownerless corporation'.[14] This suggestion initiated a lively debate over the desirability of such differentiated voting rights. A few commentators gave positive responses,[15] but the dominant view (particularly among institutional investors) expressed scepticism and outright rejection of the proposals.[16] Lord Myners later went on to suggest an even more radical proposal by recommending that shareholders be given the ability to buy and sell their voting rights independently from their shareholding—namely, a complete separation of ownership and voting rights.[17] According to this proposal, shareholders who never vote could sell their voting rights to others who do want to vote. Again, reactions to this suggestion were largely negative.[18] Finally, Lord Myners proposed introducing the option of new non-voting shares to existing shareholders, allowing them to subsequently concentrate their engagement with the company on either a voting or non-voting position, thus fostering their identification with the company.[19] It has to be noted that Myners' remarks were delivered at the height of the global financial crisis and in the context of a growing fear that liberal takeover laws could put British firms at an increased risk of falling into foreign hands. This fear is exemplified by Kraft's takeover of the British company Cadbury.[20] Lord Myners insisted that these fears were not merely xenophobic,[21] but it is well known that an effect of the crisis was the drifting of an overwhelmingly large number of Western economies towards protectionist tendencies.[22] Ultimately, the proposals did not result in legislation in the United Kingdom.

These discussions from academia and politics led, to varying degrees, to a liberalization of the relationship between share ownership and voting rights. The aforementioned reflections cannot simply be criticized as merely too 'market-believing', but it is obvious that they rely on two basic and implicit assumptions: first, they seem to assume that market forces are strong enough to form adequate prices for both full shares and mere voting rights. Second, it is assumed that the decoupling of shares and voting rights does not create other distorting effects. Already the first of these two assumptions, however, is not free from

[14] Jane Croft and Kate Burgess, 'Myners' Two-Tier Shares Plan under Fire' *Financial Times* (3 August 2009) 1.

[15] William A Allen, 'Disproportionate Voting Rights May Be the Way to Better Governance' *Financial Times* (4 August 2009) 8.

[16] Kate Burgess, 'Investors Wary of Myners' Idea on Voting Rights' *Financial Times* (4 August 2009) 16; Jonathan Russell, 'ABI Leads Attack on Myners Over Shareholder Reform' *Sunday Telegraph* (1 August 2009) 1.

[17] William Hutchings, 'Myners Proposes Sale of Voting Rights' *Financial News* (10 August 2009), available at <http://www.efinancialnews.com/story/2009-08-10/myners-proposes-sale-of-voting-rights> accessed 14 April 2015.

[18] Sam Jones, 'Big Investors Cool on Myners' Idea of Trade in Voting Rights' *Financial Times* (11 August 2009) 1.

[19] Tony Tassell, 'Myners Eyes New Non-Voting Shares' *Financial Times* (14 August 2009) 16.

[20] Jill Treanor, 'Too Many UK Firms Fall into Foreign Hands, Says Crusading Myners' *The Guardian* (24 September 2009) 31.

[21] ibid.

[22] Ulf Bernitz and Wolf-Georg Ringe (eds), *Company Law and Economic Protectionism: New Challenges to European Integration* (Oxford University Press 2010).

doubt. To be sure, the example of preference shares illustrates how the market price can adequately reflect the different voting entitlements of classes of shares.[23] However, the example of the extremely low borrowing fee[24] for shares in the context of securities lending over the record date, as previously discussed, casts doubt over the market's ability to reflect the value of voting rights in all situations.[25] There are good reasons to believe that lenders are faced with a free-rider problem, as they rely on remaining shareholders to vote, and thus entrust their own shares to the borrower at a fee that is too low.[26]

Additional questions arise when the perspective shifts from the pricing process of voting rights to the consequences felt by other market participants. Even if the pricing process works properly and produces efficient outcomes between the two parties, it imposes costs on third parties such as other shareholders and investors. All the points that were already raised in the context of the agency cost discussion become relevant here again: third parties without their own economic concern would be in a position to make decisions with implications for the financial situation of other shareholders, and potential investors could not be sure that strategic decisions would be made by actors seeking to promote the economic success of the company.[27] Vote trading may thus possibly produce an efficient exchange in bilateral relations (whereas even this is doubtful[28]). However, this would overlook the consequences for third parties.

In sum, a permanent separation between voting right and company share is to be rejected. Market failure and negative externalities to the detriment of shareholders and investors justify a general bundling rule by legal rules.

2. Self-regulation

A liberal market solution may have other advantages, however. The Coase theorem teaches us that market participants will enter into their own bargaining process and produce separate solutions based on private ordering.[29] Can we expect such a solution to also occur in the context of risk-decoupling?

A few examples may lead to optimism.[30] Consider the situation in the United States, where the business world has been waiting for a long time for the SEC to act in response to risk-decoupling strategies. In the meantime, companies themselves

[23] For more detail on preference shares, see Louise Gullifer and Jennifer Payne, *Corporate Finance Law Principles and Policy* (Hart Publishing, Oxford 2011) 59 ff.

[24] Susan E K Christoffersen and others, 'Vote Trading and Information Aggregation' (2007) 62 Journal of Finance 2897, 2912.

[25] For a similar discussion, see David Yermack, 'Shareholder Voting and Corporate Governance' (2010) 2 Annual Review of Financial Economics 103, 113.

[26] Gregor Bachmann, 'Rechtsfragen der Wertpapierleihe' (2009) 173 Zeitschrift für das gesamte Handelsrecht und Wirtschaftsrecht (ZHR) 596, 613.

[27] See Chapter V.B.1.b.

[28] See the specific interest situation for securities lending, Chapter III.B.2.b.

[29] See Ronald H Coase, *The Firm, the Market, and the Law* (University of Chicago Press 1990); Ronald H Coase, 'The Problem of Social Cost' (1960) 3 Journal of Law and Economics 1.

[30] See the note by Michael Lee, 'Empty Voting: Private Solutions to a Private Problem' [2007] Columbia Business Law Review 883.

have begun to impose disclosure obligations in their own bylaws in order to force publicity of decoupled shareholders.[31] Further, US corporate practice has frequently modified shareholder rights plans (the so-called 'poison pills', which are crucial to fend off hostile takeovers).[32] On the former, for example, Delaware-incorporated Pfizer, Inc. amended its bylaws in 2008 so that each shareholder who initiates a shareholder resolution or an election of directors is obliged to make specific disclosures about their risk exposure.[33] The amended, decisive part of the bylaws now reads as follows:

A Proponent's notice to the Secretary shall set forth as to each matter the Proponent proposes to bring before the annual meeting:

...

(f) a description of any agreement, arrangement or understanding (including any derivative or short positions, profit interests, options, hedging transactions, and borrowed or loaned shares) that has been entered into as of the date of the Proponent's notice by, or on behalf of, the Proponent or any of its affiliates or associates, the effect or intent of which is to mitigate loss to, manage risk or benefit of share price changes for, or increase or decrease the voting power of the Proponent or any of its affiliates or associates with respect to shares of stock of the Corporation, and a representation that the Proponent will notify the Corporation in writing of any such agreement, arrangement or understanding in effect as of the record date for the meeting promptly following the later of the record date or the date notice of the record date is first publicly disclosed.[34]

Sara Lee Corporation, an American consumer goods manufacturer, similarly changed its bylaws to the following:[35]

Section 10(3)

Any stockholder's notice [for proposals to the general meeting] shall set forth...(iii) as to the stockholder giving the notice, any Proposed Nominee and any Stockholder Associated Person,

...

(C) whether and the extent to which such stockholder, Proposed Nominee or Stockholder Associated Person, directly or indirectly (through brokers, nominees or otherwise), is subject to or during the last six months has engaged in any hedging, derivative or other

[31] Phred Dvorak, 'Companies Alter Bylaws To Pry Data Out of Activists—Pfizer and Others Seek Better Understanding Of Investors' Motives' *Wall Street Journal* (14 July 2008) B4.

[32] Such poison pills that defend against positive risk-decoupling are generally understood to be valid in Delaware. See Henry T C Hu, 'Financial Innovation and Governance Mechanisms: The Evolution of Decoupling and Transparency' (2015) 70 The Business Lawyer 347, 365, who refers to *In re Atmel Corporation Shareholders Litigation* (Del. Ch. May 22, 2009).

[33] See also the suggestions by Lee (n. 30) 907.

[34] Pfizer, Inc., *By-laws as Amended June 25, 2008* (Form 8-K) (26 June 2008), available at <http://www.sec.gov/Archives/edgar/data/78003/000007800308000142/pf8k0625.htm>. In 2010, the provision was slightly modified. For the current version, see Pfizer, Inc., *By-laws as Amended December 16, 2013*, available at <http://www.pfizer.com/files/investors/corporate_governance/bylaws.pdf>.

[35] See Matt Andrejczak, 'Sara Lee, Coach Set Rules to Spot Shareholder Actions' *MarketWatch* (2 April 2008) <http://www.marketwatch.com/story/sara-lee-coach-set-rules-to-deter-devious-shareholders> accessed 16 April 2015.

transaction or series of transactions or entered into any other agreement, arrangement or understanding (including any short interest, any borrowing or lending of securities or any proxy or voting agreement), the effect or intent of which is to

...

(x) manage risk or benefit of changes in the price of Company Securities for such stockholder, Proposed Nominee or Stockholder Associated Person, or

(y) increase or decrease the voting power of such stockholder, Proposed Nominee or Stockholder Associated Person in the Corporation disproportionately to such person's economic interest in the Company Securities.[36]

In the meantime, other American corporations have introduced proposals to amend their bylaws.[37] Just like the two passages cited here, the proposals would impose a comprehensive disclosure duty for every contractual arrangement, or even a tacit agreement, that decouples or intends to decouple voting right and economic risk. The disclosure duty applies only in a very specific situation, however, and that is where the shareholder, on her own initiative, makes proposals for the agenda of the general meeting (this may be for the appointment of managers or any other resolution). These initiatives are rare in the US corporate context. This is first because difficult legal and financial hurdles exist, and second because the highly dispersed ownership means that it is very difficult to persuade other shareholders to vote and to support an initiative. Only rarely will the shareholder be engaged in a 'proxy fight', in which activist shareholders compete with management (or other shareholders) to secure a maximum of proxies from other investors with the aim of reaching a majority for a specific resolution.[38] All in all, the proposed amendments to bylaws of US corporations will apply only in very limited circumstances, and are therefore of minor importance.

3. Self-regulation of the hedge fund industry

An alternative strategy of self-regulation might offer a more promising solution.[39] The hedge fund industry in its entirety will not be interested in a development where singular events of risk-decoupling are associated with the entire business sector. For this reason, the Hedge Fund Working Group, an association of the hedge fund industry, conducted a consultation in 2007 which led to an instrument

[36] Sara Lee Corporation, *By-laws as Amended March 27, 2008* (Form 8-K) (28 March 2008), available at <http://www.sec.gov/Archives/edgar/data/23666/000129993308001659/htm_26377.htm>.

[37] See Alexia Robinson, 'Addressing the Issue of Derivatives Disclosure in Advance Notice Requirements' *Research Spotlight* (16 December 2008) <https://www.sharkrepellent.net/pub/rs_20081216.html> (providing a statistical overview).

[38] April Klein and Emanuel Zur, 'Entrepreneurial Shareholder Activism: Hedge Funds and Other Private Investors' (2009) 64 The Journal of Finance 187.

[39] Generally on self-regulation of hedge funds, see Marco Lamandini, 'Self-Regulation—What Future in the Context of Hedge Funds?' in Phoebus Athanassiou (ed.), *Research Handbook on Hedge Funds, Private Equity and Alternative Investments* (Edward Elgar 2012) 244; Andreas Engert, 'Transnational Hedge Fund Regulation' (2010) 11 European Business Organization Law Review 329, 345 ff.

of self-governance.[40] Aside from deliberate self-regulation, the threat of legal action may have played a role in initiating the document.[41] The resulting Code of Conduct, entitled 'HFSB Standards', was adopted by the Working Group in 2008, and is now administered by the Hedge Fund Standard Board.[42] It can be adopted by individual hedge funds on the basis of a 'comply or explain' approach.[43] The Code also takes on risk-decoupling and securities lending:

> A hedge fund manager should not borrow stock in order to vote. The HFSB acknowledges that there might be specific situations where it should be acceptable to vote on borrowed stock, e.g. when a fund is invested in shares (and the trade has settled), but the shares have not transferred into their name.[44]

As welcome as the Code may be, it is nonetheless unsatisfactory in many respects. In principle, it seems positive in that it generally discourages voting of borrowed shares, even though exceptions are available. However, several points are problematic. First, this code only covers one part of the entire risk-decoupling problem—that of securities lending. The Code seldom mentions the other aspects of the problem. Symptomatically, the parties could not agree on a common position for the problem of positive decoupling (hidden ownership).[45] Second, the Code of Conduct is only voluntary in character, and can be disregarded when a sufficient explanation is given.[46] And third, after its adoption, the hedge fund community became disappointed with its lack of success. Only thirty-four hedge funds (out of a potential 1,000 candidates) signed up for it.[47] Of these thirty-four hedge funds, fourteen had initially been responsible for the project. These numbers were noted at a hearing in the House of Commons, which has drawn considerable attention.[48] Overall, most parties agree that the Code is not a successful project.[49] This unsuccessful attempt at self-regulation by the hedge fund industry has ultimately paved the way for regulation of the industry through the infamous EU Directive on Alternative Investment Funds.[50] This Directive, however, does not contain a single provision on the entire subject matter of risk-decoupling.[51]

[40] Hedge Fund Working Group, 'Press Release—Hedge Fund Working Group Focuses on Valuation and Risk Management Standards' (22 January 2008), available at <http://www.hfsb.org/sites/10188/files/hfwg_press_release_22_jan_08.pdf>.

[41] See James Mackintosh, 'UK Draws Up Code for Hedge Funds' *Financial Times* (11 October 2007) 1.

[42] The current standards date from 2012. Hedge Fund Standards Board, 'The Hedge Fund Standards' (2012) <http://www.hfsb.org/sites/10377/files/hedge_fund_standards_-_as_at_february_2012.pdf>.

[43] ibid. para. 1.1. [44] ibid. para. 28. [45] See ibid. para. 27.

[46] On self-regulation in this context more generally, see Lamandini (n. 39).

[47] Kit Chellel, 'Slammed Hedge Funds Shun Code to Await Make-or-Break EU Directive' *The Lawyer* (26 October 2009) 13.

[48] See James Mackintosh, 'MPs Grill Fund Managers on Bank Shorting' *Financial Times* (28 January 2009) 2.

[49] See Chellel (n. 47).

[50] Directive 2011/61/EU of the European Parliament and of the Council of 8 June 2011 on Alternative Investment Fund Managers and amending Directives 2003/41/EC and 2009/65/EC and Regulations (EC) No 1060/2009 and (EU) No 1095/2010, [2011] OJ L174/1.

[51] See Chapter IV.B.

4. Self-help in securities lending cases

Specifically for the field of securities lending, legislative inactivity may lead to other, unwanted consequences. Where self-regulation attempts do not bear fruit, securities lenders will lose their confidence in the market altogether, and thus reconsider their lending business. Evidence supporting this development has already surfaced, and a number of lenders have started to appoint special supervisors to ensure that the securities they lend out are given to responsible business participants.[52] Others, in particular institutional lenders, are reported to have stopped their lending business altogether.[53]

Whether this trend is indeed affirmed may be doubted. The incentives for lenders appear too lucrative, and they stand too rationally apathetic towards an exercise of their voting rights.[54] Data provided by the National Association of Pension Funds (NAPF) shows that British pension funds' lending business remained relatively stable between 2006 and 2014, and has even increased recently. In 2014, only 15 per cent of surveyed pension funds stated that they would never lend any shares. In 2010, the figure had been 47 per cent. At the same time, the proportion of funds that never call back shares at a vote has increased significantly (2012: 12 per cent; 2014: 20 per cent; see Table VI.1).

Table VI.1 Securities lending activity by pension funds in the United Kingdom

	2006	2007	2008	2009	2010	2011	2012	2013	2014
Never lend stock	36%	41%	25%	44%	47%	21%	33%	33%	15%
Do carry out lending activity	64%	59%	75%	56%	53%	79%	67%	67%	85%
Recall stock for contentious resolutions only	*41%*	*36%*	*34%*	*29%*	*32%*	*38%*	*33%*	*38%*	*34%*
Recall stock for all resolutions	*3%*		*4%*	*9%*	*3%*	*3%*	*2%*	*6%*	*10%*
Never recall stock	*20%*	*23%*	*33%*	*18%*	*16%*	*28%*	*12%*	*15%*	*20%*
Don't know			*4%*		*3%*	*10%*	*19%*	*8%*	*22%*
Number of respondents	39	39	53	45	38	39	42	48	50

Source: NAPF Engagement Surveys: Pension funds' engagement with companies 2006–14; own calculations

52 Amanda Gerut, 'Emerging Practices in Securities Lending and Proxy Voting Nexus' *BoardIQ* (3 April 2007); see also Henry T C Hu and Bernard S Black, 'The New Vote Buying: Empty Voting and Hidden (Morphable) Ownership' (2006) 79 Southern California Law Review 811, 896 (quoting a statement by CalPers, the largest Californian pension fund).

53 Hu and Black, 'New Vote Buying' (n. 52) 897. See also Yvan Allaire and Mihaela E Firsirotu, 'Hedge Funds as Activist Shareholders: Passing Phenomenon or Grave-Diggers of Public Corporations?' 8 (Social Science Research Network 2007) SSRN Scholarly Paper ID 961828 <http://papers.ssrn.com/abstract=961828> accessed 16 April 2015. The reason for this development may, however, also have to do with higher compliance costs and stricter regulatory requirements, for example concerning short selling. See ESMA, *Final Report—ESMA's Technical Advice on the Evaluation of the Regulation (EU) 236/2012 of the European Parliament and of the Council on Short Selling and Certain Aspects of Credit Default Swaps*, ESMA/2013/614 (3 June 2013) 70 ff., available at <http://www.esma.europa.eu/system/files/2013-614_final_report_on_ssr_evaluation.pdf> accessed 19 August 2015.

54 See Chapter III.B.2.b.

5. Risk-decoupling in existing legal frameworks

As we have seen several times in this study, case law and legal practice are understandably trying to master many aspects and dimensions of the risk-decoupling phenomenon within the limits of the existing legal tools. This concerns in particular elements of corporate law and governance, but also securities law. These efforts are briefly summarized presently. We will see that, in some instances, the existing legal framework is helpful and can be usefully applied to risk-decoupling problems, but that serious shortcomings remain. Furthermore, it should be noted that the few 'successful' experiences with traditional categories of corporate law usually take effect only *ex post*, and thus do not adequately address the real concerns resulting from risk-decoupling.

Over the past years, the courts have sought to address and solve problems of risk-decoupling. Across legal systems, two different decision-making patterns have emerged from this experience.

Frequently, where the procedure or the decision to be taken predominantly relies on formal criteria or clear threshold values, etc., court decisions are often forced to leave the specifics of risk-decoupled company shares out of consideration. By contrast, in situations where the law provides for a discretionary balancing test, judicial discretion, or substantial control, we know of several decisions that show judicial decision practice that does consider atypical situations and risk distortions.

The best examples of this are the two main decisions that were handed down by the Canadian courts concerning the empty voting problem at Telus, the Canadian telecommunications provider.[55] As we briefly saw previously, the Court of Appeal for British Columbia ruled on the validity of a request by Mason, the alleged risk-decoupled shareholder, to convene a shareholder meeting.[56] In essence, the Court upheld the request. Crucially, the court critically discussed empty voting and Mason's strategy. Nevertheless, the court concluded that it was not in a position to take into account the risk exposure for purposes of assessing whether Mason was allowed to call a meeting. Instead, the court ultimately called for regulatory action to address the issue.[57]

Two months later, the Supreme Court of British Columbia, in a separate proceeding, approved a restructuring plan as proposed by Telus. This involved a different question. Here, a substantive 'fairness test' required an assessment of whether the proposed conversion would be fair for all shareholders including Mason. The discretionary decision allowed the Court to take into account Mason's risk exposure as a relevant factor, and it consequently ruled that the 'empty voting' situation was indeed one of the factors that had to be taken into account in assessing the *fairness* of the arrangement.[58]

We thus see two diverging outcomes: the risk-decoupling situation was not considered relevant in the first case, but had an impact on the decision in the

[55] See on the background of this case Chapter III.B.1.c.
[56] *TELUS Corporation v Mason Capital Management LLC* [2012] BCCA 403.
[57] ibid. para. 81. [58] *In re TELUS Corporation* [2012] BCSC 1919 para. 366.

second. Both decisions are nevertheless not necessarily in conflict, but give a symptomatic picture of judicial practice's difficulties in handling such constellations in an appropriate way. The Court of Appeal had to apply the law with respect to assessing a required threshold for convening a meeting. It ruled in favour of legal certainty: as the statute only refers to the number of voting rights held by the applicants, the Court felt that it was not in a position to disregard this by looking at any economic incentives behind the voting rights. Furthermore, the empty voting problem is less salient in situations such as this one, where a procedural entitlement (without immediate substantive consequences) was at stake. The ability to call a meeting does not yet, in itself, lead to the implementation of the proposals made. By contrast, the Supreme Court decision concerned a substantive test of court control, involving fairness of a proposed plan of arrangement. In such a discretionary test, the competing interests are to be balanced, and the fact that one party was (irregularly) lacking economic exposure has rightly been considered as part of this test.[59]

The German *Lindner* case, as discussed previously, also belongs to the first category. Again, this case was about the formal question of whether the applicant indeed satisfied the threshold of 95 per cent required under German law for pushing through a squeeze-out of the remaining minority shareholders.[60] The problem was that a substantial part of the shares formally held was only temporarily owned by the applicant, due to a securities lending transaction.[61] Again, the German Supreme Court ruled that to assess the 95 per cent threshold, the only thing to be considered was the formal ownership of shares; the law would not allow for any consideration of the motives or risk profile behind the share ownership that could be included within the legal assessment. Thus, the squeeze-out application was held to be valid and successful.

Finally, we should mention the *Deephaven* case, briefly discussed previously, which was decided in Delaware a few years ago.[62] Again, this was about a risk-depleted shareholder's formal legal capacity to rely on certain corporate information rights. Fully in line with the cases discussed here, the Court affirmed the information powers under § 220 Delaware General Corporation Law, as the applicant formally held the shares, and the law relied solely on the ownership and not on the economic risk.[63] With remarkable foresight, however, the court added that it might have decided differently had it been not for a formal standing permission, but for a substantial shareholder entitlement instead (for example, the right to vote).[64] This *obiter dictum* corresponds to the distinction identified above between formal and substantial control decisions.

There is no rule without exception. A counter-example is *Parfi Holding*, also mentioned briefly previously. This case, also brought in the courts of Delaware,

[59] For a fuller account, see Wolf-Georg Ringe, 'Empty Voting Revisited: The *Telus* Saga' (2013) 28 Butterworths Journal of International Banking and Financial Law 154.

[60] Aktiengesetz § 327a.

[61] BGH, decision of 16 March 2009 (II ZR 302/06), BGHZ 180, 154. See on this case Chapter III.B.2.a ('examples').

[62] *Deephaven Risk Arb Trading Ltd v UnitedGlobalCom, Inc* [2005] Del Ch 2005 WL 1713067.

[63] ibid. 15.

[64] ibid. 16. See also Lee (n. 30) 886.

again concerned a merely formal authorization question, namely the standing requirement for bringing a shareholder lawsuit.[65] This time, however, the applicant was denied the right to apply, due to a lack of beneficial interest in the shares.[66] The reasoning of the Court of Chancery said there was an 'unwritten condition' that the filing of a shareholder lawsuit would be brought in the interests of the company, and that the applicant therefore needed to have proper risk exposure in the company.[67] This inherent condition was not fulfilled, according to the Court. This case illustrates the judicial creativity of a common law judge to interpret even a formal share ownership requirement in a material way, and thus to address the risk-decoupling problem as early as this stage.

Drawing these different cases together, we see put together—with some exceptions—a rough picture of how legal practice is trying to deal with the problem under existing, insufficient legal tools. Formal questions, which consider questions of standing, quorums, thresholds, and similar situations, do not normally leave judicial creativity a lot of room, and the courts are thus usually seeking to satisfy legal certainty requirements and ask for formal ownership of shares only (the examples are *Telus* [Court of Appeal], *Lindner*, and *Deephaven*). In the (rarer) situation of a substantial test, a judge may find it much easier to take into account the risk exposure of a shareholder as a criterion, for example to carry out a balancing of mutual interest or to fill in an uncertain legal term (see *Telus* [Supreme Court]). Exceptions do occur and must be accepted, as they are in the nature of the unpredictability of judicial practice.[68]

Even if such judicial pursuit of an appropriate response to risk-decoupling has merit, the situation cannot overall be considered satisfactory. First, the approach taken by the courts often follows judicial instinct and individual judicial experience. It is not free from exceptions and surprises and thus cannot satisfy the need for legal certainty. Second, it must be added that even a satisfying legal outcome and fair court decision would always suffer from the issue that it addresses the problem *ex post*. A court decision, potentially by the highest instance court, can reasonably be expected to be delivered up to several years after the risk-decoupling behaviour occurred in the market. This is not an adequate solution to cope with a defect in the fast pace of modern capital markets.[69]

There have been proposals, mainly in continental Europe, to address the problem of risk-decoupling with an increased use of fiduciary duties for shareholders.[70] We

[65] See Chapter V.D.4.

[66] *Parfi Holding AB v Mirror Image Internet, Inc* 954 A2d 911 (Delaware Court of Chancery).

[67] ibid. 939. See also before *Alabama By-Products Corporation v Cede & Co* 657 A2d 254, 265-66 (Supreme Court of Delaware); *Schilling v Belcher* 582 F2d 995, 1002.

[68] See, for example, *Parfi Holding AB v Mirror Image Internet, Inc* (n. 66). Another exception is *Crown EMAK Partners, LLC v Kurz* (2010) 992 A2d 377.

[69] See in more detail, Marcel Kahan and Edward B Rock, 'Hedge Funds in Corporate Governance and Corporate Control' (2007) 155 University of Pennsylvania Law Review 1021, 1077. See also text accompanying n. 343.

[70] Iman Anabtawi and Lynn Stout, 'Fiduciary Duties for Activist Shareholders' (2008) 60 Stanford Law Review 1255; Andrea Zanoni, 'Hedge Funds' Empty Voting in Mergers and Acquisitions: A Fiduciary Duties Perspective' (2009) 9(4) Global Jurist, article 4. This approach is particularly popular in Germany;

will consider this point further later in the chapter.[71] At this stage, it is necessary to note that fiduciary duties will also lead to court litigation, and eventually produce unpredictable court decisions *ex post*. The same applies to the equally blurred concepts of 'abuse of law'[72] or market manipulation[73] that have been mentioned in this context.

Overall, it appears that legal practice is indeed trying to exploit the acquis of existing legal instruments, but this does not lead to much overall success. Examples of an intensive examination of the phenomenon of risk-decoupling are only found at places where the courts are granted a substantive legal test. Where judicial review is limited to formal aspects, however, courts are typically denied assessment of factors such as the economic interest behind share ownership. In addition, the judicial treatment of the subject generally suffers from a timing problem. In addition to its unpredictability, such a judicial decision usually needs time and a solution is only reached long after the speedy decisions on capital markets were made.

As an example of the problem that judges are facing, let us consider a passage from one of the *Telus* decisions mentioned previously, which aptly captures the judge's frustration concerning the lack of instruments, and instead pushes for intervention by the legislature:

> The fact that Mason has hedged its position to the extent that it has is cause for concern. There is, at the very least, a strong concern that its interests are not aligned with the economic well-being of the company. That said, there is no indication that it is violating any laws, nor is there any statutory provision that would allow the court to intervene on broad equitable grounds. To the extent that cases of 'empty voting' are subverting the goals of shareholder democracy, *the remedy must lie in legislative and regulatory change*.[74]

6. Conclusion

The option to 'do nothing' unites several facets. It concerns questions of whether the market could address the problem by way of self-regulation, or whether an adequate solution is already within reach under the existing, traditional legal framework. It is doubtful whether this approach is adequate for the subject matter at hand. None of the self-regulation approaches presented here have been

see Christine Osterloh-Konrad, 'Gefährdet "Empty Voting" die Willensbildung in der Aktiengesellschaft? Überlegungen zur Proportionalität zwischen Stimmrechtseinfluss und wirtschaftlicher Betroffenheit der Aktionäre' [2012] Zeitschrift für Unternehmens- und Gesellschaftsrecht (ZGR) 35, 47 ff.

[71] See section VI.E.

[72] In this sense, see José Garrido Garcia, comment in Koen Geens and Klaus J Hopt (eds), *The European Company Law Action Plan Revisited: Reassessment of the 2003 Priorities of the European Commission* (Leuven University Press 2010) 139; Jonathan Cohen, 'Negative Voting: Why It Destroys Shareholder Value and a Proposal to Prevent It' (2008) 45 Harvard Journal on Legislation 237, 254 ff. Generally on abuse of law on the EU level, see Rita de la Feria and Stefan Vogenauer (eds), *Prohibition of Abuse of Law: A New General Principle of EU Law?* (Hart 2011).

[73] For a sceptical account, see Autorité des Marchés Financiers (AMF), *Rapport sur les opérations de prêt emprunt de titres en période d'assemblée générale d'actionnaires* (Groupe de place présidé par Yves Mansion 2008) 4.

[74] *TELUS Corporation v Mason Capital Management LLC* (n. 56) para. 81 (emphasis added).

ultimately successful. Furthermore, it must be noted that the market does not seem positioned to properly price a separation of risk and voting rights. Finally, judicial attempts to address the problem under the legal acquis have been piecemeal, unpredictable, and overall unsatisfactory.

For this reason, we will now turn to consider the various possibilities for active regulation of the problem in the future.

B. Ban and Restriction

After considering the option of 'doing nothing', at the opposite end of the regulatory strategy spectrum lies the possibility of *banning* risk-decoupling, either comprehensively or partly. In view of the fundamental problems and high costs that result from risk-decoupling, this may seem to be a palatable approach to the phenomenon.

1. Ban on decoupling

In academic writing, US scholars Robert Thompson and Paul Edelman have advocated the option of banning risk-decoupling strategies.[75] Both scholars propose introducing a comprehensive and mandatory 'one share, one vote' standard, supporting a ban on agreements that would circumvent or decouple this standard and ultimately favour an explicit restriction on vote buying.[76] These claims are supported by a theory that understands corporate voting as a mechanism of error correction for management decisions.[77] The authors reject less restrictive solutions, which they argue to be inadequate.

The suggestion of banning risk-decoupling strategies also emerged during the discussions over the reform of the European Transparency Directive.[78] The Mazars report commissioned by the European Commission recommends the adoption of a ban as the only truly effective solution. However, the report acknowledges that the Transparency Directive is probably not the right legal tool to effectuate such a ban.[79] The report distinguishes between two main strategies of how to restrict or to ban any phenomena of risk-decoupling.

- A classical strategy would be to require shareholders who have lent their shares to *recall them* before any general meeting. The report acknowledges, however,

[75] Robert B Thompson and Paul H Edelman, 'Corporate Voting' (2009) 62 Vanderbilt Law Review 129; Paul H Edelman, Randall S Thomas, and Robert B Thompson, 'Shareholder Voting in an Age of Intermediary Capitalism' (2014) 87 Southern California Law Review 1359, 1406.

[76] Thompson and Edelman ibid. 158.

[77] Thompson and Edelman ibid. 135.

[78] Directive 2004/109/EC of the European Parliament and of the Council of 15 December 2004 on the harmonisation of transparency requirements in relation to information about issuers whose securities are admitted to trading on a regulated market and amending Directive 2001/34/EC, [2004] OJ L390/38.

[79] Mazars and Marccus Partners, *Transparency Directive Assessment Report—Prepared for the European Commission Internal Market and Services DG, Final Report* (December 2009) 131, available at <http://ec.europa.eu/internal_market/securities/docs/transparency/report-application_en.pdf>.

that there are limits to this option: first, it would be generally considered burdensome; second, it may be overreaching, as it would prevent stock lending at the time of the general meeting, whereas it is not the stock lending per se which is wrong but rather the use of borrowed shares in voting; third, this option would only address empty voting based on stock lending and would thus be limited in scope.[80]

- A more radical system would be to ban empty voting altogether. In particular, voting with borrowed shares (or shares held under a temporary transfer agreement or pursuant to a scheme having a similar impact) could be prohibited. The report supports this solution as the most consistent decision to be taken in view of the principles at stake.[81]

Each variant of such a regulatory ban, however, comes with a number of serious concerns.

The first concern is that any regulatory ban may be both under-inclusive and over-inclusive. Every decision to ban a certain product is a two-dimensional black-and-white solution, which does not provide leeway for a nuanced response to the specific problem at stake in individual risk-decoupling situations. Either the risk-decoupling activity is permitted or it is not; there is no ground for an intermediate solution. Having differentiated responses developed through a holistic approach with regard to the specific problems at stake is impossible. Such a regulatory structure will not yield satisfactory responses where the problem is neither black nor white, but grey. This may be the case when shareholders have only partially, but not entirely, reduced their risk exposure with the help of derivatives.[82] In consequence, some difficult questions would arise about the exact limits of this regime: should the ban only apply to situations in which shareholders have reduced their risk entirely? How about situations in which some (small) residual risk remains? Which limit should apply to permissible hedging?

The second concern over a statutory ban relates to enforcement.[83] A comprehensive ban on risk-decoupling structures will be difficult to control and enforce.[84] This aspect has already been highlighted in the discussion of the 'one share, one vote' standard from a few years back.[85] The main problem is the possibility of circumventing the standard as enshrined in the statutory rules. The financial industry is notoriously well known for inventing new products within ever narrowing horizons.[86] In this way, new

[80] ibid. 131–2. [81] ibid. 132. [82] See Chapter III.A.

[83] Luca Enriques, Henry Hansmann, and Reinier H Kraakman, 'The Basic Governance Structure: The Interests of Shareholders as a Class' in Reinier H Kraakman and others (eds), *The Anatomy of Corporate Law: A Comparative and Functional Approach* (2nd edn, Oxford University Press 2009) 55, 60; Mike Burkart and Samuel Lee, 'One Share—One Vote: The Theory' (2008) 12 Review of Finance 1, 4.

[84] See Eddy Wymeersch, 'Shareholder(s) Matter(s)', in Stefan Grundmann and others (eds), *Unternehmen, Markt und Verantwortung—Festschrift für Klaus J. Hopt zum 70. Geburtstag am 24. August 2010* (de Gruyter, Berlin 2010) 1565, 1574.

[85] See Wolf-Georg Ringe, 'Deviations from Ownership-Control Proportionality—Economic Protectionism Revisited' in Ulf Bernitz and Wolf-Georg Ringe (eds), *Company Law and Economic Protectionism: New Challenges to European Integration* (Oxford University Press 2010) 209.

[86] Dan Awrey, 'Complexity, Innovation, and the Regulation of Modern Financial Markets' (2012) 2 Harvard Business Law Review 235.

structures allow for the creation of economically similar results. Alternatively, opportunities for circumventing regulations arise where derivatives can be configured that do not reference the full value of the underlying securities, but rather only refer to several of their economic aspects, as is the case for some credit derivatives.[87] Alternatively, derivatives could be designed to avoid referencing shares directly and instead mention the company's assets, which would economically create a similar effect. Ultimately, a ban on risk-decoupling practices would have to trigger a full 'one share, one vote' standard—a plan that was rejected by the European Commission for several years because it was considered to be economically unconvincing.[88]

Furthermore, it is unclear how regulators would ensure that a ban would not impede the economically legitimate and useful activities of a business. Both the trade with borrowed securities and the derivatives businesses undisputedly serve important functions on the capital markets.[89] The objective of restricting risk-decoupling structures for reasons of corporate governance creates the risk of catching innocent, and even desirable, situations, and thus becoming destructive and inefficient overall. To be sure, this problem could be addressed by fine-tuning the regulation, utilizing various regulatory options. For instance, regulators could implement *de minimis* thresholds, only the surpassing of which would trigger the ban, or they could design a rule that only captures already existing shareholders. Nevertheless, a prohibitive system will always risk being over-inclusive, and thereby affecting economically desirable activities.[90]

In this context, the British investment fund Hermes proposed a regulatory regime that should address the problem of voting with borrowed shares. According to Hermes, such an activity should always be counted as market manipulation and thus be banned.[91] This solution would surely have the advantage of not directly banning securities lending or restricting them in any way, as it would only target the exercise of the voting rights. Nevertheless, this proposal has been heavily criticized. In 2004–5, an independent investigation in the United Kingdom reported that such a regime would be highly impractical.[92] According to Lord Myners, the

[87] Wymeersch (n. 84).

[88] European Commission, *Commission Staff Working Document: Impact Assessment on the Proportionality between Capital and Control in Listed Companies* (2007) SEC(2007) 1705; Renée Adams and Daniel Ferreira, 'One Share–One Vote: The Empirical Evidence' (2008) 12 Review of Finance 51. See on this Chapter III.E.2.

[89] See Chapter III.B.2 and III.B.1, respectively.

[90] In this sense, AMF (n. 73) 12.

[91] Hermes Equity Ownership Services, *Letter Responding to ESMA's Call for Evidence on Empty Voting* (25 November 2011), available at <http://www.esma.europa.eu/system/files/hermes_equity_0.pdf> accessed 18 August 2015. For previously made statements, see Kit Bingham, 'Concern Grows over Borrowed Votes' *Financial News* (9 May 2005), available at <http://www.efinancialnews.com/story/2005-05-09/concern-grows-over-borrowed-votes> accessed 16 August 2015 ('By borrowing shares for voting purposes, a party misleads the market by paying only a stocklending interest rate, not a market price for the shares'); see also Kara Scannell, 'How Borrowed Shares Swing Company Votes—SEC and Others Fear Hedge-Fund Strategy May Subvert Elections' *Wall Street Journal* (26 January 2007) A1.

[92] Kit Bingham, 'Myners Rejects Calls for Curbs on Stock Lending' *Financial News* (21 March 2005) <http://www.efinancialnews.com/story/2005-03-21/myners-rejects-calls-for-curbs-on-stock-lending> accessed 16 August 2015.

chairman of the investigation, the fungibility of shares is the central problem, which makes the enforcement of the ban close to impossible. Lord Myners compared the situation with the payment of a cheque while insisting that the paid money should not be invested in the defence industry.[93] Other than Myners, commentators and practitioners do not see a basis for, and acknowledge practical obstacles for, a prohibition in the sense of the proposal by Hermes.[94] Moreover, it has been pointed out that this proposal addresses only part of the entire risk-decoupling dimension and would not extend to an equally effective derivatives structure.[95]

Another proposal to consider is the introduction of a 'purpose test' in the area of securities lending, as it applies in the United States. Such a test limits the admissibility of securities lending to a few specified purposes and can thus be regarded as a partial ban. It follows from Regulation T of the Federal Reserve Board that the execution of securities lending for institutional investors is only allowed 'for the purpose of making delivery of the securities in the case of short sales, failure to receive securities required to be delivered, or other similar situations'.[96] From this limited list of admissible purposes, it has been concluded that the borrowing of securities for other objectives—such as the exercise of voting rights—is not permissible.[97]

Theoretically, this should be implemented by requiring brokers and other intermediaries to determine the purpose of the borrowing operation, and to carry out the transaction only if it is proven to be a legitimate purpose.[98] This is supported by the fact that the standard form in the US market contains a clause stating that the borrower assures that he and any other sub-borrower borrow only in accordance with the above-described 'purpose test'.[99] However, one problem with these rules seems to be their enforcement. Thus, the SEC is self-critical and admits that although the purpose test is in force on paper, non-permitted borrowing transactions do happen still frequently.[100] This is due to the fact that the American system—probably to achieve a workable framework in the first place—keeps the 'purpose' relatively wide and vague and explicitly includes 'other similar situations'.[101] This generous

[93] 'The problem is with the fungibility of shares. It is simply not enforceable. It's like paying your cheque into the bank and saying that you don't want it invested in the defence industry.' ibid. (quoting Lord Myners).

[94] See, e.g., David Lapido, director at Lintstock, a corporate governance advisory service, quoted ibid.

[95] Cohen (n. 72) 253.

[96] Federal Reserve Board Regulation T, 12 CFR § 220.10(a).

[97] Securities and Exchange Commission, 'Concept Release on the U.S. Proxy System (Release Nos 34-62495, IA-3052, IC-29340; File No S7-14-10, 2010)' (2010) 75 Federal Register 42981, 43018: 'Within the U.S. this sort of practice appears to be limited by Regulation T, under which securities loans by institutional investors through their broker-dealers are restricted to distinct "permitted purposes" under the Federal Reserve Board's Regulation T, such as execution of a short sale.'

[98] For a more detailed account of Regulation T, see Charles E Dropkin, 'Developing Effective Guidelines for Managing Legal Risks—U.S. Guidelines' in Frank J Fabozzi and Steven V Mann (eds), *Securities Finance: Securities Lending and Repurchase Agreements* (Wiley 2005) 167, 172 ff.

[99] Securities Industry and Financial Markets Association (Sifma), 'Master Securities Loan Agreement' para. 10.5, <http://www.sifma.org/Services/Standard-Forms-and-Documentation/MRA,-GMRA,-MSLA-and-MSFTAs/MSLA_Master-Securities-Loan-Agreement-(2000-Version)/> accessed 18 August 2015.

[100] Securities and Exchange Commission (n. 97) 43019.

[101] Federal Reserve Board Regulation T, 12 CFR § 220.10(a).

interpretation de facto opens the floodgates and jeopardizes effective handling by the regulatory authority. In addition, Regulation T does not limit lending operations outside its scope, such as loan transactions outside of intermediary structures, or within the permitted exceptions.[102] Finally, it should be noted that although Regulation T prohibits the borrowing operation for the purpose of voting, it by no means targets the voting itself. Thus, it is conceivable that the borrower will subsequently change his mind or discover the possibility to use the voting rights only after having concluded the borrowing contract (at least, these would be credible submissions). In any case, repeated suspicious or problematic loan processes are reported even in the United States, which shows that the purpose test does not tackle the problem in a satisfactory manner.[103]

2. Difficulties with the record-date problem

Finally, proponents of a prohibitive regulation must accept that implementation of such a regulation, while difficult to achieve, would theoretically be possible for risk-decoupling categories that rely on the usage of derivatives and securities lending. However, it appears virtually unworkable for the third of the categories—exploitation of record-date capture.[104] If our legal frameworks intend to retain the record-date system in principle, a certain level of divergence between economic interest and voting power will be inevitable. This is simply because the record date and general meeting are separated by a certain—longer or shorter—time period. A prohibition would correspondingly be at odds with the entire system, unless the record-date system as a whole is called into question.

It lies in this logic that the Mazars report, discussed previously, modifies its call for a 'prohibition' when turning to the issue of record-date capture. Instead of an outright ban, the report advises that lenders of securities should be *legally required* to *call back their shares* before the record date.[105] Admittedly, however, such a solution would be subject to significant objections. As proponents accept, such an obligation would be seriously intrusive on the contractual freedom of market participants. Moreover, it can be argued that it would be an inconsistent intrusion because the problem lies not in borrowing the shares at the moment of the general meeting, but rather in voting with borrowed shares. Finally, the solution only captures part of the risk-decoupling problem (in the form of record-date capture), and not the deeper issues of share lending more generally and the use of derivatives.[106] Beyond these arguments, the European Securities Markets Expert Group (ESME)

[102] Securities and Exchange Commission (n. 97) 43019.

[103] See Bob Drummond, 'Double Voting in Proxy Contests Threatens Shareholder Democracy' *Bloomberg* (27 February 2006), available at <http://www.bloomberg.com/apps/news?pid=newsarchive&sid=a4OuCsU8r2Yg> accessed 18 August 2015.

[104] See Chapter III.B.3. But see Wymeersch (n. 84) 1573: 'Regular and justified practices—voting on the basis of the reference date e.g.—would become forbidden.'

[105] Mazars and Marccus Partners (n. 79) 131.

[106] This is acknowledged by the report itself: ibid. 131 f.

has raised even more serious objections. ESME argues that any positive obligation to call back shares ahead of each general meeting would potentially be very disruptive to the market, because it may result in a dramatic loss of liquidity in certain stocks during the general meeting season.[107]

Even if the *obligation* to call back lent shares were to be diluted into a legal *possibility* or an *entitlement* to call them back, it is doubtful that such a move would be successful. This is because the collective action problem on the part of the lenders, as described previously in detail,[108] does not give them any incentive to actually recall the shares. Quite the contrary, a rational lender would precisely rather not recall the shares.[109]

In this context, we should mention the efforts in the state of Delaware to separate the record dates for dividend entitlement and for voting right. A minor reform in 2009 now for the first time allows corporations to separate both dates and to select different days for them.[110] The aim of this reform was to encourage investment funds and other shareholders to make use of a right to call back their shares over the voting record date, or at least to allow such a call-back to happen.[111] In a similar vein, the SEC is currently discussing a possible reform option to require companies to make the dates and agendas for the shareholders' meeting known well in advance, so that there is sufficient time for a possible recall.[112] These reform efforts are laudable, but they do not address the root of the problem and the underlying incentives. Creating the legal possibility for a share recall alone will not change anything if the economic case for calling back the shares is not apparent.[113]

3. Conclusion

Overall, no variant of a 'prohibition' rule appears to effectively address the problem. The main issues are the lack of a specific adjustment of such a scheme to individual cases and the problematic law enforcement and avoidance possibilities. In addition to liquidity problems, the economic consequences for the derivatives and securities lending markets would be disastrous. And finally, conceptualizing a prohibition scheme would likely lead to separate rules for the three decoupling categories discussed here; a comprehensive, integrated prohibition scheme for all types of risk-decoupling would thus be hardly conceivable.

[107] European Securities Markets Expert Group (ESME), *First Report of ESME on the Transparency Directive ('TD')* (5 December 2007) 7, available at <http://ec.europa.eu/internal_market/securities/docs/esme/05122007_td_report_en.pdf>.

[108] See Chapter III.B.2.b. [109] See text accompanying n. 216.

[110] Delaware General Corporation Law § 213(a) was accordingly modified with effect from 1 August 2009.

[111] Daniel E Wolf and others, *Setting the Record (Date) Straight* (2013) Kirkland M&A Update, available at <http://www.kirkland.com/siteFiles/Publications/MAUpdate_041713.pdf>.

[112] Securities and Exchange Commission (n. 97) 42994.

[113] Bonnie J Roe, 'When the Voting Is "Empty": No Quick Fix Is Seen in Record Date Reform Proposals' *New York Law Journal* (29 November 2010).

C. Transparency

In the canon of the possible regulatory responses to the presence of risk-decoupling strategies, we will next explore the contribution of transparency, that is, enhanced publicity and disclosure requirements of such situations. Transparency plays a key role in developing an appropriate framework for the solution to the problem. In the following, I argue that transparency is indeed an adequate means to tackle many economic problems associated with risk-decoupling. However, careful consideration needs to be given to take particular account of the costs and benefits of a possible transparency regime that specifically aims at solving the issues arising here.[114] On this basis, I will develop a concrete legislative proposal.[115]

1. Transparency as a response to decoupling problems

Increased transparency is frequently the first solution of choice when new or novel problems arise in capital markets. This is not surprising, as the regulation of capital markets is essentially the regulation of information.[116] The key question is always how much information the regulator must provide market players with to enable them to make efficient decisions. On the one hand, the legislature strives to provide market participants with a good starting position, so that a liquid market may develop which allows an efficient allocation of resources. On the other hand, the capital market remains a market of private actors, which can never be exhaustively regulated.[117] If all superior knowledge of an individual was offset by comprehensive, all-encompassing information obligations, any private incentive to economic activity, to innovation and competition, would disappear.[118] Thus, capital markets regulation aims to provide investors with the most favourable conditions for making informed investment decisions, but 'no regulator promises to protect them from their own stupidity nor their own bad luck'.[119] Transparency of the markets is not an end in itself, but must always serve the pursuit of a particular purpose.[120] For example, if market distortions occur and significant information asymmetries

[114] On the problem areas, see in particular Chapter V.B, V.C, and V.D. See on the following in parts already Wolf-Georg Ringe, 'Hedge Funds and Risk-Decoupling—The Empty Voting Problem in the European Union' (2013) 36 Seattle University Law Review 1027, 1087 ff.

[115] See section VI.C.6.

[116] Alastair Hudson, *The Law of Finance* (2nd edn, Sweet & Maxwell 2013) para. 35-03.

[117] For a fundamental analysis of the basic assumptions of disclosure regulation in the European securities market, see Hendrik Brinckmann, 'Foundations' in Rüdiger Veil (ed.), *European Capital Markets Law* (Hart Publishing 2013) 209.

[118] See the seminal work by Sanford J Grossman and Joseph E Stiglitz, 'On the Impossibility of Informationally Efficient Markets' (1980) 70 American Economic Review 393. In the present context, see also Consob, *Position Paper on the Disclosure of Cash-Settled Derivatives* (8 October 2009), available at <http://www.consob.it/mainen/legal_framework/consultations/dp_cash_derivatives_20091008.pdf> accessed 15 August 2015.

[119] Hudson (n. 116) para. 35-03.

[120] This is emphasized by Callum McCarthy, 'Exigences de Transparence et Hedge Funds' (2007) 10 Banque de France • Revue de la stabilité financière 85, 86, 92.

exist, the market authority needs to intervene and to clean up the corresponding information deficits. In particular, whenever a change to established principles of investment decisions occurs, the law can, and should, help market participants to adjust their position—by allowing them either to make a new investment decision or to leave the investment objective on fair terms. For example, disclosure, particularly major shareholder notifications, and takeover regulation are two sides of the same coin:[121] disclosure regulation enables the making of informed decisions *ex ante*, before a change in investment conditions takes place, whereas takeover regulation focuses on rebalancing the opportunities of investors *ex post*, after a change in the investment conditions has occurred.[122] However, the determination of the proper balance between investor protection and burden on business remains a balancing act.

Against this background, certain areas of the capital market are subjected to specific publicity requirements. These are commonly distinguished in market entry information duties and continuous disclosure requirements on the secondary market.[123] These disclosure requirements are intended to reduce information asymmetries and to strengthen investor confidence in the capital market as a whole. In many cases, it is generally more efficient to subject the issuer (as being closer to the information) to disclosure obligations than to require investors to search for individual information for their investment decisions which may be difficult for them to access. Despite some controversial discourse,[124] the system of mandatory disclosure has prevailed in the capital market in these areas.[125]

a) *Disclosure obligation for risk-decoupling structures*

On the basis of the information asymmetries discussed previously, the idea of responding to the risk-decoupling phenomenon with an increased level of disclosure obligations thus has strong appeal. In addition to these initial reflections, information and disclosure obligations are always a less restrictive regulatory intervention when compared to prohibition laws. This choice of legal instrument would therefore also be preferable under subsidiarity and proportionality

[121] Dirk Zetzsche, 'Hidden Ownership in Europe: BAFin's Decision in Schaeffler v. Continental' (2009) 10 European Business Organization Law Review 115, 146.

[122] Hudson (n. 116) para. 36-63; Reinier H Kraakman and others, *The Anatomy of Corporate Law: A Comparative and Functional Approach* (Oxford University Press 2009) 249, 252; High Level Group of Company Law Experts, *Report on Issues Related to Takeover Bids* (2002), available at <http://ec.europa.eu/internal_market/company/docs/takeoverbids/2002-01-hlg-report_en.pdf> 45.

[123] See Alexander Hellgardt, 'Mandatory Disclosure (Securities Markets)' in Jürgen Basedow, Klaus J Hopt, and Reinhard Zimmermann (eds), *The Max Planck Encyclopedia of European Private Law* (Oxford University Press 2012) 1118.

[124] See, for example, Stephen J Choi and Andrew T Guzman, 'The Dangerous Extraterritoriality of American Securities Law' (1996) 17 Northwestern Journal of International Law & Business 207; Roberta Romano, 'Empowering Investors: A Market Approach to Securities Regulation' (1998) 107 Yale Law Journal 2359, 2401. Both advocate 'issuer choice' in such a way that the issuer of securities should have an optional right to publish securities market information.

[125] Merritt B Fox, 'Retaining Mandatory Securities Disclosure: Why Issuer Choice Is Not Investor Empowerment' (1999) 85 Virginia Law Review 1335.

considerations.[126] Not surprisingly, many commentators in academia and practice have therefore advocated for a transparency-based solution to the problems described in this book.[127] In particular, early, tentative comments from the literature suggested tightening transparency requirements as an initial step, due to the still prevailing uncertainty about the extent, significance, and weightiness of the issue.[128] These commentators hoped for a gentle and cautious approach to the problem and expected to gain access to more information in order to measure the extent of risk-decoupling activity in the market and to assess potential follow-up measures.[129]

As I have shown previously in this book, the key problem underlying risk-decoupling structures today is their lack of transparency.[130] In particular, information costs for shareholders and external investors are high because risk-decoupling structures are not disclosed to the market. Agency costs are incurred without the market knowing the level of risk exposure faced by company actors. Risk-decoupled shares are not priced adequately due to a lack of transparency, which differs from other instruments that attempt to overcome the debt–equity divide, such as preference shares.[131]

The problem perspectives and levels discussed previously indicate that there is indeed a significant lack of transparency in risk-decoupling. In particular, the considerations on information costs (Chapter V.C) and corporate finance (Chapter V.D) came to the conclusion that a lack of transparency creates substantial costs for economic activity in every company.[132] Principal-agent analysis (Chapter V.A) has also made clear that an effective disclosure scheme should meet two principal goals. First, it is necessary to protect investors external to the company, so as to reduce the cost of information for potential investments. Second, it is also important to protect the current shareholders, who are forced by the occurrence of risk-decoupling

[126] For the principles of subsidiarity and proportionality in the European context, see TEU article 5(3) and (4).

[127] In detail, see Jordan M Barry, John William Hatfield, and Scott Duke Kominers, 'On Derivatives Markets and Social Welfare: A Theory of Empty Voting and Hidden Ownership' (2013) 99 Virginia Law Review 1103 1156 ff. See also the European Corporate Governance Forum, *Paper by the Working Group on Proportionality* (June 2007) 23, 26, available at <http://ec.europa.eu/internal_market/company/docs/ecgforum/workinggroup_proportionality_en.pdf> accessed 15 August 2015.

[128] Among the many are Henry T C Hu and Bernard Black, 'The New Vote Buying: Empty Voting and Hidden (Morphable) Ownership' (2006) 79 Southern California Law Review 811; Henry T C Hu and Bernard Black, 'Empty Voting and Hidden (Morphable) Ownership: Taxonomy, Implications, and Reforms' (2006) 61 Business Lawyer 1011; Henry T C Hu and Bernard Black, 'Hedge Funds, Insiders, and the Decoupling of Economic and Voting Ownership: Empty Voting and Hidden (Morphable) Ownership' (2007) 13 Journal of Corporate Finance 343; Marcel Kahan and Edward B Rock, 'Hedge Funds in Corporate Governance and Corporate Control' (2007) 155 University of Pennsylvania Law Review 1021; Anish Monga, 'Using Derivatives to Manipulate the Market for Corporate Control' (2006) 12 Stanford Journal of Law, Business & Finance 186; Michael C Schouten, 'The Case for Mandatory Ownership Disclosure' (2009) 15 Stanford Journal of Law, Business and Finance 127; Michael C Schouten, *The Decoupling of Voting and Economic Ownership* (Kluwer 2012) 49.

[129] See, e.g., Hu and Black, 'New Vote Buying' (n. 128) 886 ('Disclosure should also provide the information required to assess the need for further empty voting reforms').

[130] See Chapter V.C.2. [131] See section VI.A.1. [132] For a summary, see Chapter V.C.3.

strategies to constantly monitor the risk structures in their investments. Hence, the concern is to avoid imposing overly burdensome monitoring obligations on investors. A comprehensive and coherent disclosure framework would in this way also strengthen investment confidence in the stock market as a whole.[133]

What would be the exact impact of a disclosure obligation, and how would it work? Generally, transparency allows for and facilitates market reaction, as private actors can respond to information and thereby either avoid or price in any negative consequences. Information disclosure and transparency requirements are therefore popular instruments among law-makers and regulators, as they (unlike a ban) do not include any rigid prohibition of a certain activity, but make the incriminating behaviour known to the market. The market can then judge itself how the previously hidden behaviour should be evaluated.

In the context of interest here, this would mean that disclosure of risk-decoupling structures would allow both shareholders and potential investors to counter-react. Primarily, it would be possible to respond to the new information by buying and selling securities—if the information is negative, thus to exit the company. Alternatively, shareholders could also use 'voice' rather than exit—for example, by forming a counter-alliance of shareholders that could sabotage the project of a risk-decoupler, formulate counter-proposals or counter-strategies, and put them on the agenda. Share lenders could be convinced, on a well-informed basis, to recall their shares. In the most egregious cases, shareholders and shareholder alliances could even initiate a media campaign to garner support and add public pressure to their cause.

In addition, a disclosure obligation would most certainly deter hedge funds and other savvy investors from entering into risk-decoupling structures in the first place. That is, the private benefits that are pursued and the agency costs that are produced are currently only seen as an attractive business model for some market actors for the very reason that they can be pursued unnoticed on the market. Disclosing these strategies could result in negative reputational consequences.

Further, it would even be conceivable that, in some cases, the disclosure of a risk-decoupling structure would provoke the opposite—a positive response in the market, such as when investors (as mentioned previously) interpret the occurrence of risk-decoupling as a helpful initiative that could reduce agency costs by granting additional leverage to shareholders in monitoring the management.[134] Thus, the beauty of any disclosure obligation would be that market publicity—without any positive or negative assessment—would leave a decision on how to assess the occurrence of risk-decoupling in a particular firm to the market actors themselves, without pre-judging them.

Finally, we have seen that one of the current problems with risk-decoupling is that many regulators across the world are unsure about the extent of its occurrence in daily life. An obligation to disclose risk-decoupling structures would give regulators an idea of their pervasiveness in practice, and would help them assess the case to evaluate the next steps.

133 See Chapter V.C.1.

134 See Chapter V.B.2.

b) Shortcomings in the existing disclosure regime

The current European regime for disclosure of major shareholdings pursuant to articles 9 ff. of the Transparency Directive hinges on the fact that the reporting party has acquired or disposed of *voting rights* in the prescribed thresholds (5, 10, 15, etc. per cent).[135]

This system is based on the assumption that the holders of such voting rights have the corresponding voting power they use for purposes we expect of utility-maximizing shareholders. As explained previously, the purpose of voting right notifications is to improve the protection of investors in the securities market, to increase their confidence in the markets, and with that to contribute to an overall good functioning of the capital market as an institution.[136] Further, transparency seeks to address potential abuses of inside information and to allow corporations to gain a better overview of their shareholder structure and control allocation in the shareholder body. At the same time, disclosure requirements play a role as an element of a 'group formation control' and thus provide (limited) protection from hostile takeover attempts.[137]

Implicitly, such reporting obligations imply that those who make a voting rights disclosure also have the corresponding motivation to that of a regular owner. In other words, a disclosure system based on voting rights with the objective of protecting investors and other market participants only makes sense where the voting rights are a meaningful piece of information and where this information can fulfil its protective purpose. But precisely this is missing when—due to a hidden risk-decoupling structure—the voting rights disclosure provides a distorted picture. Consider the following example. If shareholder A discloses the acquisition of a 10 per cent stake in company X plc, this message indicates to the capital market that A is interested in 10 per cent of the company's voting rights and is thus positively exposed in the equivalent amount and value of X's shares. This information may signal many other pieces of information to other shareholders and to investors—for example, that A may intend to build a higher stake in X or even ultimately may seek to pursue a takeover. Another possibility could be that A will be in a position (to a limited extent), through the exercise of its voting rights, to influence the company's management and strategic decisions. We may at the very least conclude that A has simply completed a positive bet on the development of the price of X shares, as the acquisition of shares is always an expectation of future positive returns.

[135] See Directive 2004/109/EC, article 9(1):

> The home Member State shall ensure that, where a shareholder acquires or disposes of shares of an issuer whose shares are admitted to trading on a regulated market and to which voting rights are attached, such shareholder notifies the issuer of the proportion of voting rights of the issuer held by the shareholder as a result of the acquisition or disposal where that proportion reaches, exceeds or falls below the thresholds of 5%, 10%, 15%, 20%, 25%, 30%, 50% and 75%.

[136] See Chapter IV.A.

[137] Eberhard Schwark in Eberhard Schwark and Daniel Zimmer (eds), *Kapitalmarkts-Kommentar* (4th edn, CH Beck 2010) vor §§ 21 ff. para. 4.

All of this information can, however, be thwarted by the fact that A may have effectuated a risk-decoupling transaction in secret. For example, this will be the case when A has only borrowed the shares and promised to return them or to transfer them further to a third person in the future. In this case, the initial disclosure following the acquisition of the voting rights will already be misleading. Alternatively, A may initially acquire the full voting rights with regular risk exposure, but may later decouple the risk by concluding a derivative contract in the way described previously. In this case, the continued disclosure without modification produces false impressions.

These gaps need to be filled. A further development of the reporting obligations should therefore provide disclosure of such negative interests, risk reductions, or other deviations from the regular full risk exposure.

The need to adapt the existing reporting regime thus draws on legal policy needs and the inadequacy of the current reporting system. To be sure, a disclosure scheme cannot solve all the problems. Much will depend on the exact details of the scheme, and there may be situations that cannot be solved by transparency alone. In the following, we shall explore the specific information needs and weigh them against the corresponding costs to develop an appropriate disclosure regime.

2. Legislative activity and reactions

Further inspiration for a concrete and appropriate development of transparency requirements may be gained from looking at first reactions by different legislatures, many of which encourage greater transparency for risk-decoupling in the market.

A number of law-makers have realized that the disclosure system plays a key role in the overall decoupling problem, in particular concerning the securities lending aspect.[138] For example, France was among the first jurisdictions to respond to the perceived empty voting problem by modifying its existing disclosure laws in 2010. The new provision addresses the problem of risk-decoupling in the form of securities lending.[139] A law enacted in 2010[140] inserted a new article, article L. 225-126, into the *Code de commerce*.[141] The article stipulates that every shareholder holding

[138] See International Organization of Securities Commissions (IOSCO), Technical Committee, *Protection of Minority Shareholders in Listed Issuers—Final Report* (June 2009) 14. For example, Australia or Hong Kong have a disclosure obligation for securities lending transactions that may have a 'material effect' on the share price of the company. In Spain, any securities lending operation needs to be reported to a special market authority; see Ben Wilkie, 'Spain: Despite the Country's Financial Woes, a Vibrant Securities Lending Market Still Exists in Spain, Even Though Short Selling Rules Are Some of the Toughest in the Western World' (2011) 18 Securities Lending Times 10.

[139] Category 2; see Chapter III.B.2.

[140] Loi 2010-1249 du 22 Octobre 2010 de Régulation Bancaire et Financière, Journal Officiel de la République Française [Official Gazette of France], 23 October 2010, p. 18984. On this new law generally, see Michel Storck and Jérôme Lasserre Capdeville, 'Panorama Général de la Loi de Régulation Bancaire et Financière' (2010) 250 Petites Affiches 3.

[141] The key passage of article L. 225-126 reads:

> [T]oute personne, . . . qui détient, seule ou de concert, au titre d'une ou plusieurs opérations de cession temporaire portant sur ces actions ou de toute opération lui donnant le droit ou lui faisant obligation de revendre ou de restituer ces actions au cédant, un nombre d'actions

borrowed shares, or shares from a similar transaction, that surpass 0.5 per cent of the voting rights of the issuer must disclose this fact to the issuer and to the French supervisor, *Autorité des Marchés Financiers* (AMF).[142] During the legislative process, the 0.5 per cent threshold proved very controversial and was modified several times.[143] The disclosure obligation arises at least three days before the date of the general meeting, provided that the lending agreement is still in force on the day of the general meeting.[144] In addition to the number of shares acquired by way of this transaction, the disclosure needs to include the identity of the lender and details about the expiry date of the agreement, its concrete way of operation, and a voting agreement, if any.[145] Finally, the issuer has to publish this information.[146]

Moreover, the new regime provides for drastic sanctions. If the borrower does not comply with the disclosure obligation, the shares will lose their voting entitlement at the general meeting.[147] In addition, a court can separately prohibit the exercise of a non-complying shareholder's voting right for up to five years. Finally, a shareholder resolution that involves a non-complying shareholder can be challenged in court and declared invalid.[148] This legislative reform draws on the original suggestions of a working group appointed by the AMF and chaired by Yves Mansion.[149]

The choice of a reference date the third day before the general meeting corresponds to the general French record date.[150] In this way, the described reform intends, in essence, to include all temporarily held shares at the moment of the record date and to disclose them to the market. The French business world has reluctantly accepted this reform, and French institutions have even suggested

> représentant plus du deux-centième des droits de vote, informe la société et l'Autorité des marchés financiers, au plus tard le troisième jour ouvré précédant l'assemblée générale à zéro heure, heure de Paris, et lorsque le contrat organisant cette opération demeure en vigueur à cette date, du nombre total d'actions qu'elle possède à titre temporaire....

An English translation is as follows:

> [A]ny person... who holds, alone or together, under one or more temporary transactions or any transaction entitling him or requiring him to sell or return the share to the transferor, a number of shares representing more than two-hundredth of the voting rights, informs the company and the AMF no later than the third business day preceding the general meeting at midnight, Paris time, the total number of shares held temporarily if when the contract organizing the transaction remains in effect to this date (author's translation).

142 See Bruno Zabala, 'Action de Concert et Transparence Préassemblées Générales: Les Nouveaux Equilibres Actionnariaux sous l'Œil du Législateur et de la Cour de Cassation' (2011) 5 Revue Lamy Droit des Affaires 110, 112.

143 Catherine Maison-Blanche and Antoine Barat, 'La Nouvelle Obligation de Transparence sur les Opérations de Détentions Temporaires Avant Tenue des Assemblées: Réflexions Préliminaires' (2011) 1/2 Revue Trimestrielle de Droit Financier 80, 83.

144 On this specific aspect of the law, see Hervé Le Nabasque, 'Commentaire des Principales Dispositions de la Loi de Régulation Bancaire et Financière du 22 Octobre 2010 Intéressant le Droit des Sociétés et le Droit Financier' [2010] Revue des Sociétés 547.

145 For a helpful form, see Instruction n° 2011-04 du 2 Février 2011 relative aux modalités de communication des opérations de cession temporaire portant sur des actions à l'AMF, available at <http://www.amf-france.org/documents/general/ 9847_1.pdf>.

146 Code de Commerce, article L. 225-126(I).

147 Code de commerce, article L. 225-126(II).

148 Zabala (n. 142) 113.

149 Autorité des Marchés Financiers (AMF), *Rapport sur les opérations de prêt emprunt de titres en période d'assemblée générale d'actionnaires* (Groupe de place présidé par Yves Mansion 2008).

150 Code de Commerce, article R. 225-85.

that their new law serve as a blueprint for the reform of the EU Transparency Directive.[151]

The French approach is a first step toward a transparency-based solution, but there are several objections. First, it is obvious that the French law deals with only part of the problem, that is, the risk-decoupling problem in the form of securities lending (category 2).[152] Because several other decoupling strategies are not included in the regime, the law facilitates arbitrage strategies. In particular, using derivatives for risk-decoupling does not fall under the scope of the French system, and even the potentially problematic trading of shares between the record date and the general meeting remains unregulated.[153]

Several other aspects of the new regime are also questionable. While the sanction of disenfranchisement applies only where disclosure is omitted, it is not tied to an abuse of the voting right. This has two important implications. First, the regulation seems to allow and even to legitimize the lending and borrowing of shares over the record date (including voting rights). The heavy sanction of disenfranchisement only applies when the duty of disclosure is not complied with. Moreover, the choice of a very low disclosure threshold seems flawed because, with a borrowed stake of 0.5 per cent of the voting rights, the potential for abuse of a risk-decoupled position, as described previously, seems very unlikely to materialize. Second, it appears questionable whether the one-off disclosure duty on the record date gives market participants sufficient information to respond. All of these issues will be revisited in the pages that follow and discussed in more detail to support the development of my own proposal later.[154]

Beyond this French advance, the European Commission increasingly saw a necessity for an EU-wide transparency obligation. In 2010, the consultation paper on Corporate Governance in Financial Institutions carefully attempted to first ask whether greater transparency as to the identity of shareholders could help reduce the problem of risk-decoupling structures.[155] The majority of respondents supported the call for enhanced transparency, for example in the realm of securities lending.[156] At the same time, it had been pointed out that the introduction of a general disclosure obligation would not be an adequate means

[151] For the responses to the consultation by BNP Paribas, see Société Générale, AMF, AFEP (p. 2), Trésor (p. 4) and AFAMI (p. 9f), available at <https://circabc.europa.eu/webdav/CircaBC/FISMA/markt_consultations/Library/company_law/transparency_requirement/> accessed 15 August 2015.

[152] See Chapter III.B.2. To be sure, a part of the record-date problem (Chapter III.B.3) is also addressed.

[153] In its response to the proposed reform of the Transparency Directive, the French bank BNP Paribas stated that it was not aware of a problem of trading between record date and general meeting. In its view, the record date according to French law was close enough to the date of the general meeting. See ibid.

[154] See sections VI.C.4 and VI.C.6.

[155] European Commission, *Green Paper on Corporate Governance in Financial Institutions and Remuneration Policies*, COM(2010) 284 final (2 June 2010), question 5.3.

[156] See generally European Commission, *Feedback Statement of the European Commission on the Summary of Responses to Commission Green Paper on Corporate Governance in Financial Institutions* (2011), available at <http://ec.europa.eu/internal_market/consultations/docs/2010/governance/feedback_statement_en.pdf>.

to solve the entire problem, as it does not focus on the cardinal point of the record date.[157] So far, the review process and this suggestion have not triggered any directive legislative activity.

Instead, the consultation paper moved the topic from the scope of company law to the field of capital markets disclosure duties. EU officials from the latter area at first graciously accepted the invitation and seemed positive about strengthening disclosure regulation. This was the reaction to a conference on the reform of the (capital markets-oriented) Transparency Directive which was held in Brussels on 11 June 2010.[158] Building on an external report,[159] a subsequently published EU working document on the reform of the Transparency Directive[160] discussed various legislative options:

1. The first option would require borrowers of shares to disclose and specify that they hold their shares as a borrower (or, more generally, under a temporary transfer agreement). This would be a simple solution, but, as the Commission acknowledges itself, it would not address all decoupling issues.[161]
2. Specifically addressing the problem of record-date capture, the Commission discussed whether to introduce a requirement saying that any sale of shares above a certain threshold (or other reduction in the net economic exposure of a shareholder of record) between the record date and the date of the general meeting should immediately be notified to the issuer and to the market in such a way that the relevant information is fully disclosed prior to the date of the general meeting.[162]
3. Another solution would be to require shareholders to immediately disclose any change, above a certain threshold, in their net economic exposure within a certain period of time before and up to a general meeting of shareholders (for instance, during the thirty days preceding a general meeting). This requirement would provide a complete picture of the shareholder base at the time when the information is most meaningful. The Commission acknowledges that such a system would be comprehensive, as it would comprise and go beyond proposal 2, but that it may be viewed as too burdensome.[163]

[157] ibid. 18.

[158] Claire Bury, Closing Remarks at the Conference on the Reform of the Transparency Directive (11 June 2010).

[159] Mazars and Marccus Partners, *Transparency Directive Assessment Report—Prepared for the European Commission Internal Market and Services DG, Final Report* (December 2009) 128, available at <http://ec.europa.eu/internal_market/securities/docs/transparency/report-application_en.pdf> accessed 12 August 2015.

[160] European Commission, *Commission Staff Working Document—The Review of the Operation of Directive 2004/109/EC: Emerging Issues*, SEC (2010) 611 (May 2010), available at <http://eur-lex.europa.eu/legal-content/EN/TXT/PDF/?uri=CELEX:52010SC0611&from=EN>.

[161] ibid. para. 10.19.

[162] ibid. para. 10.15; see also Mazars and Marccus Partners (n. 159) 131.

[163] Commission Staff Working Document (n. 160) para. 10.20.

4. Another way to improve transparency would be to require, as proposed in the Mazars Report,[164] that the economic exposure of all shareholders, above a certain threshold, be disclosed on the day of the record date, to the extent that this net economic exposure was not disclosed pursuant to a previous notification (no double notification should be required if it does not provide new information). This system would be comprehensive and would not be equally burdensome because only one extra notification would be required (subject to updates, which should be limited).[165]
5. Finally, the European Corporate Governance Forum (ECGF), an advisory body to the Commission, proposed in its February 2010 statement that a borrower of shares should notify the company prior to the general meeting that he does not have the full financial interest in the shares if he intends to exercise his voting rights on the shares. According to the ECGF, this duty to notify should apply to positions that correspond to a certain threshold, for example, 1 per cent or more of the outstanding shares with voting rights. Any false or omitted statement in this context should be dealt with under the national rules on misleading information. Furthermore, the Forum recommends introducing a rule that the company and its subsidiaries may only lend the company's own shares if the lending contract stipulates these shares will not be voted upon by the borrower. The company should disclose prior to the general meeting to what extent it and its subsidiaries have lent the company's own shares to third parties.[166]

Overall, none of the papers specifically define what constitutes 'net economic exposure'. Deducing the writers' intentions, we can assume that the term refers to the risk a shareholder factually bears with respect to a particular stake in the company, which results from the regular (positive) risk and the reduced (negative) risk potentially following from risk-decoupling mechanisms. In the normal scenario, where a shareholder only holds (long) shares, without additionally having entered into hedging transactions, the net economic exposure will correspond to the positive share position. Where the long position coincides with derivatives transactions in one of the described ways,[167] this exposure can, however, be reduced. It is important to understand that the Commission's reasoning seems to be based on the fact that borrowed shares only increase the positive risk, but not the net risk exposure. However, commentators have rightly pointed out that the decisive information relates to the *relationship* between the voting rights held by

[164] Mazars and Marccus Partners (n. 159) 131.
[165] Commission Staff Working Document (n. 160) para. 10.21.
[166] European Corporate Governance Forum, *Statement on Empty Voting and Transparency of Shareholder Positions* (20 February 2010), available at <http://ec.europa.eu/internal_market/company/docs/ecgforum/ecgf_empty_voting_en.pdf> para. 5; see Commission Staff Working Document (n. 160) para. 10.22.
[167] See Chapter III.B.1.

the shareholder and the net economic exposure, the latter alone not being very meaningful.[168] To be sure, the positive risk exposure is to be disclosed according to the regular disclosure rules for large shareholdings,[169] so that—according to the obvious reasoning by the Commission—the joint information between these two items (long and net short exposure) will yield the decisive information value. In other words, the net economic exposure is only an additional, ancillary piece of information.

The outlined proposals by the Commission and the ECGF were part of the consultation on the reform of the Transparency Directive, which was initiated in May 2010[170] and completed in 2013. Responses from the consultation participants disagreed on how to respond to this specific problem, and proved inconclusive. Many advocated in favour of more research and factual evaluation.[171] Following up on these preparatory steps, the Commission published its official proposal in October 2011.[172] Utilizing the feedback received, the proposal did not contain a direct response to the issue of empty voting, but instead included rules for *positive* decoupling only,[173] which we will discuss in more detail later.[174] The Commission proposal did not address 'empty voting' as an example for *negative* risk-decoupling mechanisms. At the same time, the regulatory responsibility for negative risk-decoupling was transferred from the European Commission to ESMA, the new European market supervisor. The latter published a 'Call for Evidence' in September of 2011 in order to evaluate the case for regulatory intervention in this field.[175] This document cited the preparatory work completed by the Commission and the inconclusiveness with respect to a possible regulatory response.[176] At the same time, it emphasized the need to strive for a comprehensive solution to the problem.[177] In December 2011, several responses prompted by the consultation

[168] Andreas Merkner and Marco Sustmann, 'Wertpapierleihe und Empty Voting—Weitergehender Transparenzbedarf im WpHG?' [2010] Neue Zeitschrift für Gesellschaftsrecht [NZG] 1170, 1174.

[169] Transparency Directive 2004/109/EC, article 9.

[170] European Commission, 'Consultation Document on the Modernisation of the Directive 2004/109/EC on the Harmonisation of Transparency Requirements in Relation to Information About Issuers Whose Securities are Admitted to Trading on a Regulated Market' (27 May 2010), available at <http://ec.europa.eu/internal_market/securities/docs/transparency/directive/consultation_questions_en.pdf>.

[171] European Commission, *Feedback Statement on the Summary of Responses to the Consultation by DG Internal Market and Services on the Modernisation of the Transparency Directive (2004/109/EC)* (17 December 2010) 23.

[172] European Commission, *Proposal for a Directive of the European Parliament and of the Council Amending Directive 2004/109/EC on the Harmonisation of Transparency Requirements in Relation to Information about Issuers Whose Securities Are Admitted to Trading on a Regulated Market and Commission Directive 2007/14/EC* COM(2011) 683 (25 October 2011), available at <http://eur-lex.europa.eu/LexUriServ/LexUriServ.do?uri=COM:2011:0683:FIN:EN:PDF> accessed 19 August 2015.

[173] ibid. 20 (draft modification of article 13).

[174] See section VI.G.

[175] European Securities and Markets Authority (ESMA), *Call for Evidence—Empty Voting* (ESMA/2011/288, 14 September 2011), available at <http://www.esma.europa.eu/system/files/2011_288.pdf> accessed 15 August 2015; see Ellen Kelleher, 'Inquiries Starting into "Empty Voting"' *Financial Times* (London, 26 September 2011) 3.

[176] ESMA ibid. paras 9–10.

[177] ESMA ibid. paras 8–12.

were published.[178] After a thorough investigation, ESMA concluded in June 2012 that there was no case for regulatory intervention for the time being.[179] The ball is thus back in the European Commission's court, and it is unclear how and when the Commission will pick up the issue. The reform of the Transparency Directive that was eventually adopted does not touch on the issue of negative risk-decoupling.[180]

3. Costs and critique

Even if the introduction of a disclosure regime is generally supported here,[181] this cannot be done in an unreflective way. Each additional regulatory requirement creates costs for business participants, and these costs have to be balanced against their expected benefits.[182]

Direct costs. The most obvious costs are so-called *compliance costs*, which are simply caused by complying with the new obligations. This includes the effort in time and substance to access information about the new rules, to make them known within a company or organization, and to implement them into the work processes—potentially using new software, employee training, etc. Beyond these firm-level costs, *legislative and regulatory activity* itself creates costs, as resources are spent and civil servants are employed to develop new rules and to monitor compliance. In this particular context, *opportunity costs* are crucial, that is, including the cost measured in terms of the value of alternatives that are forgone and not chosen.

Indirect costs. On the other hand, a new system will create *indirect costs*, such as *avoidance costs*, which are notoriously difficult to quantify. For example, issuers will be able to avoid securities regulation by not going public. If a company refrains from an initial public offering because of legal requirements that are too cumbersome, and if the company in question accordingly forgoes an otherwise optimal method of financing, this will be costly from an overall welfare perspective. Furthermore, such costs are empirically difficult to quantify.[183]

[178] These are accessible at <http://www.esma.europa.eu/consultation/Call-evidence-Empty-voting#responses>.

[179] ESMA, *Feedback Statement—Call for Evidence on Empty Voting* (ESMA/2012/415, 29 June 2012), available at <http://www.esma.europa.eu/system/files/2012-415.pdf>.

[180] Directive 2013/50/EU of the European Parliament and of the Council of 22 October 2013 amending Directive 2004/109/EC of the European Parliament and of the Council on the harmonisation of transparency requirements in relation to information about issuers whose securities are admitted to trading on a regulated market, Directive 2003/71/EC of the European Parliament and of the Council on the prospectus to be published when securities are offered to the public or admitted to trading and Commission Directive 2007/14/EC laying down detailed rules for the implementation of certain provisions of Directive 2004/109/EC, [2013] OJ L2914/13.

[181] See Chapters V.C.3 and VI.C.1.

[182] See, for example, on the costs created by the different pieces of the EU Financial Services Action Plan the study by Europe Economics, 'Study on the Cost of Compliance with Selected FSAP Measures—Final Report' (2009) <http://ec.europa.eu/finance/docs/actionplan/index/090707_cost_of_compliance_en.pdf>.

[183] See Christian Leuz, 'Was the Sarbanes–Oxley Act of 2002 Really This Costly? A Discussion of Evidence from Event Returns and Going-Private Decisions' (2007) 44 Journal of Accounting and Economics 146 in connection with the introduction of the Sarbanes–Oxley Act.

Omission of positive effects. Another, more serious cost factor is the fact that an activity that was not carried out due to regulation can create costs in such a way that its positive effects do not materialize. So, for example, in the present problem concerning the question of greater shareholder control and its potential beneficial effects: as argued previously, negative risk-decoupling may, in some situations, yield positive benefits in the form of greater management accountability to the shareholder body, and can contribute to overcoming shareholder apathy.[184] The introduction of disclosure requirements (as advocated here) may also complicate such desirable side effects.

Market responses. Additional costs may be considered, which go to the limits of technical measurability of the effects of regulation. Indirect, hardly quantifiable costs may arise by the general market reaction to regulation.[185] Due to regulation, it may be that certain products are never introduced, certain markets are never entered into, and certain companies are never restructured. In addition, the legislature can only guess what would have happened *without* having adopted a piece of regulation. Would the market participants themselves have reacted on their own, for example voluntarily agreed to some common standard, due to reputational considerations or in order to strengthen investor confidence, which arguably is in their own interest? In the case of interest here, would the hedge fund industry commit voluntarily to a type of self-control in terms of increased transparency?[186] If such reaction happens, it is realistic to expect that it does not have the same intensity as a legislatively prescribed framework, but the urge to self-regulate can be high.[187] Finally, regulation can even act to reduce costs if it gives certain market players a 'seal of approval' for their internal verification procedures. Such a seal can reduce both the costs of the awarded companies and/or the information costs of other market participants.

In light of these considerations, it becomes clear that even seemingly mild regulatory tools such as transparency and disclosure obligations may have undue and unforeseen consequences. Some statements from the literature have therefore criticized transparency as a regulatory tool for risk-decoupling problems, based on a number of considerations. In particular, in the discussion around positive risk-decoupling (*hidden ownership*), the use of disclosure requirements is questionable, since such disclosures have a direct impact on the takeover market. Additional disclosure requirements would increase the cost of corporate

[184] See Chapter V.B.2.

[185] Europe Economics (n. 182) 6 ff. See also Financial Services Authority, *Disclosure of Contracts for Difference, Consultation and Draft Handbook text, CP 07/20* (November 2007) annex 1, p. 6–10 <http://www.fsa.gov.uk/pubs/cp/cp07_20.pdf>; Isaac Alfon and Peter Andrews, 'Cost-Benefit Analysis in Financial Regulation: How to Do It and How It Adds Value' (1999) FSA Occasional Paper Series No 3, available at <http://citeseerx.ist.psu.edu/viewdoc/download?doi=10.1.1.201.978&rep=rep1&type=pdf> 10, 11; Christian Leuz and Peter D Wysocki, 'Economic Consequences of Financial Reporting and Disclosure Regulation: A Review and Suggestions for Future Research' (Social Science Research Network 2008) SSRN Scholarly Paper ID 1105398 <http://papers.ssrn.com/abstract=1105398> accessed 11 August 2015.

[186] See on corresponding (failed) attempts section VI.A.3.

[187] Europe Economics (n. 182) 7.

takeovers in this context and send out misleading signals to the market, in the sense of a non-existent undervaluation, which would trigger even more inefficient share acquisitions.[188]

Too much information. Another problem is so-called 'information overload', which is based on the realization that too much information and transparency may be counterproductive.[189] Recent findings, in particular from behavioural economics, suggest that consumers can grasp information only to a certain degree. Based on this insight, legislators and regulators are advised to ensure in particular the quality, rather than the volume, of information.[190] Practical experience comes from Switzerland, where the introduction of new transparency requirements for contracts for difference led to a wave of disclosures that has, according to many, contributed to overburdening of a manageable information level.[191] A general rule saying that the magic notion of 'more transparency' can serve as a panacea to new economic problems can therefore not be maintained.

Specifically in the context of interest here, it is conceivable that too much ongoing disclosure may supply the market with many supposedly important pieces of information that are actually irrelevant and do not achieve their purpose. For example, it is likely that an ongoing supply of information on all movements on the securities lending market causes confusion, since many transactions will be reported which are completely innocent.[192] As a result, the market could initially classify all disclosed lending transactions as suspicious. Over time, however, the market would probably sober up and as a backlash stop attaching any importance to such notifications. Both interpretations would be wrong and unintended.

Production of wrong incentives. Further, additional indirect costs could arise from the reduced incentives for hedge funds and other activist shareholders to monitor the strategies and activities of their target companies for potential profit opportunities.[193] It is the constant search for profit opportunities through

[188] Dirk Zetzsche, 'Against Mandatory Disclosure of Economic-Only Positions Referenced to Shares of European Issuers—Twenty Arguments against the CESR Proposal' (2010) 11 European Business Organization Law Review 231, 240 f. See on this further section VI.G.

[189] Troy Paredes, 'Blinded by the Light: Information Overload and Its Consequences for Securities Regulation' (2003) 81 Washington University Law Quarterly 417. See also SEC Commissioner Troy Paredes' speech at Fordham Law School on 27 October 2011: 'Simply put, it is possible for there to be too much information for investors and others to work through constructively'; Gillian Tett, 'A Guiding Light Is Needed to Cut through the Fog of Financial Data' *Financial Times* (London, 9 March 2012) 32. For a concrete case study, see Robert P Bartlett III, 'Inefficiencies in the Information Thicket: A Case Study of Derivative Disclosures during the Financial Crisis' (2010) 36 Journal of Corporation Law 1.

[190] Financial Services Authority (n. 185) annex 1 para. 43.

[191] Susan Emmenegger, 'Creeping Takeovers in Deutschland und in der Schweiz' in Stefan Grundmann and others (eds), *Unternehmen, Markt und Verantwortung—Festschrift für Klaus J. Hopt zum 70. Geburtstag am 24. August 2010* (de Gruyter 2010) 1763, 1787.

[192] European Securities Markets Expert Group (ESME), *First Report of ESME on the Transparency Directive ('TD')* (5 December 2007) 7, available at <http://ec.europa.eu/internal_market/securities/docs/esme/05122007_td_report_en.pdf> accessed 20 August 2015.

[193] Similarly, Financial Services Authority (n. 185) annex 1 para. 39.

information advantages that accounts for the business model of many (not necessarily activist) hedge funds. Other market participants can also use the information by following or copying their example, and thereby contribute to the formation of an efficient capital market.[194] At least, this is true if one agrees with the vast literature saying that hedge funds do play an economically positive, value-creating role.[195] This behaviour is invaluable in detecting underperformance and exploring undervaluations in the market. Additional disclosure obligations could scupper the attractiveness of such activity and thereby cause a decline in the efficiency and liquidity of the market.

To be sure, these objections could be taken into account by choosing a relatively high threshold for a reporting obligation of risk-decoupling activities.[196]

Legalization effect. Another fundamental objection, though not specifically based on the point of view of cost creation, is the 'legalization' effect of disclosure requirements. In this respect, a legal requirement that mandates the disclosure of certain situations where market participants have decoupled their risk from the company share could be understood as an indirect confirmation of such transactions being allowed and permissible.[197] The weight of this argument is, however, not to be overestimated.

Effectiveness and technical details. Much more important is the question of whether additional transparency requirements would actually create a remedy for the problem discussed here.[198] Indeed, some commentators argue that strengthened transparency requirements would ultimately not deter market actors from engaging in risk-decoupling strategies.[199] Here, much depends on the details, such as the time at which transparency is required, who will receive the information, what thresholds apply, etc. The answers to these and other questions are

[194] Ronald J Gilson and Reinier H Kraakman, 'The Mechanisms of Market Efficiency' (1984) 70 Virginia Law Review 549.

[195] See Chapter II.C.

[196] Financial Services Authority (n. 185) annex 1 para. 43.

[197] See Dominique Schmidt, 'Droit financier: Empty Voting' [2012] Bulletin Joly Bourse 42, on the French reform, see Christophe Clerc at the conference organized by the European Commission on the reform of the Transparency Directive on 11 June 2010, <http://ec.europa.eu/finance/securities/transparency/index_en.htm>. See also Hermes Equity Ownership Services, 'Comments to the Consultation Document on the EC Green Paper on Corporate Governance in Financial Institutions and Remuneration Policies' (2010) 9.

[198] For a sceptical view, see the Czech government's comments on the reform of the Transparency Directive:

> No, we don't see the benefits of such disclosure mechanism. The problem of empty voting is inherent to the regulation of record day and is difficult to solve effectively. If the disclosure mechanism would be established, it is not clear how the information about possible empty voting helps the issuer or indeed other shareholders. They have no possibility to influence it anyway. There is also the question how to penalize effectively the breach of such disclosure obligation (e.g. rescission of the vote?). Even if the empty voting practices would be limited or prohibited, it would be still possible to sell the shares day after the general meeting—the resulting effect is similar to the empty voting. This cannot be banned, as it would mean a strong interference with the shareholders rights. The shareholder has no particular obligation to be loyal to the company and can vote according to its own interest, even if this would mean winding up of the company. To prevent the shareholder from exercising this right is obviously hardly feasible within the rule of law system.

[199] Robert B Thompson and Paul H Edelman, 'Corporate Voting' (2009) 62 Vanderbilt Law Review 129, 156 f.

crucial in determining whether transparency can really effectively confront risk-decoupling structures. All objections raised here and in the literature, including all opinions and cost considerations, have mostly been voiced in an abstract way, often based on unreflective opinions from academia and practice, and generally based on 'transparency' as such. All of these considerations and objections will thus be addressed in the context of the individual elements of a concrete transparency regime.[200]

4. Key issues of a transparency regime

Consideration of the advantages and direct and indirect costs of a disclosure system allows us now to develop some building blocks of a transparency regime that provides a comprehensive answer to the problem of negative risk-decoupling as a whole. This section advances a number of key considerations for such a scheme. Subsequently, section VI.C.5 will align the proposal with the parallel regime for short selling and section VI.C.6 will feed all these issues together in a concrete legislative proposal. We shall address the disclosure of positive risk-decoupling in section VI.G.

a) Subject matter and addressee

First and foremost, it is important to consider the question of what, precisely, should be disclosed. We have seen in the problem discussion previously (Chapter V) that the common element to all the constellations of negative decoupling is the presence of an existing shareholder who engages in risk-decoupling and thereby creates costs for their fellow shareholders and for (external) investors.[201] What the market needs to know is that there is a significant *negative interest in shares*: essentially, the presence of short positions in shares of issuers within the scope of the Transparency Directive. Technically speaking, a well-drafted regulatory response needs to ensure that all relevant constellations, but also all potential future cases, are caught. This has two consequences. First, a comprehensive response requires that we develop a *general clause* that is able to encompass all relevant and known constellations. The law might stipulate a non-exhaustive list of examples, which could be a more concrete option. Second, a general clause of this nature needs to be *wide enough* to cover parallel, future, and presently unknown strategies.[202]

According to the findings demonstrated above, the key problem arises when: (a) existing shareholders reduce the risk inherent in their shares (category 1); and (b) market participants hold their shareholder position only on a temporary

[200] Requesting a careful, balanced analysis: Alexandros Seretakis, 'Hedge Fund Activism Coming to Europe: Lessons from the American Experience' (2014) 8 Brooklyn Journal of Corporate, Financial & Commercial Law 438.

[201] See in particular Chapter V.B, V.C, and V.D.

[202] See section VI.C.6.a.

basis or, for example, over the record date (categories 2 and 3). Both situations have to be included in a comprehensive regulatory response. Common to both is the fact that shareholders do not bear the full risk normally attached to shares. A key requirement for a regulatory solution should therefore be that the addressee of a disclosure obligation *needs to hold a substantial long position* in the first place, as only those who already have some impact on the company's decision-making would be in a position to be able to distort them to a critical extent. A basic requirement should therefore be that the obligation of transparency is only imposed on those voting rights holders who hold at least, say, 5 per cent of the voting rights of a listed company. In short, our disclosure regime should not be interested in any short position, but only in those significant short positions that are held by somebody who simultaneously holds a significant long position.

By contrast, a regulatory rule should *not* encompass non-shareholders who acquire a purely negative interest in shares. Such a rule could catch investors who engage, for example, in short selling over certain securities. It is true that these investors are also financially interested in a negative development of the share price, but the situation is not comparable to the circumstances of interest here. A non-shareholder (or a small shareholder) would neither be able to influence the voting outcomes of the general meeting in the same way as significant shareholders, nor be able to threaten to use his influence in such a way. The possibility of a situation of intra-company manipulation does not exist in the same manner.

Equally, it follows from the discussion that the present study is not concerned with the potential conflicts of interest that result from a shareholder's stake in a competitor. Recall that this was the case in the *Mylan–Perry* case discussed previously,[203] but it is not the specific problem of interest here. As we said previously, we expect that this type of conflict will, to some extent, be evened out by random distribution.[204] On the other hand, the fact that shareholders hold a stake in a competing company is a traditional conflict of interest, which is of an entirely different quality than the problems analysed here. Put differently, the regulatory problem of interest here does not result from the conflict of interest, but rather from the distorted incentive underlying the voting right. We will accordingly target the latter because other areas of corporate law specifically dealing with conflicts of interest address the former.

b) Disclosure frequency

The success of a disclosure regime is dependent upon the appropriate moment at which disclosure is fixed to occur. Only timely disclosure will allow market participants to react appropriately.

Several options are conceivable. On the one hand, the disclosure obligation could be designed in relation to an event—for instance, the obligation of

[203] See Chapter III.B.1.a. [204] In more detail, see Chapter V.B.3.

disclosure arises before the record date[205] or the general meeting.[206] Alternatively, the disclosure obligation could only be applicable to those shareholders who request an item to be placed on the agenda of the general meeting, or who request a general meeting to be held.[207] On the other hand, the obligation of disclosure could be continuous and steady, triggered whenever a specific and relevant event occurs.

Overall, the latter option—continuous disclosure—is preferable. A singular disclosure obligation leading up to the moment of a general meeting would have the advantage of placing a minimal burden on investors. Moreover, information on the risk exposure of shareholders is most relevant in the context of the general meeting. After all, it is only at this moment that the much-discussed distortion of voting incentives becomes relevant and concrete.

Nevertheless, three main reasons support the case for a continuous disclosure obligation throughout the entire business year. First, it is important to consider the short timeframe during which shareholders are expected to adequately respond to the disclosed information. If publication occurs only briefly before the general meeting, many shareholders will not be able to react promptly.[208] For example, it will not be possible for shareholders to form a viable opposition against the goals proposed by a risk-decoupled hedge fund. This will certainly be relevant when a disclosure obligation exists immediately before the general meeting, or before the record date. After the record date, shareholders are no longer able to acquire voting rights, and thus the resistance of regular shareholders who wish to acquire more shares is no longer an issue. As a consequence, the only option remaining would be an 'exit'—likely triggering a dramatic exit wave, that is, a large-scale sale of shares. This sale would provoke a massive decline of the share price, to the detriment of minority shareholders. By contrast, a decline in the share price would not concern the risk-decoupled shareholder herself in any way. Quite the contrary, a large-scale exit of shareholders would even exacerbate the risk-decoupling problem, because these activities would create fresh disparities between voting entitlements and share ownership.

[205] Luca Enriques, speaking at the Conference on the Operation of the Transparency Directive (11 June 2010); see also the position put forward in favour of the French law reform from 2010 concerning securities lending, discussed in section VI.C.2.

[206] See Deutscher Investor Relations Verband e.V. (German Investor Relations Association), *Response of Deutscher Investor Relations Verband e.V. to the EU Commission's Public Consultation on the Revision of the Transparency Directive—Appendix* (23 August 2010) 10 f., available at <https://circabc.europa.eu/sd/a/b5aff1c8-0a3d-46a9-b41a-cc6e049d7f59/German_Investor_Relations_Association_en.pdf> accessed 19 August 2015.

[207] This will, of course, be subject to the usual hurdles for convening a general meeting. For such a proposal, see Eumedion Corporate Governance Forum, *Position Paper on the Consequences of Synthetic Structures for Dutch Securities Law and Company Law* (17 November 2008) 10, available at <http://eumedion.nl/en/public/knowledgenetwork/position-papers/2008-position-paper-hidden-ownership-and-empty-voting.pdf> accessed 19 August 2015.

[208] See, e.g., Jean-François Biard, 'Proposition de Loi Relative au Régime des Prêts Emprunts de Titres' [2010] Revue de Droit Bancaire et Financier 155 (relating to the French reform, as discussed previously).

Second, and even more importantly, it is not the process of voting at the general meeting alone that is crucial for the effects of risk-decoupling strategies. At this point it is important to reconsider the previous discussions of agency and information costs.[209] As explained previously, the costs created by risk-decoupling strategies are incurred at any time, throughout the entire business year. The threat of calling a meeting is one of several options activist investors have at any given time. Otherwise, a risk-decoupled investor can informally influence the management at any moment, even on an unofficial basis.

Especially for institutional investors and hedge funds, these informal ways of influencing companies, coupled with the threat of exercising their voting power, are often much more important than the vote itself.[210] A constant dialogue, away from the public, will pressure the administration to act in a certain way. This type of influence is always available during and outside of the general meeting.[211] By exercising such informal power, a risk-decoupled shareholder puts considerable pressure on other shareholders and potential investors alike, both outside the formal meeting and during the entire business year.

Third, and relatedly, in some situations the written consent of shareholders can replace formal resolutions. For example, according to Delaware law, if the majority consents in writing, action can be taken without a meeting.[212] The same or similar rules exist in several other jurisdictions.[213]

c) *Disclosure recipient*

Next it is necessary to clarify who is to receive the information to be disclosed. The current system of capital market publicity in European law typically specifies that the relevant information must be transmitted to both the issuer and the market regulator (see e.g. Directive 2004/109/EC, articles 9(1) and 19(3)). The issuer must then publish the notifications received without delay and thus make them available to the market (ibid. article 12(6)).[214]

In the recent policy debate on the introduction of new reporting requirements, it was proposed to limit potential new requirements in a way such that information (on negative interests) should first solely be transmitted to the respective market surveillance authorities. It could then be left to the discretion of the authority to decide what of the reported information would actually be published.[215] This

[209] See Chapter V.B and V.C.

[210] As has been documented by Marco Becht and others, 'Returns to Shareholder Activism: Evidence from a Clinical Study of the Hermes UK Focus Fund' (2009) 22 Review of Financial Studies 3093.

[211] ibid.

[212] Delaware General Corporation Law § 228.

[213] Jay W Eisenhofer and Michael J Barry, *Shareholder Activism Handbook* (Aspen Publishers 2013) 9–9.

[214] See also article 16.

[215] In this sense Assonime, the Italian association of public companies, according to Latham & Watkins, *Disclosure of Cash-Settled Derivatives under Italian Securities Laws—Current Law and Proposed*

argument finds support in the risk of over-regulation and an otherwise excessive burden on the market players.[216]

The analysis carried out here, however, has shown that a high demand for information exists not only for the market supervisor, but especially also for the public and for both inside shareholders and outside, potential investors.[217] The market supervisor alone usually cannot reliably assess what information is of importance for the market and what is irrelevant. Therefore there is no reason to refrain from the general disclosure obligation. Instead, it is even more urgently needed here than in the general framework of major shareholding disclosure. The concern of overburdening the issuer can be counterbalanced by the introduction of minimum threshold values, as discussed later.

d) Disclosure threshold

It follows from the foregoing analysis (recipient and frequency) that relatively high short disclosure thresholds are required for an adequate and balanced disclosure regime. This goes hand-in-hand with the assertion that a continuous disclosure obligation is needed. If we require market participants to disclose their negative interest at all times, we need another filter to single out the disclosure information that is meaningful.

It appears that a reasonably high threshold, such as a short position of 5 per cent, should be appropriate.[218] This is based on a number of reasons.

First, it would better serve the purpose identified here, as we are concerned with shareholders who hold a particular long stake, but who at the same time have reduced or eliminated their risk. Only the kind of stake accumulated in the first instance will give a shareholder the necessary voting power to influence the target company, and only a sufficiently high-risk elimination will distort her incentives in a meaningful way. Take, for example, a 10 per cent long shareholder who has reduced her risk exposure by one percentage point. She will still be risk-exposed to 9 per cent of the share capital, which is not a significant distortion. In such a situation, the shareholder will not be induced to pervert the influence stemming from the long position for a purpose that would give raise to regulatory concerns. Instead, it can be argued that a significant difference between the long and the short position is needed, which should be around 5 per cent of the issued share capital, or more.

Second, a high threshold conforms to our goal of minimizing the administrative costs for market participants.[219] Low threshold disclosure rules for short positions

Reforms, Client Alert No 1042 (10 June 2010) 5, available at <http://www.latham.com/thoughtLeadership/disclosure-of-cash-settled-derivatives-in-italy/> accessed 19 August 2015.

[216] ibid. [217] See sections V.B.1.b, V.C.2, and V.D.2.

[218] The 5 per cent value mirrors the corresponding threshold for long position under the Transparency Directive, article 9, and also the long position required to be held in order to trigger a disclosure of negative interest (see Chapter IV.A. and section VI.C.4.a).

[219] See IOSCO, Technical Committee, *Regulation of Short Selling—Final Report* (June 2009) para. 3.23.5, available at <https://www.iosco.org/library/pubdocs/pdf/IOSCOPD292.pdf>: 'In considering the appropriate trigger level of reporting and frequency of reporting, the Technical

risk being over-inclusive and forcing the disclosure of harmless trading activity, which is not intended to influence corporate governance arrangements within a company. In particular, institutional investors might easily cross lower thresholds through normal trading positions.[220] In this way, we also take into account the high costs of additional disclosure obligations.[221]

Third, too comprehensive disclosure of short positions may provoke market overreactions. It may trigger herd behaviour or accelerate downward movements, as recently evidenced by the 2008–9 financial crisis. That is, if short positions are frequently disclosed, unsophisticated investors are more likely to sell in response to seeing a more sophisticated investor with a short position, exacerbating market declines.[222] Finally, the circumstances could reduce market liquidity because investors do not like to reveal their short positions to companies. Thus, these investors prefer to avoid taking short positions altogether.

For these reasons, a relatively high initial threshold should be preferred. An initial threshold of 5 per cent of negative interest appears reasonable.

5. Co-ordination with transparency of short selling

The disclosure obligation for negative interests in shares suggested here needs to be integrated into the existing regulatory framework.[223] In particular, it is important to consider that the EU institutions also adopted a legislative instrument concerning short selling, which is somewhat related to the issue under consideration here. This is the EU Regulation on Short Selling and Certain Aspects of Credit Default Swaps (CDS).[224] While this Regulation has a different scope and regulatory purpose, it is nevertheless essential to address its potential inconsistencies and common issues, since the Regulation goes far beyond addressing short selling (and CDS), and catches many negative interests of a different kind.[225] As we shall see in the following, there

Committee is mindful that setting a threshold too low or requiring too frequent reporting may be overly burdensome for constituents responsible for reporting' (in the context of short selling).

220 Again in the particular context of short selling disclosure, see Herbert Smith, *Reflections on the New Pan-European Regime for Short Selling and Credit Default Swaps* (2012) 4, available at <http://www.herbertsmithfreehills.com/-/media/HS/L230212219.pdf> accessed on 19 August 2015. On short selling disclosure generally, see section VI.C.5.

221 See section VI.C.3.

222 European Parliament, Committee on Economic and Monetary Affairs, *Report on the Proposal for a Regulation of the European Parliament and of the Council on Short Selling and Certain Aspects of Credit Default Swaps*, No A7-0055/2011 (19 April 2011) 45, available at <http://www.europarl.europa.eu/sides/getDoc.do?pubRef=-//EP//NONSGML+REPORT+A7-2011-0055+0+DOC+PDF+V0//EN> accessed on 19 August 2015.

223 This was requested in particular by ESMA, *Report: Mapping of the Transparency Directive – Options, Discretions and 'Gold-Plating'*, ESMA/2011/194 (7 July 2011) para. 42, available at <http://www.esma.europa.eu/system/files/2011_194.pdf>.

224 Regulation (EU) No 236/2012 of the European Parliament and the European Council of 14 March 2012 on Short Selling and Certain Aspects of Credit Default Swaps, [2012] OJ L86/1 (hereinafter Short Selling Regulation). See on this in detail Niamh Moloney, *EU Securities and Financial Markets Regulation* (3rd edn, Oxford University Press 2014) 538 ff.

225 The Short Selling Regulation was subject to an unsuccessful legal challenge by the UK Government. See case C-270/12 *United Kingdom v European Parliament and Council* ECLI:EU:C:2014:18.

are some potentially common issues of interest and conflicts with the regulatory proposal made here. This warrants a close examination of the two instruments.

a) Short selling

Short selling commonly describes a transaction of selling securities or other financial instruments that the seller does not currently own, with the objective of subsequently repurchasing them. The seller expects or hopes for an intermediate price decline of the securities, as the transaction is profitable for them where the cost of purchase is less than the proceeds which they received upon the initial short sale.[226]

During the 2008–9 global financial crisis, short selling was associated with a negative role, allegedly exacerbating a downward trend in the market.[227] Although neither theoretical nor empirical studies have found distorting effects of short selling on the development of stock prices,[228] the regulation of short selling has been on the activity list of a wide variety of legislatures and regulators over the past few years.[229]

A distinction is usually made between covered and uncovered (naked) short selling.[230] In a covered short sale, the seller usually borrows the securities first before selling them, and his subsequent purchase in the market accordingly has the objective of returning like securities to the lender. The counterpart is a naked short sale, where the seller neither owns the securities nor has a claim for delivery at the end of the same day on which the sale is completed.

b) Regulation of short selling after the financial crisis

On an international level, the attempts to regulate short selling diverge significantly. However, the more recent development is one of a certain convergence.[231]

[226] See in detail Emilios Avgouleas, 'A New Framework for the Global Regulation of Short Sales: Why Prohibition Is Inefficient and Disclosure Insufficient' (2010) 15 Stanford Journal of Law, Business and Finance 376; Henry T C Hu, 'Too Complex to Depict? Innovation, Pure Information, and the SEC Disclosure Paradigm' (2012) 90 Texas Law Review 1601, 1688 ff.

[227] See in particular Hans-Werner Sinn, *Casino Capitalism: How the Financial Crisis Came About and What Needs to Be Done Now* (Oxford University Press 2010) 153 f. See the Letter from International Organization of Securities Commissions (IOSCO) to the G20 (12 November 2008), available at <http://www.iosco.org/library/pubdocs/pdf/IOSCOPD282.pdf> accessed 19 August 2015. Contrast this with the findings from the Kay Review: *The Kay Review of UK Equity Markets and Long-Term Decision Making: Final Report* (July 2012) para. 9.24. Generally, on the economic role of short sales, see ESME, *Position on Short Selling* (19 March 2009), available at <http://ec.europa.eu/internal_market/securities/docs/esme/report_20090319_en.pdf>.

[228] For an overview, see Steven N Kaplan, Tobias J Moskowitz, and Berk A Sensoy, 'The Effects of Stock Lending on Security Prices: An Experiment' (2013) 68 Journal of Finance 1891.

[229] Moloney (n. 224).

[230] See ESMA, *Update on Measures Adopted by Competent Authorities on Short Selling* ESMA/2011/39a (24 July 2012), available at <http://www.esma.europa.eu/system/files/2011-39.pdf> accessed 19 August 2015.

[231] ESMA provides for an overview of national regulatory instruments on its website at <http://www.esma.europa.eu/page/Short-selling>. See also Fabian Walla, 'Short Selling' in Rüdiger Veil (ed.), *European Capital Markets Law* (Hart Publishing 2013) 201 ff.

Following protracted negotiations,[232] the EU institutions adopted a regulation that introduced a pan-European regulatory approach to short selling.[233] In essence, the proposal follows previous work[234] done by the Committee of European Securities Regulators (CESR)[235] and IOSCO.[236] The new regime provides for a two-tiered transparency system, encompassing all net short positions that can arise not only through short sales, but also through the use of various derivatives.[237] The threshold values are 0.2 per cent for a disclosure to the respective national supervisory authority and 0.5 per cent for public release (in both cases plus 0.1 percentage point increments).[238] The net short position shall be determined on each trading day at midnight and is to be reported by 3.30 p.m. on the following day.[239] Originally, the EU Commission had also intended that any short sale orders in the daily operations should be labelled as such in order to distinguish them from regular sales orders (flagging principle).[240] This part was not included in the final text of the regulation, however.

Overall, the Commission expects the new harmonized transparency requirements to ensure that information on short positions is provided to regulators, and that the market is complete and accurate.[241] Article 3(1) of the regulation defines a short position as follows:

(1) For the purposes of this Regulation, a position resulting from either of the following shall be considered to be a short position relating to issued share capital or issued sovereign debt:
   (a) a short sale of a share issued by a company or of a debt instrument issued by a sovereign issuer;
   (b) entering into a transaction which creates or relates to a financial instrument other than an instrument referred to in point (a) where the effect or one of the effects

[232] See European Commission, *Proposal for a Regulation of the European Parliament and of The Council on Short Selling and Certain Aspects of Credit Default Swaps*, COM(2010) 482 final (15 September 2010); European Council, *Proposal for a Regulation of the European Parliament and of the Council on Short Selling and Certain Aspects of Credit Default Swaps—Text Provisionally Agreed with the European Parliament*, Council Document 16338/11 (4 November 2011). On the various drafts, see Emilios Avgouleas, 'The Regulation of Short Sales Revisited' (2011) 5 Law and Financial Markets Review 333.

[233] See n. 224.

[234] CESR, *Model for a Pan-European Short Selling Disclosure Regime* CESR/10-088 (March 2010), available at <http://www.esma.europa.eu/system/files/10_088.pdf> accessed 19 August 2015; IOSCO, Technical Committee, *Regulation of Short Selling—Final Report* (June 2009), available at <https://www.iosco.org/library/pubdocs/pdf/IOSCOPD292.pdf> accessed 19 August 2015.

[235] The Committee of European Securities Regulators (CESR) was the predecessor of the new European regulatory body, ESMA.

[236] IOSCO is the International Organization of Securities Commissions.

[237] Short Selling Regulation (n. 224), recital 10; see Commission Proposal (n. 232) 6; Council Document 16338/11 (n. 232), recitals 6, 9.

[238] Short Selling Regulation (n. 224), articles 5(1)-(2), 6(1)-(2).

[239] ibid. article 9(2).

[240] Commission Proposal (n. 232), article 6. For a more sceptical view, see CESR, *CESR Proposal for a Pan-European Short Selling Disclosure Regime* CESR/09-581 (8 July 2009), available at <http://www.esma.europa.eu/system/files/09_581.pdf> accessed 19 August 2015; CESR, *Model for a Pan-European Short Selling Disclosure Regime* (n. 234) paras 17 ff. Flagging is required in certain jurisdictions, such as Australia, Canada, Japan, Hong Kong, and the United States.

[241] Commission Proposal (n. 232) 7.

> of the transaction is to confer a financial advantage on the natural or legal person entering into that transaction in the event of a decrease in the price or value of the share or debt instrument.[242]

The definition is an attempt to capture all positions that give their holder a negative interest in equity shares. Of the various constellations examined in the present study, securities lending alone is not included. In contrast to the original version of the Commission proposal, the regulation explicitly does not cover repurchase agreements (repos), derivatives, or securities lending.[243]

How does this compare to the disclosure system advocated here? The two instruments would have a number of issues in common, since both seek to extend disclosure not only to long but also to short positions in public companies. However, this common starting point cannot conceal that the differences prevail. First, it should be noted that both regulatory approaches have different legal policy objectives. While the regulation of short selling was mainly influenced by the experiences of the financial crisis of 2008–9 and the strengthening of market stability and investor confidence in capital markets as a whole, the concern of the present study is initially to address matters of internal governance and shareholder influence within a corporation, and accordingly individual investor protection. For the purpose of the current inquiry, it is thus important to note that the new EU regime, along with other international efforts, approaches the issue of net short positions predominantly from a *market stability* perspective, and not so much from an investor protection view or corporate governance considerations.[244] These efforts are indeed consistent and understandable, but they cannot satisfy the need identified here for the detection of negative risk-decoupling activities.

The established fundamental problem here is not one of stability as a whole, but of the protection against individual manipulation of the voting rights of shareholders. Therefore, the Short Selling Regulation, although mandating the disclosure of short positions in a related way, does not meet the requirements set out here for the individuality of the shareholder as well as to the separate disclosure of positive and negative interest or exposures. It is therefore necessary to either insert the presented requirements into the existing body of law or provide a separate reporting regime for risk-decoupled voting rights. The technical style of drafting the legislation is of less concern than the formulation of key policy goals.

In sum, we have seen that the short selling regime has a number of characteristics that would have to be reconsidered for the purposes of the present investigation. These will be discussed later. Among the main shortcomings, for the present purposes, are that the Short Selling Regulation introduces relatively low thresholds, only mandates for the disclosure of net values, and only requires disclosure to the

[242] Short Selling Regulation (n. 224) article 3(1). [243] ibid. recital 17 and article 2(1)(b).

[244] CESR, *CESR Proposal for a Pan-European Short Selling Disclosure Regime* (n. 240) para. 38: '[Disclosure of short positions is] intended to mitigate the risks posed by short selling to orderly markets and/or market abuse'.

market authority, not to the market itself. This is also a good opportunity to draw a number of lessons for the present project, and to get some clarification of what a risk-decoupling framework would have to achieve.

c) *Lessons to be drawn for the present study*

These introductory remarks allow us to develop a number of clarifications regarding when a disclosure regime for risk-decoupling situations would fundamentally differ from the market stability regime of short selling transparency. In what follows, I will pick a few policy objectives and compare them in light of the two legal instruments.

(i) High disclosure thresholds

First, the Short Selling Regulation introduces relatively *low disclosure thresholds*, which runs counter to the objective formulated previously for a risk-decoupling framework.[245] It is understandable that a market stability system requires much lower thresholds to establish a timely early warning system. The short selling lawmaker thus places particular emphasis on comprehensive and early information from the market authorities, who are to be informed well in advance of possible market uncertainties to be able to respond appropriately.

Nevertheless, even in this context, the low initial threshold values of net 0.2 per cent and 0.5 per cent have attracted criticism. Market participants have expressed concern regarding institutional investors who invest in small or medium-sized enterprises, because they may often exceed the values relatively quickly.[246] Also, low disclosure thresholds with a corresponding high volume of disclosure may lead to herding and panic reactions in the markets.[247] Accordingly, the Committee on Legal Affairs of the European Parliament requested the threshold be raised to 1 per cent.[248] A market evaluation published a few months after the Regulation came into force also renewed these criticisms.[249] As a consequence of these criticisms, the final version of the regulation now expressly provides for the possibility that the Commission has the power to adjust the thresholds to market realities if necessary, as prompted by ESMA.[250] At present, however, it appears that the thresholds are being left untouched for the near future.[251]

245 See section VI.C.4.a. 246 Herbert Smith (n. 220) 4.

247 European Parliament, Committee on Economic and Monetary Affairs (n. 222) 51; IOSCO, Technical Committee (n. 234) para. 3.19.

248 European Parliament, Committee on Economic and Monetary Affairs (n. 222) 48.

249 See ESMA, *Final Report—ESMA's Technical Advice on the Evaluation of the Regulation (EU) 236/2012 of the European Parliament and of the Council on Short Selling and Certain Aspects of Credit Default Swaps*, ESMA/2013/614 (3 June 2013) paras 22, 23, available at <http://www.esma.europa.eu/system/files/2013-614_final_report_on_ssr_evaluation.pdf> accessed 19 August 2015. But see also ibid. paras 30–2.

250 Short Selling Regulation (n. 224), articles 5(3)-(4), 6(3)-(4).

251 European Commission, *Report from the Commission to the European Parliament and the Council on the Evaluation of the Regulation (EU) No 236/2012 on Short Selling and Certain Aspects of Credit Default Swaps*, COM(2013) 885 final (13 December 2013) 2, available at <http://ec.europa.eu/finance/

If this approach was already controversial in the context of addressing market stability issues, it would be disastrous for the purposes of the present study. Any attempt to address risk-decoupling with such a small threshold would seriously over-regulate the conflict of interest here, that is, *within* the company. A shareholder holding a purely negative position of 0.2 per cent of the shares, without holding a substantial long position, has no voting power in the company and cannot eliminate any risk in the first place. As we saw above, for the purpose of the present study, the extent of voting power within the corporation is crucial.[252] Accordingly, the voting right thresholds required for the present purpose will have to be much higher. The comparison thus confirms our early decision to address significant equity-holders who significantly reduce their risk exposure.

(ii) Identity of short position holder

Second, the *identity of the market participant holding the short position* is less important under the Short Selling Regulation than it is here. It has even variously been suggested to anonymize the public disclosures: arguably, the disclosure of individual short positions does not help the regulators to uncover abusive market behaviour and market instabilities.[253] This concept would of course not be helpful in the present context of risk-decoupling, where it is essential to detect the identity of the irregular shareholder. Both the reputation of the risk-decoupler, her track record, and her potential interest in other companies are important pieces of information that will be useful in formulating an appropriate response to the risk-decoupling activity.

(iii) Gross position disclosure

Different from the short selling regime, a disclosure regulation of risk-decoupling strategies would have to reflect *gross* positions and refrain from automatic netting. This insight is based on the considerations discussed later.

As indicated above, the Short Selling Regulation and the risk-decoupling issues presented here rely on different fundamental objectives. The financial crisis of 2008–9 inspired the regulation of short sales, and the Short Selling Regulation primarily targets short sales that may be susceptible to manipulation, investor confidence, and the overall stability of the financial markets.[254] Law-makers have mainly been concerned with price stability affected by several activities: (a) the frequent use of short selling; (b) an increased supply of securities in circulation as a result of short sales and thus a self-fulfilling prophecy of falling prices; and (c) the temptation for

securities/docs/short_selling/131213_report_en.pdf>: 'ESMA considers that the current thresholds of the SSR are well-suited to generate both meaningful information for competent authorities and the market as well as a proportionate compliance burden on investors. ESMA considers that the current reporting thresholds and incremental levels for shares are appropriate and should remain unchanged'.

[252] See section VI.C.4.a.

[253] Proposed amendment 8 (on article 7(1) of the Draft Regulation) by the Committee on Legal Affairs, inserted by European Parliament, Committee on Economic and Monetary Affairs (n. 222) 50 f.

[254] See CESR, *Model for a Pan-European Short Selling Disclosure Regime* (n. 234) 5.

short sellers to accelerate price decline through targeted distribution of negative information and even higher price reductions.[255] This explains the interest of the Short Selling Regulation in the *net* position—in the net mismatch between long and short, which is alone of interest when considering market stability. By contrast, the present study looks at investors not from the angle of market stability, but from an intra-company governance perspective. In other words, the present investigation is preoccupied with individual investor protection, not market stability. This will require a different perspective on netting—investors will need to know the extent of the long position and the short position in order to evaluate the governance risk in the firm. *Gross disclosure* is therefore essential.

In addition, some fear that circumvention strategies and abuse attempts will result from the netting of long and short positions. In Hong Kong, where a disclosure regime for negative interests was introduced as early as 2003, this was one of the main reasons for insisting on having a separate disclosure of both long and short positions, and for not allowing netting between both sides.[256] Also some preparatory work in Europe argued that netting between long and short could easily be exploited, in particular in group situations where the parents and subsidiaries could engineer situations that would escape disclosure.[257] Moreover, netted information would be significantly weaker and less meaningful in comparison with separate positive and negative messages.[258]

What information do shareholders and investors really need? Information on aggregated risk exposure, as required by the Short Selling Regulation, does not satisfy the requirements that emerge from the information problem developed in the present study. Instead, this study advocates for a separate (gross) reporting requirement for a negative interest in shares.[259] Only when such a disclosure is concurrently applicable with the existing regime of positive interests pursuant to the Transparency Directive will sufficient information be provided to market players. A few examples may illustrate this concept.

Example (a) Hedge fund A holds 7 per cent of the shares in the listed company G, which it discloses in accordance with the national law implementing article 9 of the Transparency Directive. A enters into derivative transactions totalling 7 per cent of the shares of G, which eliminate its risk in the shares of G completely. Its 'net short position' is zero, so there is no reporting requirement under the Short Selling Regulation.[260] From the corporate governance angle developed here, however, it is extremely important for G's other shareholders and potential investors to learn

[255] Jennifer Payne, 'The Regulation of Short Selling and Its Reform in Europe' (2012) 13 European Business Organization Law Review (EBOR) 413.

[256] Hong Kong Securities and Futures Commission (SFC), *Proposed Amendments to The Securities (Disclosure of Interests) Ordinance—Consultation Conclusions* (March 1999) 42 f, available at <http://www.sfc.hk/edistributionWeb/gateway/EN/consultation/conclusion?refNo=98CP4> accessed 19 August 2015.

[257] CESR, *Model for a Pan-European Short Selling Disclosure Regime* (n. 234) para. 49.

[258] Securities and Futures Commission (n. 256).

[259] See Eumedion (n. 207) 9. But see Shareowners.org, *Letter in Response to SEC Concept Release on the U.S. Proxy System*, File No. S7 1410 (20 October 2010) 7.

[260] Short Selling Regulation (n. 224) articles 3(4), 5(1).

about this derivatives business. Mindful of the legal and political insights stemming from the perspective of the principal-agent conflict and information costs, as discussed previously, a duty to inform the market should be introduced in this scenario.

Example (b) Hedge fund B owns 1 per cent of the shares in G, which is not disclosure-relevant under the Transparency Directive. B enters into comparable derivatives transactions in the amount equivalent to 1.5 per cent of the shares in G. The net short position of B is -0.5 per cent, so this is to be notified under the new Short Selling Regulation both to the national regulator and to the public.[261] But it follows from our reflections above that the reasons for risk-decoupling would *not* necessarily require disclosure here. B only holds a voting position of 1 per cent, which is too small to have a lasting impact on the company's strategy or to pursue or convene a general meeting.

In addition, it is possible that netting the two positions could be misleading or ambiguous. Shareholders and investors who learn about such a notification would be unaware of how strong B's influence in G really is. There is a noticeable difference between a 0.1 per cent shareholder, who holds risk-eliminating derivatives of 0.6 per cent, and a 4.9 per cent shareholder,[262] whose risk is reduced by 5.4 per cent. Hence, having two separate notifications would be much more informative.

Example (c) Hedge Fund C holds a 10 per cent stake in G, which it discloses according to the Transparency Directive. C enters into derivatives transactions amounting to 5 per cent over shares of G, which reduce C's equity risk to that extent—namely, a partial risk elimination. Because C is far from reaching a negative 'net short position', a disclosure requirement under the Short Selling Regulation is not required, which is consistent from the perspective of market stability, as there is no incentive for C to artificially bring down the share price of G. Given our considerations here, however, distorted incentives for C's voting decisions arise. The principal-agent theory shows that C will not make optimal decisions for the benefit of all shareholders and potential investors. Because the distortion is significant, comprising five percentage points, the information is crucial to shareholders and investors.

(iv) Comprehensive definition

The key element of any disclosure framework is the substantive piece of information that needs to be disclosed. It is open to debate whether the Short

[261] ibid. articles 5(1), 6(1).

[262] This would be just under the initial disclosure threshold for long positions according to article 9 of the Transparency Directive. Most EU Member States are following this regime, although some have reduced it to 3 per cent or even to 2 per cent. See European Commission, *Report on More Stringent National Measures Concerning Directive 2004/109/EC on the Harmonisation of Transparency Requirements in Relation to Information About Issuers Whose Securities are Admitted to Trading on a Regulated Market*, SEC(2008) 3033 final, 6. The United States also has a 5 per cent initial threshold. See Securities Exchange Act 1934, Pub. L. No. 73–291, § 13(d), 48 Stat. 881 (codified as amended at 15 U.S.C. § 78j).

Selling Regulation covers all relevant instances that are essential for the present purposes.

The Regulation brings together situations of overall prevailing negative interest under the notion of 'net short position'. Such a position exists by virtue of article 3(4) of the Regulation: '[A]fter deducting any long position that a natural or legal person holds in relation to the issued share capital from any short position that that natural or legal person holds in relation to that capital'.

In turn, article 3(1) defines a 'short position' as

> (a) a short sale of a share issued by a company...or (b) entering into a transaction which creates or relates to a financial instrument other than an instrument referred to in point (a) where the effect or one of the effects of the transaction is to confer a financial advantage on the natural or legal person entering into that transaction, in the event of a decrease in the price or value of the share or debt instrument.

The term 'financial instrument' is broad and defined in the EU Market Infrastructure Directive (MiFID 2).[263]

So, overall, the Regulation covers ample ground and provides for a broad understanding of what may be 'short' positions. Nevertheless, it is obvious that a few gaps remain. Most notably, our category 2, comprising cases of share lending or repurchase agreements, is not explicitly covered by the Regulation.[264] As we saw above, the borrower of securities becomes the (temporary) owner of the security.[265] Such a temporary acquisition of full property does not fit into the Short Selling Regulation. Accordingly, it is exempted from the Regulation's disclosure obligations. Since securities lending is an important case of application of risk-decoupling in the present investigation, the definition required here will have to diverge substantially from that of the Short Selling Regulation. We saw that the disclosure of a borrowed share position is extremely controversial and treated very differently in the various Member States.[266] The disclosure regime developed here therefore needs to find a coherent approach.

In the quest for the right way forward, a law reform in Hong Kong may serve as illustration of a successful integration of the various aspects of 'negative interest'. As early as 2003, Hong Kong introduced a disclosure regime for short positions of all

[263] Directive 2014/65/EU of the European Parliament and of the Council of 15 May 2014 on markets in financial instruments and amending Directive 2002/92/EC and Directive 2011/61/EU (recast), annex I, part C, [2014] OJ L173/349.

[264] Short Selling Regulation (n. 224), recital 17 and article 2(1)(b).

[265] See Chapter III.B.2.a.

[266] See, e.g., Mazars and Marccus Partners, *Transparency Directive Assessment Report—Prepared for the European Commission Internal Market and Services DG, Final Report* (December 2009), available at <http://ec.europa.eu/internal_market/securities/docs/transparency/report-application_en.pdf> accessed 12 August 2015; see also European Commission, *Feedback Statement on the Summary of Responses to the Consultation by DG Internal Market and Services on the Modernisation of the Transparency Directive (2004/109/EC)* (17 December 2010) 41, available at <http://ec.europa.eu/finance/securities/docs/transparency/transparency-consultation-summary_en.pdf> accessed 18 August 2015; Eddy Wymeersch, 'Shareholder(s) Matter(s)' in Stefan Grundmann and others (eds), *Festschrift für Klaus J. Hopt zum 70. Geburtstag am 24. August 2010: Unternehmen, Markt und Verantwortung* (De Gruyter 2010) 1571.

types, with the aim of capturing the economic interests of a company's major shareholders and making these interests more transparent. For this purpose, the revised Securities and Futures Ordinance (SFR)[267] provides that shareholders whose stake exceeds 5 per cent need to disclose if they hold, beyond the long position, also a short position of at least 1 per cent of the same issuer's share capital.[268] Long and short positions cannot be aggregated, but they must be specified separately.[269] Remarkably, securities borrowing positions are to be explicitly included in the calculation of the short position, since section 308 defines a short position as follows:

'short position' (淡倉) means the position which a person has—
(a) where the person is the holder, writer or issuer of any equity derivatives, by virtue of which the person-
   (i) has a right to require another person to take delivery of the underlying shares of the equity derivatives;
   (ii) is under an obligation to deliver the underlying shares of the equity derivatives to another person, if called upon to do so;
   (iii) has a right to receive from another person an amount if the price of the underlying shares of the equity derivatives declines; or
   (iv) has a right to avoid or reduce a loss if the price of the underlying shares of the equity derivatives declines,

   before or on a certain date or within a certain period, whether in any case the right or obligation is conditional or absolute; or
(b) where the person is the borrower of shares under a securities borrowing and lending agreement, by virtue of which the person is under an obligation to deliver shares to another person who has lent shares, if called upon to do so, before or on a certain date or within a certain period, whether or not the obligation to deliver shares is to be settled by payment of cash or by delivery of shares or otherwise.[270]

Paragraph (a) refers to the various derivatives, whereas paragraph (b) determines that the borrower of shares holds a negative position as well. According to the Securities and Futures Commission (SFC), the Hong Kong market regulator, the borrower of securities may acquire a long and a short position at the same time, and so he may be required to issue a double notification.[271] However, a number of exceptions are stipulated.[272]

This approach appears to be a good starting point for the further analysis to come. In summary, the different points developed here will be elaborated into a concrete legislative format in the next section. For now, we can summarize that we have identified the need for: (a) a continuous disclosure obligation (b) by existing shareholders who hold a sizeable long position, such as 5 per cent of the voting

[267] Hong Kong Securities & Futures Ordinance, chapter 571, LN 12 of 2003 (1 April 2003).
[268] ibid. Part XV.
[269] See also IOSCO, Technical Committee, *Report on Transparency of Short Selling* (June 2003) 17, available at <http://www.iosco.org/library/pubdocs/pdf/IOSCOPD147.pdf> accessed 19 August 2015.
[270] Securities & Futures Ordinance (n. 267), § 308.
[271] Securities & Futures Committee, Outline of Part XV of the Securities and Futures Ordinance (Cap. 571)—Disclosure of Interests, para. 2.4.2 (6 August 2003).
[272] Securities & Futures Ordinance (n. 267), § 309.

rights, (c) along with an equally significant short position; (d) both positions should not be aggregated but disclosed separately, (e) and the definition of a short position needs to cover all relevant scenarios, including borrowed securities.

6. A concrete proposal: An integrated disclosure system

The analysis of the disclosure regime for short selling allows us now to develop our own system, which is to meet the legal policy considerations presented here. The solution advocated here for the problem of risk-decoupling is based on an integrated disclosure system for a negative interest in shares of listed companies, if only for those that are held by significant voting rights holders. The basic idea is that those interested in the company do not only, as usual, have to disclose a positive exposure in the shares to the investors and the capital market, but also need to reveal a negative interest as well. It is, however, not a question of mirroring positive and negative interest;[273] rather, we intend to mandate disclosure of a significant 'short' position which is held by an already significant 'long' shareholder.

As will be shown, this solution has considerable advantages over the previously circulated proposals: (a) it is a comprehensive solution that not only treats a portion of the risk-decoupling problem, but takes all different constellations into account; (b) it is a solution that harmonizes with the previously existing regime and does not represent a foreign element in our disclosure regime; (c) and it is also a solution that does not cause unreasonable costs for the actors involved in the capital market.

a) Details of a reporting requirement

As a first step, it is necessary to unite the different possible constellations of risk-decoupling in one common phrase.

It is a particular challenge for the wording of any piece of regulation to foresee various possible constellations and incorporate them into the legislative text in advance. This 'art of legislation' has frequently resorted to using the tool of general clauses or basic terminology, which is open to judicial interpretation.

However, specific lists with well-defined, narrow elements tend to be easily circumvented, invite regulatory arbitrage, and are usually not able to keep up with the fast pace of economic development and financial innovation. A broad general clause, by contrast, has the disadvantage of often being imprecise and not conducive to legal certainty. The task of formulating a common event for the various risk-decoupling strategies must move within this field of tension. The best solution is to find a general clause as a starting point, and to juxtapose the legislative wording with a (non-exhaustive) list of examples, which aim at both facilitating application and enforcement and limiting judicial and regulatory discretion. For the present

[273] On this see CESR, *CESR Proposal for a Pan-European Short Selling Disclosure Regime* (n. 240) para. 38.

purposes, we have chosen the term 'risk-modifying agreement' as a general clause and further substantiate this term with examples, as explained later.

A shareholder who is already within the scope of the Transparency Directive article 9, that is, a shareholder who has already crossed the threshold of a positive obligation to report by holding a long position of more than 5 per cent of the voting rights, should be subject to the disclosure obligation.[274] According to the proposal made here, such a shareholder is required to additionally disclose any risk-modifying agreement that is referenced to shares amounting to more than 5 per cent of the voting rights of the same issuer.[275] As our problem discussion, in particular the transaction and information costs perspectives, has revealed, regulatory intervention is particularly necessary for large public companies.[276] Therefore, in line with the established capital market law reporting obligations, the obligation of transparency should be introduced only for listed companies.

All of this leads us to the following proposal, which is to be inserted into the Transparency Directive 2004/109/EC (as revised).

b) A concrete proposal

Accordingly, the following new article, to be inserted into the Transparency Directive, is suggested here as follows:

Article 10a. Notification of risk-modifying agreements.

(1) The home Member State shall ensure that where a shareholder is obliged to notify according to Article 9 by reaching or exceeding the threshold of 5 per cent, such a shareholder notifies the issuer of any agreement, arrangement or mutual consent, the aim or effect of which is to modify the shareholder's risk structure with respect to the issuer, provided that such risk-modifying agreement or agreements refer to at least 5 per cent of the voting rights of the same issuer. In particular, this includes, but is not limited to, arrangements to reduce the shareholder's risk structure, to benefit from share price changes, or to modify the voting power of the shareholder. The same notification obligation shall apply to the obligation or intent to transfer shares within a specified time period to another person.

(2) The same notification obligation shall apply to any subsequent modification to the agreement.

(3) The notification to the issuer shall be effected promptly, but not later than four trading days after the shareholder

 (a) learns of the acquisition or disposal or of the possibility of exercising voting rights, or on which, having regard to the circumstances, should have learned of it, regardless of the date on which the acquisition, disposal, or possibility of exercising voting rights takes effect; or

 (b) enters into the agreement mentioned in paragraph (1).

(4) Upon receipt of the notification under paragraphs 1 or 2, but no later than three trading days thereafter, the issuer shall make public all the information contained in the notification.

[274] See section VI.C.4.a.
[275] On this value and threshold, see section VI.C.4.d.
[276] See Chapter III.C.3.

(5) A home Member State may exempt issuers from the requirement in paragraph 3 if the information contained in the notification is made public by its competent authority upon receipt of the notification, but no later than three trading days thereafter.
(6) The Commission shall, in accordance with the procedure referred to in Article 27(2), adopt implementing measures in order to take account of technical developments on financial markets and to ensure the uniform application of paragraphs 1 and 2 of this Article.

How would this proposal operate in practice? In the following, we will apply the new provision to the different risk-decoupling strategies to illustrate its practical implications and operations.

(i) Scope

The proposed regulation is addressed to 'a shareholder' who 'is obliged to notify according to article 9 by reaching or exceeding the threshold of 5 per cent'. In line with the arguments made above, this clarifies that only a shareholder who already holds a significant share of voting rights in the first place may fall within the negative disclosure duty concerning a risk-decoupling structure. In this way, it is also clarified that both disclosure obligations stand alongside one another and are in no way netted or aggregated.

Based on this requirement, draft article 10a requires the disclosure of any 'agreement, arrangement or mutual consent, the aim or effect of which is to modify the shareholder's risk structure with respect to the issuer, provided that such risk-modifying agreement refers to at least 5 per cent of the voting rights of the same issuer'. This wording is deliberately kept as broad as possible, as it strives for the disclosure of side agreements of any kind, including any non-binding understandings that do not have a formally legal character. The aim is to prevent possible circumvention and arbitrage. In terms of substance, the agreement must relate either to reducing the risk of the voting rights holder or, while maintaining the risk, to increasing the voting power. The volume of the agreement has to relate—in accordance with the above reasoning—to at least 5 per cent of voting rights. Where the voting rights holder enters into several risk-decoupling agreements, the total of which exceeds the value of 5 per cent, these have to be disclosed in their entirety.

How would this system apply to our three categories? First, on the variant of risk-decoupling by using derivatives (category 1), this would fall plainly under article 10a(1), which clarifies that it applies to an express agreement or an implied, tacit understanding. The derivative transactions presented above are able to reduce the risk of the shareholder. A delta adjustment of the reporting obligation should be considered, but does not play an important role for the typical total return swap anyway.[277]

Second, the disclosure obligations around securities lending transactions are somewhat confusing under the status quo. A *borrower* of securities must typically

[277] See Christian Renn, Christoph Andreas Weber, and Georg G Gotschev, 'Beteiligungstransparenz und dynamisches Hedging: Zur Frage einer Delta-Adjustierung der Meldepflichten' [2012] Die Aktiengesellschaft 440.

report the acquisition of a long position when exceeding the threshold values of article 9, because he becomes the full owner of the shares and also acquires the associated voting rights. Whether the *lender* needs to comply with a corresponding obligation indicating that his ownership falls below a certain threshold is less clear under the current system. Most jurisdictions seem to answer this in the affirmative when implementing or interpreting the Directive.[278]

However, UK practice appears to point in the opposite direction, as there is no notification obligation by the lender.[279] The reason is that, in a standard securities lending agreement, the lender retains a right to call back the shares at any time.[280] Technically, this means that the lender disposes of the full ownership of the shares when lending them out, but simultaneously retains a right for their redelivery, thus an acquisition of a corresponding right to reacquire them. When netting off both positions, the argument goes, the lender 'holds' the same amount of voting entitlements. This view also seems to be motivated by the policy concern that a disclosure by the lender might be misunderstood by the market and might thus lead to conflicting and confusing disclosures.[281]

In Germany, recent case law suggests that the lender does not have to notify that his ownership share has fallen below a threshold where he is still entitled to influence the voting decisions by virtue of the contractual arrangement with the borrower.[282] Following recent legislative reform, the delivery claim has to be reported additionally and separately by the lender.[283] Thus, overall it is possible that a securities lending agreement triggers one, two, or even three different disclosures.

In other Member States, the situation is even more worrying and sometimes unclear.[284] It is fair to say that this does not present a viable and coherent solution to the problem of transparency in the course of securities lending.

[278] Mazars and Marccus Partners (n. 266) 96: 'Under article 9 of the Directive, the transaction should thus be notified both by the lender and the borrower'. See on the uncertainty and lack of congruence across the EU the report by ESMA, *Final Report on draft Regulatory Technical Standards on major shareholdings and an indicative list of financial instruments subject to notification requirements under the revised Transparency Directive*, ESMA/2014/1187 (29 September 2014) paras 152 f.

[279] ibid. 124 and DTR 5.1.1R (5). [280] See Chapter III.B.2.a.

[281] Mazars and Marccus Partners (n. 266). The UK is now considering changing this and falling into line with the EU's position. See Financial Conduct Authority (FCA), *Implementation of the Transparency Directive Amending Directive (2013/50/EU) and other Disclosure Rule and Transparency Rule Changes—Consultation Paper CP 15/11* (March 2015), para. 5.8 ff.

[282] Bundesgerichtshof, decision of 16 March 2009 (II ZR 302/06), BGHZ 180, 154, 170. See also European Securities Markets Expert Group (ESME), *First Report of ESME on the Transparency Directive ('TD')* (5 December 2007) 8: 'the aim of the TD is to ascertain voting rights'. Available at <http://ec.europa.eu/internal_market/securities/docs/esme/05122007_td_report_en.pdf> accessed 20 August 2015.

[283] WpHG § 25, as reformed by the Anlegerschutz- und Funktionsverbesserungsgesetz (AnsFuG) (Investor Protection and the Functionality Improvement Act 2011). According to the official legislative reasoning, it was the explicit goal of this reform to include the redelivery claim by the lender in securities lending transactions. See Government Draft of the AnsFuG, BT-Drs. 17/3628, p. 19.

[284] In France, the current legal position on the whole subject is currently unclear. See Mazars and Marccus Partners (n. 266) 124. In the Netherlands, there is no disclosure obligation for the lender at all, if a possibility to recall the shares exists: Autoriteit Financiële Markten (AFM), *Wet op het Financieel Toezicht—Voorlichtingsbrochure aandeelhouders* (April 2009) 24–5, available at <http://www.afm.nl>; Michael Bal, 'Wet melding zeggenschap en securities lending: komt het nog goed?', in Jan T Anema

It is not the intention of the reform proposal presented here to completely dispel these doubts on the lender's disclosure obligations. Instead, the above-presented proposal aims only to properly capture the specific risk profile of the *borrower*. As mentioned, the borrower as a full ownership holder will make a long announcement according to article 9 in any event. The problem is only that third parties do not get to know that the full legal position is only temporary and, consequently, at a reduced risk. Against this background, sentence 3 of proposed article 10a makes it clear that the borrower is to be treated in the same way as the other risk-reduced shareholders. The same would apply to a repurchase agreement or an onward sale obligation. This means that borrowed stock blocks are to be reported on the borrower's side according to article 9 (if they exceed the threshold), and the borrower would have to report in accordance with article 10a(1) on top—to clearly communicate to the market that the acquired shareholder position is only temporary and ultimately not interested.

The third constellation examined here, the so-called record-date capture, does not require a separate disclosure obligation.[285] If it is carried out in the form of securities lending, the obligation of transparency just described would also meet the borrower on the record date with the same legal consequences. Conversely, if a block of shares is to be sold between the record date and the day of the general meeting, the regular reporting obligations apply—assuming a corresponding disclosure relevance—in accordance with articles 9 ff. Under transparency considerations, the record date alternative would therefore be covered, but it remains to be seen whether the legal policy concerns on this constellation will be completely eliminated.[286]

(ii) Legal consequences

If the requirements are satisfied in one of the three constellations mentioned previously, the disclosure obligation is triggered, and the shareholder needs to notify both the issuer and the market supervisor of the risk-modifying agreement. The obligation to disclose to the issuer is directly laid down in article 10a(1); the market supervisor ('competent authority') is mentioned in article 19(3), which would have to be slightly modified in order to also refer to article 10a. In line with the other notification obligations contained in the Transparency Directive, the timeframe proposed is four trading days.[287]

Equally in line with the system of the Transparency Directive, it is not the duty of the shareholder to disclose the arrangement to the public. This obligation rests with the issuer.[288] Further details could be specified by delegated law-making by the European Commission, as is usually the custom.[289]

and others (eds), *Bouwen en bezinning—Regels van wenselijk en onwenselijk financieel recht* (2007) 13. For a general assessment, see European Commission, European Commission, *Feedback Statement on the Modernisation of the Transparency Directive* (n. 266) 41.

[285] See Chapter III.B.3. [286] See section VI.D.2.

[287] The same could be achieved by modifying article 12(2) in such a way that it also refers to article 10a.

[288] Transparency Directive, article 12(6). This would have to be modified in such a way that article 12(1) also refers to article 10a.

[289] Article 12(8).

(iii) Sanctions

The success of a legal rule or system usually depends on the quality of its enforcement mechanisms. This applies particularly to the anonymous and speedy capital markets.[290]

The problem lies in the fact that EU legislation has traditionally refrained from specifying the enforcement side of legal rules, as this was entrusted to the Member States. There are several reasons behind this particular distribution of responsibilities. Officially, EU institutions cite subsidiarity concerns and the reluctance to wade into national affairs. A more realistic interpretation, however, would suggest that it is often unpractical to regulate enforcement on the EU level, as (a) national standards diverge considerably, (b) there is no EU-wide enforcement body but rather a broad variety of national enforcement styles and philosophies, and (c) political agreement on enforcement mechanisms is often difficult.

In this spirit, the Transparency Directive previously did not contain any sanctioning powers. It only included declaratory statements stating that Member States should guarantee an effective and dissuasive enforcement of the Directive.[291] In the wake of the financial crisis, however, the EU institutions became increasingly convinced that a broad divergence of enforcement methods across the Union might be problematic. Thus, in 2010, the Commission published a communication under the title 'Reinforcing sanctioning regimes in the financial services sector', which explained its increased efforts to harmonize the sanctions as well as the substantive laws in the fields of financial law.[292] At the same time, CESR reported in depth on the startling divergence of national sanctioning regimes of Member States in relation to the Transparency Directive and provided an exhaustive picture of the diversity of supervisory regimes and of the nature and level of sanctions.[293]

Against this background, the 2013 revision of the Transparency Directive introduced for the first time a separate chapter on enforcement.[294] New articles 28a and

[290] Reinier H Kraakman and others, *The Anatomy of Corporate Law: A Comparative and Functional Approach* (Oxford University Press 2009) p. 45 and ch. 9.

[291] See former article 28 and recital 37:

> In order to ensure that the requirements set out in this Directive or the measures implementing this Directive are fulfilled, any infringement of those requirements or measures should be promptly detected and, if necessary, subject to penalties. To that end, measures and penalties should be sufficiently dissuasive, proportionate and consistently enforced. Member States should ensure that decisions taken by the competent national authorities are subject to the right of appeal to the courts.

[292] European Commission, *Communication from the Commission to the European Parliament, the Council, the European Economic and Social Committee and the Committee of the Regions: Reinforcing Sanctioning Regimes in the Financial Services Sector* COM(2010) 716 final (8 December 2010), available at <http://eur-lex.europa.eu/legal-content/EN/TXT/PDF/?uri=CELEX:52010DC0716&qid=1434533872345&from=EN> accessed 15 August 2015.

[293] CESR, *Report on the Mapping of Supervisory Powers, Administrative and Criminal Sanctioning Regimes of Member States in Relation to the Transparency Directive (TD)*, CESR/09-058 (1 July 2009), available at <http://www.esma.europa.eu/system/files/09_058.pdf> accessed 19 August 2015.

[294] Directive 2013/50/EU of the European Parliament and of the Council of 22 October 2013 amending Directive 2004/109/EC of the European Parliament and of the Council on the harmonisation of transparency requirements in relation to information about issuers whose securities are admitted to trading on a regulated market, Directive 2003/71/EC of the European Parliament and of

28b laid down a minimum list of required sanctions that Member States need to offer in order to sanction the failure to notify substantial holdings. Among these is also the right to suspend the voting rights of the infringer. Article 28b(2) states that

> Member States shall ensure that their laws, regulations or administrative provisions provide for the possibility of suspending the exercise of voting rights attached to shares in the event of breaches [of notification obligations]. Member States may provide that the suspension of voting rights is to apply only to the most serious breaches.

In its reasoning, the European Commission stated that such a sanction would be most effective in sanctioning violations of disclosure obligations.[295] It was in particular the German Parliament that insisted on the adoption of this part of the reform;[296] this was probably due to the long-standing German tradition of sanctioning notification infringements with the suspension of shareholder rights, including the right to vote.[297]

This possibility should be extended to the reporting obligation in the draft article 10a developed here. The sanction would make inherent sense: other than in the case of positive risk-decoupling scenarios, where the infringer does not hold the voting rights and the sanction would not fit, the voting rights holder is the infringer in cases of negative risk-decoupling. Non-disclosure of the risk-decoupling arrangement would amount to a serious threat to investor confidence, as seen previously, and it would seem appropriate to sanction such behaviour by suspending the voting right (the exercise of which is, after all, the objective of the risk-decoupler). This could be achieved by a minimal adjustment of the text of article 28a(b) so that it also refers to new article 10a.

The loss of voting rights as a sanction due to the failure to notify stands to be distinguished from the possibility (yet to be discussed) that in individual cases the market supervisory authority mandates the suspension of the voting rights for other reasons—even where the risk-decoupler is in compliance with the disclosure requirements.[298]

the Council on the prospectus to be published when securities are offered to the public or admitted to trading and Commission Directive 2007/14/EC laying down detailed rules for the implementation of certain provisions of Directive 2004/109/EC, [2013] OJ L294/13. This reform instrument introduces new chapter VI.A 'Sanctions and Measures'.

[295] European Commission, *Proposal for a Directive of the European Parliament and of the Council Amending Directive 2004/109/EC on the Harmonisation of Transparency Requirements in Relation to Information about Issuers Whose Securities Are Admitted to Trading on a Regulated Market and Commission Directive 2007/14/EC* COM(2011) 683 (25 October 2011) 10, available at <http://eur-lex.europa.eu/LexUriServ/LexUriServ.do?uri=COM:2011:0683:FIN:EN:PDF> accessed 19 August 2015. See also European Commission, *Commission Staff Working Paper—Impact Assessment Accompanying the Document Proposal for a Directive of the European Parliament and of the Council amending Directive 2004/109/EC on the Harmonisation of Transparency Requirements in Relation to Information about Issuers Whose Securities are Admitted to Trading on a Regulated Market*, SEC(2011) 1279 final (25 October 2011) 41, available at <http://www.europarl.europa.eu/registre/docs_autres_institutions/commission_europeenne/sec/2011/1279/COM_SEC(2011)1279_EN.pdf> accessed 19 August 2015.

[296] See BT-Drucksache 17/9940 and BT-Plenarprotokoll 17/184, p. 22097.

[297] WpHG § 28.

[298] See section VI.D.

7. Summary

Overall, this section has advocated a regulatory need for additional disclosure in the area of negative interests in major shareholdings, under the heading of 'transparency'. At the same time, we have stressed that the threshold values are not to be set too low in order not to impose reporting requirements for innocent situations, and on the other hand not to burden market participants and third parties with undue costs. The result is a concrete regulatory proposal, which covers all three constellations of negative risk-decoupling discussed here and addresses the identified legal and political problems.

The proposal is underpinned by the reasoning developed previously.[299] To reiterate, it ensures that disclosure is the first and most important means to address negative risk-decoupling structures. A continuous disclosure obligation addresses most of the concerns developed in section V. In order to mitigate the disruptive effects on the market, a relatively high threshold (of 5 per cent) is appropriate; with a lower threshold, a company may not feel compelled to change its strategy. The disclosure obligation does not aggregate short and long positions, but rather mandates a separated disclosure. The definition of a 'short position' intends to cover all relevant scenarios, including borrowed securities.

D. Disenfranchisement

In addition to, and alongside, the comprehensive transparency regime that has been developed in the preceding section, it may be appropriate to sanction risk-decoupled voting right holders with a general loss of their voting rights. The inner justification for such a measure and its concrete design shall be explored later.

A few years back, a seminal academic article on the modified risk structure of shares came to the emphatic conclusion: 'Scholars (and legal rules) should recognize what is apparent from financial innovation: *not every share should be entitled to a vote*.'[300] A related, more recent analysis equally advocates for empty voting situations: 'If a hedge fund actually has an interest in lowering the share price, then [...] they should not have a vote at all.'[301] Similar to the present analysis, these pleas are based on the insight that risk-reduced, or even risk-eliminated, shareholders have entirely changed interests compared to regular shareholders, which makes voting for these shares problematic. In this context, a number of scholars have made proposals to deprive risk-decoupled shareholders of their voting right. For

[299] See Chapter V.C. and V.D.

[300] See Shaun Martin and Frank Partnoy, 'Encumbered Shares' [2005] University of Illinois Law Review 775, 813.

[301] Paul H Edelman, Randall S Thomas, and Robert B Thompson, 'Shareholder Voting in an Age of Intermediary Capitalism' (2014) 87 Southern California Law Review 1359, 1406.

instance, in the last of several articles on the subject, Professors Henry Hu and Bernard Black proposed to withdraw the voting right from every shareholder whose risk exposure is negative, by simple operation of corporate law.[302] However, they left open the question of whether a direct ban or a rebuttable legal presumption should be introduced.[303] In a similar vein, Professor David Skeel wants to grant courts a stronger role in deciding to withdraw the voting entitlement of individual shareholders.[304] A French working group chaired by Yves Mansion, board member of the AMF, also came to the conclusion that a statutory loss of the voting right is the most effective way to combat risk-decoupling strategies.[305] Even the so-called Hedge Fund Working Group, a self-organization of the sector, indirectly suggested limiting the voting rights in target companies to 'those holding economic interest'.[306]

Such forays into sanctioning risk-decoupling behaviour by denying shareholders the right to vote are to be distinguished from the loss of shareholders' voting rights as a legal consequence of the failure to comply with reporting obligations, as required by, for example, article 28b of the Transparency Directive, and as recommended previously.[307] The focus here is not the violation of a disclosure obligation, but rather whether the risk-decoupling operation itself may give rise to the shareholder losing their right to vote.

1. A general prohibition to vote?

To understand the theoretical underpinnings of this approach, we can revert to the considerations discussed previously, which draw upon the perspective of corporate finance.[308] One of the arguments developed—based on the work of Gilson and Whitehead in particular—is that risk-decoupled shares are, in substance, closer to debt than to equity.[309] Volatility risk is characteristic of equity investors, and for that very reason these investors are granted the right to vote. Where this specific risk has been eliminated, it is logical to conclude that the voting entitlement must be omitted.

In various jurisdictions, elements of legal reality correspond to this rationale. The Second Company Law Directive, for example, introduced into all EU Member States' company laws the rule that the company itself cannot exercise the

[302] Henry T C Hu and Bernard S Black, 'Equity and Debt Decoupling and Empty Voting II: Importance and Extensions' (2008) 156 University of Pennsylvania Law Review 625, 701.

[303] ibid. 702.

[304] David Skeel, 'Behind the Hedge' [2005] Legal Affairs 28.

[305] Autorité des Marchés Financiers (AMF), *Rapport sur les opérations de prêt emprunt de titres en période d'assemblée générale d'actionnaires* (Groupe de place présidé par Yves Mansion 2008) 13.

[306] Hedge Fund Working Group (HFWG), *Hedge Fund Standards Consultation Paper—Part 2: The Best Practice Standards* (9 October 2007) 61–2, available at <http://castlehall.typepad.com/risk_without_reward/files/hfwg20consultation20paper20part20ii.pdf> accessed 19 August 2015.

[307] See section VI.C.6.b.iii.

[308] See Chapter V.D.

[309] Ronald J Gilson and Charles K Whitehead, 'Deconstructing Equity: Public Ownership, Agency Costs, and Complete Capital Markets' (2008) 108 Columbia Law Review 231, 251; see Chapter V.D.4.

voting right in its own shares.[310] In a similar vein, the English law on schemes of arrangement recognizes the principle that the exercise of a right to vote requires an economic interest in the outcome of the vote, which is settled case law.[311] German law, moreover, recognizes prohibitions to vote in cases where votes are bought or otherwise abusively used.[312] Also, maybe most closely related to the matter under consideration here, the US Bankruptcy Code allows American courts to disqualify a vote that was not cast 'in good faith, or was not solicited or procured in good faith or in accordance with the provisions of [the Code]'.[313] While the Code does not define the phrase 'in good faith', case law has clarified that a vote should be disqualified when it is cast for a reason other than the distributional goal to maximize recovery on the creditor's claims.[314] In fact, therefore, this is a tool that addresses creditors' risk exposure by stripping them of their right to vote.[315] All of these instances have in common the legal principle that a voting entitlement should only be attributed to those shareholders who have a real risk exposure at stake.

The key question, then, is whether it is actually desirable to respond to our risk-decoupling analysis with a prohibition to vote. As a starting point, it should be noted that a voting ban is certainly a suitable instrument in preventing the above-described undesirable and cost-creating effects of risk-decoupling conduct. The exercise of voting rights, where risk is eliminated or reduced, has been identified above as the main problem, even if shareholders can exercise informal pressure on the administration in addition to the formal voting process at the general meeting.[316] Informal influence is mostly based on the threat to exercise the right to vote in the next general meeting. Where the shareholder lacks the right to vote, such informal influence is also clearly relativized.

Doubts arise from other quarters, however, chiefly related to similar delimitation problems that have emerged from discussions over a possible complete ban on risk-decoupling structures.[317] Just like a prohibition, a disenfranchisement rule is a

[310] Directive 2012/30/EU of the European Parliament and of the Council of 25 October 2012 on coordination of safeguards which, for the protection of the interests of members and others, are required by Member States of companies within the meaning of the second paragraph of article 54 of the Treaty on the Functioning of the European Union, in respect of the formation of public limited liability companies and the maintenance and alteration of their capital, with a view to making such safeguards equivalent, [2012] OJ L315/74, article 24(1):

> Where the laws of a Member State permit a company to acquire its own shares, either itself or through a person acting in his own name but on the company's behalf, they shall make the holding of these shares at all times subject to at least the following conditions: (a) among the rights attaching to the shares, the right to vote attaching to the company's own shares shall in any event be suspended

See also European Corporate Governance Forum, *Statement on Empty Voting and Transparency of Shareholder Positions* (20 February 2010) 2 f., available at <http://ec.europa.eu/internal_market/company/docs/ecgforum/ecgf_empty_voting_en.pdf> (accessed 19 August 2015).

[311] *Re Bluebrook Ltd* [2009] EWHC 2114; see also *In re Tea Corporation Ltd* [1904] Ch 12. On this more generally, see Louise Gullifer and Jennifer Payne, *Corporate Finance Law Principles and Policy* (Hart Publishing, Oxford 2011) 639.

[312] Aktiengesetz [AktG] §§ 136, 405.

[313] Bankruptcy Code, section 1126(e).

[314] For example, *In re Save Our Springs (S.O.S.) Alliance, Inc.*, 388 B.R. 202, 230 (Bankr. W.D. Tex. 2008).

[315] For a detailed analysis, see Christopher W Frost, 'Bankruptcy Voting and the Designation Power' (2013) 87 American Bankruptcy Journal 155.

[316] See section VI.C.4.b.

[317] See section VI.B.1.

'black and white' instrument, which offers two options: either that the shareholder is disenfranchised, or that he is not disenfranchised. Accordingly, no room for a 'grey' solution remains, which might be desirable in a partly risk-reduced situation, for example.[318] An automatic deprivation of the right to vote will therefore often yield inappropriate results.

In addition, as described previously, a reduced risk position may occasionally also produce *positive* effects, which can be subject to elimination through the imposition of a voting ban. With this, I refer to the above-described activist shareholders who may obtain additional voting power to effectively monitor the management.[319] Individual shareholders are given a way to exercise additional influence—a possibility to overcome a normalized state of 'rational apathy'. Again, an automatic prohibition or an automatic voting ban would go too far and would restrict this certainly desirable situation.[320]

Finally, we must recognize that the loss of a voting right is a far-reaching intervention and an extensive interference with the membership rights of shareholders, which should be limited to exceptional cases. Such a rule could also affect the guarantee of property in the European Convention on Human Rights and, more generally, the principle of proportionality.

2. Case-by-case regulator's decision

The sceptical discussion presented here can also serve as a more positive guide to developing an ideal response to the problem at issue, which should not be as restrictive as an outright disenfranchisement.[321] If a *general* voting ban goes too far such that individual situations are not adequately taken into account, the voting restriction should be designed in a way that it can be imposed *in individual cases.* This power could be given, for example, to national market supervisors such as the Federal Financial Supervisory Authority (BaFin) in Germany or the Financial Conduct Authority (FCA) in the United Kingdom. The role of a national regulator would draw on the transparency regime developed in this chapter and complete it. The following key points outline the benefits of these powers conferred on a regulator:

1. Any intervention of a national regulator requires the regulating body to become aware of all potentially relevant facts. In this respect, transparency and voting prohibition could be said to go hand-in-hand: the above-developed disclosure regime[322] would supply the regulator with the information on the

[318] The only possibility would be to reduce the voting power in proportion to the risk reduction.
[319] See Chapter V.B.2.
[320] In a similar vein, see Jonathan Cohen, 'Negative Voting: Why It Destroys Shareholder Value and a Proposal to Prevent It' (2008) 45 Harvard Journal on Legislation 237, 253.
[321] Similarly, in the context of the French discussion, see Alan Mason, Gabriel Flandin, and Sophie Bauquis, 'Des récentes affaires impliquant l'usage des dérivés actions' [2011] Revue Trimestrielle de Droit Financier 36, 41.
[322] See section VI.C, in particular VI.C.6.

presence of a risk-decoupling situation, on the basis of which an intervention may be initiated.

2. Furthermore, a voting restriction that can be imposed in an individual situation will cover an otherwise open gap of legal protection that remains even after the introduction of a comprehensive disclosure system. Despite the potential deterrent effect of a disclosure obligation, it is still possible for some investors to surprise shareholders by using a *well-timed stake-building strategy*. If, for example, a hedge fund reveals a risk-decoupling structure during the last possible moment before the record date, the rest of the shareholders are no longer able to react accordingly. It is inherent in the record-date system that shifts after the record date will no longer affect the voting entitlement.[323] Therefore, counter-alliances cannot be effectively formed and counter-proposals or counter-strategies cannot be formulated and put on the agenda. In this respect, depriving the hedge fund of its voting right would be the only viable option.
3. The same would be imaginable in situations in which a disclosure-based response fails to achieve an appropriate solution for *practical reasons*. For example, in the *Lindner* case discussed previously,[324] where borrowed shares were used to cross the threshold required for performing a squeeze-out, pure disclosure would not have helped the minority shareholders. In such cases, an exercise of discretion on a voting disenfranchisement would be helpful.
4. In comparison with a general statutory scheme, the greatest advantage of a system where the regulator is responsible for individual decisions is that these decisions can *account for the individual facts of the situation*. The regulator may in particular consider and take into account:
    i. the actual scope and extent of the risk-decoupling situation, in particular the extent of the voting rights owned by the investor and the risk reduced;
    ii. the timing of the situation, for example, how close to a general meeting or other decision the risk-decoupling occurs. Depending on the result, the regulator may assess how much time remains for the market to develop independent solutions, be it counter-alliances, counter-proposals, management action, or other strategies;
    iii. the potential harm of the risk-decoupled situation. The regulator will want to analyse whether the initiative was created for good reasons and in good faith, so as to, for example, control management for the benefit of all shareholders, to assess whether the risk-decoupled shareholders are likely to pursue only their own interests.

[323] See Chapter III.B.3.
[324] Bundesgerichtshof [BGH] [Federal Supreme Court], decision of 16 March 2009 (II ZR 302/06), BGHZ 180, 154. See in detail above text accompanying n. 169.

5. It becomes clear from the points discussed that the power to regulate a voting ban in individual cases complements the transparency regime and offers enforcement through real sanctions. Again, the hope is that the mere possibility of issuing a ban is enough to deter the use of risk-decoupling in the first place.
6. Finally, the path suggested here—to equip the regulator with the power of withdrawing the voting right—would harmonize with the recently reformed approach of the Transparency Directive on 'long positions'.[325] Striving to further harmonize the sanctions in the Directive, the EU introduced a new article 28b into the Transparency Directive, which stipulates that national supervisory authorities are, inter alia, empowered to suspend the exercise of voting rights if the competent authority finds that the provisions of the Directive concerning notification of major holdings have been infringed by the shareholder.[326] In this regard, the Commission is focusing on an area that has not been subject to harmonization thus far; it is based on the Commission Communication on '[r]einforcing sanctioning regimes in the financial services sector'.[327] In favour of the power to suspend voting rights, the Commission submits that the sanctions could prevent violations of transparency requirements in the most effective way.[328] It seems that a coherent legal system should have corresponding sanctions for both positive and negative interests in securities. In this respect, the solution proposed here would well complement the new approach to long positions.

By contrast, the elimination of other shareholder rights, such as the right to dividends, would appear to be unnecessary. The main economic problem that is addressed here results from an exercise of the voting right, and not the dividend right or other rights. An extension of the regulator's powers to suspend other shareholder rights would therefore be disproportionate.

All of these points taken together could lead to an additional new provision in the Transparency Directive, which may be worded as follows:

Article 28c. Sanctioning powers for risk-modifying agreements.[329]

(1) Without prejudice to the supervisory powers of competent authorities under this Directive or under national law, Member States shall ensure that in the situations

[325] Directive 2013/50/EU. See above n. 294.

[326] This is now new article 28b(2) in Directive 2004/109/EC.

[327] European Commission, *Commission Communication of 8 December 2010 on Reinforcing Sanctioning Regimes in the Financial Services Sector*, COM(2010) 716.

[328] European Commission, *Proposal for a Directive of the European Parliament and of the Council Amending Directive 2004/109/EC on the Harmonisation of Transparency Requirements in Relation to Information about Issuers Whose Securities Are Admitted to Trading on a Regulated Market and Commission Directive 2007/14/EC*, COM(2011) 683 (25 October 2011) 9, available at <http://eur-lex.europa.eu/LexUriServ/LexUriServ.do?uri=COM:2011:0683:FIN:EN:PDF> accessed 19 August 2015 ('[T]he competent authorities in the Member States should have the power to suspend the exercise of voting rights of the issuer who had breached the notification rules on major holdings, as this is the most efficient sanction to prevent a breach of these rules. In order to ensure consistent application of sanctions, uniform criteria should be set for determining the actual sanction applicable to a person or a company').

[329] Current article 28c should then become article 28d.

referred to in Article 10a, administrative sanctions and measures that can be applied include at least the power to suspend the exercise of voting rights attached to shares admitted to trading on a regulated market, if the competent authority finds that disclosure is not sufficient to address the problems resulting from the risk-modifying agreement.

(2) In making use of these powers, the competent authority shall have regard, inter alia, to
 (a) the scope and extent of the risk-decoupling situation, in particular the amount of voting rights notified under Article 9, the extent of the risk-modifying agreements notified under Article 10a, and the relationship between these two notifications;
 (b) the urgency of the situation, in particular how close to a general meeting the notification under Article 10a was made;
 (c) the intentions of the shareholder making the notification under Article 10a.

In sum, a regulator's well-defined power of suspending the voting right—targeting risk-decoupled shareholders in individual situations—seems to accompany the developed disclosure system well. Together, these two components build a helpful combination that can address all problematic situations that may arise.

3. Limitations of the approach

It is important to note that the suggested approach here—equipping the market supervisor with the power to strip shareholders of their voting rights—has its own inherent limitations.

First, law-makers will have to think about legal *remedies*, as it must be possible for shareholders to have the decision reviewed in court. When designing such a remedy, law-makers should ensure that the remedy does not call the validity of a shareholder resolution into question, as this may give rise to hold-up problems, other negative incentives, and legal uncertainty. Nevertheless, an effective legal remedy is essential, and this is not only the case from the perspective of the European Convention on Human Rights. Besides the possibility of requesting an injunction, law-makers will also have to consider the possibility of state liability claims.

Finally, we will have to consider what to do in situations where even the power to suspend voting rights *does not or not fully solve the risk-decoupling problem*. These may be situations, for example, where risk-decoupling occurs in non-listed companies, in particular close corporations, which are neither within the scope of the Transparency Directive nor under the authority of a securities market supervisor.

Another constellation might be where the market supervisor is authorized to act but is not able to make an appropriate decision—for example, for reasons of timing. For instance, when the disclosure of a risk-decoupling structure is made just hours before a general meeting, the market supervisor will not be able to make a well-funded decision. A final example could be that the market supervisor does not have access to all relevant information at the time of decision-making, or interprets certain information wrongly.

In short, even market supervisors are no magical solution to everything and have their technical and cognitive limitations. In the three scenarios just sketched out, another solution needs to be devised. To be sure, such situations will be exceptional and rare. In private companies, the personal relationship between the shareholders prevails, which provides for a number of alternative legal remedies.[330] Further, the market supervisor will actively monitor the market, aided by the information gained through the disclosure framework developed here, and carry out timely analyses and supervision. Nevertheless, a few residual situations may remain.

These are situations in which *ex post control through traditional court litigation* is the only solution. We will see next that *fiduciary duties* may be one avenue to bring a risk-decoupling case to court, claiming that the risk-decoupler violated its duties as a shareholder towards the company and/or towards the existing shareholders.[331] As a primary option, this regulatory tool is not ideal, as it brings with it all the disadvantages of lengthy *ex post* litigation. However, it may helpfully serve as a kind of 'safety net', or as a backup solution for situations where both primary instruments developed here reach their limits. If anything, this may lead to the award of some form of compensatory damages which the risk-decoupler has to pay. On a positive note, this path has the advantage of neutral court control, with sufficient time to find a balanced assessment of all relevant facts. This may be the third and missing piece of the puzzle for addressing risk-decoupling situations.

4. Summary

Overall, the loss of voting rights for risk-decoupled voting right owners appears justified based not only on the academic arguments put forward, but also on the fact that it might gain an important practical role in the market reality. According to the system developed here, we propose to harness the advantages of a targeted suspension of individual voting rights in specific situations, and to avoid the disadvantages of an overly simplified general voting disqualification. As a solution, it is advisable not to propose an automatic loss of voting rights, but instead to equip the market supervisor with the powers to decide on individual cases.

In this way, this sanction can also act on a subsidiary basis to disclosure, and only come into play in cases where the publicity regime previously developed and its market-based solution are not sufficient. Remaining cases can then subsequently be addressed by *ex post* court control, for example based on the violation of fiduciary duties. This is the final regulatory tool, to which we will turn next.

[330] See in detail Gregor Bachmann and others (eds), *Regulating the Closed Corporation* (de Gruyter 2014); Joseph A McCahery and Erik P M Vermeulen, *Corporate Governance of Non-Listed Companies* (Oxford University Press 2008).

[331] See section VI.E.

E. Fiduciary Duties

The solutions discussed above—a ban or restriction on risk-decoupling, transparency requirements, and suspension of voting rights—would be solution proposals that would require the introduction of additional, new legal rules (*de lege ferenda*). Occasionally, however, attempts have been made in the literature and court practice to find an effective response to negative risk-decoupling activities already under the existing legal framework, especially in the flexible rules provided for by company law concerning fiduciary duties of shareholders.[332] The use of an established and flexible legal instrument to address this new problem should be considered as a useful step in some cases. As we will see later, however, this legal instrument also faces a number of uncertainties and inadequacies, which is why exclusive reliance on this instrument would not yield a satisfactory answer to the problem at hand. However, fiduciary duties or other types of judicial *ex post* control may turn out useful in situations where the other two main pillars (transparency and disenfranchisement) are failing. In this way, *ex post* court control can serve as a complementary tool to support the different ways of addressing the problem.

1. Fiduciary duties as an established legal instrument

The legal concept of fiduciary duties has already been described briefly previously.[333] While most, if not all, company law systems recognize the existence of these duties for directors or managers of the corporation, fiduciary duties for shareholders are much more controversial. The basic concept is that each shareholder is required to respect a number of obligations which force him to take into account the interests of both his fellow shareholders and 'the company' itself. The shareholder is thus not completely free in how to exercise their voting rights, and cannot pursue purely selfish motives to an unlimited extent. A comparative overview shows a remarkable divergence in the various legal approaches. For example, in German law, this principle has been developed and shaped over many years by the case law, and applies to all shareholders.[334] The United States (the laws of Delaware) also recognizes such a duty, but only for large shareholders.[335] Under Israeli law, a fiduciary duty

[332] See on other tools under the existing legal framework section VI.A.5.

[333] See section VI.A.5.

[334] For the rich case law, see BGH, decision of 1 February 1988 (II ZR 75/87), BGHZ 103, 184, 193 = NJW 1988, 1579, *Linotype*; BGH, decision of 5 July 1999 (II ZR 126/98), BGHZ 142, 167, 169 = NJW 1999, 3197, *Hilgers*. See Holger Fleischer, in Karsten Schmidt and Marcus Lutter (eds), *Aktiengesetz—Kommentar* (3rd edn, Otto Schmidt 2015) § 53a paras 42 ff. For a critical view, see Friedrich Kübler and Heinz-Dieter Assmann, *Gesellschaftsrecht: Die privatrechtlichen Ordnungsstrukturen und Regelungsprobleme von Verbänden und Unternehmen* (6th edn, CF Müller 2006) 25.

[335] *Jones v HF Ahmanson & Co* 460 P2d 464, 471 f; *Kahn v Lynch Communications Systems, Inc* 638 A2d 1110, 1115 (Del 1994); *Sinclair Oil Corporation v Levien* 280 A2d 717, 720 (Del 1971).

for shareholders is even explicitly codified in the statute.[336] In contrast, the existence of such legal duties is consistently rejected, for example, in the English case law.[337] Also, Swiss law does not recognize fiduciary duties for shareholders generally, unless these also hold a position of responsibility in the company.[338]

Where it exists, the principle of fiduciary duties has several times been linked to the topic of interest here—as a potential solution to the problem of risk-decoupling in shares. The basic idea would be that the use of risk-decoupled voting rights would be contrary to the interests of the company and of the other shareholders, and would thus violate the decoupler's fiduciary duties.[339] The advantage of such an approach would be that individual case-specific considerations allow the courts to take all the specific details of the case into account, for example the interests of the voter, his risk exposure, and the impact of his behaviour on third parties.[340]

There is nothing wrong with the application and use of this type of fiduciary duties (where they are recognized by the law). It is obvious and sensible to argue, in a particular case, that the pursuit of idiosyncratic interests with risk-decoupling mechanisms may violate such a legal instrument. A duty of loyalty-based approach will especially be helpful when it comes to private firms and other companies that are not listed on the capital market, and that are therefore out of the reach of a securities regulator. For these companies, transparency requirements will only have a limited effect (see Chapter V.E.2). Furthermore, fiduciary duties may helpfully be applied in cases where all other tools fail: due to their flexibility, they can usefully fulfil a fall-back role, and can be a 'safety net' solution that comes into action where the other legal tools do not yield optimal results.

2. Individual disadvantages

Despite these advantages, the application of these judicially developed fiduciary duties as the sole solution to the problem discussed previously is not sufficient. Fiduciary duties have some disadvantages, which hamper the effective handling of the problem. These are now outlined briefly.

[336] Companies Law 5759-1999, sections 192, 193.

[337] *Northern Counties Securities Ltd v Jackson & Steeple Ltd* [1974] 1 WLR 1133, 1144.

[338] Peter Böckli, *Schweizer Aktienrecht: mit Fusionsgesetz, Börsengesellschaftsrecht, Konzernrecht, Corporate Governance, Recht der Revisionsstelle und der Abschlussprüfung in neuer Fassung unter Berücksichtigung der angelaufenen Revision des Aktien- und Rechnungslegungsrechts* (4th edn, Schulthess 2009) § 13 paras 659 f.

[339] See, in particular, Iman Anabtawi and Lynn Stout, 'Fiduciary Duties for Activist Shareholders' (2008) 60 Stanford Law Review 1255; Andrea Zanoni, 'Hedge Funds' Empty Voting in Mergers and Acquisitions: A Fiduciary Duties Perspective' (2009) 9(4) Global Jurist, article 4; Robert B Thompson and Paul H Edelman, 'Corporate Voting' (2009) 62 Vanderbilt Law Review 129. For Germany, see Christine Osterloh-Konrad, 'Gefährdet "Empty Voting" die Willensbildung in der Aktiengesellschaft? Überlegungen zur Proportionalität zwischen Stimmrechtseinfluss und wirtschaftlicher Betroffenheit der Aktionäre' [2012] Zeitschrift für Unternehmens- und Gesellschaftsrecht (ZGR) 35, 48 f; Horst Eidenmüller, 'Regulierung von Finanzinvestoren' [2007] Deutsches Steuerrecht (DStR) 2116, 2118, 2120; Christoph Kumpan and Martin Mittermeier, 'Risikoentleerte Stimmrechte—Auswirkungen von Wertpapierdarlehen im Gesellschaftsrecht' [2009] Zeitschrift für Wirtschaftsrecht (ZIP) 404, 410 f.

[340] See, in particular, Kumpan and Mittermeier ibid.

First, the temporal dimension and the retrospective character of every decision of judicial review are problems in themselves and jeopardize the possibility of finding a quick and effective solution to the problem in question.[341] Whether the shareholder has violated its fiduciary duties is rarely an easy question, in particular against the background of the principally free exercise of the voting right. Instead, such a case usually requires a lengthy and complex investigation, the implementation of which may take a long time. Where there is a lack of specific expertise, the court will often be tempted to consult experts, which extends the lawsuit even further. Finally, the litigation can be carried through multiple instances, resulting in a typical overall time span of several years. These aspects are diametrically opposed to the interests of market participants in the capital market, who are vitally interested in a quick and effective solution to their practical questions.[342] Doubts over the validity of certain shareholder resolutions, for example, can cause serious concerns over the viability of major corporate decisions such as restructuring transactions. This legal uncertainty and the risk of potentially having to reverse a transaction are the causes of significant transaction costs on a private and social level.[343]

An additional problem is that the instrument of shareholder fiduciary duties is mostly uncodified and is therefore subject to many genuine uncertainties. For example, in many legal systems the exact requirements and legal consequences of a breach of such a fiduciary duty in a particular case are actually unclear. For example, under German case law it is uncertain how the invalidity of a shareholder resolution or its contestability relates to a potential claim for damages.[344] Until these issues are resolved by regulatory design, fiduciary duties are unlikely to provide a reliable framework for the solution of risk-decoupling scenarios.

This latter point can be expanded towards a general criticism of so-called 'standards' to respond to the challenges of our economic life in the spheres of corporate law and securities regulation. It is widely accepted that the regulation of such fast-paced factual and legal matters requires clear, unambiguous rules and that these are to be preferred over broad standards or 'general clause'-like descriptions.[345] The use of such precise rules to assess individual cases lends itself to a clearer delineation of responsibilities that better meets the needs of this speedy market. This is especially true for fiduciary duties, as in the finance-oriented capital market the fiduciary obligations of equity-holders to a publicly listed firm with an anonymous body of thousands of shareholders necessarily retreat behind their financial interests. Against this backdrop, the situation can be addressed in

[341] See on this section VI.A.5.

[342] Marcel Kahan and Edward B Rock, 'Hedge Funds in Corporate Governance and Corporate Control' (2007) 155 University of Pennsylvania Law Review 1021, 1077.

[343] Helfried Labrenz, *Ökonomische Analyse der aktienrechtlichen Anfechtungsklage* (Gabler 2011) 59 ff.; Florens Sauerbruch, *Das Freigabeverfahren gemäß § 246a Aktiengesetz: eine rechtsökonomische Untersuchung* (Gabler 2008) 2 ff.

[344] See e.g. Fleischer (n. 334) para. 70.

[345] Steven M Davidoff, Alan D Morrison, and William J Jr Wilhelm, 'The SEC v. Goldman Sachs: Reputation, Trust, and Fiduciary Duties in Investment Banking' (2012) 37 Journal of Corporation Law 529, 533; more generally also James J Park, 'The Competing Paradigms of Securities Regulation' (2007) 57 Duke Law Journal 625.

a more functional way by using so-called 'bright-line rules' rather than 'general clauses'. The latter are based on a fiction of a close personal relationship between shareholder and corporation.[346]

Finally, a fiduciary duty-based approach may involve a problem in some specific constellations of risk-decoupling in the form of a collision of several conflicting fiduciary obligations. Especially in the case of securities lending, conflicting duties of the voting equity-holder can arise.[347] For example, the borrower who is exercising the right to vote may be contractually bound towards the lender of the securities to vote in his interest. However—and possibly in contradiction—a fiduciary duty emerging from his equity ownership position would commit him to a different use of the voting right.[348]

Similarly, there may be a conflict of duties for investment funds who owe fiduciary duties towards both their fellow shareholders, who invest in the same target company, as well as their own investors. Taken to the extreme, there would be the problem where a fund holds investments in two different portfolio companies which are in direct economic competition: what the fund supports in company 1 can be detrimental to its shareholder position in company 2 and cause a breach of duty there. The *Mylan–Perry* story can serve as a good illustration, although the situation was deliberately created.[349]

3. Conclusion

The overall picture shows that the duty of loyalty as a tool to address the problems raised by negative risk-decoupling has a number of limitations and is therefore usually not able to serve as a remedy of first choice.

This does not mean that fiduciary duties do not play a useful role in the toolbox of answers to risk-decoupling mechanisms. On the contrary, they may serve as a sensible 'substitutional' building block to solve some problems to which the *ex ante* legal system can anticipate no answers. As such, they are welcome as a complementary tool and a reserve solution for unforeseen problems. The foregoing discussion has, however, made it clear that fiduciary duties, in many situations, cannot always provide a satisfactory solution, are cumbersome, and are subject to time delay, legal uncertainty, and possible conflicts of fiduciary duties. Therefore, against the need for required legal clarity needed here for all actors, they can merely be of limited, substitutional use only.

[346] Davidoff, Morrison, and Wilhelm (n. 345). [347] Category 2; see Chapter III.B.2.

[348] The former *Overseas Securities Lending Agreement* of the *International Securities Lending Association (ISLA)* from 1995 specifies a type of fiduciary duty between the parties of a securities lending agreement as follows: Article 4.2.6:

> Each party undertakes that where it holds its securities of the same description as any securities borrowed by it or transferred to it by way of collateral at a time when a right to vote arises in respect of such securities, it will use its best endeavours to arrange for the voting rights attached to the securities to be exercised in accordance with the instructions of the lender or borrower (as the case may be) [...].

This Agreement has now been superseded by the Global Master Securities Lending Agreement, which takes a different approach (see clause 6).

[349] See Chapter III.B.1.a.

F. Results, Overview, and Assessment

In this chapter, we discussed several possible solutions to the problem of negative risk-decoupling and related them to the problem layers described in Chapter V. In conclusion, we saw that the instruments of the current legal framework, even in their broadest interpretation, do not suffice to adequately address the legal problems and the protection needs that were developed previously. Further, attempts at self-regulation of the market have so far borne no fruit.

Out of the proposed counter-measures, a ban or a direct restriction of risk-decoupling strategies would not do justice to the economic and legal dimensions developed here, and would also run against the occasionally potential positive effects of negative risk-decoupling situations.

Instead, this study argues for a multi-level response to risk-decoupling activities. This requires the introduction of two new instruments: a disclosure regime for negative interest for holders of significant voting right holders in listed companies, and at the same time a new authority for the market supervisor to suspend the voting rights of risk-decoupled shareholders in individual cases. These suggestions would—without a heavy administrative burden—allow a market solution in the first place, and introduce a correction by the market supervisor in individual cases. A third, subsidiary tool of *ex post* court control is available, for example based on fiduciary duties, to address those cases where the first two solutions fail to provide an adequate remedy.

We can thus speak of three pillars. All three pillars may apply in an order of priority.

1. Primarily, the issue should be handled by the disclosure system developed here. This should facilitate a market reaction and constitute a solution that would normally be adequate for most cases.
2. The disclosure obligation should be accompanied by a sanctioning regime with which European regulators should be equipped. The regime can be understood to close any loopholes in the legal protection that may remain. In contrast to a general statutory voting restriction, the regime can take into account the specific aspects of each individual situation. Where pure transparency fails to achieve an appropriate outcome—perhaps because the disclosure is made too close to the general meeting, or in threshold situations (such as *Lindner*)—the market supervisor may thus decide, with individual discretion, to strip the risk-decoupler of their voting rights.
3. In extreme solutions, where even the market supervisor is not in a position to settle the conflict situation—as in closed corporations which are not subject to its supervision, or where the regulator is not in a position to make a timely decision—*ex post* control by a court can solve the residual problems, as a 'safety net' or remedy of last resort.

This solution trio is superior to many of the answers and remedies (discussed over the course of this study) made in the literature and actual regulatory approaches taken. Table VI.2 summarizes and compares the different approaches taken or envisaged.

Table VI.2 Important solutions and reform attempts for negative risk-decoupling in comparison

Country / category	1 (Derivatives)	2 (Securities lending)	3 (Record-date capture)
Germany	./.	• ./. • *Lindner* decision allows this construction	./.
USA	• Singular, partly inconsistent court decisions[350] • Partly self-regulation in the *bylaws* or *shareholder rights plans*[351]	(Ineffective) 'Purpose Test' in *Regulation T*[352]	Separation of dividend entitlement and record date (*SEC* and *Delaware*)[353]
UK	./.	Failed self-regulation attempts in the *Stock Borrowing Code*[354] and the *Hedge Fund Working Group*[355]	./.
France	./.	Disclosure obligation for borrowed shares on the record date[356]	Disclosure obligation for borrowed shares on the record date[357]
EU	• ./. • ESMA *Call for Evidence*[358] • Discussion in Green Papers[359] and in the context of the reform of the Transparency Directive[360]		
	Proposals in the Mazars Report:		
	Transparency in the run-up to the general meeting[361]	Transparency in the run-up to the general meeting[362]	Call-back obligation for shares[363]

This overview illustrates in particular the selective character of current solutions and proposals. Law-makers, regulators, and legal practice, driven by individually relevant facts, have attempted to provide limited relief. By contrast, the developed solution model presented here is holistic and comprehensive: all of the three pillars developed here—that is, the disclosure system, the power to suspend voting rights, and *ex post* court control—all rely on a common criterion ('risk-modifying agreement'), which unites all three categories of risk-decoupling. This approach will succeed in avoiding gaps in protection and in preventing arbitrage opportunities.

The second advantage of the solution presented here is the fact that it is based on a sound legal and economic analysis, while also involving practical considerations and considerations of proportionality without overburdening the market participants. The relatively high initial thresholds proposed for the disclosure obligation

[350] E.g. *Deephaven* and *Parfi*. On both, see section VI.A.5.
[351] See section VI.A.2.
[352] See section VI.B.1.
[353] See Chapter III.B.3.c and section VI.B.2.
[354] *Stock Borrowing and Lending Code of Guidance*; see Chapter III.B.2.a and section VI.A.3.
[355] See section VI.A.3.
[356] See section VI.C.2.
[357] See section VI.C.2.
[358] See section VI.C.2.
[359] See Chapter II.D and section VI.C.2.
[360] See section VI.C.2 (p. 172 f.).
[361] See section VI.C.2.
[362] See section VI.C.2.
[363] See section VI.B.2.

of negative interests are designed to exclude insignificant matters of disclosure, and also to keep the bureaucratic demands of market participants within limits. At the same time, the three-pillar reaction system promises an efficient and powerful solution to the problem for market, authorities, and courts. Overall, a balanced system has been developed, which seeks to accommodate all concerns.

We will next consider a possible solution to positive risk-decoupling in section VI.G. The final and concluding step will be to determine the appropriate level of regulation for both positive and negative decoupling situations in Chapter VII.

G. Positive Risk-Decoupling—An Alternative Regulatory Model Targeting CfD Abuse

Finally, we need to return to the problem of positive risk-decoupling. Section V.E of this study described the need to regulate contracts for difference (CfD) market activity, refining the idea of disclosure regulation and its limits. This section continues the analysis of the different regulatory approaches and aims at identifying the most effective and balanced regulatory response to the problems caused by CfD abuse. I will argue that any CfD disclosure regulation should first be narrowed to apply only to control-affecting transactions, and second be supported by both notable sanctions and a strict reversed burden of proof applicable to CfD holders preparing to make a bid or to otherwise seek control in their target companies.

If enforcement is its Achilles heel, as the European Commission believes,[364] the attraction of intention-based regulation lies in the preciseness with which it can be applied to the activity which the regulator wants to prevent or impose obligations to. This regulatory targeting can lead to cost savings both directly and indirectly, as the number of disclosure notifications would be smaller and fewer efforts would be needed from the market to process the disclosure data into useful market information.

1. Proposed regulatory structure

a) Characteristics of the regulation and related sanctions

As discussed in Chapter V.E.2, only control-related CfD investments should be under a disclosure obligation. The motive of gaining control can be defined as an intention to acquire target shares either for takeover purposes or otherwise in order to influence the corporate decision-making. This influence on the target company's operations could be practised either directly by the CfD holder, so that he or she would aim at eventually acquiring the hedge shares before the use of control, or indirectly, by influencing the short parties in their use of voting rights of the hedge shares. Thus, large financial investments made only in hopes of monetary profits without any control-related motives would not trigger a disclosure obligation. The

[364] See Chapter V.E.2.c.

regulatory structure proposed in this study can be seen to correspond to the general US disclosure regulation making reference to control-seeking intentions. The main difference is that, under the proposal of this study, only transactions with control-seeking elements would need to be disclosed to the public. The remaining disclosure, that is, disclosure on other than control-seeking transactions, is effectively not useful to the market, as discussed in section V.E.1; on the contrary, it might even be harmful to market efficiency.

Intentions to seek control are admittedly subjective in the investment stage, although they quickly bring about objective third-party effects when executed. Using control-seeking intentions as a basis for disclosure obligation would seem to breach the paradigm of mandating disclosure of objective and verifiable historical facts.[365] Disclosure on control-seeking securities positions would, however, not be the only type of disclosure with subjective and forward-looking characteristics. For example, the regulation regarding interim management reports under the Transparency Directive specifically includes an obligation to companies' managements to disclose the 'principal risks and uncertainties for the remaining six months of the financial year' which they assess to be relevant in their business.[366] The subjectivity of the control-seeking intention does not, moreover, reduce its importance, as it is clearly different from the aim to merely gain financial profits; one can indeed blame people for their bad intentions.[367] However, the assessment of a subjective control intention does not include a *mens rea* element, so in order to fall under the disclosure obligation, investors do not need to aim at distorting or affecting the market in general or the shareholders of the specific target companies. Investors do not even need to acknowledge the potential market dangers of their activity as long as they intend to gain control via CfDs.[368]

For the disclosure obligation to be triggered there must be an intention to use the voting power either independently from or in addition to an economic interest. This control-related intention can have different forms, varying from an interest in taking over the target company to an interest in influencing the running of the company, or an interest in affecting the decisions in a shareholders' meeting. Obviously, these intentions are not visible to other market participants, or even to the short parties. If they exist, only the investors themselves are aware of them. The investment motive can initially be financial, but can change to seeking control

[365] Frank H Easterbrook and Daniel R Fischel, 'Mandatory Disclosure and the Protection of Investors' (1984) 70 Virginia Law Review 669, 702–3.

[366] Article 5(4) of Directive 2004/109/EC of the European Parliament and of the Council of 15 December 2004 on the harmonisation of transparency requirements in relation to information about issuers whose securities are admitted to trading on a regulated market and amending Directive 2001/34/EC.

[367] Compare to European Securities Markets Expert Group (ESME), *Views on the Issue of Transparency of Holdings of Cash Settled Derivatives* (November 2009) 10, available at <http://ec.europa.eu/internal_market/securities/docs/esme/tdcash_en.pdf>.

[368] Compare to market manipulation regulation with a *mens rea* requirement in the criminal offence (section 397 of the FSMA 2000) but not in the regulatory offence (section 118 of the FSMA 2000).

during the term of the CfD agreement. Nevertheless, it should be noted that there is always a turning point that will trigger the disclosure obligation.

It could be argued that there would be a need for an ultimate threshold after which even pure economic positions would trigger a disclosure obligation. This question was, surprisingly, not raised by the various consultations discussing the possibility of a 'safe harbour' alternative.[369] However, at least in the United Kingdom, current capital markets regulation already provides for such a backup threshold—the 30 per cent control threshold for a mandatory bid includes CfD positions.[370] Even though mandatory bid regulation is mainly aimed at protecting the minority shareholders of the target, there is no reason not to use it to protect market integrity as well.[371] Such a maximum threshold is absent, however, at the EU level. A separate threshold should therefore be inserted into the EU Takeover Directive. If consensus for revising the Takeover Directive is unlikely, Member States may modify their implementing laws accordingly. Remember that there is considerable freedom for implementation in filling out the requirement of an acquisition of 'control' as a trigger for the mandatory bid rule.[372]

The subjectivity of the trigger of the disclosure obligation would, under the proposed model, be compensated by enforcement. First, even though not based on a general disclosure obligation, the proposed system would include a presumption of control-seeking intention reflected in a reversed burden of proof, that is, CfD holders would be assumed to have invested in the instruments with a control purpose if they were not able to provide evidence to the contrary.[373] Second, the sanctions would cover both monetary gains achieved through the abuse of artificially low market prices and the prohibition from using the acquired voting rights, thus aiming to annul the benefits of the prohibited activity. The market supervisor would be authorized to order a fine for any breach of the disclosure obligation.[374]

In the case of a CfD takeover, the market supervisor for takeovers should be entitled to require an increased bid price. This increase would be equal to the aggregate benefit that the CfD bidder and the short party bank would have received in the offer. This benefit includes the discount to the bidder, that is, the difference

369 See Chapter V.E.2.c.

370 See Chapter V.E.2.a.ii, text accompanying n. 233.

371 High Level Group of Company Law Experts, *Report on Issues Related to Takeover Bids* (2002), available at <http://ec.europa.eu/internal_market/company/docs/takeoverbids/2002-01-hlg-report_en.pdf> 45.

372 Takeover Directive, article 5(1). See text accompanying Chapter V n. 236.

373 See Daniel Bertaccini, 'To Disclose or Not to Disclose? *CSX CORP.*, Total Return Swaps, and Their Implications for Schedule 13D Filing Purposes' (2009) 31 Cardozo Law Review 267, 292. In comparison, see Dirk Zetzsche, 'Challenging Wolf Packs: Thoughts on Efficient Enforcement of Shareholder Transparency Rules', Center for Business and Corporate Law Research Paper Series 0044 (2/2010) 25–6, available at <http://papers.ssrn.com/sol3/papers.cfm?abstract_id=1428899> accessed 23 August 2015, who argues against the reversed burden of proof in relation to takeover activity and who presents an alternative in the form of a reward model, alike to antitrust whistle-blowing. The precise details required for rebutting the burden would follow traditional rules of civil procedure.

374 See Dirk Zetzsche, 'Hidden Ownership in Europe: BAFin's Decision in Schaeffler v. Continental' (2009) 10 European Business Organization Law Review 115, 143–5.

between the initial reference price and the market price at the time of the tendering of the hedge shares (the wind-up price) multiplied with the number of hedge shares, and the premium gains of the bank, that is, the difference between the winding-up price of the CfDs and the bid price multiplied with the number of the hedge shares.[375] The increase in the bid price would be distributed to all tendering shareholders excluding the short party, which would be left in the same position as if it had sold the hedge shares after winding up to the long party in the absence of a takeover. Finally, the long party would be put into the financial position in which it would have been without the CfD toehold.[376]

The structure of enforcement in capital markets law has increasingly been discussed in the literature.[377] The present study supports the view that capital markets law should not be enforced by the general courts.[378] If there were sufficient appellate options, and if independence from the rule-making functions was guaranteed, both the specific takeover regulator in relation to takeovers and the securities markets supervisor in relation to general disclosure would be the right authorities to enforce the discussed regulation due to their expertise and more flexible way of operation.

b) Comparison to the EU and US regulatory models

The suggested regulatory model falls between the current EU approach and the US regime.[379] The revised EU Transparency Directive requires all CfD positions above the threshold to be disclosed, whereas the proposed alternative would only require the disclosure of positions where their holders are intending to use control over or to otherwise influence their target companies. This trigger can, however, be fulfilled even in the absence of any agreement, understanding, or other communication relating to the voting or investment power conveyed by the target shares or any arrangement for divesting such position—the trademarks of the US disclosure regulation. The proposed structure imposes a disclosure obligation

[375] This gain can be expected to be higher than the offer premium as the CfDs would most probably be unwound during the offer period after the market price has risen to reflect information on the offer.

[376] The 'pressure to tender' would still remain even under these sanctions.

[377] See e.g. John C Coffee Jr, 'Law and the Market: the Impact of Enforcement' (2007) 156 University of Pennsylvania Law Review 229; John Armour, 'Enforcement Strategies in UK Corporate Governance: A Roadmap and Empirical Assessment' in John Armour and Jennifer Payne (eds), *Rationality in Company Law—Essays in Honour of DD Prentice* (Hart Publishing, Oxford 2009) 71; see also John Armour and David A Skeel, 'Who Writes the Rules for Hostile Takeovers, and Why?—The Peculiar Divergence of U.S. and U.K. Takeover Regulation' (2007) 95 Georgetown Law Journal 1727; Reinier H Kraakman and others (eds), *The Anatomy of Corporate Law: A Comparative and Functional Approach* (2nd edn, Oxford University Press 2009) 295–8.

[378] See also Brian T Sullivan, 'CSX Corp. v. Children's Investment Fund Management and the Need for SEC Expansion of Beneficial Ownership' (2009) 87 North Carolina Law Review 1300, 1316, and 1318.

[379] For a US–UK comparison, see Tom Siebens and Melissa Gambol, 'Who's Hiding Behind the Hedges? Developments in the USA and UK May Limit the Use of Total Return Swaps to Conceal Equity Stakes in Public Companies' (2009) 4 Capital Markets Law Journal 172, 177.

even if the short party does not have any knowledge of, or receives no communication about, the long party's intentions. It is therefore more far-reaching than the US disclosure rules. The triggers of these rules require either voting power or investment power based on a contract, arrangement, understanding, relationship, or otherwise, or an arrangement to circumvent the disclosure obligation created with 'an accumulation of securities with a potential shift of corporate control' between the short party and the CfD holder.[380] The proposed model acknowledges first that CfD positions can be used to gain control by virtue of the market practice and irrespective of any mutual arrangement, and second that their main use is for economic purposes only. Thus, it does not link the disclosure obligation to the activities or existence of the short party, nor to the mere economic position of the long party.

The difference between the proposed regulation imposing a disclosure obligation and the US-type alternative in force in New Zealand is even greater than the difference from the US regulation, as discussed previously. This is illustrated in *Perry v Ithaca*, where the court explicitly held that the aim to avoid disclosure was a legitimate motive for entering into the CfD agreements and could not be sanctioned even if it could be argued to be against the spirit of disclosure rules.[381] The key purpose of the proposed regulation is to respect and promote the spirit of this regulatory field—summed up by the needs for investor and market protection.

In comparison with the arguments raised in *Perry v Ithaca*, it is interesting to note that the SEC has argued in favour of a distinction between the parties' motives and the commencement of a disclosure obligation in *CSX v TCI*. According to its interpretation of disclosure regulation under Rule 13d-3(b) which it had enacted, 'the long party's underlying motive for entering into the swap transaction generally is not a basis for determining whether there is "a plan or scheme to evade"'. The SEC continued by noting that the critical factor in triggering the disclosure obligation is not the motive to avoid reporting and disclosure obligation, but '[the knowledge or recklessness] in not knowing that the transaction would create a false appearance [of the beneficial ownership]'.[382] It should be noted, however, that the court in *CSX v TCI* explicitly declined this interpretation by stating that '[an] appearance of non-ownership cannot be false unless one in fact is at least a beneficial owner. That beneficial ownership would satisfy Rule 13d-3(a), thus making Rule 13d-3(b) superfluous.'[383]

380 Rule 13(d)-3; *CSX Corporation v the Children's Investment Fund Management (UK) LLP*, 562 F Supp 2d 511 (SDNY 2008), 12 June 2008, 08 CV 02764, 71.

381 *Perry Corporation v Ithaca (Custodians) Ltd* [2004] 1 NZLR 731 para. 81.

382 Brief of Amicus Curiae by the Securities and Exchange Commission in the matter CSX Corp. v. The Children's Inv. Fund Mgmt., L.L.P., et al., 08-Civ. 2764 (4 June 2008) 3, available at <http://www.chadbourne.com/files/Publication/ce4995ec-b733-4eef-89e5-d5574a182080/Preview/PublicationAttachment/ed741d95-84e9-4fb9-b0a6-c196c813e5bf/SECBrehenyLetter.pdf>, accessed 19 August 2015.

383 *CSX Corporation v the Children's Investment Fund Management (UK) LLP*, 562 F Supp 2d 511 (SDNY 2008), 12 June 2008, 08 CV 02764, 68; see also Sullivan (n. 378) 1313.

2. Reply to criticism

Although similar, the EU/UK safe harbour structure previously discussed and the regulatory solution proposed here differ in several respects. Unlike the safe harbour regulation, the proposal of this study is not based on a general disclosure obligation excluding some safe harbour cases. Instead, it focuses on a narrow group of control-affecting transactions. The structure proposed herein also takes the form-over-substance approach further as it does not rely on any artificial indicators of genuine investor motives, such as explicit clauses in the CfD agreement or declarations of innocence.[384] Instead, investors must simply know their intentions. Thus, the proposed structure is even more subjective than the EU/UK safe harbour. Nevertheless, it seems appropriate to take up some of the points of criticism that have been or might be voiced against the EU/UK solution in order to verify the soundness of our proposal.

Critics of the safe harbour approach point to its subjectivity and the resulting problem of enforcement. The European Commission noted, for example, that

> the effective implementation of this option could be problematic. Even if robust contractual agreements were created regarding explicit influence over voting rights and disposal of shares, it would be possible to circumvent the purposes of the disclosure obligation simply by changing the contract terms of the instrument immediately prior to the contract being closed. Also, such a regime would be partly based on the disclosed initial intention of the holder of the instrument. This means that (i) a holder may change its initial intention and (ii) even if holders might comply strictly with the terms of contractual arrangements, it would not with certainty prevent the building up of stakes on an undisclosed basis.[385]

In short, in addition to the concern regarding how to discover investors' intentions, the following issues were raised in the consultation.[386] First, the safe harbour was claimed to lead to increased attempts to circumvent disclosure obligations. Second, the regulation was deemed too complicated and unworkable. Third, the safe harbour would still have allowed hidden stakes to be built, which was considered a threat to the market in itself. Fourth, the mere possibility that the long party could rely on the hedging structures operating in her favour was seen to justify regulation. It is argued in the present study that these problems can be overcome with the proposed intentions-based disclosure regulation.

The disclosure system proposed here employs a reversed burden of proof in order to tackle the problem of enforcement based on the subjective criterion

[384] See Financial Services Authority, *Disclosure of Contracts for Difference, Consultation and draft Handbook text, CP 07/20* (November 2007) 49–50, available at <http://www.fsa.gov.uk/pubs/cp/cp07_20.pdf>; and Bertaccini (n. 373) 295.

[385] European Commission, *Commission Staff Working Paper—Impact Assessment accompanying the document proposal for a Directive of the European Parliament and of the Council amending Directive 2004/109/EC on the harmonisation of transparency requirements in relation to information about issuers whose securities are admitted to trading on a regulated market*, SEC(2011) 1279 final (25 October 2011) 69.

[386] See also Financial Services Authority, *Disclosure of Contracts for Difference: Feedback and policy statement on CP07/20, and further technical consultation, CP 08/17* (October 2008) 13, available at <http://www.fsa.gov.uk/pubs/cp/cp08_17.pdf> accessed 19 August 2015; see also Committee of

of intention.[387] The CfD investors would be given greater freedom, but with that freedom would also follow responsibility for compiling evidence of their intentions. If under suspicion, the investors would be required to prove their innocence or face severe sanctions. The threat of investigations would force investors to draft sufficient and genuine documentation of their decision-making process—a requirement not far from the general obligation of good governance and business practice in general corporate law. Otherwise, the precise requirements for rebutting the burden of proof would follow traditional rules known from civil litigation.

Similarly, if the investment motives changed from being purely financial to being control-seeking, this would trigger not only a disclosure obligation but also an ancillary need to prove that initial intentions were indeed only financial and that the disclosure had been timely. An investor failing to do this would be faced with sanctions. Regarding circumvention of legal obligations, strong subjectivity is not necessarily a negative aspect. Even though every regulation includes the danger of non-compliance, it can be argued that the proposed regulation would be more difficult to circumvent, since it is based not on a formal but rather a material provision of hard and convincing evidence.

It is true that the intention-based regulation does not expose all CfD transactions to the market, and that even some large transactions can remain undisclosed if they do not include an element of control. Yet, this should not be a concern as these purely economic investments would not have a market impact, as discussed in section V.E.1, and would therefore not have to be disclosed. This alleged problem is said to be increased by the market-hedging practice, which enables long parties or potential long parties to rely on their short parties to acquire a hedging block of shares.[388] This confidence would enable the CfD holder to develop his or her plans concerning these hedge shares without any communication to the short party. Under the proposed regulation, if this structure was taken advantage of and later exposed to the market after the long party had executed his or her plans, a suspicion of breach of the disclosure obligation would lead to a requirement for the CfD holder to provide counter-evidence.

In reply to the concern that a narrower disclosure regulation would lead to lower levels of compliance than an all-embracing general regulation, it is worth noting that participants in capital markets have several incentives to comply with disclosure regulation. First, the traditional risk of sanctions can be enhanced not only by increasing the number or scope of regulation, but also by increasing

European Securities Regulators (CESR), *CESR proposal to extend major shareholding notifications to instruments of similar economic effect to holding shares and entitlements to acquire shares*, CESR/09-1215b (January 2010) 15, available at <http://www.esma.europa.eu/system/files/09_1215b.pdf> accessed 19 August 2015.

387 Regulation 1/2003 article 2 operates similarly in the case of exemptions from the cartel offence, see Valentine Korah, *An Introductory Guide to EC Competition Law and Practice* (9th edn, Hart, Oxford 2007) 242. The burden of proof is then on the party claiming legality of the agreement.

388 FSA, CP 08/17 (n. 386) 13; Bertaccini (n. 373) 278.

enforcement activity, which is easier with focused regulation. Second, recent years have seen a trend of strong enforcement actions towards high-profile executives and professionals, serving as warnings to the whole industry. Last, both investors and the market demand better information than was previously the case, in particular due to a number of large-scale scandals and the financial crisis. The market quickly punishes companies and professionals if there is reason to believe that they have something to hide.[389]

Furthermore, the proposed disclosure obligation would call for increased attention from CfD investors. However, the requirement would simply be that investors would know what they were doing, that is, whether they aimed at gaining a control position with their investment. New alternatives are also not always 'unnecessarily complex': innovations must be introduced if there is a desire to further develop the legal system. Therefore, costs of learning can at times be overcome by increased ongoing efficiency, as is argued to be the case in the topic at hand.

Finally, one might suspect that risk-averse market participants could have an incentive to over-disclose their CfD positions to mitigate potential liability. This could lead to information overload, which in turn would result in market inefficiencies.[390] CfD holders can indeed develop an over-cautious disclosure practice under the proposed regulation, but our solution will compare well with both alternatives: in comparison to a no-disclosure regime (that is, the law prior to the implementation of the revised EU Directive), CfD abuse will be reduced, and therefore overall welfare gains should be expected despite some level of over-disclosure. In comparison with the revised EU full disclosure standard, we would expect the overall level of disclosure under our proposal to be lower, which would thus lead to higher efficiency gains in comparison to the revised general disclosure regime.

3. Efficiency of enforcement

We saw previously that targeted and functional regulation is not worth much if it is not enforced efficiently.[391] Powerful enforcement comprises both firm sanctions and a sufficiently high probability of getting caught. The latter component can be especially problematic in securities law, as providing evidence

389 Troy Paredes, 'Blinded by the Light: Information Overload and Its Consequences for Securities Regulation' (2003) 81 Washington University Law Quarterly 417, 429.

390 Easterbrook and Fischel (n. 365) 704.

391 See above sections VI.B.1 and VI.C.6.b.iii. See, in the present context, Coffee (n. 377) 244; Henry T C Hu and Bernard S Black, 'Empty Voting and Hidden (Morphable) Ownership: Taxonomy, Implications, and Reforms' (2006) 61 Business Lawyer 1011, 1050; and Michael C Schouten, 'The Case for Mandatory Ownership Disclosure' (2009) 15 Stanford Journal of Law, Business and Finance 127, 179; see also Easterbrook and Fischel (n. 365) 677. For a novel approach to capital markets law enforcement, see Dirk Zetzsche, 'Challenging Wolf Packs: Thoughts on Efficient Enforcement of Shareholder Transparency Rules', Center for Business and Corporate Law Research Paper Series 0044 (2/2010) 15-20 <http://papers.ssrn.com/sol3/papers.cfm?abstract_id=1428899> accessed 23 August 2015.

of a breach is particularly difficult in this field. This difficulty arises from the nature of investor decision-making and the variety of information and activities giving rise to market movements. In the field of shareholder disclosure and CfDs, these problems are connected to a complicated mixture of instruments used for mimicking shareholdings, and assessing the enforcement of our solution is therefore important.

As discussed in section VI.G.1, the proposed sanctions would be tailored to counter the expected gains of CfD abuse. The increase in bid price would result in a CfD bidder being obligated to pay the full price for all tendered shares and the loss of voting rights would correspond to those gained either directly or indirectly through the CfD arrangements. Yet, as it cannot realistically be assumed that every case of breach would be detected, the sanctions proportional to the gains are not sufficient. An additional punitive fine should be considered to increase the general probability of getting sanctioned to match the gains of abuse. The fine would be measured by the market supervisor, and its amount should be adjusted to correlate with other monetary capital markets sanctions.

For the proposed regulatory structure to be effective there must be a genuine attitude in favour of *ex post* enforcement.[392] Some market supervisors have been criticized for not using their full authority, which is essential in order for the deterrence to work.[393] It could be said that the proposed regulation relies heavily on formal sanctions and therefore does not suit capital markets enforcement generally, which has traditionally been conceived to be informal and reputation-based.[394] However, the traditional naming-and-shaming approach is not sufficient, as CfD holders abusing their position can come from very different sectors of an international market—for example, they can be hedge funds or industrial players—and the traditional regulatory approach to sanctioning would have varying effects depending on the importance of reputation to the person breaching the rules.[395] Some forms of market activity, such as CfD abuse, can lead to such serious problems that their prevention must be a priority for every regulator. It should motivate them to reform their attitudes towards formal sanctions.

A comparison with these attitudes can be found in the United States, where the SEC is known for its powerful enforcement actions as well as its severe fines and other sanctions.[396] A shift in the British outlook on enforcement can already be observed, as the UK authorities have proposed and defended a plan to increase the level of financial penalties which they can impose.[397] Moreover, the 2009 Turner Review[398]

[392] Easterbrook and Fischel (n. 365) 678.

[393] See Coffee (n. 377) 276-8; Kraakman and others (n. 377) 297.

[394] See John Armour and Jeffrey N Gordon, 'The Berle–Means Corporation in the 21st Century' (unpublished draft, on file with the author) 33–5.

[395] Similarly in Coffee (n. 377) 310.

[396] Coffee (n. 377) 268–74, 309–10; Armour and Gordon (n. 394) 23.

[397] See Financial Services Authority, *Enforcement financial penalties, Feedback on CP09/19*, PS10/4 (March 2010) 9–11, available at <http://www.fsa.gov.uk/pubs/policy/ps10_04.pdf> accessed 19 August 2015.

[398] FSA, *The Turner Review—A regulatory response to the global banking crisis* (March 2009).

signalled the end to the previous 'light-touch' regulation in the United Kingdom, promising tougher enforcement practice in the future.[399] Even if it is not necessarily suited to all types of breaches of capital markets regulations, this development is welcomed in the enforcement of the regulation limiting CfD abuse.

Yet, noble goals and policy statements are not enough, as one of the main problems with enforcement is that the supervising authorities do not have enough resources and time. It can be assumed that the easier it is to recognize non-compliance, the more efficiently the authorities can monitor and enforce the regulation.[400] A general CfD disclosure obligation, as opposed to the safe harbour model, was largely supported on this basis during the UK and EU consultations.[401] According to the proponents, every non-disclosure of CfD holdings above the set threshold can be sanctioned if observed, whereas the intention-based regulatory structures also require the abusive intention to be recognized.

The main difference between the safe harbour and the regulation proposed in this book lies in the identity of the party under the obligation to provide evidence either for the crucial intention or for the lack of it. Under the former position, the national market supervisor would have needed to show that a CfD holder had breached the law, whereas the proposal of this study is based on the reversed burden of proof falling on the investor herself. This reversal increases the deterrence of the sanctions, and it can be questioned why it is not more widely used in judging activity such as capital markets transactions where the participants plan their actions and can be prepared to provide evidence on their decisions.

In order for any type of a legal process—with any kind of procedural rules—to be initiated, the breach of law must first be detected. Even though CfDs can be abused without any formal agreements or other evidence, their effects are clearly visible.[402] Fortunately, the market practice which causes the problem also helps in identifying the problem. First, if the abuse is connected to a takeover bid, the stake of a CfD bidder is revealed by an offer document, independent of the shareholder notification disclosure regulation. This is because the offer document is required to include details on the interests of the bidder in the target.[403]

Second, if CfDs are related to other forms of influence on the target company, either by way of direct contact with the management by the CfD holder, via unusually large voting stakes exercised by investment banks for decisions peculiarly favourable to some third parties, or by a large block acquisition inducing unusual market price movements, the activity most often becomes public in a way that should attract the regulator's attention. One such market indication could be, for example, a combination of disclosure of decreasing holdings from

[399] Peter Thal Larsen, Jennifer Hughes, and George Parker, 'Turner to End Light-touch Regulation' *Financial Times* (London, 19 March 2009).

[400] See Easterbrook and Fischel (n. 365) 678–9.

[401] FSA, CP 08/17 (n. 386) 5, 13; European Commission (n. 385) 69.

[402] Zetzsche (n. 374) 141.

[403] Article 6(3)(g) of the Takeover Directive, Rule 24.3(a) of the Takeover Code.

the short party and a corresponding increasing holdings disclosure from the new large shareholder.

4. Conclusion

Even though rare in occurrence, CfD abuse can greatly disturb equity markets. It is clear that CfD positions should be under a disclosure obligation, as the combination of their characteristics and the market practice can effectively transform CfD positions into shareholdings. However, it is not equally clear how extensive CfD disclosure regulation should be.

The problems caused by CfDs include interference with market efficiency and transparency, distortion of informed investment decision-making both *ex ante* and *ex post*, and intrusions into the corporate governance dynamics of target companies. The need for regulation of CfD holdings stems from the need to overcome these problems. As it would not be feasible to completely prohibit generally beneficial market activities, such as CfD trading, disclosure has been chosen as the primary regulatory strategy to limit these problems.

The consistently introduced comprehensive disclosure requirements go too far, as they require the disclosure of innocent events that are irrelevant and unnecessary for the capital market. In this way, regulation imposes significant costs on the issuers that could have been avoided with proper consideration.

On this basis, the present study advocates for a disclosure requirement only for the cases where the positive risk-decoupling is combined with the intention to acquire control in the target company. Conversely, contracts for differences should be exempt from a duty of disclosure in all other cases. Such a 'takeover-related solution' has been discussed in the literature, but has ultimately not been included in the law. Both the EU Commission and the UK FSA had discussed such a model in detail in their consultation papers, but both opted for a comprehensive disclosure system in the end.

The beauty of a takeover law solution would be that it would require a disclosure of risk-decoupling structures only where the policy problem becomes acute. The vast majority of CfD dealings are harmless in terms of takeover plans; such trading would therefore be left untouched, and over-regulation of the sector would be avoided. Technically, this could be achieved by imposing the duty of disclosure on the risk-decoupler where a takeover intention is present. This subjective element has been considered to be problematic by most legislators, and is responsible for the fact that the comprehensive model was ultimately preferred.[404] However, this problem could be addressed, for example, by reversing the burden of proof to the disadvantage of the risk-decoupler and by adopting a sharp enforcement regime.

CfD-related market information can be divided into three categories: information on the ability to influence the use of voting rights, information on the identity

404 See Chapter V.E.2.c.

of the CfD holder, and the size of exposure and information on executed trades. Of these categories, only information concerning intentions to use control in a target company is harmful to the market and thereby needs to be under regulatory control. Identification of control-related information as the critical type of information sets the limits for the disclosure obligation. Only CfD investments made with the intention of influencing the use of voting rights in the target companies should be required to be disclosed.

In sum, the current EU regulation acknowledges the problems raised by CfDs, and attempts to remedy them with a general disclosure obligation. This regulation should be revised to tackle the actual problem—the abuse of hedging structures in the quest for corporate control. In order to achieve this, the current CfD disclosure regulation should be replaced with a more effective regulatory alternative focusing on control-related information and powered by enforcement with a reversed burden of proof.

VII
The Federal Dimension

So far in this investigation we have anticipated that the problems of positive and negative risk-decoupling should both be addressed by regulation at the EU level. This was based on the inherent assumption that related aspects are already regulated by the Transparency Directive, and so should the risk-decoupling problem at stake here be. This conclusion, however, should not be taken for granted.

All EU action is limited by constitutional constraints. In particular, proposed EU activity must have a proper legal basis, and must satisfy the requirements of subsidiarity and proportionality. Once these thresholds have been crossed, it is still important to ask whether EU activity in this field would be normatively desirable. In the following, we will explore these issues in turn.

A. Admissibility

Far too often in legislative proposals by the EU institutions, the constitutional framework of their legislative powers is given far too little attention. Legislative proposals often contain only cursory information about the legislative competence or questions of subsidiarity.

This is surprising, as the EU Treaties provide clear guidelines on these questions, and the powers of the European institutions to legislate are clearly limited by the three principles of competence (principle of conferral), subsidiarity, and proportionality.[1]

On the question of legal competence, the EU's authority of extensive capital market law legislation is no longer seriously put into question. It is based on either TFEU articles 50(2) lit. g, 53(1), or 114, depending on the predominant purpose of the respective instrument.[2] Only when setting up new European authorities and delegating powers to them do some ambiguities remain.[3] The rules proposed here would both strengthen investor protection, and thus support the freedom of

[1] See TEU article 5.

[2] Rüdiger Veil, 'Legislative Powers for Regulating Capital Markets in Europe' in Rüdiger Veil (ed.), *European Capital Markets Law* (Hart Publishing 2013) § 3 paras 4 ff.

[3] See the controversy around the European Short Selling Regulation, which grants ESMA broad powers. The CJEU has now applied more generous scrutiny than before. See case C-270/12 *United Kingdom v European Parliament and Council* ECLI:EU:C:2014:18.

establishment, and indirectly serve the completion of the internal market. A new European authority would not be up for debate, but the right to suspend voting rights would be transferred only to existing national authorities. Therefore, the proper basis of competence would appear to be, as for the original Transparency Directive, a common application of TFEU articles 50(2) lit. g and 114.

More difficult is the question of subsidiarity. Strictly speaking, the EU may act only to the extent that it is in a better position to do so than the individual Member States.[4] The Court of Justice of the European Union (CJEU) has frequently been accused of applying this requirement by imposing the burden of proof on the Member States, contrary to the wording and spirit of TEU article 5.[5] This tendency in the case law of course greatly facilitates the EU legislative process, but it may override Member States' legitimate interests.[6] The 2009 Treaty of Lisbon therefore put in place a new parliamentary monitoring and early warning system to strengthen the enforcement of subsidiarity during the law-making process.[7] The success of this new instrument is modest, and apart from only two 'yellow cards' to law-making projects raised by national parliaments, the subsidiarity control has experienced no significant upswing since the Lisbon Treaty entered into force.[8] For the question of interest here, this means that the legislative changes proposed would not be expected to meet any serious headwinds. The recently adopted reform of the Transparency Directive similarly put forward rather short explanations of why and how it complies with subsidiarity, regarding both the substantive issues and the question of enforcement.[9]

[4] See TEU article 5(3):

> Under the principle of subsidiarity, in areas which do not fall within its exclusive competence, the Union shall act only if and in so far as the objectives of the proposed action cannot be sufficiently achieved by the Member States, either at central level or at regional and local level, but can rather, by reason of the scale or effects of the proposed action, be better achieved at Union level.

[5] For example, in the famous 'Working Time Directive' case. See Case C-84/94 *United Kingdom v Council of the European Union* [1996] ECR I-5755, ECLI:EU:C:1996:431.

[6] For a critical view, see Garreth Davies, 'Subsidiarity: The Wrong Idea, in the Wrong Place, at the Wrong Time' (2006) 43 Common Market Law Review 63.

[7] On this see Robert Schütze, 'Subsidiarity After Lisbon: Reinforcing the Safeguards of Federalism?' (2009) 68 The Cambridge Law Journal 525; Philipp Kiiver, 'The Early-Warning System for the Principle of Subsidiarity: The National Parliament as a Conseil d'Etat for Europe' (2011) 36 European Law Review 98; Adam Cygan, 'The Parliamentarisation of EU Decision-Making? The Impact of the Treaty of Lisbon on National Parliaments' (2011) 36 European Law Review 480.

[8] The first yellow card concerned the proposal for the so-called 'Monti II' Regulation, COM(2012) 130 on the exercise of the right to take collective action within the context of the freedom of establishment and the freedom to provide services, of 21 March 2012; the second the Commission proposal for a Regulation on the establishment of the European Public Prosecutor's Office of 17 July 2013, COM(2013) 534 final.

[9] The final version, Directive 2013/50, only mentions this briefly in recital 29. The Commission Proposal, COM(2011) 683 final, explains this in a little more detail:

> The problems identified concerning small and medium-sized issuers derive from European Union's and national legislation and can only be addressed through changes in the legislation at the level of the European Union. In addition, only a binding legal instrument adopted at the EU level would ensure that all Member States apply the same regulatory framework based on the same principles, thereby ending the current fragmentation of the regulatory response concerning the regime for notification of major holdings. Sanctions

Finally, we should mention the principle of proportionality, which holds that Union action essentially should not go beyond what is necessary in achieving its goals.[10] The individual requirements laid down here (appropriateness, necessity, reasonableness) have to be considered when designing the shape of EU law.

B. Substantive Desirability

On the merits, it must be decided whether legislation at the EU level makes sense from a policy perspective.

First, it must be emphasized that the presence of any national elements in areas of law that are already integrated to a high degree may lead to the distortion and disruption of this relationship. Just as the European capital markets have already been widely integrated, common legal instruments have been created and an EU-wide, borderless capital market is on the horizon.[11] Thus, any national idiosyncrasy would run counter to this objective. This argument has been put forward inter alia in favour of the adoption of the European Short Selling Regulation.[12]

Apart from this argument relying on the existing acquis of the European capital markets law, it is obvious that the problem of risk-decoupling is a global one, where one must look for solutions in all economic systems that have a developed capital market. During the present study, when describing the problems, issues, and solutions, it has become clear that national legal responses cannot always be discussed in isolation, nor can they be clearly separated from one another. The economic problem under consideration here transcends borders and is found in virtually all jurisdictions in a similar form. In addition, it will frequently arise in cross-border situations: it is conceivable that a hedge fund engaging in risk-decoupling is headquartered in State A (for example the United Kingdom or the United States), but the target company in State B (such as Germany). A harmonized approach—at least on the European level—lends itself to addressing these situations.

In a common economic area like the European Union, where the free movement of capital is guaranteed and the providers and customers of financial products have unlimited freedom, separate national initiatives may be dysfunctional.[13] In such a transnational legal space, fragmented approaches may limit the effectiveness of

which are divergent and too weak risk being insufficient to effectively prevent breaches of the Transparency Directive and to ensure effective supervision and the development of a level playing field. Action at EU level can avoid divergences and weaknesses in the legal framework of sanctioning and investigative powers available to national authorities and thus contribute to the elimination of regulatory arbitrage opportunities.

[10] TEU article 5(4): 'Under the principle of proportionality, the content and form of Union action shall not exceed what is necessary to achieve the objectives of the Treaties.'

[11] See the project to create a European 'Capital Markets Union': European Commission, *Green Paper: Building a Capital Markets Union* COM(2015) 63 final, available at <http://eur-lex.europa.eu/legal-content/EN/TXT/PDF/?uri=COM:2015:63:FIN>.

[12] See International Monetary Fund, *IMF Staff Comments on EU Commission Consultation on Short Selling* (5 August 2010), available at <http://www.imf.org/external/np/eur/2010/pdf/080510.pdf>.

[13] For a similar argument, see Merrit B Fox, 'Optimal Regulatory Areas for Securities Disclosure' (2003) 81 Washington University Law Quarterly 1017, 1033.

the measures adopted and their enforcement, and trigger alternative structures and regulatory arbitrage by the market players to circumvent national legislation.[14] Such circumventions are especially easy to achieve in the mobile context of capital investments. Only a harmonized approach at European level would prevent such avoidance attempts.

Finally, it is important not to disregard the perspective of the investors. Different national regulatory approaches could lead to uncertainty in the markets and create costs and difficulties for market participants. Genuine investors who are active across the EU—typically institutional investors, such as pension funds—that hold great volumes of shares in a variety of companies from many different Member States complain about the efforts that such diverging regulation demands from them, and refer to high information, transaction, and monitoring costs.[15]

This last point leads to the foundations for the Europeanization of the financial and economic framework in the EU as a whole. In a nutshell, the declared objective of the EU financial market legislation is to integrate markets by reducing barriers and the costs of investment. In this way, the objective is to contribute to the best possible allocation of resources, and thus to achieve general welfare gains.[16] In addition, in a larger market, the cost of raising capital and the risk of market distortion stand to be reduced.[17] These basic considerations can helpfully support the claim made here. From an investor's point of view, similar legal rules across an economic territory increase trust in the capital markets and facilitate cross-border investment of capital.[18] If investors can be sure that a foreign capital

[14] Cf. European Commission, *Proposal for a Regulation of the European Parliament and of The Council on Short Selling and Certain Aspects of Credit Default Swaps*, COM(2010) 482 final (15 September 2010) 2 and recital 4. See also recital 2 of Regulation (EU) No 236/2012 of the European Parliament and of the Council of 14 March 2012 on short selling and certain aspects of credit default swaps, [2012] OJ L86/1.

[15] See, for example, the position of Eumedion, a Dutch platform for corporate governance, which represents the interests of institutional investors: *Eumedion response to the Commission Services' public consultation on short selling of 9 July 2010*, para. 8:

> [W]e would urge the Commission to introduce uniform pan-European disclosure thresholds for both public and private disclosure. A harmonised set of rules will save institutional investors with their highly diversified investment portfolio a lot of compliance costs, risks and agitation. Differences between disclosure thresholds within the European Union would lead to additional increases in the administrative burden as institutional investors would have to make costs to monitor the regulatory developments in the various Member States and would have to adopt their internal compliance systems of to implement temporary compliance measures involving manual monitoring.

See on this also Financial Services Authority, *Implementing Aspects of the Financial Services Act 2010: Feedback on CP10/11, Final Rules and Further Consultation* CP10/18 (July 2010) para. 2.14, available at <http://www.fsa.gov.uk/pubs/cp/cp10_18.pdf>.

[16] See on this in particular the seminal Financial Services Action Plan, which was the basis for integration over the past several years: European Commission, *Financial Services: Implementing the Framework for Financial Markets: Action Plan*, COM(1999) 232 (11 May 1999), in particular pp. 3 and 7, available at <http://ec.europa.eu/internal_market/finances/docs/actionplan/index/action_en.pdf>.

[17] See the seminal work by Willem Molle, *The Economics of European Integration: Theory, Practice, Policy* (5th edn, Ashgate 2006), in particular pp. 218 ff.; and Eilís Ferran, *Building an EU Securities Market* (Cambridge University Press 2004) 9 f.; 12.

[18] See already European Commission, *Proposal for a Directive of the European Parliament and of the Council on the Harmonisation of Transparency Requirements with Regard to Information about Issuers*

market has a quality level comparable to that of the domestic disclosure standard, this will reduce their information and transaction costs, and thus facilitate cross-border investment. Put differently, where an investor wanting to invest in a foreign company cannot expect to be informed in the same way as in its domestic legal system about possible risk-decoupling structures or distortions, this will create uncertainty, increased need for legal advice, and rising costs, and will consequently result in declining overall cross-border investment.

Altogether this results in an impressive number of arguments in favour of a European legal instrument.

There are very few arguments for the opposite side. At best, we could see benefits in giving Member States their own regulatory options to enable more customized regulation, tailored to the respective legal systems and the shareholder structure in the different countries. Harmonized requirements from Brussels often have the disadvantage that they can produce very different effects depending on the industry or company structure in the respective Member States.[19] However, this will not be a significant concern for the present issue. The phenomenon of risk-decoupling may become relevant in any shareholder structure or business industry. As intra-shareholder conflicts are the predominant policy issue in continental European jurisdictions, due to their relatively concentrated ownership structures, regulatory intervention in these jurisdictions would be even more important than in the Anglo-Saxon systems. As most EU Member State systems exhibit rather concentrated ownership structures, an EU-wide instrument should be strongly supported.[20]

Other known drawbacks of harmonization at the European level include the slowness of the regulatory process in the EU institutions as well as the typically resulting rigidity of an agreement once achieved.[21] The most prominent example of this is the Second Company Law Directive, which has virtually remained unchanged in its relevant parts since the 1970s, except for a few, rather technical modifications.[22] More recently, EU law-making bodies have responded to such tendencies with specifically designed review clauses that specify a particular date up to which an adopted act must be re-evaluated.[23] Furthermore, this problem can

Whose Securities Are Admitted to Trading on a Regulated Market and Amending Directive 2001/34/EC COM(2003) 138, <http://eur-lex.europa.eu/LexUriServ/LexUriServ.do?uri=COM:2003:0138:FIN:EN:PDF>.

[19] John Armour and Wolf-Georg Ringe, 'European Company Law 1999–2010: Renaissance and Crisis' (2011) 48 Common Market Law Review 125, 129.

[20] For an overview of shareholder structures, see Fabrizio Barca and Marco Becht (eds), *The Control of Corporate Europe* (Oxford University Press 2001).

[21] See Niamh Moloney, *EU Securities and Financial Markets Regulation* (3rd edn, Oxford University Press 2014) 27 ff.

[22] Second Directive 2012/30/EU, [2012] OJ L315/74. The unchanged parts include, crucially, the definition of minimum capital for public companies.

[23] See, for example, the Rome II Regulation (EC) No 864/2007 of the European Parliament and of the Council of 11 July 2007 on the law applicable to non-contractual obligations, [2007] OJ L199/40, article 30.

be mitigated to some extent by increased involvement of delegated legislation in the context of the Lamfalussy principles, which can be changed in an easier and less cumbersome way.[24]

C. Practicability

If a solution at the European level thus seems appropriate in this case, the question arises of its practical feasibility. As described previously, the subject of *negative* risk-decoupling was already on the European agenda, but was then passed on by the Commission to the European Securities and Markets Authority (ESMA) with the instruction to collect evidence.[25] It remains to be seen whether and how ESMA and/or the Commission will ultimately react. Although 86 per cent of the surveyed stakeholders spoke in favour of including measures against 'empty voting' in the Transparency Directive,[26] the subject has not been pursued further during the legislative process.[27]

To the extent that there is a political will for addressing the issue at EU level, it would make sense to implement the measures proposed here into EU legislation. This will particularly be true for the first two pillars of the present regime, which introduce a disclosure regime for negative interests and providing the power to suspend voting rights.[28] We made concrete legislative proposals above, and these could easily be implemented into the Transparency Directive.[29] The third pillar—*ex post* court control—should, however, rather be subject to national law and court procedure. The substantive elements of corporate law and governance—such as fiduciary duties—are still very much in the hands of national law-makers and case law. It appears appropriate to ensure continuity in this area.

By contrast, the issue of *positive* risk-decoupling was ultimately picked up by the EU law-making bodies, and decided, as we saw, in a comprehensive manner. The appetite for further reform is probably low, in particular after the final accomplishment of a lengthy reform process. Nevertheless, it is not unlikely that a future reform round (under the heading of deregulation) might come to the conclusion that a vast level of contracts for difference (CfD) disclosure is not required and can be exempted from the scope of application.[30]

[24] On the Lamfalussy process, see Moloney (n. 21) 898 ff.

[25] See Chapter VI.C.2.

[26] Mazars and Marccus Partners, *Transparency Directive Assessment Report—Prepared for the European Commission Internal Market and Services DG, Final Report* (December 2009) 94, available at <http://ec.europa.eu/internal_market/securities/docs/transparency/report-application_en.pdf>.

[27] The final version of the reform Directive 2013/50/EU does not deal with the problem. See the consolidated version of the Transparency Directive, as revised, article 13.

[28] See Chapter VI.C.6 and VI.D.2.

[29] See the suggestions made in Chapter VI.C.6.b and VI.D.2.

[30] See the safe harbour discussion in Chapter V.E.2.c and my proposal in Chapter VI.G.

D. Summary

In sum, there are strong arguments for the introduction of appropriate regulation at the level of the European Union. Once, and if, the political will exists, activity should be initiated by the EU legislative bodies. But it is also possible to first make an attempt at Member State level, with a view of gaining some initial practical experience so as to enrich the subsequent law-making process on the EU level.[31]

[31] This is essentially how the discovery process for regulating positive risk-decoupling evolved. See Chapter V.E.1.

VIII
Conclusion

Sophisticated players in the capital markets, including in particular activist hedge funds, often employ the strategy of risk-decoupling. Regulators worldwide are rightly on alert because risk-decoupling creates strong policy concerns. This book has distinguished positive risk-decoupling strategies—essentially, the creation of a long economic position without formally owning the shares—and negative risk-decoupling—the creation of a short position alongside holding shares, which creates distorted incentives for shareholders.

For *negative risk-decoupling*, I looked at the phenomenon from three different policy perspectives—those of agency costs, information and transaction costs, and corporate finance theory. In essence, negative risk-decoupling deviates from traditional assumptions of corporate governance and finance because it creates agency and information costs, both for internal shareholders and external investors alike. On the other hand, risk-decoupling may mitigate shareholder co-ordination problems in individual cases by allowing for the transfer of votes from the less informed to the more specialized and engaged shareholders.

The solution proposed addresses both aspects. A comprehensive regulatory response to the phenomenon should be composed of three pillars.

1. The first and most important pillar would be a comprehensive disclosure system for negative positions. Care should be taken to ensure that disclosure is meaningful and not overly burdensome. Therefore, there should be a relatively high initial disclosure threshold. By contrast, the requirement of reporting gross positions (rather than netted long and short positions) ensures that the market can clearly distinguish between the shareholder's voting influence in the company and the shareholder's economic exposure. The high initial threshold ensures that only those positions that likely have an influence on the company's strategy have to be disclosed. Moreover, daily lending activity or derivatives trading will be left untouched, avoiding a disruptive impact on the market. Based on these considerations, I develop a concrete legislative proposal to amend the European Transparency Directive. Similar considerations would apply to other jurisdictions.
2. The disclosure of negative decoupling situations should allow the market to respond adequately, and it will also strongly deter harmful decoupling activity. For the few situations where the market is unable to react, national regulators should be equipped with the power to suspend decoupled

shareholders' voting rights. This is preferable over a blanket disenfranchisement rule as regulators can assess the facts of the individual situation. Clear guidance criteria are provided.

3. The third pillar for the remaining unsolved cases would be *ex post* court litigation, mostly based on shareholders' fiduciary duties, where they exist. This would act as a 'safety net' and reserve remedy for the few cases that cannot be adequately addressed by the first two instruments.

Although conceptually similar in nature, *positive risk-decoupling* poses a number of entirely different problems. The reason is that positive decoupling is not concerned with shareholders' distorted incentives and their possible pursuit of improper purposes. Instead, the risk-decoupler here usually does not have any significant voting power. In fact, the opposite really seems to be the problem—the risk-decoupler seeks to avoid being entitled to vote, as holding voting rights may trigger disclosure obligations that the risk-decoupler seeks to circumvent. The agent here does not have any significant voting power to impose costs on the principal.

The main policy problem that was identified is therefore the circumvention of disclosure laws, which would otherwise apply to large shareholdings. It is inherently understandable that the simplest remedy to that problem would be to submit positive risk-decoupling strategies to a comparable disclosure obligation. Yet, not all dealings in contracts for differences are relevant to the policy problem, and the market should not be flooded with disclosure of innocent trading.

For these reasons, the present study develops an 'intentions-based' system of disclosure for positive risk-decoupling situations. Holders of long positions, using contracts for difference (CfDs) or other instruments, should be subject to a disclosure obligation where they have a control-related intention, in particular the objective of a CfD takeover by stealth. This subjective approach should be accompanied by a reversed burden of proof and tough enforcement action.

The concrete proposals made in this book are pitched at the European market and advocate for an EU solution to the problem. However, the policy considerations and the reasoning behind the regulatory tools would also hold true for any other jurisdiction in the world. The Securities and Exchange Commission (SEC), for example, is also considering imposing new regulatory action.[1] It is the author's hope that the present study will encourage worldwide thinking about the phenomenon.

[1] Securities and Exchange Commission, *Concept Release on the U.S. Proxy System* (Release Nos 34-62495, IA-3052, IC-29340; File No S7-14-10, 2010), (2010) 75 Federal Register 42981, 43018.

Bibliography

Ann-Kristin Achleitner, André Betzer, and Jasmin Gider, 'Do Corporate Governance Motives Drive Hedge Fund and Private Equity Fund Activities?' (2010) 16 European Financial Management 805

Renée Adams and Daniel Ferreira, 'One Share—One Vote: The Empirical Evidence' (2008) 12 Review of Finance 51

Alexander Aganin and Paolo Volpin, 'The History of Corporate Ownership in Italy' in Randall Morck (ed.), *A History of Corporate Governance around the World: Family Business Groups to Professional Managers* (University of Chicago Press 2005) 325–66

Reena Aggarwal, Pedro A C Saffi, and Jason Sturgess, 'The Role of Institutional Investors in Voting: Evidence from the Securities Lending Market' (2015) 70 Journal of Finance 2309

Anup Agrawal and Tareque Nasser, 'Blockholders on Boards and CEO Compensation, Turnover and Firm Valuation', Working Paper 2012, available at <http://ssrn.com/abstract=1443431>

Luis A Aguilar, 'Aligning the Interests of Company Executives and Directors with Shareholders' (9 February 2015), available at <http://www.sec.gov/news/statement/020915-ps-claa.html> accessed 19 August 2015

George A Akerlof, 'The Market for "Lemons": Quality Uncertainty and the Market Mechanism' (1970) 84 Quarterly Journal of Economics 488

Bram Akkermans, *The Principle of 'Numerus Clausus' in European Property Law* (Intersentia [et al.] 2008)

Armen A Alchian and Harold Demsetz, 'Production, Information Costs, and Economic Organization' (1972) 62 American Economic Review 777

Isaac Alfon and Peter Andrews, 'Cost-Benefit Analysis in Financial Regulation: How to Do It and How It Adds Value' (1999) FSA Occasional Paper Series No 3, available at <http://citeseerx.ist.psu.edu/viewdoc/download?doi=10.1.1.201.978&rep=rep1&type=pdf>

Paul Ali, Ian Ramsay, and Benjamin Saunders, 'Securities Lending, Empty Voting and Corporate Governance' [2014] Law and Financial Markets Review 326

Yvan Allaire and Mihaela E Firsirotu, 'Hedge Funds as Activist Shareholders: Passing Phenomenon or Grave-Diggers of Public Corporations?' 8 (Social Science Research Network 2007) SSRN Scholarly Paper ID 961828 <http://papers.ssrn.com/abstract=961828> accessed 16 April 2015

William A Allen, 'Disproportionate Voting Rights May Be the Way to Better Governance' *Financial Times* (London, 4 August 2009) 8

Iman Anabtawi, 'Some Skepticism About Increasing Shareholder Power' (2006) 53 UCLA Law Review 561

Iman Anabtawi and Lynn Stout, 'Fiduciary Duties for Activist Shareholders' (2008) 60 Stanford Law Review 1255

Anita Anand, 'Telus Win Scores for Shareholders' *Financial Post* (17 October 2012) <http://business.financialpost.com/2012/10/17/telus-win-scores-for-%C2%ADshareholders/>

Matt Andrejczak, 'Sara Lee, Coach Set Rules to Spot Shareholder Actions' *MarketWatch* (2 April 2008) <http://www.marketwatch.com/story/sara-lee-coach-set-rules-to-deter-devious-shareholders>

Thomas J André, Jr, 'A Preliminary Inquiry into the Utility of Vote Buying in the Market for Corporate Control' (1990) 63 Southern California Law Review 533

John Armour, 'Enforcement Strategies in UK Corporate Governance: A Roadmap and Empirical Assessment' in John Armour and Jennifer Payne (eds), *Rationality in Company Law—Essays in Honour of DD Prentice* (Hart Publishing, Oxford 2009) 71

John Armour and Brian Cheffins, 'Origins of "Offensive" Shareholder Activism in the United States' in Jonathan Koppell (ed.), *Origins of Shareholder Advocacy* (Palgrave, Basingstoke 2011) 253 ff.

John Armour and Jeffrey N Gordon, 'The Berle–Means Corporation in the 21st Century' 22 (unpublished draft, on file with the author)

John Armour, Henry Hansmann, and Reinier Kraakman, 'What Is Corporate Law?' in Reinier Kraakman and others (eds), *The Anatomy of Corporate Law: A Comparative and Functional Approach* (2nd edn, Oxford University Press 2009) 1

John Armour, Henry Hansmann, and Reinier Kraakman, 'Agency Problems and Legal Strategies' in Reinier Kraakman and others, *The Anatomy of Corporate Law: A Comparative and Functional Approach* (2nd edn, Oxford University Press 2009) ch. 2

John Armour and Wolf-Georg Ringe, 'European Company Law 1999–2010: Renaissance and Crisis' (2011) 48 Common Market Law Review 125

John Armour and David A Skeel, 'Who Writes the Rules for Hostile Takeovers, and Why? The Peculiar Divergence of U.S. and U.K. Takeover Regulation' (2007) 95 Georgetown Law Journal 1727

John Armour and Michael J Whincop, 'The Proprietary Foundations of Corporate Law' (2007) 27 Oxford Journal of Legal Studies 429

Kenneth Joseph Arrow, *The Limits of Organization* (Norton 1974)

Association Française de la Gestion financière, *Response to DG MARKT consultation on 'Fostering an appropriate regime for shareholders' rights'* (27 July 2007)

Peter Astleford and Dick Frase (eds), *Hedge Funds and the Law* (Sweet & Maxwell 2010)

Autorité des Marchés Financiers (AMF), *Rapport sur les opérations de prêt emprunt de titres en période d'assemblée générale d'actionnaires* (Groupe de place présidé par Yves Mansion 2008)

Autoriteit Financiële Markten (AFM), *Wet op het Financieel Toezicht—Voorlichtingsbrochure aandeelhouders* (April 2009), available at <http://www.afm.nl>

Emilios Avgouleas, 'A New Framework for the Global Regulation of Short Sales: Why Prohibition Is Inefficient and Disclosure Insufficient' (2010) 15 Stanford Journal of Law, Business and Finance 376

Emilios Avgouleas, 'The Regulation of Short Sales Revisited' (2011) 5 Law and Financial Markets Review 333

Gene D'Avolio, 'The Market for Borrowing Stock' (2002) 66 Journal of Financial Economics 271

Daniel Awrey, 'The Limits of EU Hedge Fund Regulation' [2011] Law and Financial Markets Review 119

Dan Awrey, 'Complexity, Innovation, and the Regulation of Modern Financial Markets' (2012) 2 Harvard Business Law Review 235

Gregor Bachmann, 'Rechtsfragen der Wertpapierleihe' (2009) 173 Zeitschrift für das gesamte Handelsrecht und Wirtschaftsrecht (ZHR) 596

Gregor Bachmann and others (eds), *Regulating the Closed Corporation* (de Gruyter 2014)

Stephen M Bainbridge, 'Director Primacy and Shareholder Disempowerment' (2006) 119 Harvard Law Review 1735

Stephen M Bainbridge, 'The Case for Limited Shareholder Voting Rights' (2006) 53 UCLA Law Review 601

Michael Bal, 'Wet melding zeggenschap en securities lending: komt het nog goed?', in Jan T Anema and others (eds), *Bouwen en bezinning—Regels van wenselijk en onwenselijk financieel recht* (Kluwer 2007) 11–17

Bank of England, *Securities Borrowing and Lending Code of Guidance* (2009), available at <http://www.bankofengland.co.uk/markets/Pages/gilts/slrc.aspx>

Paul D Barbeau and Eric Chernin, 'The CSA Proceeds with Amendments to the Early Warning Reporting Regime but Abandons Two Key Proposed Changes' (14 October 2014), available at <http://www.bennettjones.com/Publications/Updates/The_CSA_Proceeds_with_Amendments_to_the_Early_Warning_Reporting_Regime_but_Abandons_Two_Key_Proposed_Changes/> accessed 19 August 2015

Fabrizio Barca and Marco Becht (eds), *The Control of Corporate Europe* (Oxford University Press 2001)

Michael J Barclay and Clifford G Holderness, 'Private Benefits from Control of Public Corporations' (1989) 25 Journal of Financial Economics 371

Michael J Barclay, Clifford Holderness, and Dennis Sheehan, 'Dividends and Corporate Shareholders' (2009) 22 Review of Financial Studies 2423

Jordan M Barry, John William Hatfield, and Scott Duke Kominers, 'On Derivatives Markets and Social Welfare: A Theory of Empty Voting and Hidden Ownership' (2013) 99 Virginia Law Review 1103

Stephen Bartholomeusz, 'Solly in Lieu of the True Share Owners', *The Age* (23 November 2002), available at <http://www.theage.com.au/articles/2002/11/22/1037697877160.html>

Robert P Bartlett III, 'Inefficiencies in the Information Thicket: A Case Study of Derivative Disclosures during the Financial Crisis' (2010) 36 Journal of Corporation Law 1

Ronald Barusch, 'Dealpolitik: Dell Shines Spotlight on "Record Date" Anachronism' *Wall Street Journal* (1 August 2013), available at <http://blogs.wsj.com/moneybeat/2013/08/01/dealpolitik-dell-shines-spotlight-on-record-date-anachronism/> accessed 19 August 2015

Theodor Baums, 'Germany' in Theodor Baums and Eddy Wymeersch (eds), *Shareholder Voting Rights and Practices in Europe and the United States* (Kluwer Law International 1999) 109

Theodor Baums and Maike Sauter, 'Anschleichen an Übernahmeziele mit Hilfe von Aktienderivaten' (2009) 173 Zeitschrift für das gesamte Handelsrecht und Wirtschaftsrecht (ZHR) 454

Lucian Bebchuk, 'Toward Undistorted Choice and Equal Treatment in Corporate Takeovers' (1985) 98 Harvard Law Review 1695

Lucian A Bebchuk, 'Efficient and Inefficient Sales of Corporate Control' (1994) 109 Quarterly Journal of Economics 957

Lucian A Bebchuk, 'The Case for Shareholder Access to the Ballot' (2003) 59 Business Lawyer 43

Lucian A Bebchuk, 'The Case for Increasing Shareholder Power' (2005) 118 Harvard Law Review 833

Lucian A Bebchuk, 'Letting Shareholders Set the Rules' (2006) 119 Harvard Law Review 1784

Lucian A Bebchuk, Alon Brav, Robert J Jackson, Jr, and Wei Jiang, 'Pre-Disclosure Accumulations by Activist Investors: Evidence and Policy' (2013) 39 Journal of Corporation Law 1

Lucian Bebchuk, Alon Brav, and Wei Jiang, 'The Long-Term Effects of Hedge Fund Activism' (2015) 115 Columbia Law Review 1085

Lucian Bebchuk and Jesse Fried, 'Executive Compensation as an Agency Problem' (2003) 17 Journal of Economic Perspectives 71

Lucian Bebchuk and Jesse Fried, *Pay Without Performance. The Unfulfilled Promise of Executive Compensation* (Harvard University Press 2004)

Marco Becht, Julian Franks, Colin Mayer, and Stefano Rossi, 'Returns to Shareholder Activism: Evidence from a Clinical Study of the Hermes UK Focus Fund' (2009) 22 Review of Financial Studies 3093

Marco Becht, Julian Franks, and Jeremy Grant, 'Hedge Fund Activism in Europe', ECGI Finance Working Paper 283/2010

Marco Becht and others, 'The Returns to Hedge Fund Activism: An International Study', ECGI Finance Working Paper 402/2014

Ulf Bernitz and Wolf-Georg Ringe (eds), *Company Law and Economic Protectionism: New Challenges to European Integration* (Oxford University Press 2010)

Daniel Bertaccini, 'To Disclose or Not to Disclose? *CSX CORP.,* Total Return Swaps, and Their Implications for Schedule 13D Filing Purposes' (2009) 31 Cardozo Law Review 267

Marianne Bertrand and Sendhil Mullainathan, 'Are CEOs Rewarded for Luck? The Ones Without Principals Are' (2011) 116 The Quarterly Journal of Economics 901

J Carr Bettis, John M Bizjak, and Michael L Lemmon, 'Managerial Ownership, Incentive Contracting, and the Use of Zero-Cost Collars and Equity Swaps by Corporate Insiders' (2001) 36 Journal of Financial and Quantitative Analysis 345

Jean-François Biard, 'Proposition de Loi Relative au Régime des Prêts Emprunts de Titres' [2010] Revue de Droit Bancaire et Financier 155.

Kit Bingham, 'Myners Rejects Calls for Curbs on Stock Lending' *Financial News* (21 March 2005) <http://www.efinancialnews.com/story/2005-03-21/myners-rejects-calls-for-curbs-on-stock-lending> accessed 16 August 2015

Kit Bingham, 'Concern Grows over Borrowed Votes' *Financial News* (9 May 2005) <http://www.efinancialnews.com/story/2005-05-09/concern-grows-over-borrowed-votes> accessed 16 August 2015

Bernard S Black, 'Shareholder Passivity Reexamined' (1990) 89 Michigan Law Review 520

Bernard S Black, 'Agents Watching Agents: The Promise of Institutional Investor Voice' (1992) 39 UCLA Law Review 811

Board of Trade, *Report of the Company Law Committee*, Cmnd 1749 (June 1962) 207–10, available at <http://www.takeovers.gov.au/content/Resources/other_resources/downloads/jenkins_committee.pdf>

Peter Böckli, *Schweizer Aktienrecht: mit Fusionsgesetz, Börsengesellschaftsrecht, Konzernrecht, Corporate Governance, Recht der Revisionsstelle und der Abschlussprüfung in neuer Fassung unter Berücksichtigung der angelaufenen Revision des Aktien- und Rechnungslegungsrechts* (4th edn, Schulthess 2009)

Franz Böhm, *Die Ordnung der Wirtschaft als geschichtliche Aufgabe und rechtsschöpferische Leistung* (Kohlhammer, 1937)

Paul Bolster, Don Chance, and Don Rich, 'Executive Equity Swaps and Corporate Insider Holdings' (1996) 25(2) Financial Management 14

Patrick Bolton and Martin Oehmke, 'Credit Default Swaps and the Empty Creditor Problem' (2011) 24 Review of Financial Studies 2617

Fabio Braggion and Mariassunta Giannetti, 'Public Debate and Stock Prices: Evidence from the Voting Premium' (Social Science Research Network 2014) SSRN Scholarly Paper ID 2138949 <http://papers.ssrn.com/abstract=2138949> accessed 13 April 2015

William W Bratton, 'Bond Covenants and Creditor Protection: Economics and Law, Theory and Practice, Substance and Process' (2006) 7 European Business Organization Law Review (EBOR) 39

William W Bratton, 'Hedge Funds and Governance Targets' (2007) 95 Georgetown Law Journal 1375

Alon Brav and Richmond Mathews, 'Empty Voting and the Efficiency of Corporate Governance' (2011) 99 Journal of Financial Economics 289

Alon Brav, Wei Jian, Frank Partnoy, and Randall Thomas, 'Hedge Fund Activism, Corporate Governance, and Firm Performance' (2008) 63 Journal of Finance 1729

James Brickley, Ronald Lease, and Clifford Smith, 'Ownership Structure and Voting on Antitakeover Amendments' (1988) 20 Journal of Financial Economics 267

Thomas W Briggs, 'Corporate Governance and the New Hedge Fund Activism: An Empirical Analysis' (2007) 32 Journal of Corporation Law 681

Hendrik Brinckmann, 'Foundations' in Rüdiger Veil (ed.), *European Capital Markets Law* (Hart Publishing 2013) 209

David Brooks, 'Depositary Trust Company and the Omnibus Proxy: Shareholder Voting in the Era of Share Immobilization' (2014) 56 South Texas Law Review 205, 214

Bundesanstalt für Finanzdienstleistungsaufsicht (BaFin), 'No Breach of Reporting Requirements Identified in Continental AG Takeover Procedure' (21 August 2008), available at <http://www.bafin.de/SharedDocs/Veroeffentlichungen/EN/Pressemitteilung/2008/pm_080821_conti.html>

Bundesregierung, *Entwurf eines Gesetzes zur Unternehmensintegrität und Modernisierung des Anfechtungsrechts (UMAG) vom 7.1.2005*, BR-Drs 3/05

Kate Burgess, 'Investors Wary of Myners' Idea on Voting Rights' *Financial Times* (4 August 2009) 16

Mike Burkart, 'Economics of Takeover Regulation' (Stockholm School of Economics, CEPR, December 1999) 19–22 <http://www2.hhs.se/personal/MikeBurkart/papers/w_p5.pdf> accessed 15 April 2015

Mike Burkart and Samuel Lee, 'One Share—One Vote: The Theory' (2008) 12 Review of Finance 1

Mike Burkart and Samuel Lee, 'Signaling to Dispersed Shareholders and Corporate Control' (2015) 82 Review of Economic Studies 922

Guido Calabresi, *The Costs of Accidents: A Legal and Economic Analysis* (Yale University Press 1970)

Guido Calabresi and Jon T Hirschoff, 'Toward a Test for Strict Liability in Torts' (1972) 81 Yale Law Journal 1055

Guido Calabresi and Douglas Melamed, 'Property Rules, Liability Rules, and Inalienability: One View of the Cathedral' (1972) 85 Harvard Law Review 1089

Canadian Securities Administrators, *Update on Proposed Amendments to Multilateral Instrument 62-104 Take-Over Bids and Issuer Bids, National Instrument 62-103 Early Warning System and Related Take-Over Bid and Insider Reporting Issues and National Policy 62-203 Take-Over Bids and Issuer Bids*, CSA Notice 62-307 (10 October 2014)

Bidisha Chakrabarty, Pamela C Moulton, and Charles Trzcinka, 'Institutional Holding Periods', Working Paper 2013, available at <http://ssrn.com/abstract=2217588>

Richard Chang, 'Porsche: A "Hedge Fund With a Carmaker Attached"', *New York Times* (23 January 2009), available at <http://wheels.blogs.nytimes.com/2009/01/23/porsche-a-hedge-fund-with-a-carmaker-attached>

Brian Cheffins, *Company Law: Theory, Structure and Operation* (Oxford University Press 1997)

Brian R Cheffins, 'The Stewardship Code's Achilles' Heel' (2010) 73 Modern Law Review 1004

Brian Cheffins and John Armour, 'The Past, Present and Future of Shareholder Activism by Hedge Funds' (2011) 37 Journal of Corporation Law 51

Kit Chellel, 'Slammed Hedge Funds Shun Code to Await Make-or-Break EU Directive' *The Lawyer* (26 October 2009) 13

Iris H-Y Chiu, *The Foundations and Anatomy of Shareholder Activism* (Hart Publishing 2010)

Iris H-Y Chiu, 'Turning Institutional Investors into "Stewards": Exploring the Meaning and Objectives of "Stewardship"' [2013] Current Legal Problems 443

Iris H-Y Chiu, 'Reviving Shareholder Stewardship: Critically Examining the Impact of Corporate Transparency Reforms in the UK' (2014) 38 Delaware Journal of Corporate Law 983

Stephen J Choi, Jill E Fisch, and Marcel Kahan, 'The Power of Proxy Advisors: Myth or Reality?' (2010) 59 Emory Law Journal 869

Stephen J Choi and Andrew T Guzman, 'The Dangerous Extraterritoriality of American Securities Law' (1996) 17 Northwestern Journal of International Law & Business 207

Jesse H Choper, John C Coffee, and Ronald J Gilson, *Cases and Materials on Corporations* (8th edn, Wolters Kluwer Law & Business 2013)

Susan Christoffersen, Christopher Geczy, David Musto, and Adam Reed, 'Vote Trading and Information Aggregation' (2007) 62 Journal of Finance 2897

Robert C Clark, 'Vote Buying and Corporate Law' (1979) 29 Case Western Reserve Law Review 776

Clearing and Settlement Advisory and Monitoring Experts' Group, *Solving the Industry Giovannini Barriers to Post-trading within the EU* (November 2008), available at <http://ec.europa.eu/internal_market/financial-markets/docs/cesame/cesame_report_en.pdf>

Ronald Coase, 'The Nature of the Firm' (1937) 4 Economica 386

Ronald H Coase, 'The Problem of Social Cost' (1960) 3 Journal of Law and Economics 1

Ronald H Coase, *The Firm, the Market, and the Law* (University of Chicago Press 1990)

John C Coffee Jr, 'Regulating the Market for Corporate Control: A Critical Assessment of the Tender Offer's Role in Corporate Governance' (1984) 84 Columbia Law Review 1145

John C Coffee Jr, 'Law and the Market: The Impact of Enforcement' (2007) 156 University of Pennsylvania Law Review 229

Jonathan Cohen, 'Negative Voting: Why It Destroys Shareholder Value and a Proposal to Prevent It' (2008) 45 Harvard Journal on Legislation 237

Norma Cohen, 'Laxey Partners Increases British Land Stake to 9%' *Financial Times* (London, 16 July 2002) 23

Comissão do Mercado de Valores Mobiliários, *Consultation on the Modernisation of the Transparency Directive* (August 2010), available at <https://circabc.europa.eu/webdav/CircaBC/FISMA/markt_consultations/Library/company_law/transparency_requirement/public_authorities/CMVM_en.pdf>

Committee of European Securities Regulators (CESR), *Report on the Mapping of Supervisory Powers, Administrative and Criminal Sanctioning Regimes of Member States in Relation to the Transparency Directive (TD)*, CESR/09-058 (1 July 2009) <http://www.esma.europa.eu/system/files/09_058.pdf> accessed 19 August 2015

CESR, *CESR Proposal for a Pan-European Short Selling Disclosure Regime* CESR/09-581 (8 July 2009), available at <http://www.esma.europa.eu/system/files/09_581.pdf> accessed 19 August 2015

CESR, *CESR Proposal to Extend Major Shareholding Notifications to Instruments of Similar Economic Effect to Holding Shares and Entitlements to Acquire Shares*, CESR/09-1215b (January 2010) <http://www.esma.europa.eu/system/files/09_1215b.pdf> accessed 9 August 2015

CESR, *Model for a Pan-European Short Selling Disclosure Regime* CESR/10-088 (March 2010), available at <http://www.esma.europa.eu/system/files/10_088.pdf> accessed 19 August 2015

Conference Board, *Hedge Fund Activism: Findings and Recommendations for Corporations and Investors* (Research Report, R-1434-08-RR, New York 2008)

Consob, *Position Paper on the Disclosure of Cash-Settled Derivatives* (8 October 2009), available at <http://www.consob.it/mainen/legal_framework/consultations/dp_cash_derivatives_20091008.pdf> accessed 15 August 2015

Council of Institutional Investors, *Everything You Always Wanted to Know About Securities Lending, but Were Afraid to Ask* (Washington DC 2006)

Rafel Crespi and Luc Renneboog, 'United We Stand: Corporate Monitoring by Shareholder Coalitions in the UK' (CentER Discussion Paper No 2000-18, 2000), available at <https://pure.uvt.nl/portal/files/534699/18.pdf>

Jane Croft and Kate Burgess, 'Myners' Two-Tier Shares Plan under Fire' *Financial Times* (London, 3 August 2009) 1

Hans Caspar von der Crone, Eva Bilek, and Matthias Hirschle, 'Neuerungen im Offenlegungsrecht', Schweizerische Zeitschrift für Wirtschafts- und Finanzmarktrecht (SZW/RSDA) 2008, 1

Serdar Çelik and Mats Isaksson, 'Institutional Investors and Ownership Engagement' [2013] OECD Journal: Financial Market Trends 93

Adam Cygan, 'The Parliamentarisation of EU Decision-Making? The Impact of the Treaty of Lisbon on National Parliaments' (2011) 36 European Law Review 480

Steven M Davidoff, 'Taking the Preferences Out of Preferred Stock', *New York Times Dealbook* (13 September 2012)

Steven M Davidoff, 'A Standard Criticism of Activist Investors That No Longer Holds Up', *New York Times* (10 July 2013) B5

Steven M Davidoff, Alan D Morrison, and William J Wilhelm Jr, 'The SEC v. Goldman Sachs: Reputation, Trust, and Fiduciary Duties in Investment Banking' (2012) 37 Journal of Corporation Law 529

Nestor M Davidson, 'Standardization and Pluralism in Property Law' (2008) 61 Vanderbilt Law Review 1597

Paul L Davies and Klaus J Hopt, 'Control Transactions' in Reinier H Kraakman and others (eds), *The Anatomy of Corporate Law: A Comparative and Functional Approach* (2nd edn, Oxford University Press 2009) 225–73

Paul L Davies and Sarah Worthington, *Gower & Davies' Principles of Modern Company Law* (9th edn, Sweet & Maxwell 2012)

Garreth Davies, 'Subsidiarity: The Wrong Idea, in the Wrong Place, at the Wrong Time' (2006) 43 Common Market Law Review 63

Davies Ward Phillips & Vineberg LLP, *The Quality of the Shareholder Vote in Canada* (Discussion Paper, October 2010) 128 f, available at <http://www.dwpv.com/Sites/shareholdervoting/media/The-Quality-of-the-Shareholder-Vote-in-Canada.pdf>

George W Dent Jr, 'The Essential Unity of Shareholders and the Myth of Investor Short-Termism' (2010) 35 Delaware Journal of Corporate Law 97

Department for Business, Innovation & Skills (BIS), *A Long-Term Focus for Corporate Britain—A Call for Evidence* (URN 10/1225, 2010)
Deutsche Bank Markets Research, *ETF Assets to Pass $3 Trillion Milestone in 2015*, ETF Annual Review & Outlook (26 January 2015), available at <https://www.altii.de/media/modelfield_files/fondsportal/pressrelease/pdf/Deutsche_Bank_Research_ETF_Market_Review_2014_Outlook_2015.pdf>
Deutsche Börse AG, 'Deutsche Börse Extraordinarily Adjusts DAX Weightings' (29 October 2008), available at <http://deutsche-boerse.com/dbg/dispatch/en/notescontent/dbg_nav/press/10_Latest_Press_Releases/10_All/INTEGRATE/mr_pressreleases?notesDoc=FBC308516A591080C12574F000795B04> accessed 19 August 2015
Deutscher Investor Relations Verband e.V. (German Investor Relations Association), *Response of Deutscher Investor Relations Verband e.V. to the EU Commission's Public Consultation on the Revision of the Transparency Directive—Appendix* (23 August 2010) 10 f, available at <https://circabc.europa.eu/sd/a/b5aff1c8-0a3d-46a9-b41a-cc6e049d7f59/German_Investor_Relations_Association_en.pdf> accessed 19 August 2015
Charles E Dropkin, 'Developing Effective Guidelines for Managing Legal Risks—U.S. Guidelines' in Frank J Fabozzi and Steven V Mann (eds), *Securities Finance: Securities Lending and Repurchase Agreements* (Wiley 2005) 167
Bob Drummond, 'Double Voting in Proxy Contests Threatens Shareholder Democracy' *Bloomberg* (27 February 2006), available at <http://www.bloomberg.com/apps/news?pid=newsarchive&sid=a4OuCsU8r2Yg> accessed 18 August 2015
Phred Dvorak, 'Companies Alter Bylaws to Pry Data Out of Activists—Pfizer and Others Seek Better Understanding Of Investors' Motives' *Wall Street Journal* (14 July 2008) B4
Alexander Dyck and Luigi Zingales, 'Private Benefits of Control: An International Comparison' (2004) 59 Journal of Finance 537
Frank H Easterbrook and Daniel R Fischel, 'Voting in Corporate Law' (1983) 26 Journal of Law and Economics 395
Frank H Easterbrook and Daniel R Fischel, 'Mandatory Disclosure and the Protection of Investors' (1984) 70 Virginia Law Review 669
Frank Easterbrook and Daniel Fischel, 'Limited Liability and the Corporation' (1985) 52 University of Chicago Law Review 89
Frank H Easterbrook and Daniel R Fischel, *The Economic Structure of Corporate Law* (Harvard University Press 1991)
Paul H Edelman, Randall S Thomas, and Robert B Thompson, 'Shareholder Voting in an Age of Intermediary Capitalism' (2014) 87 Southern California Law Review 1359
Horst Eidenmüller, 'Regulierung von Finanzinvestoren' [2007] Deutsches Steuerrecht (DStR) 2116
Jay W Eisenhofer and Michael J Barry, *Shareholder Activism Handbook* (loose-leaf, as per supplement 2013)
Susan Emmenegger, 'Creeping Takeovers in Deutschland und in der Schweiz' in Stefan Grundmann and others (eds), *Unternehmen, Markt und Verantwortung—Festschrift für Klaus J. Hopt zum 70. Geburtstag am 24. August 2010* (de Gruyter 2010) 1763
Andreas Engert, 'Transnational Hedge Fund Regulation' (2010) 11 European Business Organization Law Review 329
Luca Enriques and Matteo Gatti, 'Creeping Acquisitions in Europe: Enabling Companies to be Better Safe than Sorry' (2015) 15 Journal of Corporate Law Studies 55
Luca Enriques, Henry Hansmann, and Reinier H Kraakman, 'The Basic Governance Structure: The Interests of Shareholders as a Class' in Reinier H Kraakman and others

(eds), *The Anatomy of Corporate Law: A Comparative and Functional Approach* (2nd edn, Oxford University Press 2009) 55

Luca Enriques, Henry Hansmann, and Reinier Kraakman, 'The Basic Governance Structure: Minority Shareholders and Non-Shareholder Constituencies' in Reinier Kraakman and others, *The Anatomy of Corporate Law: A Comparative and Functional Approach* (2nd edn, Oxford University Press 2009) 89

Luca Enriques, Gérard Hertig, and Hideki Kanda, 'Related Party Transactions' in Reinier Kraakman and others, *The Anatomy of Corporate Law: A Comparative and Functional Approach* (2nd edn, Oxford University Press 2009) 153

Matteo Erede, 'Governing Corporations with Concentrated Ownership Structure: An Empirical Analysis of Hedge Fund Activism in Italy and Germany, and Its Evolution' [2013] European Company and Financial Law Review 328

Boyd Erman, 'Fleshing Out Empty Voters' *The Globe and Mail* (16 October 2012) B2, available at <www.theglobeandmail.com/report-on-business/streetwise/telus-case-shows-more-disclosure-needed-for-empty-voting/article4614182>

Peter Esö, Stephen Hansen, and Lucy White, 'A Theory of Vote-Trading and Information Aggregation', Working Paper 2014, available at <http://www.econ.upf.edu/~shansen/votetrading.pdf>

Walter Eucken, *Grundsätze der Wirtschaftspolitik* (Tübingen 1952)

Eumedion Corporate Governance Forum, *Position Paper on the Consequences of Synthetic Structures for Dutch Securities Law and Company Law* (17 November 2008), available at <http://eumedion.nl/en/public/knowledgenetwork/position-papers/2008-position-paper-hidden-ownership-and-empty-voting.pdf> accessed 19 August 2015

Eumedion, *Eumedion Response to the Commission Services' Public Consultation on Short Selling* (9 July 2010), available at <http://www.eumedion.nl/nl/public/kennisbank/consultaties/response_ec_consultation_short_selling.pdf> accessed 19 August 2015

Europe Economics, 'Study on the Cost of Compliance with Selected FSAP Measures—Final Report' (2009) <http://ec.europa.eu/finance/docs/actionplan/index/090707_cost_of_compliance_en.pdf>

European Commission, *Financial Services: Implementing the Framework for Financial Markets: Action Plan*, COM(1999) 232 (11 May 1999), available at <http://ec.europa.eu/internal_market/finances/docs/actionplan/index/action_en.pdf>

European Commission, *Proposal for a Directive of the European Parliament and of the Council on the Harmonisation of Transparency Requirements with Regard to Information about Issuers Whose Securities Are Admitted to Trading on a Regulated Market and Amending Directive 2001/34/EC*, COM(2003) 138, <http://eur-lex.europa.eu/LexUriServ/LexUriServ.do?uri=COM:2003:0138:FIN:EN:PDF>

European Commission, *Fostering an Appropriate Regime for Shareholders' Rights—Second Consultation by the Services of the Internal Market Directorate General* (13 May 2005), available at <http://ec.europa.eu/internal_market/company/docs/shareholders/consultation2_en.pdf> accessed 19 August 2015

European Commission, *Proposal for a Directive of the European Parliament and of the Council on the Exercise of Voting Rights by Shareholders of Companies Having Their Registered Office in a Member State and Whose Shares are Admitted to Trading on a Regulated Market and Amending Directive 2004/109/EC*, COM(2005) 685

European Commission, *Commission Proposal for a Directive of the European Parliament and of The Council on the Exercise of Voting Rights by Shareholders of Companies Having Their Registered Office in a Member State and Whose Shares are Admitted to Trading on a Regulated Market and Amending Directive 2004/109/EC*, COM(2005) 685 final (1 May 2006)

European Commission, *Report on the Implementation of the Directive on Takeover Bids*, SEC(2007) 268 (21 February 2007)

European Commission, *Commission Staff Working Document: Impact Assessment on the Proportionality between Capital and Control in Listed Companies* (2007) SEC(2007) 1705

European Commission, 'Impact Assessment on the Directive on the Cross-Border Transfer of Registered Office' SEC(2007) 1707

European Commission, *Fostering an Appropriate Regime for Shareholders' Rights—Third Consultation Document of the Services of the Directorate General Internal Market and Services* (April 2007), available at <http://ec.europa.eu/internal_market/company/docs/shareholders/consultation3_en.pdf>

European Commission, *Synthesis of the Comments on the Third Consultation Document of the Internal Market and Services Directorate-General 'Fostering an Appropriate Regime for Shareholders' Rights'* (September 2007), available at <http://ec.europa.eu/internal_market/company/docs/shareholders/consultation3_report_en.pdf>

European Commission, *Report on More Stringent National Measures Concerning Directive 2004/109/EC on the Harmonisation of Transparency Requirements in Relation to Information About Issuers Whose Securities are Admitted to Trading on a Regulated Market*, SEC (2008) 3033 final

European Commission, *Consultation Document on the Modernisation of the Directive 2004/109/EC on the Harmonisation of Transparency Requirements in Relation to Information about Issuers whose Securities are Admitted to Trading on a Regulated Market*, 27 May 2010, available at <http://ec.europa.eu/internal_market/securities/docs/transparency/directive/consultation_questions_en.pdf>

European Commission, *Report to the Council, the European Parliament, the European Social and Economic Committee and the Committee of the Regions on the Operation of Directive 2004/109/EC on the Harmonisation of Transparency Requirements in Relation to Information about Issuers whose Securities are Admitted to Trading on a Regulated Market*, COM(2010) 243

European Commission, *Green Paper—Corporate Governance in Financial Institutions and Remuneration Policies*, COM(2010) 284 final

European Commission, *Feedback Statement: Summary of Responses to Commission Green Paper on Corporate Governance in Financial Institutions* (2010), available at <http://ec.europa.eu/internal_market/consultations/docs/2010/governance/feedback_statement_en.pdf> accessed 19 August 2015

European Commission, *Commission Staff Working Document—The Review of the Operation of Directive 2004/109/EC: Emerging Issues*, SEC (2010) 611 (May 2010), available at <http://eur-lex.europa.eu/legal-content/EN/TXT/PDF/?uri=CELEX:52010SC0611&from=EN>

European Commission, *Proposal for a Regulation of the European Parliament and of The Council on Short Selling and Certain Aspects of Credit Default Swaps*, COM(2010) 482 final (15 September 2010)

European Commission, *Corporate Governance in Financial Institutions: Lessons to be Drawn from the Current Financial Crisis, Best Practices* (Commission Staff Document SEC(2010) 669, 2010)

European Commission, *Communication from the Commission to the European Parliament, the Council, the European Economic and Social Committee and the Committee of the Regions: Reinforcing Sanctioning Regimes in the Financial Services Sector*, COM(2010) 716 final (8 December 2010), available at <http://eur-lex.europa.eu/legal-content/EN/

TXT/PDF/?uri=CELEX:52010DC0716&qid=1434533872345&from=EN> accessed 15 August 2015

European Commission, *Feedback Statement on the Summary of Responses to the Consultation by DG Internal Market and Services on the Modernisation of the Transparency Directive (2004/109/EC)* (17 December 2010), available at <http://ec.europa.eu/finance/securities/docs/transparency/transparency-consultation-summary_en.pdf> accessed 18 August 2015

European Commission, *Green Paper—The EU Corporate Governance Framework*, COM (2011) 164

European Commission, *Proposal for a Directive of the European Parliament and of the Council Amending Directive 2004/109/EC on the Harmonisation of Transparency Requirements in Relation to Information about Issuers Whose Securities Are Admitted to Trading on a Regulated Market and Commission Directive 2007/14/EC* COM(2011) 683 (25 October 2011), available at <http://eur-lex.europa.eu/LexUriServ/LexUriServ.do?uri=COM:2011:0683:FIN:EN:PDF> accessed 19 August 2015

European Commission, *Commission Staff Working Paper—Impact Assessment Accompanying the Document Proposal for a Directive of the European Parliament and of the Council amending Directive 2004/109/EC on the Harmonisation of Transparency Requirements in Relation to Information about Issuers Whose Securities are Admitted to Trading on a Regulated Market*, SEC(2011) 1279 final (25 October 2011) 41, available at <http://www.europarl.europa.eu/registre/docs_autres_institutions/commission_europeenne/sec/2011/1279/COM_SEC(2011)1279_EN.pdf> accessed 19 August 2015

European Commission, *Communication from the Commission to the European Parliament, the Council, the European Economic and Social Committee and the Committee of the Regions, Action Plan: European Company Law and Corporate Governance—A Modern Legal Framework for More Engaged Shareholders and Sustainable Companies*, COM(2012) 740 final

European Commission, *Report from the Commission to the European Parliament and the Council on the Evaluation of the Regulation (EU) No 236/2012 on Short Selling and Certain Aspects of Credit Default Swaps*, COM(2013) 885 final (13 December 2013), available at <http://ec.europa.eu/finance/securities/docs/short_selling/131213_report_en.pdf>

European Commission, *Proposal for a Directive of the European Parliament and of the Council amending Directive 2007/36/EC as regards the Encouragement of Long-term Shareholder Engagement and Directive 2013/34/EU as regards Certain Elements of the Corporate Governance Statement*, COM(2014) 213 final

European Commission, *Green Paper: Building a Capital Markets Union* COM(2015) 63 final, available at <http://eur-lex.europa.eu/legal-content/EN/TXT/PDF/?uri=COM:2015:63:FIN>

European Corporate Governance Forum, *Paper by the Working Group on Proportionality* (June 2007), available at <http://ec.europa.eu/internal_market/company/docs/ecgforum/workinggroup_proportionality_en.pdf> accessed 15 August 2015

European Corporate Governance Forum, *Statement on Empty Voting and Transparency of Shareholder Positions* (20 February 2010), available at <http://ec.europa.eu/internal_market/company/docs/ecgforum/ecgf_empty_voting_en.pdf> (accessed 15 August 2015)

European Council, *Proposal for a Regulation of the European Parliament and of the Council on Short Selling and Certain Aspects of Credit Default Swaps—Text Provisionally Agreed with the European Parliament*, Council Document 16338/11 (4 November 2011)

European Financial Reporting Advisory Group (EFRAG), 'Distinguishing between Debt and Equity—Discussion Paper' (2008) <http://www.iasplus.com/en/binary/efrag/0801liabequitydp.pdf>

European Parliament, *The Use of Shareholder Voting Rights During the General Assembly of Company Shareholders—Study IP/A/ECON/2008-32* (December 2009), available at <http://www.europarl.europa.eu/RegData/etudes/etudes/join/2009/429978/IPOL-ECON_ET%282009%29429978_EN.pdf> accessed 13 August 2015

European Parliament, Committee on Economic and Monetary Affairs, *Report on the Proposal for a Regulation of the European Parliament and of the Council on Short Selling and Certain Aspects of Credit Default Swaps*, No A7-0055/2011 (19 April 2011), available at <http://www.europarl.europa.eu/sides/getDoc.do?pubRef=-//EP//NONSGML+REPORT+A7-2011-0055+0+DOC+PDF+V0//EN> accessed on 19 August 2015

European Securities and Markets Authority (ESMA), *Report: Mapping of the Transparency Directive –Options, Discretions and 'Gold-Plating'*, ESMA/2011/194 (7 July 2011) para. 42, available at <http://www.esma.europa.eu/system/files/2011_194.pdf>

ESMA, *Call for Evidence—Empty Voting* (ESMA/2011/288, 14 September 2011), available at <http://www.esma.europa.eu/system/files/2011_288.pdf>

ESMA, *Discussion Paper: An Overview of the Proxy Advisory Industry. Considerations on Possible Policy Options*, ESMA/2012/212 (22 March 2012)

ESMA, *Feedback Statement—Call for Evidence on Empty Voting* (ESMA/2012/415, 29 June 2012), available at <http://www.esma.europa.eu/system/files/2012-415.pdf>

ESMA, *Update on Measures Adopted by Competent Authorities on Short Selling* ESMA/2011/39a (24 July 2012), available at <http://www.esma.europa.eu/system/files/2011-39.pdf> accessed 19 August 2015

ESMA, *Final Report—ESMA's Technical Advice on the Evaluation of the Regulation (EU) 236/2012 of the European Parliament and of the Council on Short Selling and Certain Aspects of Credit Default Swaps*, ESMA/2013/614 (3 June 2013), available at <http://www.esma.europa.eu/system/files/2013-614_final_report_on_ssr_evaluation.pdf> accessed 19 August 2015

ESMA, *Final Report on Draft Regulatory Technical Standards on Major Shareholdings and an Indicative List of Financial Instruments Subject to Notification Requirements under the Revised Transparency Directive*, ESMA/2014/1187 (29 September 2014)

European Securities Markets Expert Group (ESME), *First Report of ESME on the Transparency Directive ('TD')* (5 December 2007), available at <http://ec.europa.eu/internal_market/securities/docs/esme/05122007_td_report_en.pdf>

ESME, *Views on the Issue of Transparency of Holdings of Cash Settled Derivatives* (November 2009), available at <http://ec.europa.eu/internal_market/securities/docs/esme/tdcash_en.pdf>

ESME, *Position on Short Selling* (19 March 2009), available at <http://ec.europa.eu/internal_market/securities/docs/esme/report_20090319_en.pdf>

Judith Evans and Jonathan Eley, 'Democratising Finance: How Passive Funds Changed Investing' *Financial Times* (London, 31 January 2015) FTMoney 10

Eugene Fama, 'Efficient Capital Markets: A Review of Theory and Empirical Work' (1970) 25 Journal of Finance 383

Mark C Faulkner, *Securities Lending and Corporate Governance* (2005), available at <http://www.bankofengland.co.uk/markets/Documents/gilts/slcgjun05.pdf>

Mark Faulkner, *An Introduction to Securities Lending* (4th edn, London 2007)

Federal Trade Commission, *Statement of the Federal Trade Commission In the Matter of Third Point*, File No. 121-0019, 24 August 2015, available at <https://www.ftc.gov/system/files/documents/public_statements/777341/150824thirdpointcommstmt.pdf>

Rita de la Feria and Stefan Vogenauer (eds), *Prohibition of Abuse of Law: A New General Principle of EU Law?* (Hart 2011)

Eilís Ferran, *Building an EU Securities Market* (Cambridge University Press 2004)

Eilís Ferran, 'After the Crisis: The Regulation of Hedge Funds and Private Equity in the EU' (2011) 12 European Business Organization Law Review 379

Eilís Ferran and Look Chan Ho, *Principles of Corporate Finance Law* (2nd edn, Oxford University Press 2014)

Financial Conduct Authority (FCA), *Implementation of the Transparency Directive Amending Directive (2013/50/EU) and other Disclosure Rule and Transparency Rule Changes—Consultation Paper CP 15/11* (March 2015)

Financial Services Authority (FSA), *Private Equity: A Discussion of Risk and Regulatory Engagement* (FSA Discussion Paper 06/6, 2006)

FSA, *Disclosure of Contracts for Difference, Consultation and draft Handbook text, CP 07/20* (November 2007) <http://www.fsa.gov.uk/pubs/cp/cp07_20.pdf>

FSA, *Disclosure of Contracts for Difference: Feedback and Policy Statement on CP07/20, and Further Technical Consultation, CP 08/17* (October 2008) <http://www.fsa.gov.uk/pubs/cp/cp08_17.pdf> accessed 19 August 2015

FSA, *The Turner Review—A Regulatory Response to the Global Banking Crisis* (March 2009)

FSA, *Enforcement Financial Penalties, Feedback on CP09/19*, PS10/4 (March 2010) 9–11 <http://www.fsa.gov.uk/pubs/policy/ps10_04.pdf> accessed 19 August 2015

FSA, *Implementing Aspects of the Financial Services Act 2010: Feedback on CP10/11, Final Rules and Further Consultation* CP10/18 (July 2010), available at <http://www.fsa.gov.uk/pubs/cp/cp10_18.pdf>

FSA, *Conduct of Business Sourcebook (Stewardship Code) Instrument 2010*, FSA 2010/57

Financial Stability Board, *Potential Financial Stability Issues Arising from Recent Trends in Exchange-Traded Funds (ETFs)* (12 April 2011), available at <http://www.financialstabilityboard.org/wp-content/uploads/r_110412b.pdf>

Jill E Fisch, 'Securities Intermediaries and the Separation of Ownership from Control' (2010) 33 Seattle University Law Review 877

Daniel R Fischel, 'Organized Exchanges and the Regulation of Dual Class Common Stock' (1987) 54 University of Chicago Law Review 119

Holger Fleischer, 'Finanzinvestoren im ordnungspolitischen Gesamtgefüge von Aktien-, Bankaufsichts- und Kapitalmarktrecht' [2008] Zeitschrift für Gesellschafts- und Unternehmensrecht (ZGR) 185

Holger Fleischer, 'Proxy Advisors in Europe: Reform Proposals and Regulatory Strategies' (2012) 9 European Company Law 12

Holger Fleischer and Klaus-Ulrich Schmolke, 'Zum beabsichtigten Ausbau der kapitalmarktrechtlichen Beteiligungstransparenz bei modernen Finanzinstrumenten' [2010] Neue Zeitschrift für Gesellschaftsrecht 846

Chris Flood, 'Hedge Funds Remain a Popular Choice' *Financial Times* (London, 8 June 2015) FTFm 12

Chris Flood, 'Dark Side of ETFs Erode Active Managers' Outperformance' *Financial Times* (London, 10 August 2015) FTfm 2

Chris Flood, 'Time to Re-examine the Entire ETF Ecosystem' *Financial Times* (London, 26 October 2015) FTfm 6

Florida State Board of Administration, *Corporate Governance—Annual Report 2006* (2007)

Merritt B Fox, 'Retaining Mandatory Securities Disclosure: Why Issuer Choice Is Not Investor Empowerment' (1999) 85 Virginia Law Review 1335

Merrit B Fox, 'Optimal Regulatory Areas for Securities Disclosure' (2003) 81 Washington University Law Quarterly 1017

Tamar Frankel, 'The Legal Infrastructure of Markets: The Role of Contract and Property Law' (1993) 73 Boston University Law Review 389

Tamar Frankel, 'The New Financial Assets: Separating Ownership from Control' (2010) 33 Seattle University Law Review 931

Derek French, Stephen W Mayson, and Christopher Ryan, *Mayson, French & Ryan on Company Law* (32nd edn, Oxford University Press 2015)

Jesse M Fried, 'The Uneasy Case for Favoring Long-Term Shareholders' (2015) 124 Yale Law Journal 1554

Christopher W Frost, 'Bankruptcy Voting and the Designation Power' (2013) 87 American Bankruptcy Journal 155

Eirik G Furubotn, 'The New Institutional Economics and the Theory of the Firm' (2001) 45 Journal of Economic Behavior & Organization 133

Eirik G Furubotn and Rudolf Richter, *Economics, Cognition, and Society: Institutions and Economic Theory—The Contribution of the New Institutional Economics* (2nd edn, University of Michigan Press 2010)

José-Miguel Gaspar, Massimo Massa, and Pedro Matos, 'Shareholder Investment Horizons and the Market for Corporate Control' (2005) 76 Journal of Financial Economics 135

Koen Geens and Carl Clottens, 'One Share One Vote: Fairness, Efficiency and EU Harmonisation Revisited' in Koen Geens and Klaus J Hopt (eds), *The European Company Law Action Plan Revisited* (Leuven University Press 2010) 145

Koen Geens and Klaus J Hopt (eds), *The European Company Law Action Plan Revisited: Reassessment of the 2003 Priorities of the European Commission* (Leuven University Press 2010)

Sean Geraghty and Harriet Smith, 'Shareholder Activism as a Strategy for Hedge Funds' in Peter Astleford and Dick Frase (eds), *Hedge Funds and the Law* (Sweet & Maxwell 2010) ch. 8

Amanda Gerut, 'Emerging Practices in Securities Lending and Proxy Voting Nexus' *BoardIQ* (3 April 2007)

Ronald J Gilson, 'Controlling Shareholders and Corporate Governance: Complicating the Comparative Taxonomy' (2006) 119 Harvard Law Review 1641

Ronald J Gilson and Bernard Black, *The Law and Finance of Corporate Acquisitions* (2nd edn, Foundation Press 1995)

Ronald J Gilson and Jeffrey N Gordon, 'The Agency Costs of Agency Capitalism: Activist Investors and the Revaluation of Governance Rights' (2013) 113 Columbia Law Review 863

Ronald J Gilson and Reinier Kraakman, 'The Mechanisms of Market Efficiency' (1984) 70 Virginia Law Review 549

Ronald J Gilson and Reinier Kraakman, 'Market Efficiency After the Fall: Where Do We Stand Following the Financial Crisis?' in Claire A Hill and Brett H McDonnell (eds), *Research Handbook On The Economics Of Corporate Law* (Edward Elgar 2012) 456

Ronald J Gilson and Reinier Kraakman, 'Market Efficiency After the Financial Crisis: It's Still a Matter of Information Costs' (2014) 100 Virginia Law Review 313

Ronald J Gilson and Curtis Milhaupt, 'Sovereign Wealth Funds and Corporate Governance: A Minimalist Solution to the New Mercantilism' (2008) 60 Stanford Law Review 1345

Ronald J Gilson and Charles K Whitehead, 'Deconstructing Equity: Public Ownership, Agency Costs, and Complete Capital Markets' (2008) 108 Columbia Law Review 231

Kimberly Gladman and Beth M Young, 'The Dangers of Dual Share Classes', Harvard Law School Forum on Corporate Governance and Financial Regulation (21 May 2012), available at <http://blogs.law.harvard.edu/corpgov/2012/05/21/the-dangers-of-dual-share-classes/>

Marc Goergen, Marina Martynova, and Luc Renneboog, 'Corporate Governance Convergence: Evidence from Takeover Regulation Reforms in Europe' (2005) 21 Oxford Review of Economic Policy 243

Wulf Goette and others (eds), *Münchener Kommentar zum Aktiengesetz* (3rd edn, CH Beck 2008)

Simon Goldstone, 'Will Genuine CFD Trading Be Caught by the EU Market Abuse Regulation?' (2015) 30 Butterworths Journal of International Banking and Financial Law 550

Royston Miles Goode, *Principles of Corporate Insolvency Law* (4th edn, Sweet & Maxwell 2011)

Zohar Goshen, 'The Efficiency of Controlling Corporate Self-Dealing: Theory Meets Reality' (2003) 91 California Law Review 393

Sebastian Goslar and Klaus von der Linden, 'Grenzen des Rechtsmissbrauchseinwands gegen Gestaltungen beim Aktienrechtlichen Squeeze out' [2009] Betriebs-Berater 1986

Sanford J Grossman and Oliver D Hart, 'Takeover Bids, the Free-Rider Problem, and the Theory of Corporation' (1980) 11 Bell Journal of Economics 42

Sanford J Grossman and Oliver D Hart, 'The Costs and Benefits of Ownership: A Theory of Vertical and Lateral Integration' (1986) 94 Journal of Political Economy 691

Sanford J Grossman and Joseph E Stiglitz, 'On the Impossibility of Informationally Efficient Markets' (1980) 70 American Economic Review 393

Stefan Grundmann, *European Company Law—Organization, Finance and Capital Markets* (2nd edn, Intersentia 2012)

Louise Gullifer and Jennifer Payne, *Corporate Finance Law Principles and Policy* (Hart Publishing, Oxford 2011)

Matthias Habersack, *Die Mitgliedschaft—subjektives und 'sonstiges' Recht* (Munich 1996)

Paul Halpern, Michael Trebilcock, and Stuart Turnbull, 'An Economic Analysis of Limited Liability in Corporation Law' (1980) 30 The University of Toronto Law Journal 117

Dean F Hanley, '2009 Updates to Delaware General Corporation Law—Part 2: Elimination of "Empty Voting"', Foley Hoag Business Alert, 29 April 2009, available at <http://www.foleyhoag.com/publications/alerts-and-updates/2009/april/2009-updates-to-delaware-general-corporation-law-part-2-elimination-of-empty-voting>

Pamela Hanrahan, Ian Ramsay, and Geof Stapledon, *Commercial Applications of Company Law 2011* (12th edn, CCH 2011)

Henry Hansmann and Reinier Kraakman, 'Toward Unlimited Shareholder Liability for Corporate Torts' (1991) 100 Yale Law Journal 1879

Henry Hansmann and Reinier Kraakman, 'The Essential Role of Organizational Law' (2000) 110 Yale Law Journal 387

Henry Hansmann, Reinier Kraakman, and Richard Squire, 'Law and the Rise of the Firm' (2006) 119 Harvard Law Review 1333

Richard Hasen, 'Vote Buying' (2000) 88 California Law Review 1323

Shmuel Hauser and Beni Lauterbach, 'The Value of Voting Rights to Majority Shareholders: Evidence from Dual Class Stock Unifications' (2004) 17 Review of Financial Studies 1167

Dietmar Hawranek, 'Kafka und die Cash-Optionen' [Kafka and the Cash Options], *Der Spiegel* (3 November 2008) 82, available at <http://www.spiegel.de/spiegel/print/d-61822082.html>

Hedge Fund Standards Board, 'The Hedge Fund Standards' (2012) <http://www.hfsb.org/sites/10377/files/hedge_fund_standards_-_as_at_february_2012.pdf>

Hedge Fund Working Group, *Hedge Fund Standards Consultation Paper—Part 2: The Best Practice Standards* (9 October 2007), available at <http://castlehall.typepad.com/risk_without_reward/files/hfwg20consultation20paper20part20ii.pdf> accessed 19 August 2015

Hedge Fund Working Group, 'Press Release—Hedge Fund Working Group Focuses on Valuation and Risk Management Standards' (22 January 2008), available at <http://www.hfsb.org/sites/10188/files/hfwg_press_release_22_jan_08.pdf>

Eveline Hellebuyck, 'Activist Hedge Funds and Legal Strategy Devices' in Antoine Masson and Mary J Shariff (eds), *Legal Strategies* (Berlin/Heidelberg 2010) 277

Michael A Heller, 'The Boundaries of Private Property' (1998) 108 Yale Law Journal 1163

Alexander Hellgardt, 'Mandatory Disclosure (Securities Markets)' in Jürgen Basedow, Klaus J Hopt, and Reinhard Zimmermann (eds), *The Max Planck Encyclopedia of European Private Law* (Oxford University Press 2012) 1118

Herbert Smith, *Reflections on the New Pan-European Regime for Short Selling and Credit Default Swaps* (2012), available at <http://www.herbertsmithfreehills.com/-/media/HS/L230212219.pdf> accessed on 19 August 2015

Herbert Smith Freehills, 'US Federal Appeals Court Limits Extraterritorial Application of Anti-Fraud Provisions of the U.S. Federal Securities Laws' 2 September 2014, available at <http://www.herbertsmithfreehills.com/-/media/Files/ebulletins/2014/20140902%20-%20Alert%20re%20Second%20Amendment%20Circuit%20Porsche%20decision.htm>

Svea Herbst-Bayliss, 'Activist Investors Get More Respect amid Strong Returns' Thomson Reuters (17 November 2013) <http://www.reuters.com/article/2013/11/18/us-investment-summit-activism-idUSBRE9AH02K20131118>

Hermes Equity Ownership Services, *Letter Responding to ESMA's Call for Evidence on Empty Voting* (25 November 2011) <http://www.esma.europa.eu/system/files/hermes_equity_0.pdf> accessed 18 August 2015

High Level Group of Company Law Experts, *Report on Issues Related to Takeover Bids* (2002), available at <http://ec.europa.eu/internal_market/company/docs/takeoverbids/2002-01-hlg-report_en.pdf>

High Level Group of Company Law Experts, *Final Report on a Modern Regulatory Framework for Company Law in Europe* (4 November 2002) 34 <http://ec.europa.eu/internal_market/company/docs/modern/report_en.pdf> accessed 19 April 2015

Andrew Hill, 'Neither a Borrower…' *Financial Times* (London, 18 December 2009) 18

Albert O Hirschman, *Exit, Voice, and Loyalty: Responses to Decline in Firms, Organizations, and States* (Harvard University Press 1970)

David Hirshleifer and Siew Hong Teoh, 'Herd Behaviour and Cascading in Capital Markets: A Review and Synthesis' (2003) 9 European Financial Management 25

Jack Hirshleifer, 'The Private and Social Value of Information and the Reward to Inventive Activity' (1971) 61 American Economic Review 561

Jack Hirshleifer, 'Exchange Theory: The Missing Chapter' (1973) 11 Economic Inquiry 129

Jack Hirshleifer and John G Riley, 'The Analytics of Uncertainty and Information—An Expository Survey' (1979) 17 Journal of Economic Literature 1375

Jay Hoffman and Melissa Ghislanzoni, 'Empty Voting—Waiting for a Regulatory Response' *Miller Thomson Securities Practice Note* (2012), available at <http://www.millerthomson.com/en/publications/newsletters/securities-practice-notes/fall-2012/empty-voting-waiting-for-a-regulatory>

Clifford Holderness and Dennis Sheehan, 'The Role of Majority Shareholders in Publicly Held Corporations: An Exploratory Analysis' (1988) 20 Journal of Financial Economics 317

Wolfgang Hölters (ed.), *Aktiengesetz—Kommentar* (2nd edn, Munich 2014)

Hong Kong Securities and Futures Commission (SFC), *Proposed Amendments to The Securities (Disclosure of Interests) Ordinance—Consultation Conclusions* (March 1999), available at <http://www.sfc.hk/edistributionWeb/gateway/EN/consultation/conclusion?refNo=98CP4> accessed 19 August 2015
Klaus J Hopt, 'Modern Company and Capital Market Problems: Improving European Corporate Governance After Enron' in John Armour and Joseph McCahery (eds), *After Enron: Improving Corporate Law and Modernising Securities Regulation in Europe and the US* (Hart Publishing 2006) 445
House of Commons Treasury Committee, *Banking Crisis: International Dimensions, 2008–9*, HC 615, available at <http://www.publications.parliament.uk/pa/cm200809/cmselect/cmtreasy/615/615.pdf> accessed 9 March 2015
House of Lords European Union Committee, 10th Report of Session 2009–2010, 'The Future Regulation of Derivatives Markets: Is the EU on the Right Track?' dated 31 March 2010 <http://www.publications.parliament.uk/pa/ld200910/ldselect/ldeucom/93/93.pdf> accessed 9 March 2015
Hendrik Houthakker and Peter Williamson, *The Economics of Financial Markets* (Oxford University Press 1996)
Henry T C Hu, 'Hedging Expectations: "Derivative Reality" and the Law and Finance of the Corporate Objective' (1995) 73 Texas Law Review 985
Henry T C Hu, ' "Empty Creditors" and the Crisis', *Wall Street Journal* (New York, 10 April 2009) A13
Henry T C Hu, 'Too Complex to Depict? Innovation, Pure Information, and the SEC Disclosure Paradigm' (2012) 90 Texas Law Review 1601
Henry T C Hu, 'Debt, "Debt Governance," and the Decoupling Framework: "Empty Creditors," "Hidden Non-Interests," and the Matter of Evidence', conference manuscript, June 2013
Henry T C Hu, 'Financial Innovation and Governance Mechanisms: The Evolution of Decoupling and Transparency' (2015) 70 Business Lawyer 347
Henry T C Hu and Bernard Black, 'The New Vote Buying: Empty Voting and Hidden (Morphable) Ownership' (2006) 79 Southern California Law Review 811
Henry T C Hu and Bernard S Black, 'Empty Voting and Hidden (Morphable) Ownership: Taxonomy, Implications, and Reforms' (2006) 61 Business Lawyer 1011
Henry T C Hu and Bernard S Black, 'Hedge Funds, Insiders, and the Decoupling of Economic and Voting Ownership: Empty Voting and Hidden (Morphable) Ownership' (2007) 13 Journal of Corporate Finance 343
Henry T C Hu and Bernard S Black, 'Equity and Debt Decoupling and Empty Voting II: Importance and Extensions' (2008) 156 University of Pennsylvania Law Review 625
Henry T C Hu and Bernard S Black, 'Debt, Equity and Hybrid Decoupling: Governance and Systemic Risk Implications' (2008) 14 European Financial Management 663
Alastair Hudson, *The Law of Finance* (2nd edn, Sweet & Maxwell 2013) ch. 40.
William M Humphries, 'Leveraged ETFs: The Trojan Horse Has Passed the Margin-Rule Gates' (2010) 34 Seattle University Law Review 299
William Hutchings, 'Myners Proposes Sale of Voting Rights' *Financial News* (10 August 2009) <http://www.efinancialnews.com/story/2009-08-10/myners-proposes-sale-of-voting-rights> accessed 14 April 2015
Jacques Iffland and Nadia Gilliard, 'Les nouvelles règles en matière de publicité des participations importantes', [2007] Zeitschrift für Gesellschafts- und Kapitalmarktrecht (GesKR) 365

Institute of Chartered Secretaries and Administrators, ICSA Response to the Consultation on Modernisation of the Directive 2004/109/EC (Transparency Requirements for Listed Companies) (20 August 2010), available at <http://ec.europa.eu/finance/securities/transparency/index_en.htm>

Institutional Shareholder Services Inc. (ISS), *U.S. Corporate Governance Policy: 2013 Updates* (16 November 2012) 4, available at <http://www.issgovernance.com/file/files/2013USPolicyUpdates.pdf> accessed 17 August 2015

ISS, *Best Practice Principles for Providers of Shareholder Voting Research & Analysis—ISS Compliance Statement* (10 June 2014), available at <http://www.issgovernance.com/file/duediligence/BPP-ISS-ComplianceStatement-1406010.pdf>

International Corporate Governance Network (ICGN), *Share Lending Vis-à-Vis Voting—a Report* (2004)

ICGN, *Global Governance Principles* (2014), available at <https://www.icgn.org/file/65/download?token=DY_GHtEO>

ICGN, *Guidance on Securities Lending* (2015), available at <https://www.icgn.org/file/599/download?token=Vu6g-24p>

International Monetary Fund, *IMF Staff Comments on EU Commission Consultation on Short Selling* (5 August 2010), available at <http://www.imf.org/external/np/eur/2010/pdf/080510.pdf>

International Organization of Securities Commissions (IOSCO), Technical Committee, *Report on Transparency of Short Selling* (June 2003), available at <http://www.iosco.org/library/pubdocs/pdf/IOSCOPD147.pdf> accessed 19 August 2015

IOSCO, Letter from IOSCO to the G20 (12 November 2008), available at <http://www.iosco.org/library/pubdocs/pdf/IOSCOPD282.pdf> accessed 19 August 2015

IOSCO, Technical Committee, *Protection of Minority Shareholders in Listed Issuers—Final Report* (June 2009)

IOSCO, Technical Committee, *Regulation of Short Selling—Final Report* (June 2009), available at <https://www.iosco.org/library/pubdocs/pdf/IOSCOPD292.pdf> accessed 19 August 2015

International Securities Lending Association (ISLA), *Overseas Securities Lending Agreement* (1995)

International Securities Lending Association, *Global Master Securities Lending Agreement* (2010, with minor changes in 2012), available at <http://www.isla.co.uk/wp-content/uploads/2015/08/GMSLA_2010_amendments_July_2012-1.pdf>

International Swaps and Derivatives Association, Brief of Amici Curiae by International Swaps and Derivatives Association, Inc. and Securities Industry and Financial Markets Association in the matter CSX Corp. v. The Children's Inv. Fund Mgmt., LLP, et al., 08-Civ. 2764 (2 June 2008) 11–15, available at <http://www.sifma.org/WorkArea/DownloadAsset.aspx?id=1708> accessed 15 April 2015

International Swaps and Derivatives Association, *Derivatives Usage Survey*, Research Notes 2/2009, April 2009, available at <http://www.isda.org/researchnotes/pdf/ISDA-Research-Notes2.pdf>

International Swaps and Derivatives Association, 'The Empty Creditor Hypothesis', Research Notes 3/2009, 17 December 2009

Doron Israeli, Charles M C Lee, and Suhas Sridharan, 'Is There a Dark Side to Exchange Traded Funds (ETFs)? An Information Perspective' Working Paper 2015, available at <http://ssrn.com/abstract=2625975> accessed 20 August 2015

Katayun I Jaffari and Whitney W Deeney, 'One Share, One Vote? Not Necessarily: Manipulation of the SEC Proxy System to Effect Empty Voting' *Legal Intelligencer* (25 February 2011) 7

Michael C Jensen and William H Meckling, 'Theory of the Firm: Managerial Behavior, Agency Costs and Ownership Structure' (1976) 3 Journal of Financial Economics 305

Steve Johnson, 'Fidelity Eyes Stock Loans Exit' *Financial Times* (London, 8 April 2013) FTfm 1

Steve Johnson, '"Protectionist" French Law Alarms Investors' *Financial Times* (FT.com, 22 February 2015)

Christine Jolls, Cass Sunstein, and Richard Thaler, 'A Behavioral Approach to Law and Economics' (1998) 50 Stanford Law Review 1471

Sam Jones, 'Big Investors Cool on Myners' Idea of Trade in Voting Rights' *Financial Times* (London, 11 August 2009) 1

Marcel Kahan and Edward Rock, 'Hedge Funds in Corporate Governance and Corporate Control' (2007) 155 University of Pennsylvania Law Review 1021

Marcel Kahan and Edward B Rock, 'The Hanging Chads of Corporate Voting' (2008) 96 Georgetown Law Journal 1227

Avner Kalay, Oğuzhan Karakaş, and Shagun Pant, 'The Market Value of Corporate Votes: Theory and Evidence from Option Prices' (2014) 69 Journal of Finance 1235

Avner Kalay and Shagun Pant, 'Time Varying Voting Rights and the Private Benefits of Control' (Social Science Research Network 2009) SSRN Scholarly Paper ID 1102832 <http://papers.ssrn.com/abstract=1102832> accessed 13 April 2015.

Steven N Kaplan, Tobias J Moskowitz, and Berk A Sensoy, 'The Effects of Stock Lending on Security Prices: An Experiment' (2013) 68 Journal of Finance 1891

Roberta S Karmel, 'Voting Power without Responsibility or Risk: How Should Proxy Reform Address the Decoupling of Economic and Voting Rights' (2010) 55 Villanova Law Review 93

Dionysia Katelouzou, 'Worldwide Hedge Fund Activism: Dimensions and Legal Determinants' (2015) 17 University of Pennsylvania Journal of Business Law 789

David A Katz and Laura A McIntosh, '13(d) Reporting Inadequacies in an Era of Speed and Innovation' *New York Law Journal* (24 September 2015)

John Kay and others, *Kay Review of UK Equity Markets and Long-Term Decision Making: Final Report* (July 2012), available at <https://www.gov.uk/government/consultations/the-kay-review-of-uk-equity-markets-and-long-term-decision-making>

Thomas Keijser, *Financial Collateral Arrangements: the European Collateral Directive Considered from a Property and Insolvency Law Perspective—An Academic Essay in Law* (Kluwer 2006)

Ellen Kelleher, 'Enquiry Starting into Empty Voting' *Financial Times* (London, 25 September 2011) 3

Maiju Kettunen and Wolf-Georg Ringe, 'Disclosure Regulation of Cash-Settled Equity Derivatives—An Intentions-Based Approach' [2012] Lloyd's Maritime and Commercial Law Quarterly 227

Rakesh Khurana and Andy Zelleke, 'You Can Cap the Pay, but the Greed Will Go On' *The Washington Post* (8 February 2009) B01

Philipp Kiiver, 'The Early-Warning System for the Principle of Subsidiarity: The National Parliament as a Conseil d'Etat for Europe' (2011) 36 European Law Review 98

Michael Klausner, 'The Contractarian Theory of Corporate Law: A Generation Later' (2006) 31 Journal of Corporation Law 779

April Klein and Emanuel Zur, 'Entrepreneurial Shareholder Activism: Hedge Funds and Other Private Investors' (2009) 64 Journal of Finance 187

Lars Klöhn and Philip Schwarz, 'The Regulation of Proxy Advisors' (2013) 8 Capital Markets Law Journal 90

Bruce Kobayashi and Larry Ribstein, 'Outsider Trading as an Incentive Device' (2006) 40 UC Davis Law Review 21

Valentine Korah, *An Introductory Guide to EC Competition Law and Practice* (9th edn, Hart, Oxford 2007)

Reinier H Kraakman and Henry Hansmann, 'Property, Contract, and Verification: The Numerus Clausus Problem and the Divisibility of Rights' (2002) 31 The Journal of Legal Studies S373

Reinier Kraakman and others, *The Anatomy of Corporate Law: A Comparative and Functional Approach* (2nd edn, Oxford University Press 2009)

Friedrich Kübler and Heinz-Dieter Assmann, *Gesellschaftsrecht: Die privatrechtlichen Ordnungsstrukturen und Regelungsprobleme von Verbänden und Unternehmen* (6th edn, CF Müller 2006)

Rainer Kulms, 'A Shareholder's Freedom of Contract in Close Corporations—Shareholder Agreements in the USA and Germany' (2001) 2 European Business Organization Law Review 685

Christoph Kumpan and Martin Mittermeier, 'Risikoentleerte Stimmrechte—Auswirkungen von Wertpapierdarlehen im Gesellschaftsrecht' [2009] Zeitschrift für Wirtschaftsrecht [ZIP] 404

Peter V Kunz, 'Kapitalmarktrechtliche Beteiligungstransparenz im Lichte moderner Finanzinstrumente—Perspektive der Schweiz', in Holger Fleischer, Susanne Kalss, and Hans-Ueli Vogt (eds), *Konvergenzen und Divergenzen im deutschen, österreichischen und schweizerischen Gesellschafts- und Kapitalmarktrecht* (Mohr Siebeck 2011) 181

Helfried Labrenz, *Ökonomische Analyse der aktienrechtlichen Anfechtungsklage* (Gabler 2011)

Simon Lack, *The Hedge Fund Mirage: The Illusion of Big Money and Why It's Too Good to Be True* (John Wiley 2012)

Kevin M LaCroix, 'Second Circuit Affirms Porsche Securities Suit Dismissal; Domestic Transaction Necessary but Not Sufficient to Invoke U.S. Securities Laws' D&O Diary, 18 August 2014, available at <http://www.dandodiary.com/2014/08/articles/securities-litigation/second-circuit-affirms-porsche-securities-suit-dismissal-domestic-transaction-necessary-but-not-sufficient-to-invoke-u-s-securities-laws/>

Hilde Laga and Floris Parrein, 'Corporate Governance in a European Perspective' in Koen Geens and Klaus J Hopt (eds), *The European Company Law Action Plan Revisited* (Leuven University Press 2010) 79

Marco Lamandini, 'Self-Regulation—What Future in the Context of Hedge Funds?' in Phoebus Athanassiou (ed.), *Research Handbook on Hedge Funds, Private Equity and Alternative Investments* (Edward Elgar 2012) 244–67

Peter Thal Larsen, Jennifer Hughes, and George Parker, 'Turner to End Light-touch Regulation' *Financial Times* (London, 19 March 2009)

Latham & Watkins, *Disclosure of Cash-Settled Derivatives under Italian Securities Laws—Current Law and Proposed Reforms,* Client Alert No 1042 (10 June 2010), available at <http://www.latham.com/thoughtLeadership/disclosure-of-cash-settled-derivatives-in-italy/> accessed 19 August 2015

Kin-Wai Lee, 'Corporate Voluntary Disclosure and the Separation of Cash Flow Rights from Control Rights' (2007) 28 Review of Quantitative Finance and Accounting 393

Michael Lee, 'Empty Voting: Private Solutions to a Private Problem' [2007] Columbia Business Law Review 883

Hervé Le Nabasque, 'Commentaire des Principales Dispositions de la Loi de Régulation Bancaire et Financière du 22 Octobre 2010 Intéressant le Droit des Sociétés et le Droit Financier' [2010] Revue des Sociétés 547

Christian Leuz, 'Was the Sarbanes–Oxley Act of 2002 Really This Costly? A Discussion of Evidence from Event Returns and Going-Private Decisions' (2007) 44 Journal of Accounting and Economics 146

Christian Leuz and Peter D Wysocki, 'Economic Consequences of Financial Reporting and Disclosure Regulation: A Review and Suggestions for Future Research' (Social Science Research Network 2008) SSRN Scholarly Paper ID 1105398 <http://papers.ssrn.com/abstract=1105398> accessed 11 August 2015.

Saul Levmore, 'Voting with Intensity' (2000) 53 Stanford Law Review 111

Martin Lipton, 'Dealing with Activist Hedge Funds', The Harvard Law School Forum on Corporate Governance and Financial Regulation, 21 November 2013, available at <http://blogs.law.harvard.edu/corpgov/2013/11/21/dealing-with-activist-hedge-funds-2/>

Yair Listokin, 'Corporate Voting versus Market Price Setting' (2009) 11 American Law & Economics Review 608

Niklas Luhmann, *Vertrauen: Ein Mechanismus zur Reduktion sozialer Komplexität* (4th edn, Lucius & Lucius 2000)

Andrew Lumsden and Saul Fridman, 'Proxy Voting and Vote Selling' (2009) 61 Keeping Good Companies 332

Jonathan R Macey and Jeffry M Netter, 'Regulation 13D and the Regulatory Process' (1987) 65 Washington University Law Quarterly 131

James Mackintosh, 'UK Draws up Code for Hedge Funds' *Financial Times* (11 October 2007) 1

James Mackintosh, 'MPs Grill Fund Managers on Bank Shorting' *Financial Times* (28 January 2009) 2

James Mackintosh, 'It's Easy to Only Just Beat a Poor Index' *Financial Times* (16 July 2012) 24

Ananth Madhavan, 'Exchange-Traded Funds: An Overview of Institutions, Trading, and Impacts' (2014) 6 Annual Review of Financial Economics 311

Steven Maijoor, 'The ESA's Role in Financial Consumer Protection', speech at CNMV Conference, La Nueva Financiera Regulacion, Madrid, 15 October 2014, ESMA/2014/1265, available at <http://www.esma.europa.eu/system/files/2014-1265_keynote_speech_-_the_esas_role_in_financial_consumer_protection_cnmv_conference_madrid_-_steven_maijoor.pdf>

Catherine Maison-Blanche and Antoine Barat, 'La Nouvelle Obligation de Transparence sur les Opérations de Détentions Temporaires Avant Tenue des Assemblées: Réflexions Préliminaires' (2011) 1/2 Revue Trimestrielle de Droit Financier 80

Ajay Makan, 'ETFs Under Fire over Revenues Generated by Securities Lending' *Financial Times* (10 May 2012) 33

Alfred Manes, 'Insurance: Principles and History' in Edwin Seligman and Alvin Johnson (eds), *Encyclopaedia of the Social Sciences*, volume VIII (New York 1932) 95

Henry G Manne, 'Some Theoretical Aspects of Share Voting. An Essay in Honor of Adolf A. Berle' (1964) 64 Columbia Law Review 1427

Henry G Manne, 'Mergers and the Market for Corporate Control' (1965) 73 Journal of Political Economy 110

David Marais, 'Decoupling Voting Rights from Economic Interest: The Case of Empty and Negative Voting' (2015) 18 Trinity College Law Review 180

Dante A Marinucci, 'Empty Creditor Syndrome and Vivisepulture: Preventing Credit-Default-Swap Holders from Pushing Companies into Premature Graves by Refusing to Negotiate Restructurings' (2012) 62 Case Western Reserve Law Review 1285

Harry M Markowitz, 'Portfolio Selection' (1952) 7 Journal of Finance 77

Harry M Markowitz, *Portfolio Selection: Efficient Diversification of Investments* (2nd edn, Wiley 1991)

Shaun Martin and Frank Partnoy, 'Encumbered Shares' [2005] University of Illinois Law Review 775

Alan Mason, Gabriel Flandin, and Sophie Bauquis, 'Des récentes affaires impliquant l'usage des dérivés actions' [2011] Revue Trimestrielle de Droit Financier 36

Mazars and Marccus Partners, *Transparency Directive Assessment Report—Prepared for the European Commission Internal Market and Services DG, Final Report* (December 2009) 124, available at <http://ec.europa.eu/internal_market/securities/docs/transparency/report-application_en.pdf>

Joseph A McCahery and Erik P M Vermeulen, *Corporate Governance of Non-Listed Companies* (Oxford University Press 2008)

Callum McCarthy, 'Exigences de Transparence et Hedge Funds' (2007) 10 Banque de France • Revue de la stabilité financière 85

Roger McCormick and Harriet Creamer, *Hybrid Corporate Securities: International Legal Aspects* (Sweet & Maxwell 1987)

Charlie McCreevy, 'Shifting up a gear—Transatlantic Cooperation in Financial Services' (Speech 07/125 at the US Chamber of Commerce, 2007)

Ben McFarlane, 'The Numerus Clausus Principle and Covenants Relating to Land' in Susan Bright (ed.), *Modern Studies in Property Law*, vol 6 (Hart 2011) 311–31

Julius Melnitzer, '"Empty Voting" Clouds Shareholder Rights Law' *Financial Post* (14 November 2012), available at <http://business.financialpost.com/2012/11/14/empty-voting-clouds-shareholder-rights-law/>

Andreas Merkner and Marco Sustmann, 'Wertpapierleihe und Empty Voting—Weitergehender Transparenzbedarf im WpHG?' [2010] Neue Zeitschrift für Gesellschaftsrecht 1170

Thomas W Merrill and Henry E Smith, 'Optimal Standardization in the Law of Property: The Numerus Clausus Principle' (2000) 110 Yale Law Journal 1

Ernst-Joachim Mestmäcker, *Verwaltung, Konzerngewalt und Rechte der Aktionäre* (CF Müller 1958)

Wayne H Mikkelson and Richard S Ruback, 'An Empirical Analysis of the Interfirm Equity Investment Process' (1985) 14 Journal of Financial Economics 523

Jonathan Miller and Matthew DiRisio, 'The Potential Implications of Decoupling Shareholders' Economic and Voting Interests in Corporate Control Contests' [2008] International Corporate Governance Review 4

Millstein Center for Corporate Governance and Performance, Yale School of Management, *Voting Integrity: Practices for Investors and the Global Proxy Advisory Industry—Policy Briefing no 3* (2009) 11–12, available at <http://web.law.columbia.edu/sites/default/files/microsites/millstein-center/Voting%20Integrity%20Policy%20Briefing%20No%203%2002%2027%2009.pdf>

Richard Milne, Michael Mackenzie, and Nicole Bullock, '"Push-button Perils" Investment: Exchange Traded Funds' *Financial Times* (6 June 2011) 7

Willem Molle, *The Economics of European Integration: Theory, Practice, Policy* (5th edn, Ashgate 2006)

Niamh Moloney, *EU Securities and Financial Markets Regulation* (3rd edn, Oxford University Press 2014)

Anish Monga, 'Using Derivatives to Manipulate the Market for Corporate Control' (2006) 12 Stanford Journal of Law, Business & Finance 186

Kevin J Murphy, 'Explaining Executive Compensation: Managerial Power versus the Perceived Cost of Stock Options' (2002) 69 University of Chicago Law Review 847

Paul Myners, *Review of the Impediments to Voting UK Shares* (Report to the Shareholder Voting Working Group, London 2004)

Paul Myners, *Review of the Impediments to Voting UK shares: An Update on Progress* (Report to the Shareholder Voting Working Group, London 2005)

Paul Myners, *Review of the Impediments to Voting UK shares: An Update on Progress Three Years on* (Report to the Shareholder Voting Working Group, London 2007)

Eugenio de Nardis and Matteo Tonello, 'Know Your Shareholders: The Use of Cash-Settled Equity Derivatives to Hide Corporate Ownership Interests' The Conference Board no DN-009 (July 2010)

Charles Nathan, '"Empty Voting" and Other Fault Lines Undermining Shareholder Democracy: The New Hunting Ground for Hedge Funds' (2007) 15 The Corporate Governance Advisor 1

Niels Nauhauser, 'Index- ETFs bergen stets ein Kontrahentenrisiko', *Börse Online* (12 January 2010), available at <http://www.genios.de/presse-archiv/artikel/BONL/20101202/index-etfs-bergen-stets-ein-kontrah/A48508382.html>

Tatiana Nenova, 'The Value of Corporate Voting Rights and Control: A Cross-Country Analysis' (2003) 68 Journal Financial Economics 325

Mette Neville, 'Shareholder Activism: The Suspicious Shareholder', in Hanne Søndergaard Birkmose, Mette Neville, and Karsten Engsig Sørensen (eds), *The European Financial Market in Transition* (Alphen aan den Rijn 2012) 217

Paula Niall and Pauline Skypala, 'Regulatory Spotlight Turns on Lending Business' *Financial Times* (London, 23 January 2012) FTfm 8

Rachel Nolan, 'VW Stock Price Anomaly "Must Not Be Allowed"' *Der Spiegel* (29 October 2008) <http://www.spiegel.de/international/the-world-from-berlin-vw-stock-price-anomaly-must-not-be-allowed-a-587293.html> accessed 19 August 2015

Office for National Statistics, *Statistical Bulletin: Ownership of UK Quoted Shares* (2012), available at <http://www.ons.gov.uk/ons/dcp171778_327674.pdf>

Kingsley T W Ong and Eugene Y C Yeung, 'Repos & Securities Lending: The Accounting Arbitrage and Their Role in the Global Financial Crisis' (2011) 6 Capital Markets Law Journal 92

Christine Osterloh-Konrad, 'Gefährdet "Empty Voting" die Willensbildung in der Aktiengesellschaft? Überlegungen zur Proportionalität zwischen Stimmrechtseinfluss und wirtschaftlicher Betroffenheit der Aktionäre' [2012] Zeitschrift für Unternehmens- und Gesellschaftsrecht (ZGR) 35

Dan Palmon and Fred Sudit, 'Empowering Democracy in Corporate Governance by Unbundling Shareholders' Voting Rights from Their Return on Investment Rights' (2008) 5 International Journal of Disclosure and Governance 93

Dan Palmon and Ephraim F Sudit, 'Shareholders Groups, Unbundled Rights, and Corporate Democracy: A Commentary' (2011) 20 Group Decision and Negotiation 133

Panagiotis Kon. Panagiotou, 'The Disruption of the Principle of Indivisibility of the Share and the Assignment of Autonomous Voting Rights' (2015) 36 Company Lawyer 67

Troy Paredes, 'Blinded by the Light: Information Overload and Its Consequences for Securities Regulation' (2003) 81 Washington University Law Quarterly 417

James J Park, 'The Competing Paradigms of Securities Regulation' (2007) 57 Duke Law Journal 625

Jennifer Payne, 'The Regulation of Short Selling and Its Reform in Europe' (2012) 13 European Business Organization Law Review (EBOR) 413

Jennifer Payne, *Schemes of Arrangement: Theory, Structure and Operation* (Cambridge University Press 2014)

Murray A Pickering, 'The Problem of the Preference Share' (1963) 26 Modern Law Review 499

Arthur R Pinto, 'The European Union's Shareholder Voting Rights Directive from an American Perspective: Some Comparisons and Observations' (2009) 32 Fordham International Law Journal 587

John Plender, 'The Waning Power of Equity Ownership' *Financial Times* (23 April 2012) FTFm 24

John Plender, 'Activist Animals Sought for Governance Jungle' *Financial Times* (London, 8 June 2015) FTFm 13

Richard A Posner, 'The Rights of Creditors of Affiliated Corporations' (1976) 43 University of Chicago Law Review 499

Susanne Preuss, 'Ein Hedge-Fonds namens Porsche' ['A Hedge Fund called Porsche'], *Frankfurter Allgemeine Zeitung* (29 October 2008), <http://www.faz.net/aktuell/wirtschaft/unternehmen/vw-aktien-ein-hedge-fonds-namens-porsche-1711580.html>

Ludwig Raiser, 'Vertragsfunktion und Vertragsfreiheit', in: Ernst v. Caemmerer (Hrsg.), *Hundert Jahre Deutsches Rechtsleben, Festschrift zum 100jährigen Bestehen des Deutschen Juristentages 1860-1960,* (CF Müller 1960) vol 1, 101

Juan Ramirez, *Handbook of Corporate Equity Derivatives and Equity Capital Markets* (Wiley 2011)

Christian Renn, Christoph Andreas Weber, and Georg G Gotschev, 'Beteiligungstransparenz und dynamisches Hedging: Zur Frage einer Delta-Adjustierung der Meldepflichten' [2012] Die Aktiengesellschaft 440

David Ricketts, 'Traditional Index Funds Lose to ETFs' *Financial Times* (London, 6 February 2012) 9

Jonathan Rickford, 'Invisible Hand or Dead Hand?—Reflections on the EU "One Share One Vote"' in European Policy Forum (ed.), *One Share One Vote? Tomorrow's Companies: One Universal Model or Tailored Equity Structures?* (London 2006) 67

Mark S Rieder, 'Kein Rechtsmissbrauch beim Squeeze-out' [2009] Zeitschrift für Unternehmens- und Gesellschaftsrecht 981

Wolf-Georg Ringe, 'Deviations from Ownership-Control Proportionality—Economic Protectionism Revisited' in Ulf Bernitz and Wolf-Georg Ringe (eds), *Company Law and Economic Protectionism* (Oxford University Press 2010) 209

Wolf-Georg Ringe, 'Hedge Funds and Risk-Decoupling—The Empty Voting Problem in the European Union' (2013) 36 Seattle University Law Review 1027

Wolf-Georg Ringe, 'Empty Voting Revisited: The *Telus* Saga' (2013) 28 Butterworths Journal of International Banking and Financial Law 154

Wolf-Georg Ringe, 'Changing Law and Ownership Patterns in Germany: Corporate Governance and the Erosion of Deutschland AG' (2015) 63 American Journal of Comparative Law 493

Wolf-Georg Ringe, 'Shareholder Activism: A Renaissance' in Jeffrey N Gordon and Wolf-Georg Ringe (eds), *The Oxford Handbook of Corporate Law and Governance* (forthcoming, Oxford University Press 2016), available at <http://www.oxfordhandbooks.com/>

Susanna K Ripken, 'The Dangers and Drawbacks of the Disclosure Antidote: Toward a More Substantive Approach to Securities Regulation' (2006) 58 Baylor Law Review 139

Alexia Robinson, 'Addressing the Issue of Derivatives Disclosure in Advance Notice Requirements' *Research Spotlight* (16 December 2008) <https://www.sharkrepellent.net/pub/rs_20081216.html>

Bonnie Roe, 'When the Voting Is "Empty": No Quick Fix is Seen in Record Date Reform Proposals' *New York Law Journal* (29 November 2010) 9

Mark J Roe, 'A Political Theory of American Corporate Finance' (1991) 91 Columbia Law Review 10

Mark J Roe, *Strong Managers, Weak Owners: The Political Roots of American Corporate Finance* (Princeton University Press 1996)
Mark J Roe, 'Corporate Short-Termism—In the Boardroom and in the Courtroom' (2013) 68 Business Lawyer 977
Mark Roe and Federico Venezze, 'A Capital Market, Corporate Law Approach To Creditor Conduct' (2013) 112 Michigan Law Review 59
Roberta Romano, 'Empowering Investors: A Market Approach to Securities Regulation' (1998) 107 Yale Law Journal 2359
Paul Rose, 'The Corporate Governance Industry' (2007) 32 Journal of Corporation Law 887
Paul Rose, 'On the Role and Regulation of Proxy Advisors' (2011) 109 Michigan Law Review First Impressions 62
Michael Rozeff, 'Growth, Beta and Agency Costs as Determinants of Dividend Payout Ratios' (1982) 5 Journal of Financial Research 249
Bernard Rudden, 'Economic Theory v. Property Law: The Numerus Clausus Problem' in John Eekelaar and John Bell (eds), *Oxford Essays in Jurisprudence: Third Series 1987* (Clarendon Press 1987) 239–63
Jonathan Russell, 'ABI Leads Attack on Myners Over Shareholder Reform' *Sunday Telegraph* (1 August 2009) 1
Rachel Sanderson, 'Italy Makes U-turn on Loyalty Shares' *Financial Times* (FT.com, 5 February 2015)
Paolo Santella, Enrico Baffi, Carlo Drago, and Dino Lattuca, 'Legal Obstacles to Institutional Investor Activism in the EU and in the US' (2012) 23 European Business Law Review 257
Sara Lee Corporation, *By-laws as Amended March 27, 2008* (Form 8-K) (28 March 2008), available at <http://www.sec.gov/Archives/edgar/data/23666/000129993308001659/htm_26377.htm>
Florens Sauerbruch, *Das Freigabeverfahren gemäß § 246a Aktiengesetz: eine rechtsökonomische Untersuchung* (Gabler 2008)
Kara Scannell, 'How Borrowed Shares Swing Company Votes—SEC and Others Fear Hedge-Fund Strategy May Subvert Elections' *Wall Street Journal* (26 January 2007) A1
Schaeffler KG, 'Angebotsunterlage, Freiwilliges öffentliches Übernahmeangebot (Barangebot) der Schaeffler KG an die Aktionäre der Continental Aktiengesellschaft' [Formal Voluntary Takeover Bid] (30 July 2008) 16 <http://www.bafin.de/SharedDocs/Downloads/DE/Angebotsunterlage/schaeffler.pdf?__blob=publicationFile&v=5> accessed 10 August 2015
Kay-Michael Schanz and Christoph Schalast (eds), 'Schaeffler KG/Continental AG im Lichte der CSX Corp.-Entscheidung des US District Court for the Southern District of New York' (Frankfurt School of Finance and Management—Working Paper Series, Working Paper No. 100, July 2008) 13 <http://www.frankfurt-school.de/clicnetclm/fileDownload.do?goid=000000227192AB4>
Dominique Schmidt, 'Droit financier: Empty Voting' [2012] Bulletin Joly Bourse 42
Karsten Schmidt, *Gesellschaftsrecht* (4th edn, Heymanns 2002)
Karsten Schmidt and Marcus Lutter (eds), *Aktiengesetz—Kommentar* (3rd edn, Otto Schmidt 2015)
Michael D Schmitz, 'Shareholder Vote Buying—A Rebuttable Presumption of Illegality' [1968] Wisconsin Law Review 927
Wolfgang Schön, 'The Distinct Equity of the Debt-Equity Distinction' (2012) 66 Bulletin for International Taxation (IBFD Bulletin) 490

Wolfgang Schön and others, 'Debt and Equity in Domestic and International Tax Law—A Comparative Policy Analysis' [2014] British Tax Review 146

Michael C Schouten, 'The Case for Mandatory Ownership Disclosure' (2009) 15 Stanford Journal of Law, Business and Finance 127

Michael C Schouten, *The Decoupling of Voting and Economic Ownership* (Kluwer 2012)

Robert Schütze, 'Subsidiarity After Lisbon: Reinforcing the Safeguards of Federalism?' (2009) 68 The Cambridge Law Journal 525

Steven L Schwarcz, 'The Governance Structure of Shadow Banking: Rethinking Assumptions about Limited Liability' (2014) 90 Notre Dame Law Review 1

Eberhard Schwark and Daniel Zimmer (eds), *Kapitalmarkts-Kommentar* (4th edn, CH Beck 2010)

Heike Schweitzer, 'Sovereign Wealth Funds—Market Investors or "Imperialist Capitalists"? The European Response to Direct Investments by Non-EU State-controlled Entities' in Ulf Bernitz and Wolf-Georg Ringe (eds), *Company Law and Economic Protectionism* (Oxford University Press 2010) 250

SCM Private, 'SCM Private Research Reveals UK Retail Fund Managers Controlling over £241 Billion, Can Lend Out up to 100% of Funds Yet Investors Are Kept in the Dark' (1 September 2011), <http://www.independentinvestor.info/PDF-Downloads/ETF-MUTUAL-FUNDS-WRAP-ACCOUNTS-FUNDS-08/doc.2133-%20SCM%20 2011%20UK%20fund%20stock%20lending.pdf>

Securities and Exchange Commission, Brief of Amicus Curiae by the Securities and Exchange Commission in the matter CSX Corp. v. The Children's Inv. Fund Mgmt., L.L.P., et al., 08-Civ. 2764 (4 June 2008) 2, 4, available at <http://www.chadbourne.com/files/Publication/ce4995ec-b733-4eef-89e5-d5574a182080/Preview/PublicationAttachment/ed741d95-84e9-4fb9-b0a6-c196c813e5bf/SECBrehenyLetter.pdf>, accessed 19 August 2015

Securities and Exchange Commission, Press Release 2009-165, *SEC Charges Perry Corp. with Disclosure Violations in Vote Buying Scheme* (21 July 2009), available at <http://www.sec.gov/news/press/2009/2009-165.htm>

Securities and Exchange Commission, *Concept Release on the U.S. Proxy System* (Release Nos 34-62495, IA-3052, IC-29340; File No S7-14-10, 2010), (2010) 75 Federal Register 42981

Securities and Exchange Commission, *Disclosure of Hedging by Employees, Officers and Directors*, SEC Release No 339723 (9 February 2015), available at <https://www.sec.gov/rules/proposed/2015/33-9723.pdf> accessed 19 August 2015

Securities Industry and Financial Markets Association (Sifma), 'Master Securities Loan Agreement', <http://www.sifma.org/Services/Standard-Forms-and-Documentation/MRA,-GMRA,-MSLA-and-MSFTAs/MSLA_Master-Securities-Loan-Agreement-(2000-Version)/> accessed 18 August 2015

Ulrich Seibert, 'Gute Aktionäre—schlechte Aktionäre—"Aktive Finanzinvestoren" und Stimmrecht', in Lutz Aderhold and others (eds), *Festschrift für Harm Peter Westermann zum 70. Geburtstag* (2008) 1505

Christoph Seibt, 'Verbandssouveränität und Abspaltungsverbot im Aktien- und Kapitalmarktrecht—Revisited: Hidden Ownership, Empty Voting und andere Kleinigkeiten' [2010] Zeitschrift für Unternehmens- und Gesellschaftsrecht 795

Alexandros Seretakis, 'Hedge Fund Activism Coming to Europe: Lessons from the American Experience' (2014) 8 Brooklyn Journal of Corporate, Financial & Commercial Law 438

Jonathan Shapiro and Gretchen Friemann, 'How Deutsche Bank's Name Sparks Fear' *The Australian Financial Review* (21 June 2014) 36

Shareowners.org, *Letter in Response to SEC Concept Release on the U.S. Proxy System*, File No. S7 1410 (20 October 2010)

William F Sharpe, 'Capital Asset Prices: A Theory of Market Equilibrium Under Conditions of Risk' (1964) 19 Journal of Finance 425

Shearman & Sterling LLP, ISS, and ECGI, *Proportionality between Ownership and Control in EU Listed Companies: Comparative Legal Study* (External Study, commissioned by the European Commission, May 2007), available at <http://ec.europa.eu/internal_market/company/docs/shareholders/study/final_report_en.pdf>

Anil Shivdasani, 'Board Composition, Ownership Structure, and Hostile Takeovers' (1993) 16 Journal of Accounting and Economics 167

Andrei Shleifer and Robert W Vishny, 'Large Shareholders and Corporate Control' (1986) 94 Journal of Political Economy 461

Andrei Shleifer and Robert W Vishny, 'A Survey of Corporate Governance' (1997) 52 Journal of Finance 737

Tom Siebens and Melissa Gambol, 'Who's Hiding Behind the Hedges? Developments in the USA and UK May Limit the Use of Total Return Swaps to Conceal Equity Stakes in Public Companies' (2009) 4 Capital Markets Law Journal 172

Hans-Werner Sinn, *Casino Capitalism—How the Financial Crisis Came About and What Needs to be Done Now* (Oxford University Press 2010)

David Skeel, 'Behind the Hedge' [2005] Legal Affairs 28

Pauline Skypala, 'Fund Managers Cannot be Stewards' *Financial Times* (London, 19 March 2012) FTFm 6

Tom Stabile, 'Fraud-chasing Profiteers Raise Questions', *Financial Times* (14 May 2012) FTfm 11

Samuel Stadelmann and Noël Bieri, 'Die Offenlegung von Finanzinstrumenten nach Art. 20 Börsengesetz' [2010] GesKR 310

George Stigler, 'The Economics of Information' (1961) 69 Journal of Political Economy 213

Stock Lending and Repo Committee, *Summary of Meeting Held at the Bank of England on 9 October 2002* (11 December 2002), available at <http://www.bankofengland.co.uk/markets/Documents/gilts/slrcdec02.pdf>

Michel Storck and Jérôme Lasserre Capdeville, 'Panorama Général de la Loi de Régulation Bancaire et Financière' (2010) 250 Petites Affiches 3

Michael Stothard, 'French Companies Fight Back Against Share Legislation' *Financial Times* (London, 17 April 2015) 19

Lynn A Stout, 'The Mythical Benefits of Shareholder Control' (2007) 93 Virginia Law Review 789

David Stowell, *An Introduction to Investment Banks, Hedge Funds, and Private Equity: The New Paradigm* (Elsevier 2010)

Brian T Sullivan, 'CSX Corp. v. Children's Investment Fund Management and the Need for SEC Expansion of Beneficial Ownership' (2009) 87 North Carolina Law Review 1300

Simon Targett, 'Top Pension Funds Plan Securities Lending Code' *Financial Times* (London, 14 June 2004) 1

The Takeover Panel, *Practice Statement No. 26: Shareholder Activism* (9 September 2009) <http://www.thetakeoverpanel.org.uk/wp-content/uploads/2008/11/PS26.pdf> accessed 19 August 2015

Tony Tassell, 'Myners Eyes New Non-Voting Shares' *Financial Times* (14 August 2009) 16

Gillian Tett, 'A Guiding Light Is Needed to Cut through the Fog of Financial Data' *Financial Times* (London, 9 March 2012) 32

Ingo Theusinger and Daniel Möritz, 'Empty Voting als moderner Stimmenkauf?' [2010] Neue Zeitschrift für Gesellschaftsrecht 607

Robert Thompson and Paul Edelman, 'Corporate Voting' (2009) 62 Vanderbilt Law Review 129

James Tobin, 'Liquidity Preference as Behavior Towards Risk' (1958) 25 Review of Economic Studies 65

Roman Tomasic, Stephen Bottomley, and Rob McQueen, *Corporations Law in Australia* (2nd edn Sydney 2002)

Jill Treanor, 'Too Many UK Firms Fall into Foreign Hands, Says Crusading Myners' *The Guardian* (24 September 2009) 31

Pablo Triana and Mari Subrahmanyam, 'Another Troublesome Feature of CDS Usage' *Financial Times* (London, 9 April 2012) 11

George G Triantis and Ronald J Daniels, 'The Role of Debt in Interactive Corporate Governance' (1995) 83 California Law Review 1073

Rita Trichur, 'Telus Looks to Regulator in Share-consolidation Spat' *The Globe and Mail* (27 April 2012), available at <http://www.theglobeandmail.com/globe-investor/telus-looks-to-regulator-in-share-consolidation-spat/article4102877/>

Frederick Tung, 'Leverage in the Board Room: The Unsung Influence of Private Lenders in Corporate Governance' (2009) 57 UCLA Law Review 115

Rüdiger Veil, 'The Reform of the Transparency Regime in European Capital Markets Laws' [2013] European Company and Financial Law Review 18

Rüdiger Veil, 'Legislative Powers for Regulating Capital Markets in Europe' in Rüdiger Veil (ed.), *European Capital Markets Law* (Hart Publishing 2013) § 3

Marco Ventoruzzo and others, *Comparative Corporate Law* (West Academic Publishing 2015)

Fabian Walla, 'Short Selling' in Rüdiger Veil (ed.), *European Capital Markets Law* (Hart Publishing 2013) 201.

John Waples, 'Ritblat Hits at CSFB and Laxey for Vote "Conspiracy"' *Sunday Times* (London, 21 July 2002) 1

Harm P Westermann, *Vertragsfreiheit und Typengesetzlichkeit im Recht der Personengesellschaften* (Berlin and Heidelberg 1970)

Richard Whish, *Competition Law* (6th edn, Oxford University Press 2009)

Charles K Whitehead, 'The Evolution of Debt: Covenants, the Credit Market, and Corporate Governance' (2009) 34 Journal of Corporation Law 641

Herbert Wiedemann, *Die Übertragung und Vererbung von Mitgliedschaftsrechten bei Handelsgesellschaften* (Munich 1965)

Ben Wilkie, 'Spain: Despite the Country's Financial Woes, a Vibrant Securities Lending Market Still Exists in Spain, Even Though Short Selling Rules Are Some of the Toughest in the Western World' (2011) 18 Securities Lending Times 10

Oliver E Williamson, *The Economic Institutions of Capitalism* (Free Press 1985)

Oliver E Williamson, 'The New Institutional Economics: Taking Stock, Looking Ahead' (2000) 38 Journal of Economic Literature 595

Jaap Winter, 'The European Union's Involvement in Company Law and Corporate Governance', in Koen Geens and Klaus J Hopt (eds), *The European Company Law Action Plan Revisited* (Leuven University Press 2010) 140

Daniel E Wolf and others, 'Setting the Record (Date) Straight', Kirkland M&A Update, 17 April 2013, available at <http://www.kirkland.com/siteFiles/Publications/MAUpdate_041713.pdf>

Simon Wong, 'Why Stewardship Is Proving Elusive for Institutional Investors' (2010) 25 Butterworths Journal of International Banking and Financial Law 406

Simon Wong, 'Barriers to Effective Investor Engagement' *Financial Times* (London, 16 January 2012) 6

Eddy Wymeersch, 'Shareholders in Action: Towards a New Company Paradigm?' (2007) 4 European Company Law 50

Eddy Wymeersch, 'Shareholder(s) Matter(s)' in Stefan Grundmann and others (eds), *Festschrift für Klaus J. Hopt zum 70. Geburtstag am 24. August 2010: Unternehmen, Markt und Verantwortung* (De Gruyter 2010) 1571

Victor Yeo and others, *Commercial Applications of Company Law in Singapore* (3rd edn, North Ryde 2008)

David Yermack, 'Shareholder Voting and Corporate Governance' (2010) 2 Annual Review of Financial Economics 103

Bruno Zabala, 'Action de Concert et Transparence Préassemblées Générales: Les Nouveaux Equilibres Actionnariaux sous l'Œil du Législateur et de la Cour de Cassation' (2011) 5 Revue Lamy Droit des Affaires 110

Andrea Zanoni, 'Hedge Funds' Empty Voting in Mergers and Acquisitions: A Fiduciary Duties Perspective' (2009) 9(4) Global Jurist, article 4

Dirk Zetzsche, 'Hidden Ownership in Europe: BAFin's Decision in Schaeffler v. Continental' (2009) 10 European Business Organization Law Review 115

Dirk Zetzsche, 'Challenging Wolf Packs: Thoughts on Efficient Enforcement of Shareholder Transparency Rules', Center for Business and Corporate Law Research Paper Series 0044 (2/2010) 15–20 <http://papers.ssrn.com/sol3/papers.cfm?abstract_id=1428899> accessed 23 August 2015

Dirk Zetzsche, 'Against Mandatory Disclosure of Economic-only Positions referenced to Shares of European Issuers—Twenty Arguments against the CESR Proposal' (2010) 11 EBOR 231

Luigi Zingales, 'The Value of the Voting Right: A Study of the Milan Stock Exchange Experience' (1994) 7 Review of Financial Studies 125

Luigi Zingales, 'What Determines the Value of Corporate Votes?' (1995) 110 Quarterly Journal of Economics 1047

Luigi Zingales, 'Learning to Live With Not-So-Efficient Markets' (2010) 139(4) Daedalus 31

Index